Adobe® Acrobat® 6 PDF

FOR DUMMIES®

by Greg Harvey

WILEY

John Wiley & Sons, Inc.

Adobe® Acrobat® 6 PDF For Dummies®

Published by
John Wiley & Sons, Inc.
111 River Street
Hoboken, NJ 07030-5774
www.wiley.com

Copyright © 2003 by John Wiley & Sons, Inc., Hoboken, New Jersey

Published by John Wiley & Sons, Inc., Hoboken, New Jersey

Published simultaneously in Canada

For general information on our other products and services, please contact our Customer Care Department within the U.S. at 877-762-2974, outside the U.S. at 317-572-3993, or fax 317-572-4002. For technical support, please visit www.wiley.com/techsupport.

Wiley publishes in a variety of print and electronic formats and by print-on-demand. Some material included with standard print versions of this book may not be included in e-books or in print-on-demand. If this book refers to media such as a CD or DVD that is not included in the version you purchased, you may download this material at http://booksupport.wiley.com. For more information about Wiley products, visit www.wiley.com.

Library of Congress Control Number: 2003105653

ISBN 978-0-7645-3760-8 (pbk); ISBN 978-0-7645-4432-3 (ebk)

10 9 8 7 6 5 4

1O/SR/QX/QT/IN

About the Author

Greg Harvey, the author of more than 50 computer books, has had a long career of teaching business people in the use of IBM PC, Windows, and Macintosh software application programs. From 1983 to 1988, he conducted hands-on computer software training for corporate business users with a variety of training companies (including his own, PC Teach). From 1988 to 1992, he taught university classes in Lotus 1-2-3 and Introduction to Database Management Technology (using dBASE) in the Department of Information Systems at Golden State University in San Francisco.

In mid-1993, Greg started a new multimedia publishing venture called mind over media. As a multimedia developer, he hopes to enliven his future computer books by making them into true interactive learning experiences that will vastly enrich and improve the training of users of all skill levels. You can send him e-mail at gharvey@mindovermedia.com and visit his Web site at www.mindovermedia.com.

In 1999, Greg began graduate school at the California Institute of Integral Studies (CIIS) in San Francisco. In the summer of 2000, he received his master's degree in philosophy and religion in the area of Asian and Comparative Studies. Currently, he has finished all his coursework in the Ph.D. program at CIIS and is getting ready to begin work on his dissertation in the area of Chinese and Tibetan end-of-life religious beliefs.

Dedication

To Chris for his unflagging support and encouragement

Author's Acknowledgments

Let me take this opportunity to thank all the people, both at Wiley Publishing, Inc., and at Mind over Media, Inc., whose dedication and talent combined to get this book out and into your hands in such great shape.

At Wiley Publishing, Inc., I want to thank Steve Hayes and Tiffany Franklin for their considerable help in getting this project underway, Christine Berman for her tremendous expertise as project editor, and Jean Rogers for her great skill as the copy editor, for making sure that the project stayed on course and made it into production so that all the talented folks on the Production team could create this great final product.

At Mind over Media, I want to give a special thanks to Michael Bryant, the person primarily responsible for the updating and reorganizing all the material for this 6.0 version of the software covered in this new edition of the book (fantastic job, Michael!).

Publisher's Acknowledgments

We're proud of this book; please send us your comments through our online registration form located at www.dummies.com/register/.

Some of the people who helped bring this book to market include the following:

Acquisitions, Editorial, and Vertical Websites

Project Editor: Christine Berman

Acquisitions Editor: Tiffany Franklin

Copy Editor: Jean Rogers

Technical Editor: Gordon Kent

Editorial Manager: Leah Cameron

Vertical Websites Manager: Laura VanWinkle

Vertical Websites Supervisor: Richard Graves

Editorial Assistant: Amanda Foxworth

Cartoons: Rich Tennant, www.the5thwave.com

Production

Project Coordinators: Nancee Reeves, Regina Snyder

Layout and Graphics: Seth Conley, Carrie Foster, LeAndra Hosier, Michael Kruzil, Janet Seib

Proofreaders: Laura Albert, Angel Perez, Carl Pierce, Kathy Simpson, Techbooks Production Services

Indexer: Techbooks Production Services

Publishing and Editorial for Technology Dummies

> **Richard Swadley,** Vice President and Executive Group Publisher
>
> **Andy Cummings,** Vice President and Publisher
>
> **Mary C. Corder,** Editorial Director

Publishing for Consumer Dummies

> **Kathleen Nebenhaus,** Vice President and Executive Publisher

Composition Services

> **Debbie Stailey,** Director of Composition Services

Contents at a Glance

Table of Contents

Introduction

• •

*A*dobe PDF (Portable Document Format) is just now starting to fulfill its promise as a truly transportable file format that enables people to share sophisticated electronic documents across a wide array of otherwise incompatible computer platforms without requiring access to either the software that generated the documents or the fonts used in the documents. Part of the proof of this statement is evidenced in the ever-growing presence of PDF documents, especially on the World Wide Web.

Nowadays, you can hardly browse the Web without encountering sites that present some of their online information as PDF files. In fact, so many sites offer their standard reports, registration and feedback forms, and industry white papers as downloadable PDF files that few seasoned business users remain unfamiliar with the PDF format (even if they're not exactly sure what it is) or the free Adobe Reader software used to open, read, and print documents saved in it.

Beyond the popularity of PDF for information-sharing on the Internet, PDF is also becoming increasingly popular as the format to use for prepress documents, eBook publishing, document review, and document archiving. To ready PDF files for these additional roles, you naturally graduate from the world of the free Adobe Reader and Acrobat eBook Reader to that of Acrobat 6. Acrobat 6 (which, unlike the free Adobe Reader, you must purchase) is Adobe's latest version of its all-in-one utility for editing, annotating, and managing documents saved in PDF.

As the name Acrobat implies, this utility enables you to juggle the many roles it can assign PDF files with relative ease. All that's required of you is a keen sense of the role or roles you want your PDF document to fulfill along with a careful reading of the pertinent sections of this book.

About This Book

This book is your complete introductory reference to the reading, writing, and managing of PDF files for any and all of their many purposes, from preparing prepress documents for printing on sophisticated imagesetters to publishing your life story as an eBook for sale on the bevy of online bookstores. Because the way you make, prepare, and sometimes even read a PDF file varies according to the purpose you have in mind for it, you will find that this book's information emphasizes more the purpose you ultimately have in mind for the PDF file than the features used to accomplish this purpose in the various programs such as Acrobat, Adobe Reader, and the Acrobat eBook Reader.

As a result, this book is not meant to be read from cover to cover. Each discussion of a topic briefly addresses the question of how a particular feature enables you to accomplish your purpose before launching into how to use it. In Acrobat, as with most other sophisticated programs, there is usually more than one way to do a task. For the sake of your sanity, I have purposely limited the choices, usually by giving you only the most efficient ways to do a particular task. Later on, if you're so tempted, you can experiment with alternative ways of doing a task. For now, just concentrate on performing the task as described.

As much as possible, I've tried to make it unnecessary for you to remember anything covered in another section of the book. From time to time, however, you come across a cross-reference to another section or chapter in the book. For the most part, such cross-references are meant to help you get more complete information on a subject, should you have the time and interest. If you have neither, no problem; just ignore the cross-references as if they never existed.

How to Use This Book

As a reference to all things PDF, you should start out by looking up the topic you need information on (either in the Table of Contents or the Index) and then refer directly to the section of interest. Most topics are explained conversationally. Many times, however, my regiment-commander mentality takes over, and I list the steps you need to take to accomplish a particular task in a particular section.

What You Can Safely Ignore

When you come across a section that contains the steps you take to get something done, you can safely ignore all text accompanying the steps (the text that isn't in bold) if you have neither the time nor the inclination to wade through more material.

Whenever possible, I have also tried to separate background or footnote-type information from the essential facts by exiling this kind of junk to a sidebar. These sections are often flagged with icons that let you know what type of information you will encounter there. You can easily disregard text marked this way. (I discuss the icons used in this book a little later.)

Foolish Assumptions

I'm going to make only two assumptions about you (let's see how close I get): You have a need to create and use PDF files in your work, and you have access to Acrobat 6. Some of you are working on PCs running some version of Windows or Windows NT. Others of you are working on Macintosh computers running one of the later versions of the Mac operating system. Note that there are rather specific system requirements for Acrobat 6 whether you use a Windows or Macintosh computer. These requirements are covered in Chapter 1.

Beyond that, it's anyone's guess what brings you to Acrobat and PDF. Some of you need to know how to convert all your paper documents into PDF files. Some of you need to know how to save your graphics files as PDFs. Others of you need to know how to create PDF form files in which users can submit important data. Still others of you need to know how to create and publish PDF files as eBooks for sale and distribution on the World Wide Web. Regardless of your needs, you will be able to find the information you require somewhere in the pages of this book.

How This Book Is Organized

This book is organized into five parts, the first four of which cover all the basics of reading, making, and managing PDF files. The fifth part, the indispensable Part of Tens, recaps important Acrobat and PDF enhancements and resources. You should not, however, get too hung up about following along with the structure of the book; ultimately, it doesn't matter at all if you find out how to use Paper Capture to convert printed documents to PDF before you find out how to use PDFMaker 6.0 to convert your Word documents, or if you figure out how to archive your PDF documents in a searchable collection before you discover how to create interactive forms for collecting data online. The important thing is that you find the information — and understand it when you find it — when you need to do what needs getting done.

In case you're interested, here's a synopsis of what you find in each part of this book.

Part 1: Presenting Acrobat and PDF Files

Part I looks at what makes PDF files tick and the most common ways of accessing their information. Chapter 1 covers the many purposes of PDF documents in today's business world. Chapter 2 lays out essential information about using the different Adobe programs that enable you to read and print PDF documents. Chapter 3 acquaints you with the interface of Acrobat 6, Adobe's utility for preparing and editing PDF documents.

Part II: The Wealth of Ways for Creating PDF Files

Part II looks at the many ways of making PDF files. Chapter 4 gives you vital information on how to use and customize the Acrobat Distiller to create the PDF document suited to just the purpose you have in mind. Chapter 5 covers the ins and outs of converting Microsoft Office documents (specifically those created with Word, Excel, and PowerPoint) to PDF. Chapter 6 covers capturing paper documents as PDF files primarily by scanning them directly into Acrobat 6. Chapter 7 tells you how to capture Web pages as PDF files. Chapter 8 covers the printing of all or part of your PDF files on printers you have in-house.

Part III: Reviewing, Editing, and Securing PDFs

Part III covers a mixture of techniques for reviewing, editing, and protecting your PDF files. Chapter 9 introduces you to the many ways for annotating the PDF documents that you send out for online review and introduces the new e-mail-based and browser-based review features in Acrobat 6. Chapter 10 covers editing PDF files in Acrobat 6. Chapter 11 tells you how to secure your PDF documents and protect them from further changes. Chapter 12 acquaints you with the different ways you can extract contents in your PDF files for repurposing with the other software programs you use. Chapter 13 gives you the ins and outs of cataloging your PDF files by creating searchable collections that you can distribute across networks or on CD-ROM.

Part IV: PDFs as Electronic Documents

Part IV covers the different roles of electronic PDF files. Chapter 14 covers the creation and usage of PDF documents as interactive forms that you can fill out and whose data you can extract. Chapter 15 acquaints you with creating and preparing PDF files as eBooks for sale and distribution on the World Wide Web. Chapter 16 gives you information on how you can turn PDF documents into online presentations by adding multimedia elements, including audio and video clips.

Part V: The Part of Tens

As is the tradition in these *For Dummies* books, the last part contains lists of the top ten most useful facts, tips, and suggestions. Chapter 17 gives you a list of my top ten third-party (that is, not developed by Adobe Systems) add-in programs for augmenting and enhancing the program's already considerable features. Chapter 18 gives you a list of my top ten online resources for discovering even more about Acrobat and PDF files!

Conventions Used in This Book

The following information gives you the lowdown on how things look in this book — publishers call these the book's *conventions* (no campaigning, flag-waving, name-calling, or finger-pointing is involved, however).

Keyboard and mouse

Although most of the keyboard and mouse instructions given in the text are self-explanatory, there are a few important differences between the typical Windows and Macintosh keyboards and mice that are worth noting here. For example, keystroke shortcuts in Acrobat 6 and Adobe Reader 6 in Windows often use the Ctrl key in combination with one or more letter keys. The Macintosh, however, substitutes its ⌘ key (called the Command key, the one with the apple and the cloverleaf icon) for the Windows Ctrl key (rather than using its Control key). Also, because the Macintosh keyboard has no Alt key, its Option key is routinely substituted in all shortcuts using the Alt key.

Regarding the mouse, Windows favors a two-button (left- and right-button) mouse, whereas Macintosh favors a single-button mouse. As a result, while you access shortcut (or context) menus in Acrobat in Windows by clicking the right mouse button (a technique commonly known as right-clicking), you hold down the Control (not the ⌘) key as you click the mouse on the Macintosh (a technique commonly known as Control+clicking). Note that if you do have a two button mouse on the Macintosh, the right-clicking technique applies.

Other than these common keyboard and mice anomalies, it's pretty much the same whether you are working with PDFs in Acrobat and Adobe Reader on a Windows or Macintosh machine. In the few cases where there are differences in Acrobat's capabilities across the platforms, I have duly noted them in the text, usually in the form of a tip or warning (described in the next section).

Special icons

The following icons are strategically placed in the margins to point out stuff you may or may not want to read.

This icon alerts you to nerdy discussions that you may well want to skip (or read when no one else is around).

This icon alerts you to shortcuts or other valuable hints related to the topic at hand.

This icon alerts you to information to keep in mind if you want to meet with a modicum of success.

This icon alerts you to information to keep in mind if you want to avert complete disaster.

Where to Go from Here

If you've never had any prior experience with PDF files, I suggest that, right after getting your chuckles with the cartoons, you go first to Chapter 1 and find out what you're dealing with. If you're already familiar with the ins and outs of PDF files, but don't know anything about how you go about creating them, jump to Chapter 4, where you find out how to get started using Acrobat's Create PDF features and using the Acrobat Distiller. Then, as specific needs arise (like "How do I annotate PDF documents in Acrobat 6?" or "How do I protect PDF files from further changes?"), you can go to the Table of Contents or the Index to find the appropriate section and go right to that section for answers.

Part I

Presenting Acrobat and PDF Files

The 5th Wave   By Rich Tennant

"...and I'd also like to thank Doug Gretzel here for all his work in helping us develop our interactive, multimedia stapling division."

In this part . . .

Adobe's PDF (Portable Document Format) is characterized as a truly universal file format that preserves all the original document's formatting — including its fonts, graphics, and layout — across a wide array of different computer platforms. This part of the book is where you find out how PDF came to warrant this lofty characterization.

In Chapter 1, you discover the many platforms that support documents saved as PDFs, the many uses for PDF documents in your work, the different classes of PDF files that you will be dealing with, along with a general overview of the process you follow in saving documents as PDF files. In Chapter 2, you get the lowdown on how to use the various PDF reader software programs offered by Adobe Systems, including Acrobat 6, Adobe Reader, and Acrobat eBook Reader. Chapter 3 rounds out Part I by introducing you to the interface of Acrobat 6, the Adobe program that not only enables you to view and print PDF files but edit them as well.

Chapter 1

The Ins and Outs of PDF Files

I'm so enthusiastic about Adobe PDF files that I think the abbreviation PDF should stand for Pretty Darn Fantastic instead of the more mundane Portable Document Format. In PDF files, you not only see the first inklings of a truly paperless office (or as close as we're likely to get), but also the delivery of a truly universal file format; that is, one truly capable of being opened and used on any of the many computer operating systems currently in use.

In this chapter, you get introduced to what makes PDF files so special and how they can be used to your advantage, especially in office environments that mix and match different computer platforms. As part of this process, you also get acquainted with the different versions of PDF files and how they can be tailored to fit the particular needs of those who use the documents.

The Purpose of PDF Files

PDF, as the name Portable Document Format implies, was developed by Adobe Systems as a means for digital file exchange. The main idea behind the file format is to enable all computer users to be able to open, review, and print the documents saved in it. This means that users who work on computers that don't have the software with which the files were originally created can still see the document as it was originally designed and laid out, including all its fonts and graphics.

The key to this digital file interchange is the nifty little software program known as Acrobat (although Adobe originally named it Carousel when it first appeared in 1993). A free form of this software, known as the *Adobe Reader,* is available from Adobe Systems for all the major personal computing devices and most versions of all the operating systems known to humankind. As of this writing, these forms include:

- ✔ Microsoft Windows machines with the following versions: Windows 3.1, Windows 95 (OSR 2.0), Windows 98 SE, Windows Millennium Edition, Windows NT 4.0 (with Service Pack 5), Windows 2000, or Windows XP

- ✔ Macintosh computers with version 7.5.3, 8.1–8.6, 9.1–9.2, or OS X of the Macintosh operating system

- ✔ Palm handhelds with OS 3.0 or later

- ✔ Pocket PC computers with Windows CE or Windows 2002

- ✔ IBM AIX workstations with IBM AIX 4.2.1

- ✔ HP 9000 Series workstations (model 700 or higher) with HP-UX 9.0.3

- ✔ SGI workstations with Silicon Graphics IRIX 5.3

- ✔ DEC workstations with DEC OSF/1, version 4

- ✔ Sun Solaris SPARCStations with Sun OpenWindows 3.0 or later, Motif 1.2.3 or later, OpenLook 3.0, or CDE 1.0 or later

- ✔ Computers running versions of Linux including Red Hat Linux 5.1 or Slackware Linux 2.0

Acrobat 6 and Adobe Reader are both major upgrades to the Acrobat software family. Consequently, backward-compatibility with older operating systems is limited. In order to run Acrobat 6 on Windows you must use one of the following operating systems: Microsoft Windows 98 Second Edition, Windows NT Workstation 4.0 with Service Pack 6, Windows 2000 Professional with Service Pack 2, Windows XP Professional or Home Edition, or Windows XP Tablet PC Edition. Macintosh users must use OS X versions 10.2.2–10.2.6.

All you have to do to get the appropriate version of Adobe Reader for your current operating system is point your Web browser to the following page on the Adobe Systems Web site at

```
www.adobe.com/products/acrobat/readstep2.html
```

and in the Step 1 of 2 area of the Adobe Reader download page choose your language, your connection speed (dial-up or broadband), and your computer platform. After you choose your computer platform, the Step 2 of 2 area appears. Note that the selections you make in Step 1 determine the version of

Adobe Reader best suited for your computer system. If your current system is compatible with Adobe Reader, you are offered two choices: either the Basic or Full versions if you chose dial-up as your connection speed, or Full if you chose broadband. The Basic version is 8.7MB and can typically take up to 30 minutes or more to download with a 56K modem. The Full version of Adobe Reader has enhanced features that are described in the Step 2 of 2 dialog box and weighs in at a hefty 15.3MB — not a big deal if you have broadband Internet access but worth the consideration if you use a modem to connect to the Web. After choosing your desired version of Adobe Reader, click the Download button. After downloading the Adobe Reader to the desktop of your computer platform, double-click the icon representing the compressed version of the program to unpack and install it on your computer.

After you install the Adobe Reader on your computer, you can then open, review, and print any PDF file that you get, regardless of what application programs were used in generating its text and graphics, and regardless of the computer platform on which these programs ran. (See Chapter 2 for details on how to access and review PDF files with the Adobe Reader.)

Adobe Reader comes in two versions with very different feature sets that you can compare during the process of downloading the program. Adobe also created not two, but three different versions of Acrobat 6: Professional, Standard, and Elements. In order to compare the different features of these products, Adobe provides an Acrobat family features matrix page on their Web site. Go to the following page on Adobe's Web site to view this important information:

```
www.adobe.com/products/acrobat/matrix.html
```

Benefits of Using PDF Files

The most important benefit derived from the use of PDF files is that anyone whose computer is equipped with Adobe Reader can open, read, and print them. This essentially enables you to concentrate on the software tools that you have at hand and feel are best suited for producing the document without having to worry about whether or not your client or coworker has the same software available to them. As you'll soon see, this is only one of the many important uses to which you can put your PDF files with Acrobat 6. Keep in mind that the availability of many features described in the following sections depend on which version of Adobe Reader or Acrobat 6 you are using. For that reason, it's a good idea to go to the Acrobat family features page described in the previous section to familiarize yourself with all of Adobe's new Acrobat products.

What you designed is what they see

Because you are assured that your PDF files will essentially appear on-screen and print as you originally designed them, no matter the computer on which they're opened or the printing device to which they're output, you don't have to hold back on your design, avoiding the use of certain more decorative fonts and/or complex layouts. Figures 1-1 and 1-2 illustrate this situation. In Figure 1-1, you see a PDF file as it appears when opened with Adobe Reader on a computer running Windows. Figure 1-2 shows the same PDF file as it appears when opened on a Macintosh computer. As you can see, they are both comparable in terms of the appearance of their fonts and their layout.

PDF files in the review cycle

While PDF debuted as a universal file format for viewing and printing documents on various types of computers and printers, thanks to advances to the Acrobat software (and here I'm referring to the full-fledged Acrobat program that you must pay for rather than the freebie Adobe Reader available for download), you can now make PDF files an integral part of your design review process. After converting a document to PDF, you can disseminate copies of it to each of the people from whom you need feedback or approval before you put it into use. Each of these people can then add their feedback by adding comments or actually marking up the PDF document in Acrobat 6.

You can then collect their feedback and make the necessary changes either to the PDF version of the file in Acrobat 6 or to the original document (prior to PDF conversion) in the program used in its creation. If managers, coworkers, or clients are required to sign off on the document (either in its original or revised form), they can indicate their approval by stamping the document with their approval or by digitally signing off on it, as shown in Figure 1-3. (See Chapter 9 for details on how to use PDF files in a review cycle and Chapter 11 for details on how to use digital signatures.)

Providing forms, both paper and electronic

With the widespread reliance on the World Wide Web for getting and submitting crucial information, PDF files have taken on another important use, that of providing forms to fill in both online and after printing. Acrobat 6 makes form creation about as easy as it can be.

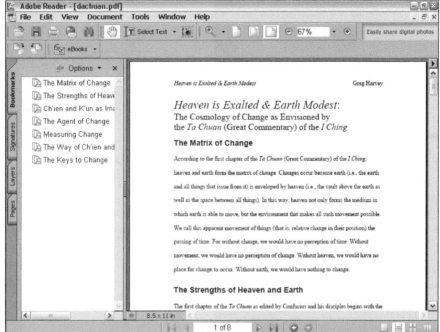

Figure 1-1:
A PDF
document
as it
appears in
the Adobe
Reader 6 on
a computer
running
Windows.

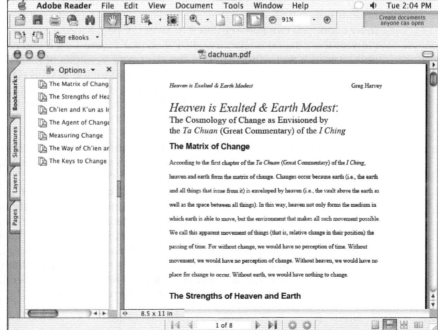

Figure 1-2:
The same
PDF
document
as it
appears in
the Adobe
Reader 6
on a Mac
computer.

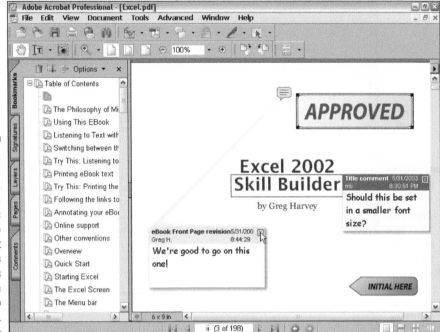

Figure 1-3:
With
Acrobat 6,
you can add
comments
and mark up
text that
needs
revising, as
well as give
your stamp
of approval.

If you need to make certain paper forms available on your company's intranet or your public Web site so that users can download, print, and then fill them in by hand, you can use Acrobat 6 to scan the paper forms and immediately convert their digital images into PDF files (see Figure 1-4). If you need to be able to search and edit the text in the electronic versions of these forms, you can use the Paper Capture feature — Acrobat's version of OCR (Optical Character Recognition) software — to convert the text image into searchable and editable fonts. (See Chapter 6 for details on scanning paper forms and converting them into PDF files with Acrobat 6.)

If you need to get feedback or process informational or order forms directly from your company's intranet or its public Web site, you can use Acrobat 6 to design the electronic forms. Acrobat 6 makes it possible to add all types of interactive fields, including text boxes, combo boxes (also known as drop-down list boxes), check boxes, radio buttons, and command buttons (that users can select to do things such as submit their information or clear the form). With the addition of a simple CGI (Common Gateway Interface) script (courtesy of your friendly IT personnel or Internet service provider), you can store the data submitted by way of your PDF forms in text files that your favorite database or spreadsheet program can read and store. (See Chapter 14 for details on creating interactive PDF forms for use online.)

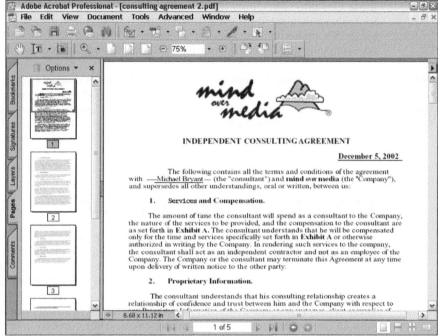

Figure 1-4:
Acrobat 6
makes it
easy to scan
and convert
paper forms
to PDFs,
which can
then be
distributed
for
download
from your
Web site.

You don't have to use the World Wide Web or a company intranet to be able to fill in electronic PDF forms that you create with Acrobat 6. Users who have Acrobat 4 or later installed on their computers can open and fill in these electronic forms using this version or later of Acrobat.

Document archiving

Let's face it: Paper archives are not just bulky and heavy, but they also degrade quickly and are a veritable nightmare to search. For this reason alone, out of all the possible uses for Adobe's Portable Document Format, archiving your documents as PDF files may prove to be the most important to you. Imagine all your paper contracts, correspondence, company reports, and the like stored as collections on CD-ROMs, from which you can retrieve individual files through searches for keywords or for vital statistics such as author name, client name, or job number.

You can use the Paper Capture feature in Acrobat 6 on the Windows or Macintosh platform to scan and convert such paper documents into searchable PDF files. After you do that, Acrobat makes it easy for you to organize these files into collections (known officially as catalogs), which you can index for truly speedy retrieval using the Acrobat 6 search feature. (See Chapter 6 for details on converting paper documents to PDF and Chapter 13 for details on cataloging and indexing your files prior to storing them on various media.)

The Paper Capture feature in Acrobat 6 for Windows restricts you to scanning and converting paper documents of no more than 50 pages in length. If you know that you must scan and convert documents longer than 50 pages on the Windows platform, you need to purchase the standalone module, Acrobat Capture 3 for Windows NT, 2000, or XP or Acrobat Capture 2.0 for Windows 95/98.

PDF in the prepress workflow

One of the most obvious uses for PDF files is in the prepress workflow, during which documents that require professional printing are checked for potential printing errors and readied for conversion from electronic images to the film or plates used in the final printing of the document using high-end imageset-ters (a process known in the industry as *preflight*). Acrobat 6 (Professional version only) contains a number of prepress-related printing options, along with an overprinting preview and an on-screen color correction feature.

These specialized print options and error-checking features in Acrobat 6 are designed to help professional graphic artists and service bureau personnel in finding and eliminating potentially costly printing problems. Most users not directly involved in this end of the business will have no reason to fool with these printing options or use these specialized preview features. (If, for some unknown reason, you are interested in knowing more about these prepress features, refer to Chapter 8.)

Always check with your service bureau personnel to find out what, if any, prepress options they want you to use prior to sending them your PDF files for preflight. Some houses definitely prefer that you not use *any* of these pre-press options, so it's always good to check it out ahead of time.

Quick and easy Web site retrieval

If you are involved with your company's Web design or you are a Web freak who travels frequently and is therefore bereft of a way to stay connected to the Net, you can use the Acrobat 6 Web Capture feature to copy and convert to PDF specific Web pages or even entire Web sites that are of interest to you (see Figure 1-5). After you've converted a set of Web pages or an entire Web site into PDF files, you can then browse them from your hard drive with Acrobat or Adobe Reader without being connected to the Internet.

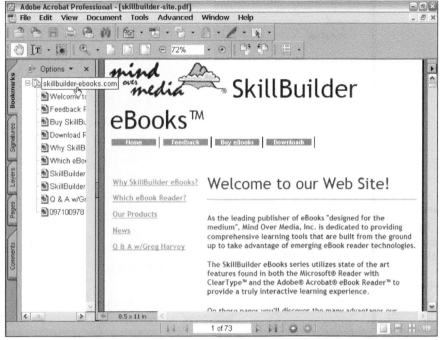

Figure 1-5:
Acrobat 6
makes it a
snap to
capture
Web pages
as PDF files.

As both a road warrior and Web enthusiast, you can use this feature to keep up on the latest online information right from the comfort of your portable computer at those times when you're traveling or just waiting to travel.

If you work as a Web designer, the Web Capture feature provides a perfect means for distributing your Web pages for approval to your client or coworkers. If they have Adobe Reader or Acrobat 6 on their computers, they can even annotate the pages with their suggestions in the form of notes and markups or even give you that final nod of approval using the stamp feature. (See Chapter 7 for details on retrieving and converting Web pages to PDF.)

PDF files as slide shows and multimedia presentations

Another application for PDF files is to use them to create and distribute slide shows and multimedia presentations (see Figure 1-6). Acrobat 6 enables you to add interactivity to your slides in the form of hyperlinks, buttons, and slide transitions. You can also use the program to add sound and/or digital movie files to the slides that your users can play back for a true multimedia experience. Note that Acrobat 6 now supports slide shows and greeting eCards created in Adobe Photoshop Elements 2.0 and Photoshop Album 1.0.

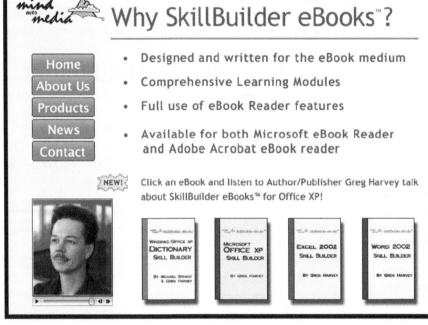

Figure 1-6:
You can play
slide shows
saved as
PDF files in
full-screen
mode.

To enhance the online slide show or multimedia presentation, Acrobat 6 supports a full-screen mode that the user can invoke with none of the screen clutter normally associated with using Acrobat and Adobe Reader (full-screen mode hides the menus, toolbars, scroll bars, status bar, and in Windows, even the omnipresent Task bar). When a user views your slide show or presentation in full-screen mode, you can set it up so that Acrobat automatically advances through each page after a set time interval, using a slide transition of your choice.

If you normally use Microsoft PowerPoint to create your slide shows, you can convert them into PDF files at the touch of a button. You can then use Acrobat 6 to add any extra interactivity and then distribute them for playback on any computer on which the free Adobe Reader 6 is installed.

The Different Types of PDF Files

In addition to the many different uses for the Adobe Portable Document Format described in this chapter, PDF files also give you a great deal of flexibility when you want to reuse their content for other purposes. For example, you can use various PDF formats to distribute a graphically rich report with lots of tables and pictures for printing or viewing on a computer monitor, and then "repurpose" that same content for viewing in a Web page or on a hand-held device where such graphics are prohibitive. This fabulous chameleon act is possible because Adobe PDF files support three basic document structure types: *unstructured, structured,* and *tagged.* PDF documents that are created from these types of documents create the following PDF files:

✔ **Unstructured PDF:** These PDFs have no logical structure tree to define or further describe the author's content. All document information is treated as a single unit with just the author's text and paragraph structure recognized. Basic text formatting, tables, and lists are not recognized.

✔ **Structured PDF:** These PDFs recognize the author's text and paragraph structure but also have a logical structure tree that defines basic text formatting, such as font attributes. Tables and lists are not recognized.

✔ **Tagged PDF:** These PDFs have a logical structure tree that includes all the attributes of structured PDFs and also includes definitions such as document styles and stories (this allows tables and lists to be recognized) and dependencies among various document elements that allow the text to be reflowed. (For more information on reflowing text, see Chapter 15.)

To understand document structure types, you need to look under the hood of your favorite word processor or page layout program. As you create your document, these programs can provide a logical structure tree and tags that define how your document appears when printed or viewed on-screen. I say *can provide* because programs such as Notepad in Windows and Macintosh, which are simple text editing programs with no formatting ability, don't provide for a logical structure tree and so create unstructured documents. You can get an idea of how a document structure tree works using the Document Map feature in Microsoft Word. Open a document and choose View⇨Document Map. The program displays the document's structure tree as hierarchies of headings, paragraphs, and so on. Word then adds tags to this tree that define paragraph styles, font types, font attributes, and allow you to use this structure tree to navigate the document by clicking different structure elements.

The support of document structure types enables you to create unstructured, structured, and tagged PDF files with Acrobat 6. The subsequent result is that the more structured your original document, the more you can reliably reuse your content for other purposes using Adobe PDF. To find out more about PDF file types, see "Understanding how structure types affect flexibility" in the online Acrobat help module. To access the online help guide, choose Help⇨Complete Acrobat 6.0 Help or choose Complete Acrobat 6.0 Help on the How To Window.

Chapter 2

Accessing PDF Files

· ·

In This Chapter

▶ Viewing PDF files with Adobe Reader 6

▶ Viewing PDF files with Acrobat 6

▶ Reading PDF files with Acrobat eBook Reader

▶ Browsing PDF files in your Web browser

· ·

A s this chapter proves, there's more than one way to open and read a PDF file. You have a choice between using Adobe Reader, which comes in two flavors; Basic and Standard (both of which are free), or if you've purchased the full-blown Acrobat 6 (which also comes in two versions; Standard or Professional) for creating and editing PDF files, you can, of course, use it as well. In addition, Adobe also introduced a new product this year for the enterprise sector called Acrobat Elements. The program allows you to view and create, but not edit, PDF documents and must be bulk purchased in lots of 1000. See Chapter 5 for more information on creating PDF documents with Acrobat Elements. As if these weren't enough browsing choices, you can also open and view your PDF files in common Web browsers, such as Internet Explorer and Netscape Navigator on all Windows operating systems and Macintosh OS 9.2.2 and earlier. Note that as of this writing, in order to use the Windows version of Acrobat 6 or Adobe Reader for in-browser viewing of PDF documents, you must have Internet Explorer 5 or later. In-browser viewing of PDF files is also not supported in Mac OS X. As of this writing, Adobe plans to add that functionality in the near future for Mac OS X users. In the meantime, you can configure Acrobat 6 or Adobe Reader as Helper applications in OS X versions of Internet Explorer and Netscape Navigator.

Perusing PDF Files in Adobe Reader

The most common way to view PDF files is by using Adobe Reader (formerly called Acrobat Reader). Adobe Systems offers this program as a free download for a wide number of different computer platforms. As of this writing, the most current version of Adobe Reader is version 6.0. Adobe Reader coincides with the release of Acrobat 6 and utilizes many of the same feature enhancements and improvements to the User Interface (UI) that characterize the latest version of the full-blown product. If you're using Windows XP or Mac OS X, Adobe Reader is automatically selected when you specify your operating system on the Adobe download page. Note that the Macintosh version of Adobe Reader (and also Acrobat 6 Standard and Professional versions) only runs on the Jaguar version of Mac OS X, because the minimum system requirement for the Macintosh version is 10.2.2.

Adobe Reader can open and read all PDF files created with earlier versions of Acrobat. Be aware, however, that earlier versions of Acrobat Reader cannot open and read PDF files created with the later versions of Adobe Acrobat unless you specify compatibility with earlier versions when you create a PDF. Consequently, you also lose newer Acrobat functionalities when you create backward compatible PDF files. See Chapter 4 for more information on creating PDF documents. As Table 2-1 indicates, each version of Adobe Acrobat creates its own version of PDF files. Later versions of Acrobat can read files created in earlier versions, but not vice versa.

Table 2-1	Versions of Acrobat and Their PDF Files	
Acrobat Version	*PDF File Version Created*	*Year Released*
Acrobat 1.0	PDF 1.0	1993
Acrobat 2.0	PDF 1.1	1994
Acrobat 3.0	PDF 1.2	1996
Acrobat 4.0	PDF 1.3	1999
Acrobat 5.0	PDF 1.4	2001
Acrobat 6.0	PDF 1.5	2003

As you can see in Table 2-1, you can tell which version of Acrobat produced a particular PDF file version because the sum of the digits in the PDF file version equals the number of the Adobe Acrobat version that created it. For example, you know that a PDF file in version 1.3 was likely created with Acrobat 4 because the sum of its file version numbers, 1 and 3, is 4.

When you're viewing PDF files in Acrobat on a Windows computer, you can tell what version of PDF file you're dealing with by choosing File⇨Document Properties to open the Document Properties dialog box. Select Description in

the list box in the PDF Information area of the Description palette and you
find the PDF version. Note that the file version listed will not always tally with
the version of Acrobat that created the file because engineering a PDF for
backward compatibility is possible.

When creating a PDF file with the Acrobat Distiller in Acrobat 6, you can make
it possible for viewers using earlier versions of Acrobat Reader to open your
files by selecting a Compatibility setting in the Adobe PDF Settings dialog box
for an earlier version of Acrobat. This setting provides compatibility with
Acrobat versions 3.0 through 6.0 and their corresponding PDF versions,
which ensures that your files will reach a wider audience.

Downloading and launching Adobe Reader 6

Adobe Reader 6 (formerly Acrobat Reader) is available in two flavors: Basic
and Full. The Full version gives you the added functionality of local, network,
or Internet PDF searches, Accessibility features, eBook support, and
Multimedia enhancements.

All you have to do to get the appropriate version of Adobe Reader for your
current operating system is point your Web browser to the following page on
the Adobe Systems Web site:

```
www.adobe.com/products/acrobat/readstep2.html
```

This URL takes you to the Download Adobe Reader page, where all you have
to do is make a selection from each of three drop-down lists provided in the
Step 1 of 2 dialog box:

1. **Select the Language of the Adobe Reader (English in most cases).**

2. **Select the Platform (or operating system) that your computer uses
   (that is, Windows Me, Windows NT, Windows 2000/XP, Mac 8.6,
   Mac 9.x, OS X, and so on).**

3. **Choose a Connection speed that you use to access the Internet (dial-up
   or broadband).**

Note that the selections you make in Steps 2 and 3 above determine the
version of Adobe Reader best suited for your computer system. After you
choose your Connection speed, the Step 2 of 2 dialog box appears and displays the result of your Platform and Connection speed choices. If your

current operating system is compatible with Adobe Reader 6 and you chose dial-up as your connection speed, you are offered two choices: either the Basic or Full version. If you chose broadband as your connection speed, only the Full version is offered. Earlier platform/operating system choices that are not compatible with Adobe Reader provide the appropriate version of the older Acrobat Reader program for download.

The Basic version of Adobe Reader is 8.7MB in size and can typically take up to 30 minutes or more to download with a 56K modem. The Full version of Adobe Reader has enhanced features described in the Step 2 of 2 dialog box and weighs in at a hefty 15.3MB (20.9MB for the Mac version). Downloading the Full version is not a big deal if you have broadband Internet access, but it may be worth considering the Basic version if you use a modem to download from the Web.

After choosing your desired version of Adobe Reader, click the Download button, select a download location in the Browse for Folder dialog box, and wait until the Adobe Reader file is downloaded on your computer. Then double-click its installer icon to decompress the Reader files and install them on your hard drive (on the Mac, the Adobe Reader Installer actually downloads the Reader files and installs them when you double-click the Adobe Reader Installer icon).

After installing Adobe Reader on your hard drive, you can launch the Reader with or without also opening a PDF file. To launch the program without also opening a PDF on the Windows platform, choose Start➪Programs➪Adobe Reader (Start➪All Programs➪Adobe Reader in Windows XP).

To launch Adobe Reader on the Macintosh in OS X, follow these steps:

1. **Click the Finder icon on the Dock to open the Finder and click the Applications button on the Finder toolbar.**

2. **Double-click the Adobe Reader file icon in the Applications folder.**

After you launch Adobe Reader , you can then open PDF files for viewing and printing by choosing File➪Open and selecting the PDF file to open in its Open dialog box.

In addition to simply double-clicking a PDF file icon you can also launch Adobe Reader and open a PDF file for viewing by dragging a PDF file icon onto an Adobe Reader shortcut on the Windows or Macintosh desktop. Note that when you install Adobe Reader on a Windows machine, the installer automatically creates a desktop shortcut called Adobe Reader 6.0.

To create such a desktop shortcut on the Macintosh (where it's called an *alias*), click to select the Adobe Reader icon (located in the Applications folder on your hard drive), press ⌘+M to create an Adobe Reader 6.0 alias, and then drag this alias icon onto the Macintosh desktop.

Figure 2-1 shows you how the Adobe Reader window appears on a Windows computer when you launch the Reader and simultaneously open a PDF file within it. Note that in this particular case, the PDF file that opens takes up the full width of the program window up to the Navigation pane, which displays the bookmarks in this document.

You can have more than one PDF file open at a time in Adobe Reader 6. To open multiple files when launching Adobe Reader 6, Ctrl+click individual PDF file icons or lasso a group of them and then drag the entire selection onto the Adobe Reader desktop shortcut (alias). To do this from the Open dialog box, Ctrl+click or lasso the group before you click the Open button.

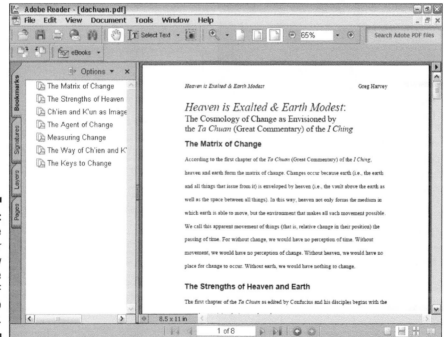

Figure 2-1:
The Adobe Reader window with the open PDF file used to launch it.

The Adobe Reader window

As you can see in Figure 2-2, the Adobe Reader window is divided into three areas:

- ✔ Menu and toolbars at the top of the screen
- ✔ Document pane with scroll bars to the right and bottom and a status bar to immediate left at the bottom
- ✔ Navigation pane with tabs for its four palettes: Bookmarks, Signatures, Layers, and Pages.

Toolbars

Menu bar

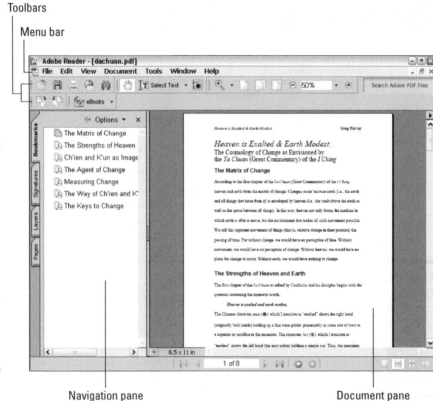

Figure 2-2:
The Adobe
Reader
window is
divided into
three areas:
menu and
toolbars
above;
Document
and
Navigation
panes
below.

Navigation pane   Document pane

The menu bar contains standard application menus: File through Help. To select a menu and display its items, you click the menu name (or you can press the Alt key plus the underlined letter in the menu name, the so-called *hot key,* in the Windows version). To select a menu item, you drag down to highlight it and then press Enter, or you click it (in the Windows version, you can also select an item by typing its hot key). Menus on the Macintosh version display hot keys with the cloverleaf symbol that represents the Command key. You can select these commands simply by holding down the Command key plus the appropriate hot key without opening the menu.

The Adobe Reader toolbars

Directly beneath the menu bar, you see a long toolbar with an almost solid row of buttons. The toolbar may appear on two rows, depending on your screen resolution, when you install and open Adobe Reader for the first time. As Figure 2-3 indicates, this toolbar is actually five separate toolbars, File through Tasks. Note the Tasks toolbar is a single button with a pop-up menu for acquiring, opening, or accessing help on eBooks. This is one example (and the only one you see in Adobe Reader 6) of several new single-button Tasks toolbars. The rest are covered in the section about toolbars in Chapter 3.

The File toolbar, shown in Figure 2-3, displays buttons and labels. You can gain more space on the upper toolbar area by hiding the File Toolbar labels. To do so, right-click the toolbar area and choose Tool Button Labels to remove the checkmark from the context menu.

Figure 2-3:
The space below the menu bar of the Adobe Reader window contains five toolbars side by side.

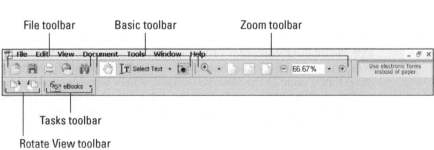

Four of the buttons shown in the toolbars in this figure sport downward-pointing shaded triangles. These downward-pointing triangles (formerly titled More Tools in previous versions of Acrobat) are buttons that, when clicked, display a pop-up menu with additional related tools or commands. In Adobe Reader, these buttons, from left to right, are as follows:

✓ **The Select Text tool:** Right next to the Hand tool in the Basic toolbar, its pop-up menu button enables you to choose either Text or Image and also the Expand This Button option to add both menu items as buttons on the toolbar.

✓ **The Zoom In tool:** The first button in the Zoom toolbar. Its pop-up menu button enables you to select the Zoom In tool if you're using one of the other Zoom tools, the Zoom Out tool (Shift+Z) for zooming out on an area, or a new Dynamic Zoom tool that enables you to dynamically (without incremental changes) zoom in and out by clicking on a viewing area and dragging the mouse up or down.

✓ **The Viewing button:** Shows the current page magnification setting as a percentage in the Zoom toolbar.

✓ **The Read an eBook tool:** The only button on the Tasks toolbar. Its pop-up menu lets you open an eBook in your library (called My Bookshelf) and display an online guide to reading eBooks in the How To window.

Another similar option you may encounter on these pop-up menus is the Show (insert name) Toolbar command that displays, by default, all the menu commands in a floating toolbar window that can be docked anywhere in the toolbar area. To hide this floating toolbar, click its Close button. If the toolbar has been docked, uncheck the Show Toolbar command on the original tool-bar button pop-up menu to hide it. The next time you select this command, the toolbar will appear in its last displayed state, either floating or docked.

Users of Acrobat Reader 5 or earlier may notice that Adobe has consolidated the Find and Search tools into a single Search tool button on the File Toolbar. I find this most gratifying, because I can never remember the difference between a Find and a Search. The Acrobat 6 Search feature is very clear. It enables you to do fast text searches in either the current PDF document, a PDF file on your computer or local network, and even on the Internet when you're using the Full version of Adobe Reader. Clicking the button opens the Search PDF pane in the How To window, where you specify search criteria and then click the Search button. Search results are then displayed in the Search PDF pane. See the "Adobe Reader Document pane" section, later in this chapter, to find out more on the new How To window.

Table 2-2 lists the buttons on each of these toolbars and describes their functions.

Table 2-2		The Toolbars of Adobe Reader 6	
Toolbar	*Icon*	*Name*	*Use It To . . .*
File		Open	Display the Open dialog box.

Toolbar	Icon	Name	Use It To . . .
		Save a Copy	Display the Save a Copy dialog box.
		Print	Open the Print dialog box.
		E-mail	Open your e-mail client and attach the current PDF to a new e-mail.
		Search	Open the Search PDF pane in the How To window.
Basic		Hand tool (H)	Move the PDF document to different areas of the viewing window or of the document itself, depending on your zoom setting; the Hand tool changes to an arrow over menus and buttons, and to a pointing finger over hyperlinks.
		Select Text tool (V)	Select text or images in the document for copying to the Clipboard.
		Snapshot tool	Select text or graphics in the document for copying to the Clipboard by drawing a marquee around your selection.
Zoom		Zoom In tool (Z)	Zoom in on the area that you point to with the magnifying glass icon.
		Actual Size	Resize the zoom magnification setting to 100%.
		Fit in Window	Resize the zoom magnification setting so that you see the entire document.
		Fit Width	Resize the zoom magnification setting so that the width of the document fills the entire Document pane.
		Zoom Out	Decrease the magnification (to see more of the entire document) by set intervals of 25% or less.
	120%	Magnification Level	Display the current magnification level as a percentage of the actual size (100%). To change the magnification, type a number in the Magnification Level text box or select a preset zoom value from the pop-up menu.

(continued)

Table 2-2 *(continued)*

Toolbar	Icon	Name	Use It To . . .
		Zoom In	Increase the magnification (to see more detail and less of the entire document) by set intervals of 25% or less.
Tasks		Read an eBook	Go online to acquire eBooks.
Rotate View		Rotate Clockwise	Reorient the current page by rotating it 90 degrees to the right (clockwise).
		Rotate Counter-clockwise	Reorient the current page by rotating it 90 degrees to the left (counterclockwise).
Navigation		First Page	Jump to the beginning of a multipage document.
		Previous Page	Jump to the previous page in a multi-page document.
		Next Page	Jump to the subsequent page in a multipage document.
		Last Page	Jump to the end of a multipage document.
View History		Previous View	Go to the last page you visited.
		Next View	Go back to the page that was current when you clicked the Previous View button.

The Adobe Reader Document pane

The Adobe Reader Document pane is where your PDF files load for viewing. How much document text and graphics appear in this pane depends upon a number of factors:

- The size of the pages in the document (displayed in the Page Size indicator in the status bar at the bottom of the Document pane — see Figure 2-4)

- The size of your computer monitor

- The current zoom (magnification) setting in Adobe Reader (shown in the Magnification Level button in the Viewing toolbar)

Musical toolbars

You don't have to leave the five Adobe Reader toolbars in the original arrangement. You can move them to new rows or even move them out of the top area of the screen so that they float on top of the Navigation or Document pane. To move a toolbar, you drag it by its separator bar (the slightly raised vertical bar that appears before the first button in each toolbar). As you drag, a dark outline appears at the mouse pointer until you release the mouse button and plunk the toolbar down in its new position. Note that when you release the toolbar in the Navigation or Document pane area, the Adobe Reader reshapes the toolbar so that its buttons are no longer in a single row and gives the toolbar its own title bar. You can move the floating toolbar by clicking the title bar and dragging the window to a new location, but you can't change the shape of the toolbar. To close a floating toolbar, click its close button. To dock a floating toolbar, drag it by its title bar until its outline assumes a single-row shape, and then drop it in place. These features also apply to the Navigation toolbar, which is not displayed by default in Adobe Reader or Acrobat 6.

Of these factors, you can change only the current zoom setting either with the buttons in the Viewing toolbar (see Table 2-2) or the options on the View menu. Zoom out to get an overview of the document's layout. Zoom in to make the text large enough to read.

The How To window is a new feature in both Adobe Reader and Acrobat 6 that provides help and dialog boxes for common tasks, displays the online help guide for both programs, and takes up a significant portion of the Document window. To quickly display or hide the How To window in both the Windows and Macintosh versions of Adobe Reader and Acrobat 6, press F4. See Chapter 3 to discover more about the How To window.

The best way to zoom in on some document detail (be it lines of text or a graphic) is to click the Zoom In tool (or press Z, its hot key) and then use the magnifying-glass pointer to draw a bounding box around the desired text or graphic. When you release the mouse button, Adobe Reader zooms in on the selected area so that it takes up the entire width of the Document pane.

At the bottom left of the Document pane, you find the status bar, which gives you valuable information about the current PDF file you're viewing. The status bar also enables you to advance back and forth through the pages and to change how the pages are viewed in the Document pane (the default setting is a single page at a time). Figure 2-4 helps you identify the status bar buttons.

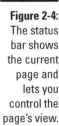

Figure 2-4:
The status
bar shows
the current
page and
lets you
control the
page's view.

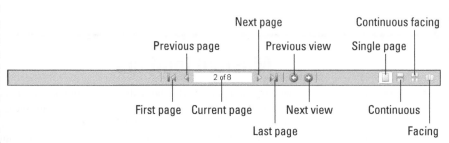

The Adobe Reader Navigation pane

The Navigation pane to the left of the Document pane contains four Tab palettes in Adobe Reader 6:

- ✔ **The Bookmarks palette:** Shows the overall structure of the document in an outline form. Note, however, that not all PDF files that you open in Adobe Reader have bookmarks because this is a feature that the author of the document must decide to include prior to or when actually making the PDF file. (See Chapter 4 for more on this topic.)

- ✔ **The Signatures palette:** Displays your digital signature or any others that exist in a PDF document signature form field. (See Chapter 11 for more info on signing and securing PDF documents.)

- ✔ **The Layers palette:** Enables you to view any content layers that the author has inserted, such as headers and footers or watermarks, in the current PDF document. (For more on this new feature, see Chapter 10.)

- ✔ **The Pages palette (formerly the Thumbnails palette):** Shows little representations of each page in the PDF document you're viewing. Note that Adobe Reader generates thumbnails for each page in a PDF document, whether or not the author embedded them at the time when the PDF was made.

Adobe Reader offers you several ways to open and close the Navigation pane (which may or may not be displayed automatically when you first open the PDF file for viewing):

- ✔ If the Navigation Pane is closed, click any of the Navigation Tabs on the left side of the document pane to open the Navigation Pane and display that palette.

- ✔ If the Navigation Pane is open, you can close it by clicking the Close button (X) on the Options bar at the top of the pane.

✔ Click the Navigation Pane button (the double-headed arrow) at the beginning of the status bar in the Document pane to open or close the Navigation Pane.

✔ Press F6 (Windows or Mac).

Note that you can manually resize the Navigation pane to make it wider or narrower. Position the Hand tool mouse pointer on its border or on the Navigation Pane button at the beginning of the Status bar. When the tool changes to a double-headed arrow, drag right (to make the pane wider) or left (to narrow it). Adobe Reader remembers any width changes that you make to the Navigation pane, so that the pane resumes the last modified size each time you use the Reader.

You might be tempted to increase the width of the Navigation pane because it isn't wide enough to display all the text in the headings in the Bookmarks palette. Rather than reduce the precious real estate allotted to the Document pane in order to make all the headings visible, you can read a long heading by hovering the Hand tool mouse pointer over its text. After a second or two, Acrobat displays the entire bookmark heading in a highlighted box that appears on top of the Navigation pane and extends as far as necessary into the Document pane. As soon as you click the bookmark link or move the Hand tool off the bookmark, this highlighted box disappears. You can also choose Wrap Long Bookmarks on the Options menu at the top of the Bookmarks pane which automatically adjusts the width of bookmark text to the current width of the Navigation pane.

Using the Bookmarks palette

The Bookmarks palette gives you an overview of the various sections in many PDF documents (see Figure 2-5). Adobe Reader indicates the section of the document that is currently being displayed in the Document pane by highlighting the page icon of the corresponding bookmark in the Bookmarks palette.

In some documents you open, the Bookmarks palette will have multiple nested levels (indicating subordinate levels in the document's structure or table of contents). When a Bookmarks palette contains multiple levels, you can expand a part of the outline to display a heading's nested levels by clicking the Expand button that appears in front of its name. In Windows, Expand buttons appear as boxes containing a plus sign. On the Macintosh, Expand buttons appear as shaded triangles pointing to the right. Note that you can also expand the current bookmark by clicking the Expand Current Bookmark button at the top of the Bookmark palette.

Expand Current Bookmark

Options menu

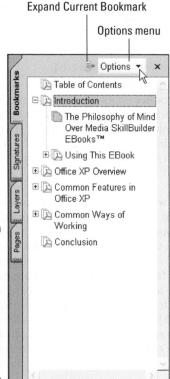

Figure 2-5:
The
Navigation
pane
opened
with the
Bookmarks
palette
selected.

When you expand a particular bookmark heading, all its subordinate topics appear in an indented list in the Bookmarks palette, and the Expand button becomes a Collapse button (indicated by a box with a minus sign in it in Windows and by a downward-pointing shaded triangle on the Mac). To hide the subordinate topics and tighten up the bookmark list, click the topic's Collapse button. You can also collapse all open subordinate topics by selecting Collapse Top-Level Bookmarks on the Options menu.

Using the Pages palette

The Pages palette shows you tiny versions of each page in the PDF document you're viewing in Adobe Reader (see Figure 2-6). You can use the Navigation pane's vertical scroll bar to scroll through these thumbnails to get an overview of the pages in the current document, and sometimes you can even use them to locate the particular page to which you want to go (especially if that page contains a large, distinguishing graphic).

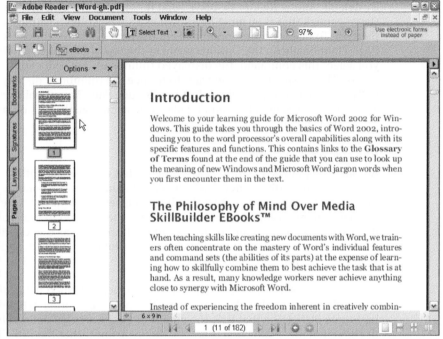

Figure 2-6:
The
Navigation
pane
opened with
the Pages
palette
selected.

Note that Adobe Reader displays the number of each page immediately beneath its thumbnail image in the Pages palette. The program indicates the current page that you're viewing by highlighting its page number underneath the thumbnail. The program also indicates how much of the current page is being displayed in the Document pane on the right with the use of a red outlining box in the current thumbnail (this box appears as just two red lines when the box is stretched as wide as the thumbnail).

You can zoom in and out and scroll up and down through the text of the current page by manipulating the size and position of this red box. To scroll the current page's text up, position the Hand tool on the bottom edge of the box and then drag it downward (and, of course, to scroll the current page's text down, you drag this outline up). To zoom in on the text of the page in the Document pane, position the Hand tool on the sizing handle located in the lower-right corner of the red box (causing it to change to a double-headed diagonal arrow) and then drag the corners of the box to make the box smaller so that less is selected. To zoom out on the page, drag the corner to make the box wider and taller. Of course, if you stretch the outline of the red box so that it's as tall and wide as the thumbnail of the current page, Adobe Reader responds by displaying the entire page in the Document pane, the same as if you selected the Fit in Window view.

By default, Adobe Reader displays what it considers to be large thumbnails (large enough that they must be shown in a single column within the Pages palette). To display more thumbnails in the Pages palette, choose Reduce Page Thumbnails on the Options menu at the top of the Pages palette. When you select this command, the displayed thumbnails are reduced in 33% increments. This means that if you want to reduce the thumbnail display substantially, you have to repeatedly select the Reduce Page Thumbnails command. To increase the size of the thumbnails, choose Enlarge Page Thumbnails on the Options menu.

Using the Article palette

Acrobat 6 supports a feature called *articles* that enables the author or editor to control the reading order when the PDF document is read online. This feature is useful when reading text that has been set in columns, as are many magazine and newspaper articles, because it enables you to read the text as it goes across columns and pages as though it were set as one continuous column. Otherwise, you end up having to do a lot of zooming in and out and scrolling, and you can easily lose your place.

To see if the PDF file you're reading has any articles defined for it, choose View⇔Navigation Tabs⇔Articles. Doing this opens a floating Articles palette in its own dialog box that lists the names of all the articles defined for the document. If this dialog box is empty, then you know that the PDF document doesn't use articles. Note that you can dock this palette on the Navigation pane and add its tab beneath the one for the Pages palette by dragging the Articles tab displayed in the dialog box and dropping it on the Navigation pane.

To read an article listed on the Articles tab, double-click the article name in the list or click its name in the list and then click the Read Article item on its pop-up menu. The first part of the text defined in the article appears in fit-width viewing mode at the Adobe Reader 's default maximum-fit setting, and the mouse pointer changes to a Hand tool with a down arrow on it. After reading the first section of the article, you continue to the next section either by pressing the Enter key (Return on Mac) or by clicking the Hand tool pointer. Adobe Reader indicates when you reach the end of the article by placing a horizontal bar under the arrowhead of the down arrow on the Hand tool. If you then click the Hand tool again or press Enter (or Return), Adobe Reader returns you to the start of the article (indicated by a horizontal bar appearing at the top of the shaft of the down arrow). To return to normal viewing mode after reading an article, click one of the regular viewing buttons on the Zoom toolbar — Actual Size, Fit in Window, or Fit Width — or its corresponding menu option on the View menu (you can even use the View⇔Fit Visible command, which resizes the text and graphics in the document — without page borders — and has no comparable button).

To change the magnification used in reading an article in a PDF file, before you start reading the article, choose Edit➪Preferences or press Ctrl+K (⌘+K on the Mac). In the Preferences dialog box that appears, click Page Display in the left window, and then select a new magnification setting from the Max Fit Visible Zoom drop-down list. Click OK to close the Preferences dialog box and change the magnification.

Navigating PDF documents

Between the buttons on the Navigation toolbar at the top, the navigation buttons on the status bar, the Bookmarks and Pages palettes in the Navigation pane to the left, and the scroll bars on the Document pane to the right, you have quite a few choices in how you navigate a PDF document in Adobe Reader. The following list describes the most popular ways to move through the pages of a PDF document:

- **To move a page at a time:** Press the → or ← key, click the Next Page button in the Navigation toolbar or the status bar to move forward, or click the Previous Page button to move back.

- **To move to the last page:** Press the End key or click the Last Page button in the Navigation toolbar or the status bar.

- **To move to the first page:** Press the Home key or click the First Page button in the Navigation toolbar or the status bar.

- **To move to a specific page:** Drag the scroll button in the Document pane's vertical scroll bar until the page number appears in the ScreenTip; click the Current Page indicator in the status bar, type the page number, and press Enter; or scroll to the page's thumbnail in the Pages palette and click it.

- **To scroll through sections of text (about half a page at a time):** Press the Page Down key (to move forward) or the Page Up key (to move back).

- **To scroll continuously through the text:** Click and hold down the down (to move forward) and up (to move back) scroll arrows on the vertical scroll bar in the Document pane.

Changing the page viewing mode

Normally, Adobe Reader displays a single page of the PDF document at a time so that when you scroll from the end of one page to the next page, the next page seems to replace the previous one. You can, if you want, change the page viewing mode from single to continuous paging, wherein you see a steady stream of pages as you scroll through the document. To change from single-page to continuous-page viewing, click the Continuous button on the right side of the status bar or choose View➪Continuous.

As part of continuous paging, you can also display facing pages (with verso or left-hand pages on the left, and recto or right-hand pages on the right). To display a PDF document with continuous facing pages, click the Continuous - Facing button on the status bar or choose View➪Page Layout➪Continuous - Facing. A new addition to the status bar is the Facing button that displays two full pages side by side in the document window.

Reading text in full-screen mode

If you're like me and your computer isn't equipped with a mega-size monitor, you may want to make the most of your screen real estate by viewing the PDF document in full-screen mode. When you switch to full-screen viewing, the program removes all the screen controls, including the menu bar, toolbars, Navigation pane, status bar, and yes, even the ubiquitous Windows taskbar.

To view a PDF document in full-screen mode, press Ctrl+L (⌘+L on the Macintosh), or choose View➪Full Screen. To get out of full-screen mode and return to your regular viewing settings (replete with menus, toolbars, and so on), press the Escape key (usually marked Esc on your keyboard) or press Ctrl+L again.

Note that when viewing a PDF document in full-screen mode, Adobe Reader always displays a single page at a time (no matter what page viewing mode you were using prior to selecting full-screen mode). Because full-screen mode hides all menus and toolbars, you normally need to rely on keystroke shortcuts to alter the magnification and move through the document text. Here are some of the more useful keystroke shortcuts for doing just that:

- **Ctrl++ (Ctrl plus the plus key) and Ctrl+– (Ctrl plus the minus key):** Increase magnification by 25% by pressing Ctrl++; decrease magnification by 25% by pressing Ctrl+–.

- **Ctrl+0:** Select the Fit in Window view.

- **Ctrl+1:** Select the Actual Size view.

- **Ctrl+2:** Select the Fit Width view.

- **Ctrl+3:** Select the Fit Visible view (this enlarges the document so that it takes up as much of the screen width as possible).

- **Page Down or Ctrl+↓:** Scroll down the text (and move to the next page in the Fit in Window view).

- **Page Up or Ctrl+↑:** Scroll up the text (to the previous page in the Fit in Window view).

Note that if you use Fit Visible, the view that enlarges the document to the highest degree, you can use the arrow keys to scroll either up, down, left, or right through the document.

Reading text in the fit-visible viewing mode

Reading a PDF document in full-screen viewing mode is fine as long as you don't mind having to navigate the pages with keystroke shortcuts. If, however, you prefer using the various Adobe Reader screen controls (including the scroll bars and the navigating buttons on the Navigation toolbar and on the Document window status bar), you're out of luck.

To make online viewing as comfortable as possible while still retaining access to the Adobe Reader screen controls, try viewing the document text in the fit-visible viewing mode. This viewing mode is very similar to the fit-width mode, except that it doesn't retain the space for the document's left and right margins, using this margin space instead to further boost the magnification of the document's text and graphics.

To use this viewing mode, you need to choose View➪Fit Visible or press Ctrl+3 (⌘+3 on the Macintosh) because the viewing mode does not have a button on the Viewing toolbar. Note that the four page view modes (Fit Page, Actual Size, Fit Width, and Fit Visible) also appear at the bottom of the Zoom toolbar magnification drop-down list.

Reading reflowed text at larger magnifications

As part of the new accessibility features in Adobe Reader 6, the program is equipped with a Reflow command that you can use to prevent document text from disappearing off the page at larger magnifications. This feature is a godsend for visually impaired users who otherwise wouldn't be able to read the text on the screen at all, and it can be a real boon for anyone, particularly when reading a PDF document that uses especially ornate and decorative fonts that can be very difficult to decipher given the current screen resolution.

Figures 2-7 and 2-8 illustrate how beneficial reflowing the text can be when doing online reading in Adobe Reader 6. In Figure 2-7, I selected the Fit Visible command on the Adobe Reader View menu and then increased the magnification setting to 200%. As you can see, at this magnification, you would have to do a lot of horizontal as well as vertical scrolling to read the text. Figure 2-8 shows what happens when you use the Reflow command by choosing View➪ Reflow. Note how, when this viewing setting is turned on, all the lines of text now fit within the screen width. Although you have to do more vertical scrolling to get through the reflowed text at this magnification, you won't be forced to do any horizontal scrolling at all.

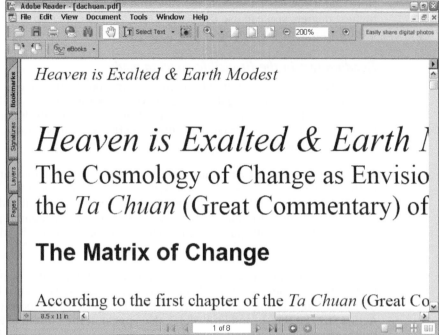

Figure 2-7:
Viewing PDF document text in fit-visible mode at 200% magnification.

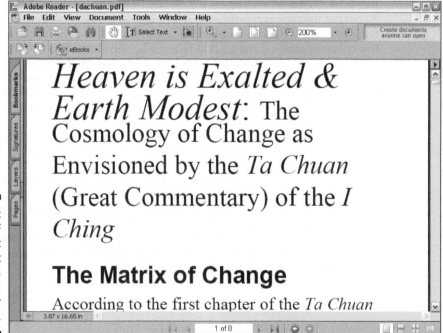

Figure 2-8:
PDF document text at 200% magnification after reflowing.

Getting a non-tagged PDF to reflow

Note that the Reflow feature works only on tagged PDF documents that have been prepared with one of the latest versions of an Acrobat Distiller including, of course, the Distiller in Acrobat 6 and PDFMaker for Microsoft Office 2000 and XP (see Chapter 15 for more on tagged files). If the PDF file you're viewing isn't tagged, you can tell right away because the Reflow command on the View menu is grayed out and not available for use. To convert such a PDF file to a tagged version for use with the Reflow feature with Acrobat 6, choose Advanced⇨ Accessibility⇨Add Tags to Document (the Accessibility items are available on the Advanced menu when you perform a Complete installation of Acrobat 6).

You can turn on the reflow viewing mode by choosing View⇨Reflow or by pressing Ctrl+4 (⌘+4 on the Mac). While viewing the PDF document with Reflow turned on, you can increase or decrease the magnification settings, and Adobe Reader will immediately reflow the text to accommodate the increase or decrease in magnification.

To get out of reflow viewing mode, simply select one of the other viewing modes — Actual Size, Fit in Window, Fit Width, or Fit Visible — from the View menu or the Viewing toolbar (remember, Fit Visible is available only on the View menu). When you select one of these other viewing modes, Adobe Reader automatically reduces the magnification setting to accommodate the text in the mode.

Using bookmarks to locate a particular spot in the document

Instead of just aimlessly scrolling through the PDF text, you may want to find a particular place in the text. If the document has bookmarks, you can often use their links to go right to the spot you want. Simply display the Bookmarks palette in the Navigation pane, expand the topic of interest, and then click the heading at which you want to start reading. When you click a bookmark link, Adobe Reader displays that heading in the Document pane.

If you scroll through the text of a PDF document in the Document pane and then decide that you want to find your place in the bookmarks, click the Reveals Bookmark for the Current Page button (the one with the arrow pointing toward the tiny sheet of paper) located to the immediate left of the Options menu at the top of the Bookmarks palette. When you click this button, Adobe Reader highlights the bookmark in the Bookmarks palette corresponding to the heading closest to your place in the text displayed in the Document pane.

Using Search to locate a particular spot in the document

If your document doesn't have bookmarks (and not all PDF files do), you can use the Adobe Reader (Full version only) Search function to search for a heading, key term, or identifying phrase. To search for text with the Search feature, click the Search button in the File toolbar or choose Edit⇔Search to open the Search PDF pane in the How To window. Enter the word or phrase you want to locate in the document in the What Word or Phrase Would You Like to Search For? text box in the Search PDF pane, and then click the Search button or press Enter to search for it in the document. The program then scans the entire document and displays the results in a list box. The word or phrase is highlighted in each occurrence in the Results list, and you can then click the highlighted term to highlight and move to that occurrence in the document. If no matching text is located, you receive a warning dialog box indicating that this is the case.

To find subsequent occurrences after you close the Search dialog box, press Ctrl+G (⌘+G on the Mac). You can use this keystroke shortcut until you reach the final occurrence of the term in the document, at which point the command stops working.

To narrow your search by preventing Adobe Reader from finding matches for your search text within other, longer words (such as the occurrence of *her* in the word *whether*), select the Match Whole Words Only check box in the Search PDF pane before you begin the search. To narrow your search to exact case matches, select the Match Case check box. To search for a term in the Bookmarks or Comments in a PDF file, check the appropriate check boxes. The Search PDF pane also provides two radio buttons that specify where you would like to perform your search. Select the In the Current PDF Document radio button to search the document displayed in the document window or select the All PDF Documents In radio button and then choose a location on your computer or LAN (Local Area Network). You can even select the Search PDFs on the Internet link at the bottom of the pane to perform your search on the Internet. This feature is powered by Google, the well-known Internet search engine, but keep in mind that you are searching across all PDF documents on the Internet, so the time it takes to perform your search depends on your Internet connection speed. For more information on the Adobe Reader/Acrobat 6 Search feature, see Chapter 13.

Perusing PDF Files in Acrobat 6

It should come as little or no surprise to discover that viewing PDF files in Adobe Acrobat 6 is no different from viewing them in Adobe Reader. After all, the free, giveaway Adobe Reader is simply a trimmed-down version of the full-fledged, must-be-purchased Acrobat 6, lacking all Acrobat's editing tools (they being what you pay for) but none of the browsing tools.

This means that if you have Acrobat 6 installed on your computer (and I'm assuming that you do or will shortly, otherwise why invest in this book?), you can dispense with Adobe Reader altogether and use Acrobat 6 as your exclusive PDF editing *and* viewing program. Of course, this means that for details on how to view and browse your PDF files in Acrobat 6, you need to back up and read the earlier information on perusing PDF documents in Adobe Reader, because all of it pertains to using Acrobat 6 to view PDF documents. (For information on using Acrobat 6's editing features to create, edit, and proof PDF files that can then be distributed to readers using Adobe Reader, refer to the chapters in Parts II and III of this book.)

Reading eBooks with Adobe Reader and Acrobat 6

Adobe has added eBook support to their new releases of Acrobat 6 and Adobe Reader. By *support,* I mean that you can use either program to log onto secure eBook servers, purchase and download eBooks that are encrypted so that authors and publishers are protected with respect to copyrights, and even migrate your old Adobe Acrobat eBook Reader library to the new Acrobat Bookshelf feature. These enhancements mark the end of the Adobe Acrobat eBook Reader program, which has been discontinued (the name was too long anyway). The following sections show you how to use Adobe Reader or Acrobat 6 to specifically read Adobe eBooks.

If you are using the Basic version of Adobe Reader, you must go online and download the eBooks plug-in in order to access My Bookshelf and use eBooks. To get the plug-in, choose Help➪Updates and in the Adobe Reader plug-ins page choose the eBooks package and click Update. The plug-in is downloaded and automatically installed in your Basic version of Adobe Reader.

I want my DRM

The first thing you have to do in order to start downloading and enjoying the huge selection of Adobe eBooks available on the Internet is activate a DRM (Digital Rights Management) account with Adobe. DRM is a system architecture used to prevent unauthorized copying and distribution of copyrighted materials. The system uses security and encryption to lock content and limit its distribution to only those who pay for the content. You cannot purchase or download Adobe eBooks without activating a DRM account with Adobe.

Adobe allows you to activate Acrobat or Adobe Reader on *only* two devices: a computer and a PDA (Personal Digital Assistant) running Palm OS. The computer can be a desktop or laptop and the limitation applies to cross-platform machines — so if you have both Windows and Macintosh computers, you have to decide which platform you want to use for eBook consumption. Consider these choices carefully because it's a one shot deal. If you know you want to read eBooks on your desktop computer, activate your desktop of choice. If you plan on reading eBooks while traveling with a laptop, make sure to activate that machine. Again, you can only activate one of your computers!

Using the Adobe DRM Activator

Adobe makes it a snap to perform this very important eBook DRM business through My Bookshelf in both Adobe Reader and Acrobat 6. As I mentioned earlier, My Bookshelf is a separate module that replaces the Adobe Acrobat eBook Reader Library and can be accessed by either Acrobat 6 or Adobe Reader. To do so, choose File➪My Bookshelf. The first time you open My Bookshelf, an Alert box appears, suggesting that you go online to activate a DRM account. Click OK in this alert box to open your browser and go to the Adobe DRM Activator Web page, as shown in Figure 2-9.

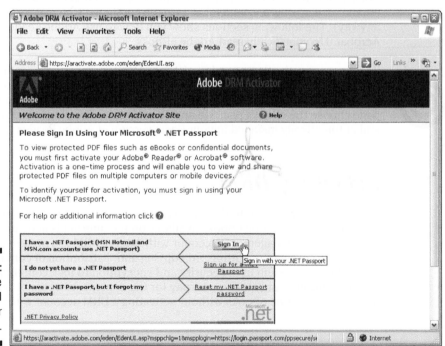

Figure 2-9:
The Adobe DRM Activator Web site.

The Adobe DRM Activator site uses Microsoft's .NET Passport service to create an online identity for you when performing secure transactions on the Internet. If you don't have a .NET Passport you can click the I Do Not Yet Have a .NET Passport link and easily register yourself. Note that you also have the option of signing into the Adobe DRM Activator using your Adobe ID (acquired if you've ever done business at the Adobe Store online). Scroll to the very bottom of the Web page (it's not shown in Figure 2-9) and click the tiny I Prefer Not to Sign in Using Microsoft .NET Passport link. With ID in hand, follow these steps to activate your computer or Palm OS device:

1. **Click the Sign In button.**

   A new page appears with a form for signing into the Adobe DRM Activator.

2. **Fill in the E-Mail Address and Password text boxes then click the Sign In button on this page.**

   After signing in, the Adobe DRM Activator page appears where you can perform three important functions: activate Adobe Reader or Acrobat, activate Adobe Reader on your Palm OS device, and migrate eBooks from the Adobe Acrobat eBook Reader (both Windows and Macintosh versions of the eBook Migration Utility are provided).

3. **Click the Activate or Activate Palm OS Device button.**

After clicking the desired Activate button, a lot of behind the scenes digital tinkering occurs between the DRM Activator and your computer or Palm device that results in an alert box telling you Adobe Reader or Acrobat has been successfully activated. You can now start using My Bookshelf to purchase and download eBooks.

You can access the Adobe DRM Activator page to perform any of its functions at any time by choosing Tools➪eBook Web Services➪Adobe DRM Activator in Adobe Reader, or by choosing Advanced➪eBook Web Services➪Adobe DRM Activator in Acrobat 6. On the eBook Web Services submenu, you also find the Adobe eBook Central command that takes you online to Adobe's eBook Web site, where you can get all manner of eBook information and support, access online booksellers, and even find out how to use online lending libraries or create your own lending library using Adobe's Content Server software.

Dusting Off My Bookshelf

My Bookshelf, similar to the one shown in Figure 2-10, is a separate module used to access and organize your Adobe eBook collection. You can open My Bookshelf in either Adobe Reader or Acrobat 6 by choosing File➪My Bookshelf or by selecting My Bookshelf on the Read an eBook drop-down list on the Tasks toolbar. Whichever program you use (either Adobe Reader or Acrobat 6) to open My Bookshelf is the program that is used to view selected eBooks.

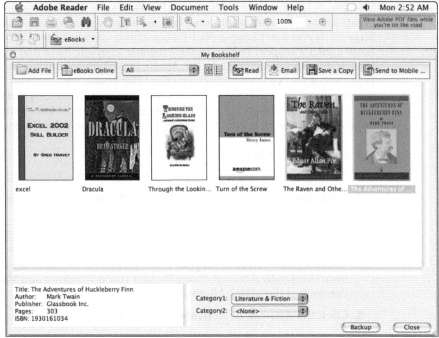

Figure 2-10:
Viewing
an eBook
collection
in My
Bookshelf.

As you can see in Figure 2-10, My Bookshelf displays collected eBooks as individual thumbnails for each book in the display area. You can use My Bookshelf as a repository for regular PDF files as well as eBooks. When you select an eBook, its vital statistics appear in a window in the lower-left corner of My Bookshelf. To open an eBook or PDF document you've added to My Bookshelf and view it in Adobe Reader or Acrobat 6, double-click its thumbnail display. At the top of My Bookshelf is a button bar with the following buttons and functions:

- ✔ **Add File:** Use this button to add a PDF document to My Bookshelf. After clicking the button, browse for the desired PDF and click OK. You can then access and manage the file in the same manner as eBooks.

- ✔ **eBooks Online:** Use this to go online to the Adobe eBook Central Web site and from there navigate to the Adobe eBook Mall, where you can purchase or borrow eBooks from the online Lending Library.

- ✔ **Categories:** Use this drop-down list to sort the display of eBooks in My Bookshelf by either All eBooks, All Documents, or any of six default categories provided such as Fiction, History, Romance, and so on. You can also choose Edit Categories on this drop-down list to create custom categories, as well as delete categories in the Bookshelf Categories dialog box. To assign a category to an eBook or document, select the item in the My Bookshelf display window, and then choose up to two categories in the drop-down lists provided at the bottom of the My Bookshelf window.

- **Thumbnail View:** Use this to display thumbnails of all the eBooks and PDF files stored in My Bookshelf. Double-click a thumbnail icon to open that eBook or document.

- **Detail View:** Use this to display a list of all the eBooks and PDF files stored in My Bookshelf. The detailed list includes title, author, access information, and category. Double-click an item in this list to open that eBook or document.

- **Read:** Select an eBook or PDF document in My Bookshelf and click this button to open the item in Adobe Reader or Acrobat 6.

- **E-mail:** Click this button to e-mail a copy of an eBook to another person. This functionality is set up by the eBook retailer and instructions are automatically entered in the body of the e-mail for the recipient to follow in order to gain access to the e-mailed PDF eBook.

- **Save a Copy:** Click this button to create and save a copy of an eBook in a directory on your hard drive. Restrictions on the ability to copy or the number of copies that can be made are set forth in the individual eBook permissions. See the "Viewing eBook permissions" section, later in this chapter, for more information.

- **Send to Mobile Device:** Use this button to transfer an encrypted copy of an eBook to a Palm OS hand-held device. You must have a DRM activated installation of Adobe Reader for Palm OS on the destination handheld in order to transfer and view a purchased eBook on it. You can't use this button to transfer regular PDF files to a Palm device. Use your Palm Hot Sync software instead. *Note:* This button appears automatically in My Bookshelf only if you have a Palm device cradle attached to your computer when you install Acrobat 6 or Adobe Reader.

Viewing Adobe eBooks

When reading an eBook in Acrobat 6 or Adobe Reader, you use the same viewing and navigational tools (including keyboard shortcuts) that you use when viewing regular PDF documents. In addition, Adobe has added a new viewing mode, called Facing mode, that is particularly well-suited to reading eBooks. Facing mode presents two eBook or PDF document pages at a time side by side in the document window, emulating the look of an opened book. Figure 2-11 shows an eBook viewed in Facing mode. The normal viewing modes found on the View menu (Actual Size, Fit Page, and so on) can be applied to pages viewed in Facing mode. Paging through an eBook is easily accomplished via the navigational buttons found on the status bar at the bottom of the document window.

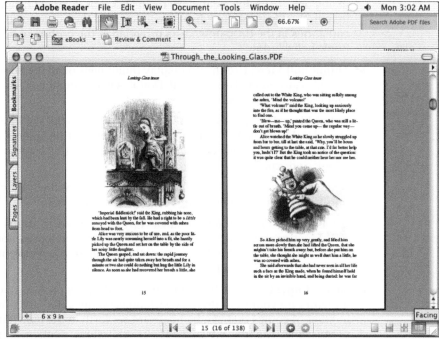

Figure 2-11:
Using
Facing
mode to
view an
eBook in
Adobe
Reader.

Adobe has also added two features to Acrobat 6 and Adobe Reader. The new automatic scrolling makes it easier to scan through pages in an eBook, and the new Read Out Loud feature enhances accessibility for visually impaired readers by reading eBook or PDF document text out loud.

To use automatic scrolling, choose View➪Automatically Scroll. The document window begins a continuous vertical scroll to the end of the document. To momentarily stop the scrolling, click and hold the mouse button. Releasing the mouse button continues automatic scrolling. To completely halt automatic scrolling, press Esc before the end of the document. Note that there is no control over scrolling speed and the scrolling movement blurs the text and degrades readability somewhat. This feature is best used to scan for a particular place in an eBook where you want to start reading.

The Read Out Loud (formerly Read Aloud in the Adobe Acrobat eBook Reader) uses your Windows or Macintosh speech engine to read an eBook or PDF document text out loud through your computer speakers. To use Read Out Loud, choose View➪Read Out Loud, and then choose either Read This Page Only, or Read to the End of Document on the Read Out Loud context menu. This context menu also provides Pause and Stop commands for the Read Out Loud feature. To specify the default voice, volume, and speech attributes, choose Edit➪Preferences, and then select Reading in the list box in the Preferences dialog box. In the Reading palette that appears, specify options in the Read Out Loud Options area.

When you're reading an eBook, you can look up the definitions of words using the Select Text tool. Choose the Select Text tool on the Basic toolbar and drag to select a single word in an eBook or PDF document, and then right-click and choose Look Up "selected word" on the context menu. Acrobat automatically takes you online to Dictionary.com and instantly looks up the definition of your selected word on that Web site. This feature is especially handy if you're blessed with broadband (always on) Internet access. If you've only got dial-up access to the Web, it's probably quicker to use the old fashioned method — grab your dog-eared copy of Webster's and look the word up yourself.

Improving readability

You can utilize Adobe's CoolType technology to improve the on-screen readability of eBooks and other PDF documents. CoolType is a font and image smoothing process that increases the contrast of text and images on their background. The technology works particularly well on flat-screen LCD computer monitors or handheld devices. To adjust CoolType settings, follow these steps:

1. **Choose Edit➪Preferences (Acrobat➪Preferences on Mac) to open the Preferences dialog box.**

2. **Select Smoothing in the list box to display the Smoothing palette, as shown in Figure 2-12.**

3. **Select the Use CoolType (Recommended for Laptops/LCD Screens) check box.**

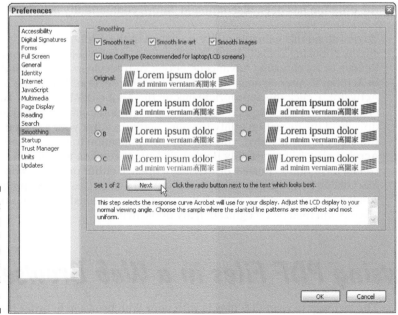

Figure 2-12: Specifying CoolType settings to improve eBook readability.

4. **Select one of the example radio buttons (A-F) that is most readable on your monitor, and then click the Next button.**

5. **Select one of the example radio buttons (A-D) that is most readable on your monitor, and then click OK to save your CoolType settings.**

Note that you can also experiment with readability settings for the type of content you're viewing by selecting different combinations of the Smooth Text, Smooth Line Art, and Smooth Images check boxes in the Preferences dialog box.

Viewing eBook permissions

All Adobe eBooks you purchase and download have permissions built in as part of their DRM (Digital Rights Management) architecture. These permissions are set by the publisher of the eBook and specify how many times you can print and copy an eBook, as well as the eBook expiration date. To view permissions set for a particular eBook, open the eBook from My Bookshelf and choose File⇨Document Properties. In the Document Properties dialog box that appears, choose Security in the list box to display the Security settings for your selected eBook.

Migrating eBooks from Adobe Acrobat eBook Reader

Adobe provides a utility on the DRM Activator Web site that enables you to migrate eBooks you've previously purchased using the Adobe Acrobat eBook Reader into My Bookshelf. Note that if you don't use this utility to move previously purchased eBooks into My Bookshelf, you'll have no choice but to use Acrobat eBook Reader in order to access these older books, and because the program has been discontinued, future compatibility is not guaranteed.

To download this valuable utility, go online to the Adobe DRM Activator Web site by choosing Tools⇨eBook Web Services⇨Adobe DRM Activator in Adobe Reader, or by choosing Advanced⇨eBook Web Services⇨Adobe DRM Activator in Acrobat 6. After signing in (see the preceding section, "Using the Adobe DRM Activator"), click the appropriate link on the Adobe DRM Activator Web page (Windows and Macintosh versions of the migration utility are provided) to download the migration utility to your computer. After your selected version of the utility is downloaded, you can run the application to migrate your Adobe Acrobat eBook library to My Bookshelf. Note that when you run this utility, you *cannot* have Adobe Reader or Acrobat 6 open. If either program is open, an alert dialog box will stop the process and tell you to close those programs and run the migration utility again. When the process is finished, your old library eBooks will then be recognized in My Bookshelf.

Browsing PDF Files in a Web Browser

The last way to read PDF files is with your Web browser. In order for your Web browser to be able to open PDF files, it needs a special PDFViewer plug-in that is automatically installed when you perform a complete install of Acrobat 6 or download and install the Full version of Adobe Reader on your computer. The programs have a detect and repair feature that automatically checks for the browser plug-in when you launch Acrobat 6 or Adobe Reader 6, so you're sure to get this plug-in one way or another.

The Acrobat 6 PDFViewer plug-in is not supported on browsers running under Mac OS X, though the Acrobat 5 version of the plug-in works perfectly on the Macintosh for OS 9.2.2 and earlier using both Netscape Navigator and Internet Explorer. Adobe has stated that it will make an OS X version of the PDFViewer available in the near future. For now, OS X users must configure their browsers to use Acrobat 6 or Adobe Reader as a helper application in order to download and view PDF files.

Figure 2-13 shows you how Internet Explorer 6 looks when you open a PDF file in it. Note how the Adobe Reader toolbars are integrated into the normal Internet Explorer 6 user interface, along with the Adobe Reader Navigation bar, complete with the palette tabs for Bookmarks and Pages. If you're using Internet Explorer 5.0 or greater as your Web browser, you also get the PDFMaker plug-in, in addition to the PDFViewer plug-in, when you install Acrobat 6. This plug-in adds a Create PDF button to the browser toolbars that allows you to create PDF documents from Web pages you're viewing in the browser.

Figure 2-13: Opening an online PDF file for viewing in Internet Explorer 6.0 on Windows XP.

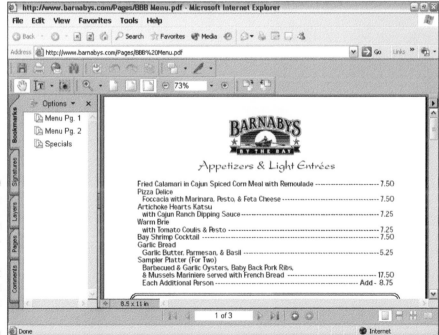

If you have Acrobat 6 (the one you have to buy) installed on your computer instead of just the freebie Adobe Reader, the additional toolbars (Basic Tools, Commenting, and Editing) and palette tabs (Comments and Signatures) not found in Adobe Reader are also added to the Web browser's user interface.

You can save a copy of the PDF document that you're viewing online with the Web browser to your hard drive by clicking the Saves a Copy of the File button (the one with the disk icon at the very beginning of the very first toolbar). In the Save a Copy dialog box that appears, specify the folder where you want the copy saved, and then click the Save button to make the copy. After the PDF document is saved on your hard drive, you can then open it for reading with Acrobat 6 or Adobe Reader.

Chapter 3

Getting Acquainted with Acrobat 6

*Y*ou can think of Acrobat 6 as the full-Monty edition of Adobe Reader 6. Adobe Reader acts as the free viewer for the PDF files that you prepare with Acrobat 6 (which will put you back about U.S. $250 unless you're upgrading from a previous version). As the full-featured Acrobat product goes, its user interface, while similar to a great degree with that of Adobe Reader 6, is still a wee bit more fun-filled and jam-packed than that of Adobe Reader (which is covered at length in Chapter 2).

In this chapter, you find out what makes Acrobat 6 so special that it's worth all the bucks. As part of this orientation process, you start to discover all the ways you can use Acrobat 6 to put your PDF files into the hands of all of those freeloaders using Adobe Reader.

Launching Acrobat 6

When you install Acrobat 6 on a Windows computer, the installer automatically puts a shortcut to the program on the desktop called Adobe Acrobat 6.0. To launch Acrobat 6, double-click this shortcut, or if you have a PDF file you want to edit with the program, drag its file icon onto this shortcut or double-click the PDF file icon to start Acrobat and open the file for editing. You can also launch the program from the Start menu by choosing Start➪Programs➪ Adobe Acrobat 6.0 (in Windows XP, choose Start➪All Programs➪Adobe Acrobat 6.0).

If you plan on using Acrobat regularly, you should add an Adobe Acrobat 6.0 button to the Quick Launch toolbar on the Windows Taskbar. That way, you can launch the program from the Windows Taskbar with a single click of the Acrobat button, even when another application program is running full-screen. To add an Adobe Acrobat 6.0 button to your Quick Launch toolbar, simply drag the Adobe Acrobat 6.0 desktop shortcut to the place on the Quick Launch toolbar where you want the Adobe Acrobat 6.0 button to appear, and then release the mouse button. Note that the Quick Launch feature does not appear by default on the Windows XP Taskbar. To enable this feature, right-click the Taskbar, choose Properties, and select the Show Quick Launch check box in the Taskbar and Start Menu Properties dialog box.

You can easily add an Acrobat 6.0 alias to the Dock in the Macintosh OS X by following these steps:

1. **Open Acrobat 6 by double-clicking its icon in the Applications folder.**

2. **Right-click if you have a two-button mouse (when will Steve Jobs get a clue about single-button mice?) or ⌘+click the Acrobat icon on the Dock and choose Keep in Dock on the context menu that appears.**

After creating an Acrobat 6.0 alias on the Dock, you can launch the program by clicking the program icon on the Dock, or you can launch it and open a PDF file for editing by dragging its file icon and dropping it on the same program icon.

Opening PDF files for viewing or editing

Acrobat 6 and the Adobe Reader 6 enable you to open multiple PDF files at a time. The easiest way to open more than one PDF file is from the Open dialog box, which you can display by choosing File⇨Open on the Acrobat menu, by clicking the Open button (the very first button on the File toolbar), or by pressing Ctrl+O (⌘+O on the Macintosh).

In the Open dialog box, first select the folder that contains the PDF files you want to open, and then select the multiple PDF files using one of the following methods:

✔ To select a cluster of files, lasso them by dragging a bounding box around the group with the Arrowhead mouse pointer (Windows only).

✔ To select a bunch of files in a single column or row, click the first one to select it and then hold down Shift when you click the last one.

✔ To select individual files not all in a cluster, single column, or single row, hold down the Ctrl (⌘ on the Mac) key as you click each file icon or name.

Figure 3-1 shows the Open dialog box in Windows after selecting several individual PDF files for opening in Acrobat 6. When you click the Open button after selecting multiple files for opening, all the selected files open in Acrobat in alphabetical order by filename, although only the one whose filename is last in this sequence is actually displayed in Acrobat's document window.

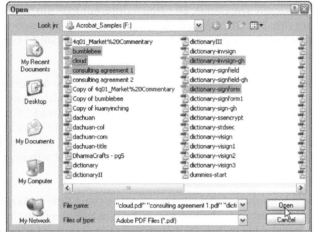

Figure 3-1:
Selecting
multiple PDF
files to open
in Acrobat 6.

To display one of the files that's currently open but not visible on the screen in the Acrobat document window, choose Window on the Acrobat menu bar and then type the number or click the name of that PDF file displayed at the bottom of the Window menu.

Arranging open PDF files in the Acrobat window

When you're working with more than one file in Acrobat, you can use the Tile or Cascade options on the Window menu to display part of all the open files in the Acrobat document window. You have a choice between two tiling options, Horizontally or Vertically. When you choose Window⇨Tile⇨ Horizontally, Acrobat arranges the open document windows one on top of the other. When you choose Window⇨Tile⇨Vertically, Acrobat arranges the open document windows side by side.

Generally speaking, vertical tiling is usually more useful than horizontal tiling, given that computer monitors are wider than they are tall, so that when you place them side by side, you can see more of the document's text and graphics. Tiling is very useful when you want to copy text and graphics from one PDF document to another using the drag-and-drop method.

When you choose Window⇨Cascade, Acrobat arranges the open document windows in a cascade. When you cascade the open document windows, the title bars and the tabs of the palettes on the Navigation pane are visible for all the files, although you can only see part of the contents of the first file (that is, alphabetically speaking). To bring a different PDF file to the front, simply click its title bar. The cascade arrangement is useful when you need to see all the names of the PDF files that are open and you want to copy text and graphics using the Copy and Paste commands.

To end a tiled or cascading window arrangement, click the Maximize button on the active document (the one whose title bar is highlighted and its file-name is not grayed out). As soon as you maximize the active PDF document window in Acrobat in Windows, all the other document windows are automat-ically maximized as well. In Acrobat on the Mac, however, this is not the case, and you must still manually maximize the other document windows when you activate them.

When you have a number of PDF files open at the same time in Acrobat, their document titles are listed at the bottom of the Window menu on the Acrobat menu bar. To select a file and make it current in the document window, choose its name on the Window menu or press Alt+W and then the keyboard shortcut number that appears next to the document title on the Window menu.

Closing open PDF files

Of course, you can close any document open on the Acrobat screen by clicking its Close button, by choosing File⇨Close, or by pressing Ctrl+W (⌘+W on the Mac). When you have multiple files open in a tiled or cascading arrangement in Acrobat, you have to be cognizant of which file is active when you close it, or you can end up accidentally closing a file that you still want to use.

To activate a particular document for closing (or editing, for that matter) when ordered in a tiled or cascading arrangement, click its title bar to high-light the title bar and activate the document window (on Acrobat in Windows, you can do this by pressing Ctrl+F6) or select its filename on the Window menu.

Acrobat 6 has a very useful menu command, Window⇨Close All, that you can use to close all the document windows that you have open at that time. Of course, Acrobat stops and prompts you to save changes to any file or files in the group it's closing in which you have edits that have yet to be saved.

Getting Comfy with the Acrobat 6 Interface

Adobe has given quite a makeover to the Acrobat 6 UI (User Interface) and feature set. For the most part, the improvements entail adding depth to features that were already present in Acrobat 5 and reorganizing menus and toolbars in a more intuitive fashion. While the initial effect may be disconcerting to "old school" users of Acrobat, the enhanced usability quickly becomes apparent. Because Adobe Reader 6 is essentially a watered-down version of Acrobat 6, you're already good friends with the basic interface enhancements if you've read the sections pertaining to viewing files with the Adobe Reader 6 in Chapter 2. If you skipped over that material, you may want to give it a quick look before reading the Acrobat 6-specific stuff in the following sections of this chapter.

Acrobat 6, despite its obvious similarity with Adobe Reader 6 in terms of viewing and navigating PDF documents, offers you a much richer interface with which to work, given its ability to both generate and edit PDF files. In the remaining sections of this chapter, you find important information about the features in the Acrobat 6 interface that make the program the powerful PDF generating and editing tool that it is.

What's good on the Acrobat 6 menus today?

The Acrobat 6 menus (File, Edit, View, Document, Tools, Advanced, Window, and Help) contain all the commands found on the Adobe Reader 6 menus; however, the items in the Acrobat 6 menus vary greatly from those found on Adobe Reader. The variance is due to the fact that Acrobat 6 has many more commands than Adobe Reader 6; in addition, Acrobat 6 sports a new Advanced menu (Adobe Reader does not have this menu) that contains many of the commands currently sprinkled throughout the Adobe Reader 6 menu set. You find, even in cases where the menu items seem to match exactly between the programs, that the options offered on the Acrobat 6 menus are either more numerous or their functions are tailored specifically to suit the program's editing abilities. The follow sections give you a menu-by-menu description of the most salient Acrobat 6 menu items.

Fun stuff on the File menu

The File menu in Acrobat 6 (shown in Figure 3-2) is home to the common command items for opening, closing, and saving PDF files. Because you can edit PDF files in Acrobat 6, this menu contains a Save option for saving editing changes, as well as a Save As command for renaming, saving copies, and changing file formats (Adobe Reader 6 has only a Save as Copy command that enables users to save to disk a copy of the PDF document that they're viewing, and a Save as Text command that converts the current PDF file to Rich Text Format). Acrobat 6 also lets you use the Save as Certified Document command to vouch for the contents of a document by digitally signing it. (See Chapter 11 for more on Certified documents.)

Figure 3-2:
Examining
the File
menu in
Acrobat 6.

Among the items for opening, closing, and saving files and the standard print (Page Setup and Print) and exiting commands (Exit on Windows and Quit on the Mac), are various new File menu commands categorized in the following areas:

✔ **PDF Creation/Viewing:** Use the Create PDF command to easily create a new PDF file from either another file, multiple files, your scanner, a Web Page, or an item in the Clipboard. Choosing any of the commands on the Create PDF submenu opens a dialog box that enables you to select your source items for PDF creation. The My Bookshelf command lets you access your Adobe eBook library and read eBooks within Acrobat 6. The new support for EBX encryption that Adobe uses to secure its eBooks, previously available only in the Acrobat eBook Reader, is also supported in the Adobe Reader 6 Full version.

✔ **E-mail:** Use the E-mail command to open your default e-mail program and attach the current PDF document to a new message. You can also use the Send by E-mail for Review command to initiate an e-mail review of the current PDF document. Choosing the command opens a dialog box where you enter a return e-mail address that reviewers will use to send Comments from a review of an attached PDF back to you. The e-mail address you enter is saved for future reviews. When reviewers receive and open the PDF file in Acrobat 6, they use the Send Comments to Review Initiator command to send their comments back to you.

✔ **Comment/Review:** In addition to sending PDF files for review and receiving comments via e-mail as described in the preceding bullet, you can also use the Upload for Browser-Based Review command (Windows only) to send a PDF file to a specified server on a local network, company intranet, or the Web. Others can then review the online document in their Web browsers and provide comments that are uploaded and stored in an Online Comments Repository that you, as the initiator, can review. You use the Export Comments to Word command to create a Microsoft Word document containing comments attached to the current PDF file. Note that the PDF file must be tagged using the Accessibility options in order to use this command. See Chapter 2 for more on creating tagged PDF files and Chapter 9 for more on annotating and reviewing PDF files.

✔ **Printing:** Use the Print with Comments command to select print formatting options for a PDF file and its annotations in the Summarize Options dialog box. Here you choose the page layout, the specific comments and how they are sorted in the printout, and font size of printed comments. The PrintMe Internet Printing command enables you to send the current PDF file to the PrintMe online printing service — a new company offering Mobile and Internet printing that lets any user with Internet access print their documents to any fax machine or PrintMe-enabled printer, regardless of location.

The Reduce File Size command is a much-needed improvement on previous methods of optimizing a PDF document so that it is the smallest possible size. To optimize a PDF file in previous versions of Acrobat, you either used the Save As command (optimizing was accomplished by replacing the current document by saving under the same name), or you used the multi-stepped Optimize command in Acrobat 5. The Reduce File Size command is a simple one-click operation with the added feature of allowing you to set backwards compatibility with earlier versions of Acrobat. Note that if you really like to tinker with all the optimizing options available for reducing the size of a PDF document, you can choose Advanced⇨PDF Optimizer for a look at some truly advanced optimizing options.

Don't forget the very valuable Revert item on the File menu. You can use the File⇨Revert command to dump all the edits that you've made since you last saved your PDF document. Click the Revert button in the alert dialog box that appears, asking you if you want to revert to the previously saved version of the file, and Acrobat opens this last-saved version without bothering to save your edits.

Edification on the Edit menu

The Acrobat 6 Edit menu (shown in Figure 3-3) is pretty standard stuff, with the usual items for undoing and redoing, copying, cutting and pasting, and searching. A new addition to the Edit menu in both Acrobat 6 and Adobe Reader 6 is the Check Spelling command that lets you perform a spell check in the comments and form fields of the current PDF file. The Check Spelling command also enables you to add or delete words in the spell checker custom dictionary by choosing the appropriate command on the Check Spelling submenu. Another new addition to the Edit menu is the Look Up Definition command, which is activated when you open an eBook and gives you the definition of a selected word in the eBook. You'll find that the Acrobat 6 Edit menu mainly differs from the Adobe Reader 6 menu in its inclusion of additional Preferences menu items, and additional general preference settings that you can set for the PDF document you're editing in the Preferences dialog box. You also get the new Add Bookmark command that lets you, oddly enough, add a bookmark to the current PDF document.

Undo 'Signature' field property change	Ctrl+Z
Redo	Shift+Ctrl+Z
Cut	Ctrl+X
Copy	Ctrl+C
Paste	Ctrl+V
Delete	
Copy File to Clipboard	
Select All	Ctrl+A
Deselect All	Shift+Ctrl+A
Check Spelling	▸
Add Bookmark	Ctrl+B
Look Up Definition...	
Search	Ctrl+F
Search Results	▸
Preferences...	Ctrl+K

Figure 3-3: Exploring the Edit menu in Acrobat 6.

Variations on the View menu

The View menu (shown in Figure 3-4) is one of the areas that Adobe has completely reworked in Acrobat 6 by altering the UI (User Interface) to improve usability and give a more intuitive feel to the program. For example, the options for the way the document pages are displayed (single-page, continuous, or continuous with facing pages) in the Acrobat Document window, as well as options for rotating the pages, are now consolidated on submenus under the commands Page Layout and Rotate View. The options for changing the page magnification, page fit, and reflow are all grouped together in the second section of the View menu. In the second-to-last section of this menu, you find items for using, displaying, and hiding a layout grid for aligning graphics and form fields, making those items Snap to Grid, and displaying or hiding Rulers and Guides for graphic and form field layout. (See Chapter 14 to find out more about interactive forms in Acrobat 6.) These menu consolidations create space on the View menu for the following new feature categories:

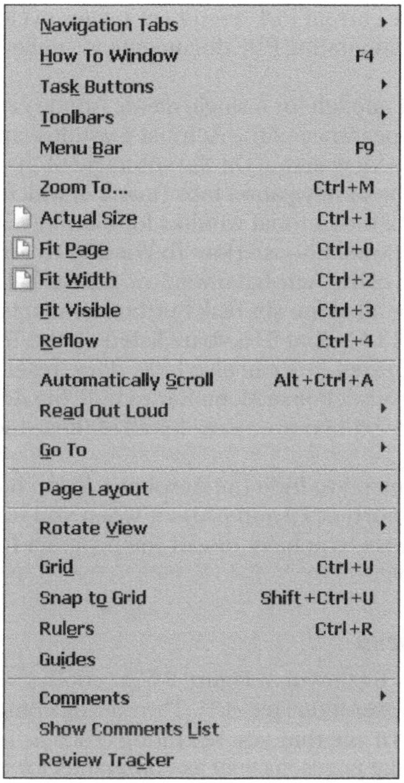

N̲avigation Tabs	▶
H̲ow To Window	F4
Tas̲k Buttons	▶
T̲oolbars	▶
Menu B̲ar	F9
Z̲oom To...	Ctrl+M
Act̲ual Size	Ctrl+1
Fit P̲age	Ctrl+0
Fit W̲idth	Ctrl+2
F̲it Visible	Ctrl+3
R̲eflow	Ctrl+4
Automatically S̲croll	Alt+Ctrl+A
Rea̲d Out Loud	▶
G̲o To	▶
Page Lay̲out	▶
Rotate V̲iew	▶
Gri̲d	Ctrl+U
Snap t̲o Grid	Shift+Ctrl+U
Rule̲rs	Ctrl+R
Gui̲des	
Co̲mments	▶
Show Comments L̲ist	
Review Tra̲cker	

Figure 3-4: Visiting the View menu in Acrobat 6.

✔ **eBooks:** The Automatically Scroll and Read Out Loud options are Acrobat eBook Reader features that Adobe integrated in Acrobat 6 and Adobe Reader 6. These features allow you to automatically scroll down the current document or have your speech-enabled computer read PDF document text out loud. As with the Acrobat eBook Reader, the features work for both eBooks and regular PDF files.

✔ **Comment/Review:** At the bottom of the View menu are three options that aid the initiator of a PDF review cycle or the reviewers themselves. The Comments options displays a submenu with over a dozen different criteria that you can use to display reviewer comments, which are pop-up windows that are attached to the current PDF document. Also available are commands to Open and Close these pop-up windows and specify their display in relation to the source document. Use the Show Comments List command to open the Comments tab in a floating window that displays all comments in a list that you can sort, search, change status, and filter. Choose the Review Tracker command to open the Review and Comment pane in the How To window on the right side of the document window. Here you can display and manage comments that different reviewers have attached to the current PDF document. You can also e-mail, remind, and invite more reviewers to the current PDF document review cycle. See Chapter 9 for more info on annotating PDF documents for review purposes.

As if all of these features weren't enough for a single menu, Adobe created five new options for changing the appearance of the Acrobat 6 window and placed them all in the first section of the View menu. On the submenu of the Navigation Tabs command, choose any of the 11 navigation tabs (many of which are normally displayed on the left side of the Acrobat window for viewing in the Navigation Pane) as floating windows. Choose How To Window to display the How To window in the right side of the Acrobat 6 window. On the Task Buttons submenu, you can choose any or all of the six Task Buttons for display in the toolbar area. Choose any of the 13 Acrobat 6 toolbars listed on the Toolbars submenu for display as floating boxes. You can also hide, dock, reset, and lock currently displayed toolbars. Finally, choose Menu Bar to hide the Acrobat Menu bar and give yourself a tiny bit of more space for all of those toolbars.

When using the Menu Bar command to hide the Acrobat 6 Menu bar, you must remember its keystroke shortcut F9 and press it when you want to redisplay the Menu bar. Otherwise, you have to exit the program to get a new Acrobat window with a Menu bar.

Delights on the Document menu

The Document menu in Acrobat 6 (shown in Figure 3-5) is another example of Adobe's efforts to improve the User Interface (UI). The editing command items that affect all the pages in the PDF file that you're editing (such as inserting, replacing, extracting, and deleting pages, as well as commands for cropping and rotating pages) are consolidated on the submenu of the Pages option.

Consolidating all the Page option commands on the Document menu makes room for the following sets of options that are either new features or reshuffled/renamed commands formerly displayed on other menus in Acrobat 5:

✔ **Pages:** Contains commands on a submenu that enable you to Insert, Extract, Replace, Delete, Crop, or Rotate pages in the current PDF document. Choose Set Page Transitions to specify transitions between pages when creating a PDF Presentation. See Chapter 16 for more information.

✔ **Add Headers & Footers:** Create, position, and format the text of headers and footers in a PDF file. See Chapter 10 for more information.

✔ **Add Watermark and Background:** Select a source image, specify page range, position, appearance, and preview a watermark or background for a PDF file. For more information, see Chapter 10.

✔ **Add a Comment:** Annotate a PDF document by inserting a comment.

✔ **Compare Documents:** Compare the visual or textual differences in an older and newer version of the same document.

✔ **Summarize Documents:** Specify the page layout of a PDF file and its attached comments.

✔ **Import/Export Comments:** Import or export comments to and from other PDF files, or export comments in the current PDF document to Microsoft Word.

✔ **File Attachments:** Import files that are attached to the current PDF document.

✔ **Security:** Restrict the ability to open or edit a PDF file. You can also encrypt a document by using certificates, display restriction, and security levels in the current document. See Chapter 11 for more about security.

✔ **Digital Signatures:** Use this command to digitally sign, validate, and create signature fields in a PDF document. See Chapter 11.

✔ **Paper Capture:** Apply OCR (Optical Character Recognition) to scanned text files so that you can search the text.

✔ **Preflight:** Choose from an extensive list of preflighting profiles so that you can validate the content of a PDF file prior to sending it to press. For more information, see the section on PDF in the press workflow in Chapter 1.

Treats on the Tools menu

The Tools menu is yet another example of Adobe's great effort to consolidate the Acrobat 6 menu items. The veritable smorgasbord of useful tools from Acrobat 5 (not to worry — they've all been reshuffled to various other menus, most notably the View menu) has been removed to make room for the addition of six new tool sets. While the Tools menu is in a dead heat with the Window menu for shortest menu on the bar, as shown in Figure 3-6, its options and submenus (some of these options have five submenus!) give you access to the Basic toolbar set and all the tools that aren't accessible through the default toolbar display in Acrobat 6. For those of you who can't possibly bear the idea of clicking a toolbar button (or would rather not clutter up your Acrobat window with scads of seldom-used tool buttons), this menu is a godsend. Because all the tools on the Tools menu have corresponding toolbar buttons, you can find out about the Basic tools in Chapter 2 and the rest later in this chapter.

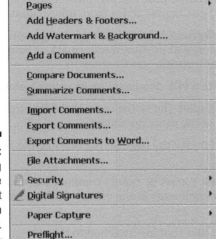

Figure 3-5:
Discovering
the
Document
menu in
Acrobat 6.

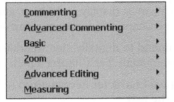

Figure 3-6:
Touring the
Tools menu
in Acrobat 6.

Angst (just kidding) artifice on the Advanced menu

The Advanced menu (shown in Figure 3-7) seems to contain all the more esoteric options formerly sprinkled throughout the Adobe 5 menus, as well as a bevy of new and improved options. Here is your veritable smorgasbord of features. There are so many options that it may be the first time in history a menu (the first section anyway) has been alphabetized. Starting at the top of the Advanced menu, you find the following menu items:

- ✔ **Accessibility:** Enables you to do a Quick Check or Full Check of the current document to see if its structure contains tags for reflowing the document text. If it doesn't, you can choose Add Tags to Document to do so. See Chapter 2 for information on viewing reflowed text in Acrobat.

- ✔ **Acrobat Distiller:** Opens, you guessed it, the Acrobat Distiller. For more on this very important Acrobat component, see Chapter 4.

- ✔ **Batch Processing:** Select or edit one of the many batch processes that enables you to perform particular tasks, such as printing or setting basic security options for a whole bunch of PDF files at one time.

✔ **Catalog:** Enables you to create a full-text index of a single PDF document or a collection of PDF documents that can then be searched by using the Search command.

✔ **Document Metadata:** Use the Document Metadata command to view and edit the metadata information (such as Title, Author, Description, and so on) that is embedded in the current PDF document.

✔ **eBook Web Services:** Use the Adobe eBook Central command to go online to Adobe's eBook Web site. Choosing Adobe DRM Activator logs you on to Adobe's secure servers to create an eBook purchaser account that enables you to download commercial eBooks.

✔ **Export All Images:** Lets you extract all the images in the current PDF document as single images in either JPEG, PNG, TIFF, or JPEG2000 file format.

✔ **Forms:** Use these commands to perform advanced form use or creation functions. Choose Import Forms Data to bring form data into the current PDF document from another PDF form; choose Export Forms Data to send form data to another PDF form; choose Fields⇨Create Multiple Copies or Fields⇨Duplicate to speed up the process of field creation when building a PDF form; and choose Templates to attach, edit, or delete a Page Template when creating a PDF form. See Chapter 14 for more on creating interactive PDF forms.

✔ **JavaScript:** Lets you access Acrobat's JavaScript editor, where you can view, create, edit, and debug JavaScript actions for your PDF forms. See Chapter 14 for more on using JavaScript actions in interactive PDF forms.

✔ **Links:** Use the Create from URLs in Document command to convert all the decipherable URLs (Uniform Resource Locators) to active hyperlinks. Use the Remove All Links from Document command to do just that. See Chapter 7 for more on creating links in a PDF document.

✔ **Manage Digital IDs:** Use the commands on this menu to view and edit your personal Digital ID, as well as those of others who are referred to in Acrobat as Trusted Identities. See Chapter 11 to discover the ins and outs of securing PDF documents.

✔ **PDF Optimizer:** Choose PDF Optimizer to open the PDF Optimizer dialog box, where you can choose from a comprehensive array of options to compress images, embed or remove fonts, and compress, discard, or remove various PDF document features that bulk up its size in order to reduce the size of a PDF document to optimum levels. You can find out all about the PDF Optimizer by clicking Complete Acrobat 6.0 Help in the How To window or by choosing Help⇨Complete Acrobat 6.0 Help to open the Acrobat 6.0 online help guide. In the Contents tab window, choose Publishing in Electronic Formats and then select Optimizing Adobe PDF Files.

✔ **Web Capture:** Use this command to convert Web pages from the Internet into PDF documents. See Chapter 7 for more on this excellent Acrobat feature.

Well, that's all the alphabetizing fun I have for you courtesy of Adobe. The bottom sections of the Advanced menu contains these unalphabetized commands:

- ✔ **Use Local Fonts:** This command is turned on by default. When fonts aren't embedded in a PDF file, Acrobat uses font substitutions based on your computer's system fonts. To see how your PDF document will look on a computer that doesn't have your fonts, turn off this feature by clicking the command to remove the check mark. You can then preview how substituted fonts will appear and decide which fonts to embed.

- ✔ **Proof Setup:** This command and its associated commands (Proof Colors, Overprint Preview, Separation Preview, and Transparency Flattener Preview) in the last section of the Advanced menu allow you to setup, proof, and preview color separations and overprints on your computer screen for high-end commercial print output as opposed to printing out hard copy proofs. Keep in mind that the reliability of these features depends on the quality of your monitor, use of ICC profiles for color management, and the ambient lighting of your work environment. If you're a printing business professional, this will all make sense. If not, leave it up to the professionals to develop proofs of your printed PDF document. The Transparency Flattener Preview command lets you preview how transparent graphic object layers will appear when flattened. Note that you must have a Postscript printer to use this option.

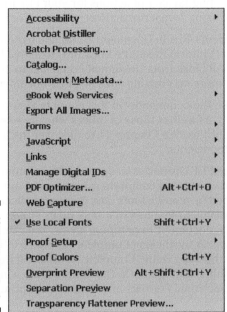

Figure 3-7:
Aiming
at the
Advanced
menu in
Acrobat 6.

Wonders on the Window menu

The Window menu (shown in Figure 3-8) contains the items you need for arranging and selecting document windows for the PDF files you're editing. See the "Arranging open PDF files in the Acrobat window" section earlier in this chapter for more information. It also contains the Split command that allows you to view the same PDF document in two viewing panes, the Clipboard Viewer for displaying items you've copied to the Clipboard, and Full Screen View for displaying the current document so that it fills your entire monitor and hides all menus, tools, display windows, and navigation control. You can toggle Full Screen View on and off by pressing Ctrl+L (⌘+L on the Mac).

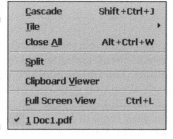

Figure 3-8:
Walking
through the
Window
menu in
Acrobat 6.

Happiness on the Help menu

The Help menu (shown in Figure 3-9) shows the various options for getting online help with Acrobat 6. The first Help menu item, How To, lets you display the new Acrobat 6 How To window. This help panel, which opens up on the right side of the Acrobat window, is similar to the Microsoft Office Help window. The default set provides links to important help topics, such as Create PDF, Review & Comment, Secure, Sign, and so on. Clicking a link displays the corresponding help topics. You can also access the Complete Acrobat 6.0 Help database and choose whether or not the How To window is displayed when you start Acrobat 6.

The About Adobe Acrobat 6.0 item displays the program splash screen that shows your version number, along with your license information, including your serial number. (You need to click the splash screen to get rid of it, by the way.) The About Adobe Plug-ins command lets you view the presence and status of all plug-ins available in your current Acrobat 6 installation. The About Third-Party Plug-Ins option displays a submenu showing all the third-party (that is, not made by Adobe Systems) plug-ins installed for your copy of Acrobat 6. (Two third-party plug-ins, Preflight and PrintMe Internet Printing, are installed when you first install Acrobat 6 on your computer.)

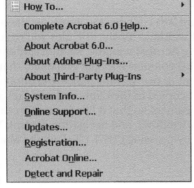

Figure 3-9:
Helping
yourself to
the Help
menu in
Acrobat 6.

The System Info command creates a report of your current computer system and Acrobat 6 installation, opens your e-mail client, and attaches the report to an e-mail for sending to Adobe Tech Support. The Online Support, Updates, Registration, and Adobe Online commands all launch your Web browser and connect you to the appropriate pages on the Adobe Systems Web site. Choose the Online Registration option to register your copy of Acrobat 6 (of course, you need to do this only once, right after you first install Acrobat 6 on your computer). The Detect and Repair feature starts a Windows or Macintosh diagnostic routine that optimizes Acrobat's performance.

Tons o' toolbars!

Acrobat 6 contains all the toolbars found in Adobe Reader 6 plus seven more: Advanced Commenting, Advanced Editing, Commenting, Edit, How To, Measuring, and Tasks. Figure 3-10 shows these extra toolbars in a custom display without the Acrobat 6 default toolbars. I've docked the extra toolbars in the order they appear on the Toolbars menu for clarity. To see this menu, choose View⇨Toolbars. The seventh toolbar found in Acrobat 6 and not Adobe Reader 6 is the Properties toolbar, which is also shown in Figure 3-10, though not activated. (The Properties toolbar comes alive when you select certain editing tools and allows quick access to that tool's functions.) For a complete rundown on the toolbars and buttons that both Acrobat and Adobe Reader share, see Chapter 2). The buttons on these extra toolbars are designed to give you quick access to every editing tool in Acrobat 6 (which are totally absent from Adobe Reader), and you will undoubtedly make much use of them as you work in the program. Table 3-1 gives a brief description of the function of each of these tools.

Figure 3-10:
A custom display of the toolbars used for editing and commenting in Acrobat 6 that don't appear in Adobe Reader 6.

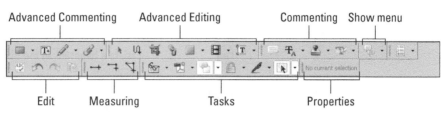

Table 3-1		The Complete Set of Editing Toolbars in Acrobat 6	
Toolbar	*Icon*	*Tool Name*	*Use This Tool To . . .*
Advanced Commenting		Drawing Markup	Draw rectangles, ovals, clouds, and polygons, as well as lines and arrows. You can also attach notes to these markups.
	T+	Text Box	Mark up your PDF document with comments written in a text box.
		Pencil Markup	Draw freehand markups in your PDF document.
		Attachments	Attach images, sounds, and movies as comments in your PDF document.
Advanced Editing		Select Object	Select objects, such as links, comments, and form fields, in your PDF document.
		Article	Create articles in the document that designate the order in which portions of the text are to be read by using the Article palette in Adobe Reader 6.

(continued)

Table 3-1 *(continued)*

Toolbar	Icon	Tool Name	Use This Tool To . . .
		Crop	Crop pages in the PDF document.
		Link	Create a hyperlink in the PDF document.
		Button	Add form fields and form objects, such as check boxes and buttons, to your PDF document.
		Movie	Insert a digital movie for playback in the PDF document.
		TouchUp Text	Edit portions of the PDF document. Its More Tools button accesses the TouchUp Text, TouchUp Object, and TouchUp Order tools.
Commenting		Note	Annotate text in the PDF document. Its More Tools button accesses the Note, FreeText, Sound Attachment, and File Attachment tools.
		Indicate Text Edits	Mark up text in the PDF document. Use the commands on the pop-up menu to insert, replace, highlight, cross out, or underline text, or to add a note to selected text.
		Stamp	Apply an electronic rubber stamp; Approved, Confidential, Received, and many other stamps in various visual styles are available.
		Highlight Text	Mark up your PDF document with an electronic colored marker. Choose Highlight, Cross-out, or Underline from the button's pop-up menu.
		Show	View comments and change their display. Use the pop-up menu to sort by type, reviewer, and so on. Display or hide pop-up comments and connector lines, and change the alignment of pop-up comments.

Toolbar	Icon	Tool Name	Use This Tool To . . .
Edit		Spell Check Comments and Form Fields	Spell check comments and form fields that you add to a PDF document.
		Undo/Redo	Click these two buttons when you want to undo or redo a change you've made to your PDF document.
		Copy	Copy a selection in the current PDF document to the Clipboard.
How To		How To	Display all the items that appear on the How To window on the pop-up menu on the How To button.
Measuring		Distance	Accurately measure the distance between two points. Click the first point, move the mouse pointer to the second point, and click again. Distance is displayed in the Properties toolbar.
		Perimeter	Accurately measure the distance between multiple points by clicking each point you want to measure and double-clicking the last point. Perimeter distance is displayed in the Properties toolbar.
		Area	Accurately measure the area between line segments that you draw. Click at least two points and then click the first point again. The measurements (shown in square inches) are displayed in the Properties toolbar.
Tasks		eBooks	Open eBook topics in the How To window, go online to purchase eBooks, or display My Bookshelf by choosing an option from this button's pop-up menu.

(continued)

Table 3-1 *(continued)*

Toolbar	Icon	Tool Name	Use This Tool To . . .
		Create PDF	Open the Create PDF topics in the How To window or actually create a PDF from a file, multiple files, a Web page, a clipboard image, or a scanner by choosing an option from this button's pop-up menu.
		Review and Comment	Open the Review and Comment topics in the How To window or use reviewing tools on a PDF document already in a review cycle by choosing an option from this button's pop-up menu.
		Secure	Open the Security Topics in the How To window or Restrict and Encrypt a PDF document or view current security settings by choosing an option from this button's pop-up menu.
		Sign	Open the Signature Topic in the How To window or digitally Sign, Validate, or Create a Blank Signature Field in a PDF document by choosing an option from this button's pop-up menu.
		Advanced Editing	Open the Advanced Editing Topics in the How To window or Hide or Display the Advanced Editing toolbar by choosing an option from this button's pop-up menu.
Properties Bar		Current Tool	Edit properties of certain tools or objects, such as links, media clips, measuring tools, and bookmarks. Choose View⇨Toolbars⇨Properties Bar to display the floating toolbar.
Zoom		Loupe	Displays the Loupe Tool window where you view specific areas of a PDF document under high magnification using the mouse pointer to navigate.

Getting all the help you need

The Complete Acrobat 6.0 Help guide, as it's now called, is an interactive hypertext application filled with pages and pages of information (it is called *complete,* after all) that you can read online or print out for later and repeated reference. To open the Adobe Acrobat 6 Help file, choose Help⇨ Complete Acrobat 6.0 Help. If you have the How To window open, you can also click the Complete Acrobat 6.0 Help link there.

As shown in Figure 3-11, when the Complete Adobe Acrobat 6.0 Help file opens, it displays a Help splash page in a large document viewing area on the right side of the window and a navigation pane on the left. The navigation pane has three tabs at the top: Contents, Search, and Index. The Contents tab is selected by default and contains a scrolling list of hyperlinked topics highlighted with blue arrows. Clicking one of these headings displays that topics subheadings in the viewing window. Each topic also has an Expand button (plus sign on Windows, triangle on Mac). Clicking the Expand button next to a Contents topic expands the list to display subtopics that you can click to display the topic information in the viewing window.

Figure 3-11: The Complete Acrobat 6.0 Help application provides online help in Acrobat 6 and Adobe Reader 6.

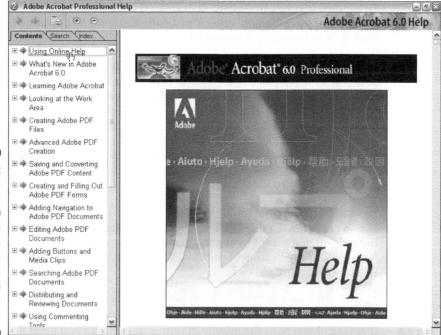

The Search tab enables you to enter search criteria in the Find Pages Containing text box. Enter your text and click the Search button. Result are displayed in the scrolling list; you can then click a topic to display its information in the viewing window.

Clicking the Index tab displays each letter, A through Z, with an Expand button next to each letter. To find a help topic by name in the index, click the Expand button in front of the first letter in your help topic to display all the topics in the Help guide that start with that letter. For example, to find information on using the Find command in Acrobat 6, click the Expand button next to the letter F, and then locate the topic you want in the alphabetical list under F. You can also use the Show drop-down list to choose one letter and display all the topics for that one letter in the navigation pane. Clicking any of these links displays their information in the viewing window. Note that many of the articles in the Help guide contain links that, when clicked, take you to related topics.

Viewing the How To window

Adobe Acrobat 6 and Adobe Reader 6 provide a new feature, called the How To window, that supplements the Complete Acrobat 6.0 Help guide. The How To window appears by default in Acrobat 6 on the right side of the screen, but you have to manually open it in Adobe Reader 6 by choosing View↪ How To Window or by pressing F4.

The How To window, shown in Figure 3-12, gives you quick access to a number of everyday tasks you might perform in Acrobat 6. For example, clicking the Create PDF heading displays a list of links to every method of creating a PDF file in Acrobat 6. The articles give you quick step-by-step procedures, and related information links appear with many of the articles. At the top of the window is a Home button that takes you back to the How To Homepage (shown in the figure), Back and Forward buttons, and a Hide button to close the display, thus giving you all the navigational tools you need to easily browse the How To database.

You can change where the How To window appears on the screen by right-clicking the How To title bar and choosing Docked Left, Docked Right, or Hide. If you don't want to see the How To window every time you launch Acrobat 6, at the bottom of the How To window, deselect the Show How To Window at Startup check box.

Every button on the Task toolbar (see the "Tons o' toolbars!" section, earlier in this chapter) has a How To topic on its pop-up menu that corresponds to that task. If you're in the middle of one of these tasks and need a quick reference guide, choose the How To command on the Task button pop-up menu to open the How To window and get some quick help.

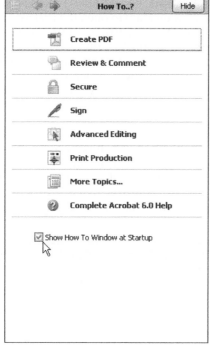

Figure 3-12: The How To window gives you quick access to help with everyday tasks.

Making quick use of keyboard shortcuts

Acrobat 6 is chock-full of keyboard shortcuts, which is great for a person like me who likes having access to commands directly from the keyboard (it really bugs me to have to keep taking my hand off the keyboard in order to click menu commands and toolbar buttons). The Cheat Sheet card at the front of this book is full of what I consider to be the most important keyboard shortcuts when you use Acrobat 6 on a steady basis. Of course, the Cheat Sheet is designed to tear out of the book so that you can put it up on your bulletin board or keep it close by your keyboard as you work. In this section, I want to say only a few words specifically about using the shortcut keys to select the various tools from the Basic Tools, Zoom, Commenting, Advanced Commenting, Advanced Editing, and Measuring toolbars, which you use extensively in your routine editing of PDF files.

Someone at Adobe decided that the keystrokes documented in the following table were confusing to new users, so the keyboard shortcuts are not activated by default in Acrobat 6 (much to the chagrin of seasoned users, who might think Adobe did away with this valuable feature when they first launch the new program). To make these keystrokes work, choose Edit⇨Preferences or press Ctrl+K (Acrobat⇨Preferences or ⌘+K on Mac) to open the Preferences dialog box. Choose General on the scroll list to display those options in the dialog box, and in the Miscellaneous area, select the Use Single-Key Accelerators to Access Tools check box, and then click OK. Note that when the feature is activated, the ToolTips that appear when you hover the mouse pointer over a button tool show not only the tool's name but its keystroke shortcut, or *single-key accelerators,* as Adobe likes to call them. What'll they think of next?

This section makes a lot more sense if you turn on single-key accelerators, as described in the preceding paragraph. Table 3-2 shows you the shortcut keystrokes for all the tools in Acrobat 6 that use this feature. Note how all the shortcuts are single letters of the alphabet, used alone, without the usual combination key like Ctrl, Alt, or ⌘ on Mac. Note, too, that not all of these letters are mnemonic. (How'd they get N for the Pencil tool and S for the Note tool?)

Table 3-2	Shortcut Keys for Selecting Acrobat 6 Tools	
Toolbar	*Tool*	*Shortcut Key*
Basic Tools	Hand	H
	Select Text	V
	Snapshot	G
Zoom	Zoom In	Z
Commenting	Note	S
	Indicate Text Edits	E
	Stamp	K
	Highlight Text	U
Advanced Commenting	Rectangle	D
	Text Box	X
	Pencil	N
	Attach File	J
Advanced Editing	Select Object	R
	Article	A
	Crop	C

Toolbar	Tool	Shortcut Key
	Link	L
	Form	F
	Movie	M
	TouchUp Text	T
Measuring	Distance	B

To select any of the tools on these toolbars, type the letter of its shortcut key. Acrobat then selects the tool on the toolbar (indicated by highlighting the button as though it were depressed), and the mouse pointer changes to the shape associated with the tool you selected. For example, the pointer changes to a magnifying glass when you select the Zoom In or Zoom Out tool, and it changes to an I-beam when you select the TouchUp Text tool.

Many of the Acrobat toolbar buttons have hidden tools that you can view and select by clicking on their associated pop-up menus. When the single-key accelerators feature is turned on, you can cycle through and select these different tools by holding down the Shift key and pressing the keystroke shortcut for the primary (unhidden) tool. For example, the Select Text tool also has the hidden tools Select Table and Select Image. Press V to choose the Select Text tool or hold down the Shift key and tap the letter V to toggle through all three tools in the order that they appear on the pop-up menu. As you cycle through the menu list, each tool icon is highlighted on the toolbar button to indicate that tool is selected.

Part II

The Wealth of Ways for Creating PDF Files

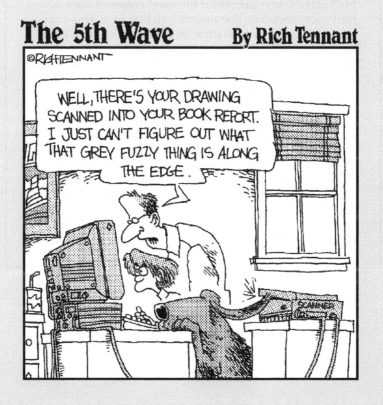

The 5th Wave   By Rich Tennant

WELL, THERE'S YOUR DRAWING SCANNED INTO YOUR BOOK REPORT. I JUST CAN'T FIGURE OUT WHAT THAT GREY FUZZY THING IS ALONG THE EDGE.

In this part . . .

Given the universal nature of the Adobe PDF (Portable Document Format), it should come as little surprise to find out that there are many ways to turn the documents created with the various software programs you use into PDF files. This part of the book introduces you to all the major ways to convert both your electronic and paper documents to PDF files.

In Chapter 4, you encounter the most common ways to turn your electronic documents into PDF files. This chapter includes vital information on the most common ways to convert to PDF, how to customize the settings used in making these conversions, as well as how to automate the conversion process. In Chapter 5, you find out how to turn Microsoft Office documents into PDF files using the PDFMaker 6.0 utility (automatically installed in Word, Excel, and PowerPoint when you install Acrobat 6 on your computer). In Chapter 6, you discover how to convert paper documents into PDF files by scanning them into Acrobat 6. In Chapter 7, you find out how to capture Web pages on your company's intranet or the Internet and save them as PDF files (for later viewing and printing in Acrobat or Adobe Reader). Finally, in Chapter 8, you find out how to print all or part of the PDF files that you make using these many methods.

Chapter 4

Distilling PDF Files

. . . .

. . . .

*P*DF files don't grow on trees, but oftentimes it does seem as though they are produced by every piece of software that you use. The first problem is understanding how exactly to go about producing PDF versions of your files, given the software you're using. (See Chapter 5 for details on producing PDFs with Microsoft Office programs and Chapter 10 for details on Acrobat 6's new ability to convert AutoCAD and Microsoft Visio files to PDF.) Then, after you do understand the software's procedure, you still have to understand what settings to apply in the Acrobat Distiller utility to produce exactly the type of PDF file you want.

In this chapter, you find out how to use the Acrobat Distiller (the Distiller utility is included as part of the Acrobat 6 program) to produce the type of PDF files you need. You also discover how to customize the basic settings and automate the PDF distillation process.

Common Ways to Create PDF Files

With the advent of Acrobat 6, Adobe Systems has significantly simplified the process of creating PDF files. In the good old days of PDF production (in other words, when Acrobat 3 was the latest version), you had little choice but to print a PostScript file from whatever application program you were using to create the file to be converted to PDF. You then had to run this file through the Acrobat Distiller.

Of course, you can still perform this two-part process with Acrobat 6 (which is generally referred to as *manually distilling* the PDF file), and, in fact, the rest of this chapter is devoted to giving you the information you need to create PDF files using this good old-fashioned way. You need to know how to do manual PDF distilling primarily because it gives you the most freedom over the settings that produce exactly the type of PDF file you need. Also, in understanding how to customize the settings in the Acrobat Distiller, you almost always understand how to customize the distilling settings available in your native application software in order to produce precisely the PDF file you require.

Put away that PDFWriter!

Up through version 4 of Acrobat, Adobe distributed a utility called PDFWriter (no longer automatically installed in Acrobat 6) that enabled you to create PDF files from popular application software such as Word, Excel, and PowerPoint in Office 97. Be aware that the PDF files created with the PDFWriter are PDF 1.2 files, meaning that they lack all the current quality and security features offered in the PDF 1.4 (generated by Acrobat 5) and 1.5 files (generated by Acrobat 6).

The PDFWriter is suitable only for the creation of the simplest, text-only PDF documents, completely lacking in interactivity, and please don't use it to produce prepress PDF documents because its 1.2 file format provides no support for embedded EPS graphics (which can really mess up your workflow). Instead, use either the Acrobat Distiller described in this chapter or, if you're converting Microsoft Office documents, the PDFMaker utility that's automatically installed with Acrobat 6 (described in Chapter 5).

Using Create PDF in Acrobat 6

Acrobat 6 includes a File menu command, Create PDF, that you can use to open files saved in the HTML file format (that is, as Web pages) and simple text files, as well as a number of common graphics file formats including bitmap (*.bmp or *.rle), CompuServe GIF (*.gif), JPEG (*.jpg, *.jpeg, or *.jpe), PCX (*.pcx), PNG (*.png), and TIFF files (*.tif). Note that Acrobat 6 can now open Microsoft Office, AutoCAD, MS Visio, and MS Project files using the Create PDF command as well.

To open one of these file types as a PDF file, follow these steps:

1. **Launch Acrobat 6 and then choose File⇨Create PDF⇨From File.**

   The Open dialog box appears.

2. **Browse to the folder that contains the text, HTML, or graphics file or files that you want to open as PDF files in Acrobat 6, and then click their file icons.**

   To restrict the file listing in a folder to just files of the type you want to open in Acrobat, click the file type in the Files of Type drop-down list. To select multiple files in the folder you open in the Open dialog box, Ctrl+click each one or, if they're listed sequentially in the list, click the first one and then Shift+click the last one.

3. **Click the Open button in the Open dialog box.**

As soon as you click the Open button, Acrobat opens the selected files as PDF files (indicated by the appearance of the .pdf extension after the original file-name in the Acrobat title bar). To save a file opened as a PDF in its new format, choose File⇨Save to open the Save As dialog box, and then click the Save button. To change the folder where the file is saved, select the new folder on the Save In drop-down list. To save the file with a new filename, select the File Name text box and edit the original filename (leaving the .pdf file extension) before you click the Save button.

In Windows, you can convert any of the file types listed at the beginning of this section to PDF from the desktop, a folder window, or Explorer by simply right-clicking the file and choosing Convert to Adobe PDF on the context menu. Options for converting the file and e-mailing it to someone or combining a group of selected files in Acrobat are also provided on the context menu.

Acrobat 6 enables you to open and convert multiple files to PDF using the Create PDF commands on the File menu. To do so, follow these steps:

1. **Choose File⇨Create PDF⇨From Multiple Files to open the Create PDF from Multiple Documents dialog box.**

2. **Click the Browse button in the Add Files area, choose the file(s) you want to combine in a new PDF document in the Open dialog box that appears, and then click the Add button.**

   Files can be selected individually or grouped in the Open dialog box. When you click the Add button, selected files appear in the Files to Combine list box on the right side of the Create PDF from Multiple Documents dialog box.

3. **Select a file(s) in the Files to Combine list box and use the Remove, Move Up, or Move Down buttons in the Arrange Files area to specify the order in which selected files appear in the converted PDF document.**

4. **To append all open PDF documents to your multiple files selection in a new PDF document, select the Include All Open PDF Documents check box.**

5. **To append the recent PDF files listed on the File menu to your multiple files selection in a new PDF document, select the Include Most Recent List of Files to Combine check box.**

6. **Click OK to create a new multiple document PDF file.**

Converting graphics files to PDFs by choosing File⇨Create PDF⇨From File does not produce the same quality PDF graphics files as distilling them from their native application or manually distilling them with the Acrobat Distiller. Reserve this method for Windows graphics that you can't convert into PostScript files or that you intend to use only in online PDF documents or files that will be printed only on in-house printers. Never use this quick-and-dirty method to produce PDF files that you intend to send out for professional printing; they lack the encoded PostScript necessary to produce the quality that prepress demands.

Using the Acrobat 6 Distiller

You use the PDF file Distiller that launches from within Acrobat 6 to convert only two kinds of files: Those saved as PostScript files (usually printed to PostScript using the application's Print command) or those saved in the EPS (Encapsulated PostScript) file format. This means that before you can use the Acrobat Distiller, you must have the files you want to convert saved in one of these two file formats.

Assuming that you have your files readied in these formats, you perform the following general steps to turn them into PDFs:

1. **Launch the Acrobat 6 program.**

2. **Choose Advanced⇨Acrobat Distiller to launch the Acrobat Distiller.**

   The Acrobat Distiller program window appears, as shown in Figure 4-1.

3. **In the Adobe PDF Settings section, select the name of the job option that uses the desired distilling settings from the Default Settings drop-down list.**

   (See the following sections, "To every PDF there is a purpose . . ." for details on the default Adobe PDF settings, and "Making Adobe PDF settings of your very own" for details on creating customized Adobe PDF settings.)

4. **Choose File⇨Open from the Acrobat Distiller menus or press Ctrl+O (⌘+O on the Mac).**

   The Acrobat Distiller - Open PostScript File dialog box opens.

Figure 4-1:
The Acrobat
Distiller
program
window as it
appears
when you
launch it in
Acrobat 6.

5. **In the Acrobat Distiller - Open PostScript File dialog box, browse to the folder that contains the PostScript or EPS file that you want to convert to PDF, click the file icon, and then click the Open button.**

   If you're distilling an EPS (Encapsulated PostScript) file rather than a plain old PostScript file, don't forget to select EPS files rather than the default PostScript files in the Files of Type (Show on the Mac) drop-down list.

As soon as you click the Open button in the Open PostScript File dialog box, the Acrobat Distiller begins distilling the selected PostScript file. The program displays the progress of the file distillation in the Progress bar in the middle of the Acrobat Distiller window. If you discover that you're distilling the wrong file, click the Cancel Job button. If, for any reason, you need to pause the distilling job, click the Pause button in the Acrobat Distiller. When you're ready to complete the job, click the Resume button (which replaces Pause as soon as you pause the job).

After the Acrobat Distiller finishes the job, it displays the destination of the resulting PDF file, the name of the source PostScript file, and the time it took to do this distillation job in a list box at the bottom of the Acrobat Distiller window (see Figure 4-2). Distiller automatically saves the new PDF file using the same name and location as the PostScript source file.

If you want Distiller to prompt you for a new name and destination folder for your newly converted PDF file, you can specify that in the Acrobat Distiller Preferences dialog box. Choose File⇨Preferences on the Acrobat Distiller menus or press Ctrl+K (⌘+K on the Mac). In the Acrobat Distiller Preferences dialog box, select the Ask for PDF File Destination check box, and then click

OK. After selecting this check box, upon the completion of each PDF distillation you perform with the Acrobat Distiller, Acrobat will automatically open the Specify PDF File Name dialog box so that you can edit the filename in the File Name text box and navigate to a new destination folder if so desired.

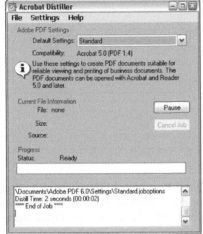

Figure 4-2:
Statistics
on the
completed
distilling job
appear in
the list box
at the
bottom of
the Acrobat
Distiller
program
window.

Upon completion of a distilling job, the Acrobat Distiller window remains open so that you can repeat this process and distill more PostScript files if you wish. When you're finished distilling files, close the Acrobat Distiller by clicking its Close button or by choosing the File➪Exit (Quit on the Mac) command from its menus. After closing the Acrobat Distiller, you can open the distilled PDF file and check out the results in Acrobat 6 by choosing File➪Open.

If you don't already have an authoring program that creates EPS or PostScript files, such as Adobe Illustrator, installed on your computer, you can simply double-click an EPS or PostScript file to open Acrobat Distiller and automatically convert a file to PDF. The conversion occurs in a single instance so the default settings in Acrobat Distiller are automatically applied. If you have a bunch of PostScript files to convert, you can easily batch process them by selecting all the files you want to distill in a folder and double-clicking them. Note that if you do have Illustrator or similar program installed, you just open all the selected files in that program.

To every PDF there is a purpose . . .

The six preset Adobe PDF settings in the Acrobat Distiller represent what Adobe considers to be the optimal distilling settings for creating the basic types of PDF files:

✔ **Standard:** This is the default preset job option that is automatically used in distilling your file unless you select one of the other preset options or a custom setting of your own design. Use this job option to generate PDF files for business documents that will be printed and read. This job option converts all colors to sRGB, downsamples images to 150 dpi, and provides Acrobat 5 (PDF 1.4 file) compatibility.

✔ **High Quality:** Use this job option to generate PDF files with higher image resolution for improved printing quality. For example, use the High Quality setting for a document containing photographic images (as opposed to clipart) that you want to print on an in-house laser printer or archive on CD-ROM. This job option leaves all colors unchanged, down-samples images to 300 dpi but provides high-quality JPEG compression, and embeds all fonts used in the source document. This job option (as well as PDF/X1a, PDF/X3, and Press Quality) produces PDF files of the largest file size. When converting especially large and graphically complex documents, you may end up generating enormous PDF files that are impossible to deliver to your service bureau (in such cases, you have to split the document up into smaller, separate files that, once distilled, you can successfully send).

✔ **PDF/X1a:** Use this job option to generate a PDF that's destined for a professional prepress work flow and that has the same settings as High Quality. PDF/X1a is an ISO (International Organization for Standardization) standard for digital graphic content exchange used in the printing industry. This setting creates a report and produces a PDF file only if it is compliant with the PDF/X1a standard. You can get more information about this feature by choosing Help⇨Complete Acrobat 6.0 Help to open the help guide, clicking the Search tab, and typing **About PDF/X** in the Find Pages Containing text box.

✔ **PDF/X3:** Use this job option to generate a PDF that's destined for a professional prepress work flow and that has the same settings as High Quality. PDF/X3 is an ISO standard for digital graphic content exchange used in the printing industry. This setting creates a report and produces a PDF file only if it is compliant with the PDF/X3 standard. You can get more information about this feature by choosing Help⇨Complete Acrobat 6.0 Help to open the help guide, clicking the Search tab, and typing **About PDF/X** in the Find Pages Containing text box.

✔ **Press Quality:** Use this job option to generate prepress PDF files are intended for high-end printing by a professional printer or service bureau. This job option leaves all colors unchanged and downsamples images to 300 dpi, but provides high-quality JPEG compression and embeds all fonts used in the source document.

✔ **Smallest File Size:** Use this job option to generate PDF files to be posted on your online Web site on the Internet, a corporate intranet, or a network server for online reading or for quick downloading. This job option converts all colors to RGB, downsamples images to 100 dpi, and does not allow font embedding. Of the six presets, this job option produces PDF files of the smallest file size.

You can use any of these six default Adobe PDF settings as is or as the starting point for creating customized Adobe PDF settings that take into consideration special online display or printing parameters that you need to meet.

The Acrobat Distiller retains the distilling settings last used even after you close the program so that they are in effect the next time you use the Acrobat Distiller. This means that if, for example, you distill a file using the Press Quality job option, Press Quality will be selected as the new default preset (instead of the original Standard default). This makes it imperative that you check the Adobe PDF Settings field each time you open the Acrobat Distiller before you set about distilling files with it. Otherwise, you may end up wasting time distilling a huge file ready for professional printing with the Press Quality preset when you only needed to generate a smaller, compact file for your Web site with the Smallest File Size preset.

Automatically displaying your distilled file in Acrobat

Normally, when you manually distill a PDF file with the Acrobat Distiller, the program does not automatically display the new PDF file in Acrobat 6. If you want to automatically check out the results of each distillation you perform with Acrobat Distiller, you need to select the View PDF When Using Distiller check box in the Acrobat Distiller - Preferences dialog box.

To open this dialog box, shown in Figure 4-3, choose File⇨Preferences from the Acrobat Distiller menu or press Ctrl+K (⌘+K on the Mac). Then select the View PDF When Using Distiller check box and click OK. After selecting this check box, upon the completion of each PDF distillation you perform with the Acrobat Distiller, Acrobat automatically closes the Acrobat Distiller window and displays the newly distilled PDF in the Acrobat 6 Document window.

Figure 4-3: Changing the Output options in the Acrobat Distiller - Preferences dialog box.

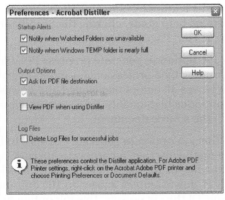

As you see in Figure 4-3, the Output Options section in the Acrobat Distiller - Preferences dialog box also includes an option called Ask to Replace Existing PDF File. Select this option to make sure that the Acrobat Distiller always prompts you if you are about to inadvertently replace an existing PDF file with the one you've just distilled with the Acrobat Distiller. Note that the Distiller program won't allow you to select both the Ask for PDF File Destination and the Ask to Replace Existing PDF File check boxes in the Acrobat Distiller - Preferences dialog box. When you click the Ask for PDF File Destination check box, the program immediately grays out the Ask to Replace Existing PDF File check box. The assumption is that if you have the Acrobat Distiller prompt you for the destination of the new PDF, you will notice any filename conflict in the process of selecting the file's destination folder.

Making Adobe PDF settings of your very own

The best way to go about creating your own Adobe PDF settings for distilling PDF files is to select the preset job option with the settings closest to the ones you want to customize in the Acrobat Distiller, and then make appropriate changes to individual settings. For example, to create a custom job option for distilling PDF files for pamphlets with a special trim size and binding that will be professionally printed by a service bureau using a particular typesetter, you would start by selecting Press Quality in the Default Settings drop-down list under the Adobe PDF Settings area in the Acrobat Distiller window. Then you would open the Press Quality- Adobe PDF Settings dialog box by choosing Settings➪Edit Adobe PDF Settings on the Acrobat Distiller menus or by pressing Ctrl+E (⌘+E on the Mac).

Changing the General options

When you first open the Adobe PDF Settings dialog box in the Acrobat Distiller, the dialog box opens with the General tab selected, as shown in Figure 4-4. Note that the particular settings selected on the General tab (and the four other tabs in the Adobe PDF Settings dialog box, for that matter) reflect the optimal values assigned to whatever preset job option is selected at the time you open the dialog box (this being the Press Quality job option in the example shown in Figure 4-4).

You then begin customizing the values for whatever settings need changing in your custom job option. On the General tab, these settings include:

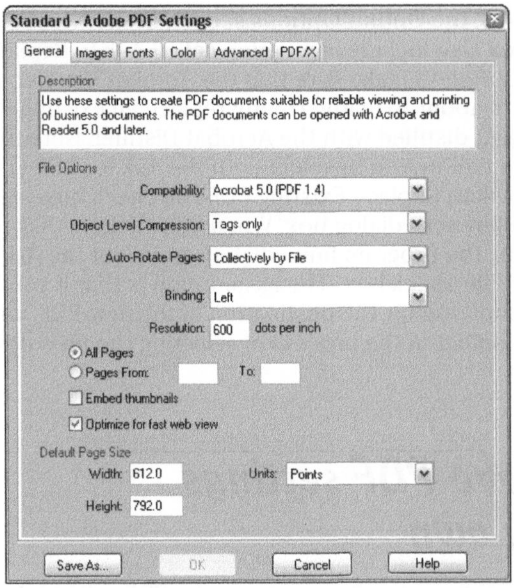

Figure 4-4:
The options
on the
General tab
of the
Standard -
Adobe PDF
Settings
dialog box.

✔ **Description:** Use this text box to type a description of your custom distiller settings. The entered description is displayed in the Acrobat Distiller dialog box when you select your custom setting from the Default Settings drop-down list.

✔ **Compatibility:** Specifies the PDF file version for the final distilled document and thereby its level of Adobe Reader compatibility. You have a choice between Acrobat 6.0 (PDF 1.5), Acrobat 5.0 (PDF 1.4), Acrobat 4.0 (PDF 1.3), and Acrobat 3.0 (PDF 1.2). When creating a job option for distilling prepress PDFs, stay with the default value of Acrobat 5.0 (PDF 1.4) unless your service bureau specifically tells you that it can handle PDF 1.5 files, or if you need the highest level of file encryption (PDF 1.4 and 1.5 files support 128-bit file encryption — the highest level of security available). Don't select Acrobat 3.0 (PDF 1.2) unless you are creating a custom job option for online files that requires Acrobat Reader 3.0 compatibility to reach the widest possible audience.

✔ **Object Level Compression:** Specifies that small objects in a PDF files, such as tags, be consolidated so that they can be efficiently compressed. Choose Off to not compress a document's structural information. The resulting PDF file will retain accessibility features and the ability to navigate and interact with bookmarks using Acrobat 5 and later. Choose Tags Only to compress the document's structural information. The resulting PDF can be viewed and printed using Adobe 5, but accessibility, navigation, and bookmarks are visible only in Acrobat 6.

✔ **Auto-Rotate Pages:** When selected, automatically rotates the pages of the distilled PDF file to match the orientation of the text. You can choose to apply the Individually to Pages or the Collectively by File setting.

✔ **Binding:** Specifies how pages and thumbnails are displayed in the Adobe Reader when the two-page and continuous page viewing options are selected. This setting has no effect on the printed binding edge. You have a choice between the Left option (the default) used for all European languages, and the Right option for this setting.

✔ **Resolution:** Specifies the print resolution to be used in the distilled PDF file when this setting is *not* specified by PostScript commands in the source file. Most of the time, you can leave the default 600 dpi (dots per inch) setting as is. If you change the value to match that of the printer with which the PDF file will be printed, you must enter a value in its text box that is between 72 and 4000 dpi.

✔ **Page Range:** Specifies the range of pages in the source document to be distilled in the final PDF file. The default setting is the All radio button. To set a range of pages, select the From radio button and then enter starting and ending page values in the From and To text boxes.

✔ **Embed Thumbnails:** Creates thumbnail images and embeds them as part of the distilled file for use in navigating the file's text in Adobe Reader. Note that Adobe Reader 6 automatically creates thumbnails whether or not this option is selected. Users of earlier versions of Adobe Reader will not have them unless this option is selected. Be aware, however, that embedding thumbnails does increase the PDF file size, especially for documents with many pages.

✔ **Default Page Size:** Specifies the size of the pages in the final PDF document when this information is not specified by the PostScript commands in the source file. By default, the Width and Height values for the Default Page Size setting are displayed in points. When modifying the page size values in the Width and Height text boxes, be sure to select the appropriate units (Picas, Inches, or Centimeters) in the Units drop-down list.

Changing the Images options

The settings on the Images tab of the Adobe PDF Settings dialog box, shown in Figure 4-5, determine in large part both the quality and the size of the distilled PDF file. As you can see in Figure 4-5, the Images settings for a job option fall into three broad categories: Color Images, Grayscale Images, and Monochrome Images.

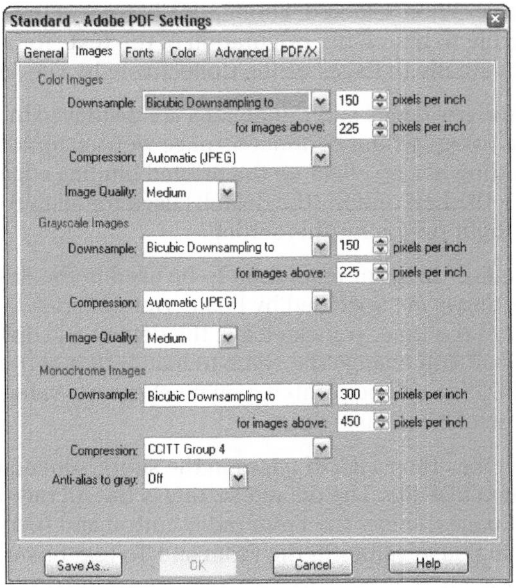

Figure 4-5:
The options
on the
Images tab
of the
Standard -
Adobe PDF
Settings
dialog box.

Note that when modifying the Color Images, Grayscale Images, and Mono-chrome Images settings, you have the ability to change the type of down-sampling and the rate, as well as the type of compression (and in terms of color and grayscale images, the quality as well). *Downsampling* refers to a process of applying a mathematical algorithm to a bunch of pixels in the images to determine how to combine them into fewer (but larger) pixels at a new resolution; in other words, changing the resolution (in pixels per inch) of an image to make the file size smaller and the print quality lower. *Compression* refers to the applying of a mathematical algorithm to the pixels in your images in order to eliminate redundant pixels. There are two types of com-pression: *Lossless,* which results in no loss of image integrity, and *lossy,* which removes pixels from the image that can't be retrieved, and thus results in some degradation of the image quality. In Acrobat, you apply compression and downsampling to bitmap images such as photos. If you are converting text and line art (vector graphics), you use only compression.

In terms of the type of downsampling applied to bitmap images, you have the following choices:

✓ **Bicubic Downsampling To:** This is the default option, and it uses a weighted average to come up with a new pixel color value at a new reso-lution. This type of downsampling takes the longest but gives the best results for high-end images with fine color gradations.

✔ **Average Downsampling To:** This option averages the color pixel values in a particular area to replace them with a new color value at a new resolution.

✔ **Subsampling To:** This option uses the color pixel value of a pixel at the center of a particular region as the replacement value for the pixels in that region.

When using any of these types, you must specify a threshold value that tells the Acrobat Distiller which images to downsample and gives the lowest image resolution to which they can be resampled.

In terms of the type of compression for color and grayscale images, you have a choice among the following options:

✔ **Automatic:** This is the default option, and it leaves the decision as to which type of compression (JPEG or ZIP) to apply to the images in the distilled file to Acrobat Distiller. This is the best setting in cases where you have documents that are a mixture of bitmap and vector graphics.

✔ **JPEG:** This option is a lossy compression scheme best used for photos in which image data is analyzed in 8 x 8 pixel blocks and redundant pixels are permanently removed.

✔ **ZIP:** This option is a lossless compression best used on text and line art or vector graphics in which the image size is reduced while the image integrity is preserved.

When you choose the Automatic or JPEG option for compression, you can set the Quality setting to Maximum (the default), High, Medium, Low, or Minimum. Note that the higher the setting on this list (with Maximum at the top), the better the image quality, the less the compression, and the larger the final file size. The lower the setting on this list (with Minimum at the bottom), the lower the image quality, the higher the compression, and the smaller the file size.

When you choose ZIP compression, you can choose between 8-bit (the default) and 4-bit. Always select the type that is equal to or greater than the bit depth of your images, or you will lose image integrity (note that 4-bit images have 16 colors or shades of gray and 8-bit images have 256 or more colors or shades of gray).

For monochrome (that is, black and white) images in the source file, you can choose between ZIP (the default), two types of CCITT (Consulting Committee on International Telephony and Telegraph) developed for compressing FAX transmissions, and Run Length (or RLE for Run-Length Encoding) developed for compressing images with large separate areas of black and white. All of these Monochrome compression settings are of the lossless type and are pretty comparable in terms of size and quality, so in most cases, you can stay with the ZIP default.

The last setting that you can change in the Monochrome Images area is the Anti-Alias to Gray setting. Select this check box to have the Acrobat Distiller smooth jagged lines (also known as *jaggies*) on text and black-and-white images. When you check this option, Acrobat Distiller lets you select the bit depth for the anti-aliasing (that is, the levels of gray to be generated): 4-bit (the default) for 2 levels, 8-bit for 4 levels, or 8-bit for 256 levels of gray.

Changing the Fonts options

The options on the Fonts tab of the Adobe PDF Settings dialog box (shown in Figure 4-6) enable you to determine which fonts are embedded in the distilled PDF file. By default, all presets (except for the Smallest File Size preset) automatically check the Embed All Fonts check box. When this option is checked, Acrobat Distiller includes all the fonts used in the source document as part of the final PDF file. This is essential when creating a custom job option for distilling prepress PDF files, because nothing can mess up your artwork or upset your service bureau more than delivering PDF files without the necessary fonts.

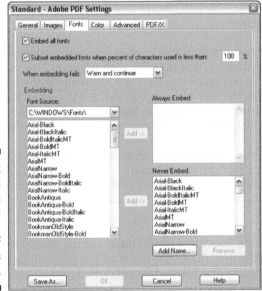

Figure 4-6:
The options on the Fonts tab of the Standard - Adobe PDF Settings dialog box.

To help cut down on the bloat caused by embedding fonts in the final PDF file, the Fonts tab has the Subset Embedded Fonts When Percent of Characters Is

Less Than check box that, when checked, tells Acrobat Distiller to embed only the characters in a font that are actually used in the source document. This means that if your source document uses only 15 characters in Bodoni Bold, only the PostScript commands for generating those 15 characters, and not for the entire character set, are included in the final PDF file.

The percentage field to the immediate right of this Subset Embedded Fonts check box enables you to set the threshold percentage at which the entire character set is embedded. The 100% default setting means that the only time that all the characters are embedded is when they are all needed (and you should leave this percentage at 100% whenever you use the Subset Embedded Fonts option).

Directly beneath the Embed All Fonts and the Subset Embedded Fonts check boxes, you find a When Embedding Fails drop-down list box that tells Acrobat Distiller what warning to display or action to take if, for some reason, font embedding fails while distilling a PDF file (usually because the font is not installed on the computer on which the job option is being used).

If you intend to create prepress PDF files with the custom job option you're building, be sure to select Cancel Job on the When Embedding Fails drop-down list so that no prepress PDF file can be created without the necessary fonts. If you don't mind that Acrobat or Adobe Reader does some font substitution in the final file, you can select the Ignore option. If you want to be informed each time font embedding fails during a distilling job, select the Warn and Continue option instead.

If you prefer to handpick which fonts are to be embedded during the PDF file distilling and which are not, you use the Embedding section of the Fonts tab instead of the Embed All Fonts option. To indicate which fonts to embed, select the location of the fonts in the Font Source drop-down list (by default, this is set to `C:\Windows\Fonts\`, which displays all the fonts installed on your computer). Click the name of each font you want to specify in the list box on the left to select it, and then click either the Add button to the left of the Always Embed list box to add the font there, or click the Add button to the left of the Never Embed list box to put the selected font there.

To ensure that font embedding doesn't fail when distilling a file with your custom job option, make sure to list all the possible locations where fonts are installed on your system (including networked drives if fonts are stored on a special volume). To do this, choose Settings⇨Font Locations on the Acrobat Distiller menu (upon closing the Adobe PDF Settings dialog box) or press Ctrl+L (⌘+L on the Mac), and then use the Add button in the Acrobat Distiller - Font Locations dialog box (see Figure 4-7) to select and add all the font folders on your computer system that should be used in font embedding.

Font substitution 101

If you don't embed certain fonts in the final PDF document, then the Acrobat Distiller does the best it can at font substitution using what's known as the Multiple Master typeface. In font substitution, Acrobat Distiller matches serif fonts with serif fonts and sans-serif with sans-serif fonts and tries to pick available substitute fonts whose use have little or no impact on the line and page layout of the final document. It does an okay job with substituting straightforward,

non-decorative fonts and a less-than-stellar job with substituting those highly decorative or script-type fonts with which you just love to embellish your documents. So if your document uses simpler fonts, you can get away with not embedding the fonts. But if you're using decorative or script-type fonts, you should embed the fonts to guarantee the best results in the final PDF document.

Figure 4-7:
Specifying
all the font
folders
on the
computer
system to
aid in font
embedding.

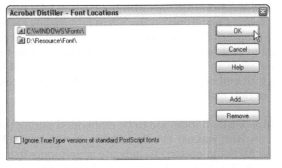

Not all fonts you install on your computer give you the *license* (that is, the legal right) to embed them in the PDF files you distill. For example, Adobe lets you embed the fonts you license from it with impunity. Agfa/Monotype, on the other hand, does not. You need to check the license that came with the fonts you installed. Also, when you intend to send the PDF file out to a service bureau or professional printer, check with those folks, because they may have special standing licenses that cover the fonts you're using in a document they're printing so that you can embed the fonts without violating the law!

You may be wondering how you can tell which fonts have been embedded and which, if any, have been substituted when viewing a PDF file in Acrobat 6. To check on which fonts are embedded in the PDF document you're viewing, open the Document Fonts dialog box by choosing File⊏>Document Properties or by pressing Ctrl+D (⌘+D on the Mac). When you select this command, the Document Properties dialog box opens, as shown in Figure 4-8. Click Fonts in the scroll box on the left to display a listing of all fonts that are embedded in the file in the viewing window on the right.

The easiest way to spot substitute fonts in the file you're viewing in Acrobat is to toggle off the Advanced⇨Use Local Fonts command (press Ctrl+Shift+Y on Windows or ⌘+Shift+Y on the Mac). When you turn this setting off, Acrobat Distiller ignores the local fonts on your computer and then displays the substitute fonts. Any fonts that the program can't substitute are indicated with bullets, and, of course, if all the fonts are embedded in the file, the PDF document is not affected by turning this setting off.

Changing the Color options

The Color tab on the Press - Adobe PDF Settings dialog box (shown in Figure 4-9) enables you to specify how colors are managed in the distilling process and, most importantly, whether or not you want the colors in the source document converted into what graphic designers call another *color space* (that is, converted to the sRGB — or Red, Green, Blue — model used by computer monitors to display colors).

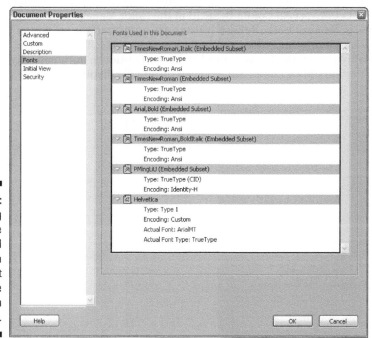

Figure 4-8: Examining the embedded fonts in a PDF file that you're viewing in Acrobat 6.

Color 101

Color and color management are about the most obtuse of topics (they must give Ph.D.s in the field). In a nutshell, monitors produce colors additively using the RGB, or Red, Green, and Blue, model (just like your color TV), and color printing produces colors subtractively using the CMYK model that combines Cyan, Magenta, Yellow, and BlacK inks. The problem lies in rectifying the large gamut of colors in the RGB model with the more limited and quite different range of the CMYK model. Enter ICC (International Color Consortium) color management, which profiles the range of colors that every device involved in the displaying and printing of colors can produce so that colors are displayed or printed consistently across all devices. To discover more about the wonderful world of color and color management, go to http://studio.adobe.com/learn/tips/phstamecmb/main.html and then follow the links to the articles on color and color management. Note that you may need to fill out a simple registration form to access Adobe's Expert Center, but it's well worth the effort.

As you would expect, when building a custom job option using either the Standard or Smallest File Size preset, the Acrobat Distiller automatically selects Convert All Colors to sRGB in the Color Management drop-down list. This is because both of these presets are optimized for on-screen viewing instead of printing. When you build a custom job option using the Press Quality preset, the Leave Color Unchanged option is automatically selected so that no CMYK colors are changed during file distillation.

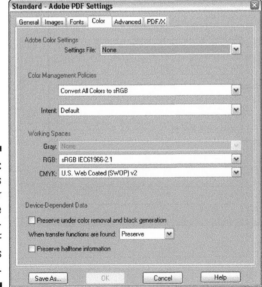

Figure 4-9: The options on the Color tab of the Standard - Adobe PDF Settings dialog box.

The rest of the options on the Color tab of the Adobe PDF Settings dialog box should be approached with great caution. Always check with your service bureau partners before making modifications to these settings, such as selecting a color management settings file from the Settings File drop-down list (None is the default setting for all six presets), selecting one of the tag options in the Color Management drop-down list (Tag Everything for Color Management or Tag Only Images for Color Management), or, for heaven's sake, fooling with any of the Device Dependent options.

Changing the Advanced options

As the name implies, the Advanced tab of the Adobe PDF Settings dialog box (shown in Figure 4-10) contains a bunch of check box options, most of which, I'm happy to report, you won't ever have to monkey with. In case you're the least bit curious, Prologue.ps and Epilogue.ps, just as their names imply, are the beginning and ending files in between which is sandwiched the file with the PostScript codes that actually produce the text and images in your document. DSC, by the way, is an acronym for Document Structuring Conventions files. These are the types of files created by QuarkXPress, and they must be converted into a PostScript or EPS file before distilling, or else the Acrobat Distiller will burp something silly.

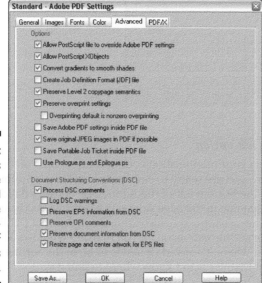

Figure 4-10: The options on the Advanced tab of the Standard - Adobe PDF Settings dialog box.

Changing the PDF/X options

The PDF/X tab options of the Adobe PDF Setting dialog box, shown in Figure 4-11, are even more arcane than the Advanced tab options to those (like me) who don't jump up and down for joy that Adobe has finally provided this functionality in Acrobat 6. Suffice it to say that these options enable you to specify criteria that Distiller uses when checking to see if your PDF file is compliant with PDF/X1a or PDF/X3 standards. If your PDF is not destined for high-resolution print production, fagetaboudit! On the other hand, if this subject makes you tingle all over, you can get more information about this feature by choosing Help➪Complete Acrobat 6.0 Help to open the help guide, clicking the Search tab, and then typing **About PDF/X** in the Find Pages Containing text box.

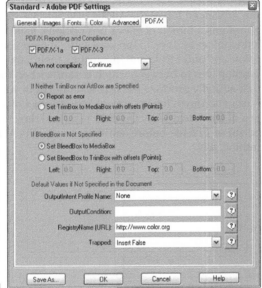

Figure 4-11:
The options
on the
PDF/X tab
of the
Standard -
Adobe PDF
Settings
dialog box.

Saving your custom job option

When you finish making your modifications on the various tabs of the Adobe PDF Settings dialog box, you are ready to save your custom job option. Click the Save As button on the bottom left of the Adobe PDF Settings dialog box and then edit the default filename in the Save Adobe PDF Settings As dialog box. Be careful not to modify the .joboptions file extension in Acrobat Distiller for Windows (you may not see file extensions if you're using Windows XP) and don't change the folder where it's saved (it needs to be in the Settings folder; otherwise, the Acrobat Distiller won't know where to find it).

After editing the filename, click the Save button and then click the Close button in the Adobe PDF Settings dialog box to close it and return to the Acrobat Distiller window. The name of the custom job option you just defined now appears in the Default Settings drop-down list, along with the six presets, so that you can select it anytime you need to in distilling your PDF files.

To access a custom option that you need to delete, copy, or share with a coworker, go to your computer's operating system and open the Settings folder found inside the Distiller (it's misspelled as Distillr on Windows) folder within the Acrobat 6.0 folder and find the Adobe PDF settings file there. You can also Add or Delete custom job option settings by choosing the appropriate command on the Settings menu in Acrobat Distiller.

Selecting security settings for the new PDF file

Whenever you create a PDF file with the Acrobat Distiller, you can restrict access to its contents by assigning a password to it, and, further, you can control what other Acrobat and Adobe Reader users can and cannot do with it by restricting the file permissions. To add these kinds of securities to a file in Acrobat Distiller, choose Settings⇨Security on the Acrobat Distiller menus or press Ctrl+S (⌘+S on the Mac) to open the Acrobat Distiller - Security dialog box, as shown in Figure 4-12. You do this after you designate which Adobe PDF settings to use but before you specify which source file to distill.

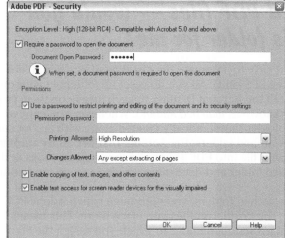

Figure 4-12:
Modifying
the options
in the
Acrobat
Distiller -
Security
dialog box.

To prevent anyone who doesn't know the secret password from even being able to open the final PDF document, select the Requires a Password to Open Document check box and then enter the password in the Document Open Password text box. To prevent anyone who has the password for opening the document from changing the password and/or the permissions you set for the file, select the Use a Password to Restrict Printing and Editing of the Document and Its Security Settings check box and enter a password in the Permissions Password text box (make sure you don't assign the same password here that you assigned for opening the PDF file).

When setting the permissions for the file, you have the following choices on the drop-down lists:

- ✔ **Printing Allowed:** Select None to prevent users from printing any part of the PDF document in either Acrobat 6 or Adobe Reader 6. Choose Low Resolution to enable users to print a lower quality PDF that prevents reproduction of the PDF with different security settings. Note that this setting is available only for PDF files compatible with PDF versions 1.4 or 1.5 where 128 bit encryption is supported. Choose High Resolution to allow printing at any resolution, including high output commercial printers.

- ✔ **Changes Allowed:** Choose None to prevent any changes in a PDF file or any of the following self-explanatory allowed changes: inserting, deleting, and rotation of pages, fill in of form fields and signing, commenting, or any except extracting of pages.

Automated PDF files — would you watch this folder for me?

Acrobat 6 makes it easy to automate the distilling of PostScript files (the print-to-disk kind and the EPS kind). All you do is set up folders in your operating system and then tell the Acrobat Distiller to keep an eye on them (such folders are thereafter known as *watched folders*). Whenever you copy a PostScript file into the In subfolder (automatically created along with an Out subfolder) within one these watched folders, the Acrobat Distiller utility automatically distills the PostScript file into PDF as soon as the program looks at the contents of the watched folder and determines the file's ready for distilling.

When setting up watched folders, you determine which Adobe PDF settings to use in distilling the PostScript files you place there. This means that you can set up a Standard watched folder to which you assign the Standard job option or one of your custom Adobe PDF settings based on its settings, as well as a Press Quality watched folder to which you assign the Press Quality PDF Setting or one of its variants. Then, to distill a PDF file using the Standard settings, you just drop the PostScript file into the Standard watched folder. To distill a PDF file using the Press Quality settings, you drop it into the Press Quality watched folder.

To set up watched folders on your hard drive, follow these steps:

1. **In your operating system, create and name the folder you want watched.**

2. **Launch Acrobat 6, and then launch the Acrobat Distiller by choosing Advanced⇨Acrobat Distiller.**

3. **Choose Settings⇨Watched Folders on the Acrobat Distiller menus or press Ctrl+F (⌘+F on the Mac).**

   The Watched Folders dialog box appears, as shown in Figure 4-13.

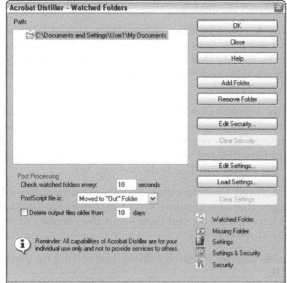

Figure 4-13: Setting up watched folders in the Acrobat Distiller - Watched Folders dialog box.

4. **Click the Add Folder button, and then in the Browse for Folder dialog box that opens, select the folder that you created and click OK.**

   After the Browse for Folder dialog box closes, the folder you selected is displayed in the list box of the Watched Folders dialog box. (Windows XP displays the directory path of the watched folder.)

5. **Click the folder you created to select it.**

6. **Click the Load Settings button to display the Load Adobe PDF Settings dialog box. Click the name of the Adobe PDF Setting to be applied to the files distilled in this folder, and then click the Open button.**

   Skip this step if you want to use the current Adobe PDF Setting specified in Distiller.

7. **If you want to modify any of the settings in the job option you selected for the watched folder, click the Edit Settings button and modify the settings as desired.**

8. **If you want to assign a password to the file or change the file permissions, click the Edit Security button and assign these settings in the Security dialog box.**

   (See the "Selecting security settings for the new PDF file" section, earlier in this chapter, for details, and be sure to jot down your password and store it in a safe place.)

9. **To add another watched folder, click the Add Folder button again and then repeat Steps 5 through 8.**

10. **By default, the Acrobat Distiller checks the watched folders you define every ten seconds to see whether or not they contain a new file to distill. To modify this interval (usually to lengthen it), click inside the Check Watched Folders Every text box and enter the number of seconds there.**

11. **By default, the Acrobat Distiller automatically moves all PostScript files that it distills in your watched folders into a folder marked Out (the PDF versions, however, remain in the watched folder). To have the PostScript files deleted after they're distilled, select the Deleted option from the PostScript File Is drop-down list.**

12. **To have the Acrobat Distiller automatically clear processed files in the watched folders that are so many days old, select the Delete Output Files Older Than check box and then enter the number of days (10 by default) in the Days text box.**

13. **After you finish adding watched folders and setting up their parameters, click OK.**

    The Watched Folders dialog box closes.

Note that watched folders are not designed to serve as the clearing house for all of your PDF distilling across the entire corporate network. If your company needs to set up just such a clearing house, look into purchasing Adobe's Acrobat Distiller Server that is made for just that kind of bulk processing using watched folders.

Making Acrobat Distiller your printer

You don't have to launch the Acrobat Distiller in order to use it and its Adobe PDF settings (including the custom Adobe PDF settings described earlier in the "Making Adobe PDF settings of your very own" section) to distill your PDF files. In fact, with certain application software, you don't even need to create a print-to-file PostScript or Encapsulated PostScript file in order to do the distilling. All you have to do is select the Acrobat Distiller as your printer in the program's Print dialog box.

Figure 4-14 illustrates this process using Microsoft Word 2002 in Windows. Select Adobe PDF as the printer from the Name drop-down list in the Word Print dialog box. To select the type Adobe PDF settings (called Conversion Settings in Microsoft programs), click the Properties button in the Print dialog box and then click the Adobe PDF Settings tab in the Adobe PDF Document Properties dialog box. Here, you can change the Adobe PDF settings to use (Standard in this example) in the Default Settings drop-down list and even edit these Adobe PDF settings by clicking the Edit button — see Chapter 5 for details.

Figure 4-14:
Making the
Acrobat
Distiller the
printer in
a program
like Word
causes the
Acrobat
Distiller
utility to run
in the
background
as it creates
the PDF file.

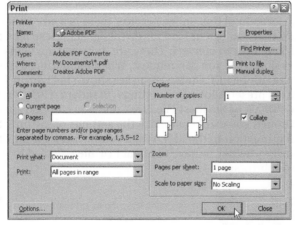

After selecting the Adobe PDF settings/conversion settings to use and clicking the OK button to close the Adobe PDF Document Properties dialog box, you have only to click the OK button in the Print dialog box to run the Acrobat Distiller. Prior to distilling the file, the Acrobat Distiller opens a Save PDF File As dialog box that enables you to rename and to relocate the new PDF file if you wish (otherwise, the new file carries the same filename as the original Word file with a .pdf extension and is automatically saved on the desktop of your computer). Then, after you click the Save button, the Acrobat Distiller completes the distilling, finally opening the converted PDF file in Acrobat 6.0.

PDF Files Courtesy of Adobe PDF Online

Adobe Systems offers a subscription service available worldwide called Create Adobe PDF Online that you can use to distill your source files. This subscription service costs $9.99 a month or $99.99 a year for creating an unlimited number of PDF files (you can also sign up for a trial subscription to this service that lets you create up to five PDF files for free).

You can submit a wide variety of different file formats to be converted to PDF, including HTML pages, Microsoft Office files, AutoCAD, Corel WordPerfect, and a whole bunch of graphics formats, including all those created by Adobe's many graphics and page layout programs (basically all the file formats supported by Acrobat 6). Note, however, that you can't submit native QuarkXPress files for converting (you need to convert them to PostScript files as you do with any other unsupported file format). You can get a complete list of all the file formats supported by the Create Adobe PDF Online service by visiting its Web site.

To sign up for this service or try it out free, go the following Web address:

```
http://createpdf.adobe.com
```

Note that for subscribers of this online service, there is a size limit of 100 pages per PDF file that you can upload for distilling, and these files must take no longer than 15 minutes to convert. There are, however, no limits on the amount of conversions that you can request. When submitting a file for distilling at the Create Adobe PDF Online Web site, shown in Figure 4-15, you can select any of the six preset Adobe PDF settings (Standard, High Quality, Press Quality, PDFX1a, PDFX3, or Smallest File Size), and you can also specify file permissions (although you can't customize the settings of the presets or assign password protection to the file). When submitting a file for distilling, you can also specify whether to have the final PDF file e-mailed to you or displayed in your Web browser.

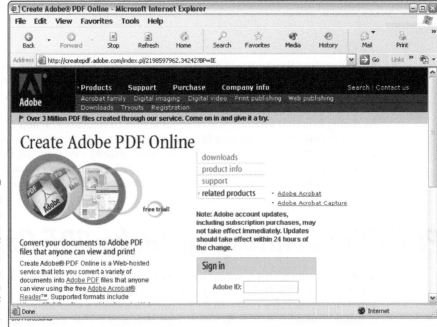

Figure 4-15: Using the Create Adobe PDF Online subscription service to create PDF files.

Chapter 5

Converting Microsoft Office Documents

* * *

* * *

*A*crobat 6 makes it a snap to convert Microsoft Office documents created and saved in the Word, Excel, or PowerPoint file formats to PDF files so that they can partake of all the benefits offered by this universal file format. When you install Acrobat 6 on a Windows or Macintosh computer on which these Microsoft Office applications (Office 2000 and XP on Windows and Office X on Macintosh) have already been installed, Acrobat 6 enhances the Word, Excel, and PowerPoint interface by adding three one-touch buttons (the Convert to Adobe PDF, Convert to Adobe PDF and E-mail, and Convert to Adobe PDF and Send for Review buttons) to the Office toolbars, as well as an Acrobat menu to the Office menus. Note that on Office X for Macintosh, you don't get the PDF reviewing features.

As you discover in this chapter, you can use the Convert to Adobe PDF buttons and the additional Acrobat menu to convert your native Microsoft Office documents into PDF documents in a flash. The best thing about this enhanced PDF conversion functionality is that you retain the ability to use any of the preset Adobe PDF Settings (Standard, Press Quality, High Quality, PDF/X1a, PDF/X3, and Smallest File Size) for distilling, as well as all the custom Adobe PDF Settings you create. Even more importantly, you can have the paragraph styles used in your Word documents automatically converted into bookmarks in the resulting PDF documents, and on the Windows platform, you can have your Word documents automatically converted into tagged PDF documents so that their text can reflow when viewed in Acrobat 6 or Adobe Reader 6.

Using PDFMaker in Microsoft Office for Windows

With the release of Acrobat 6, gone are the days of having to select the Acrobat Distiller as the name of your printer in the Print dialog box in Word, Excel, or PowerPoint in order to convert the native Office document file format into PDF (although you can still make perfectly good PDF files that way). Figure 5-1 shows the two sets of controls that are automatically added to the Microsoft Word, Excel, and PowerPoint 2000 and 2002 interfaces when you install Acrobat 6 on your computer.

Figure 5-1: Examining the Acrobat menu and PDFMaker 6.0 toolbar in Word 2002.

All you have to do in order to convert the current document open in Word, Excel, or PowerPoint into a PDF document is follow these three simple steps:

1. **Choose Adobe PDF➪Convert to Adobe PDF in the Office application or click the Convert to Adobe PDF button on the PDFMaker 6.0 toolbar.**

   An Acrobat PDFMaker alert dialog box appears, telling you that PDFMaker needs to save the document before continuing and asking whether or not you'd like to save the document and continue. Click Yes. The Save Adobe PDF File As dialog box appears.

2. **Edit the filename of the converted PDF file in the Name text box and select the folder on your hard drive in which to save it.**

   If you don't edit the filename, PDFMaker gives the new PDF file the same name as its Office counterpart but with the .pdf filename extension. Note that by default, filename extensions aren't displayed in Windows XP.

3. **Click the Save button.**

PDFMaker does the rest. As it converts the open document in the Office application to PDF, an Acrobat PDFMaker alert dialog box appears to keep you informed of the progress in converting the document's text and graphics in a progress bar. As soon as PDFMaker finishes the document conversion indicated on the progress bar, this Acrobat alert dialog box disappears.

To view the PDF document you just converted, launch Acrobat 6, and then choose File➪Open and select the newly converted PDF file (or better yet, open the PDF file's folder in the My Documents or the My Computer window and then just drag its file icon onto the Acrobat 6.0 desktop shortcut). Figure 5-2 shows the Word document (that first made its appearance in the background of Figure 5-1) as it looks in Acrobat 6 after its conversion to PDF.

Automatically viewing the converted PDF in Acrobat

If you'd like to view the converted PDF file automatically in Acrobat 6 as soon as the PDFMaker completes the Office-to-PDF file conversion in your Office application, select the View Result in Acrobat option before you invoke the Convert to Adobe PDF button or select the Convert to Adobe PDF item on the Acrobat menu. In the Office application, choose Adobe PDF➪Change Conversion Settings to open the Acrobat PDFMaker dialog box. Select the View Adobe PDF Result check box on the Settings tab and click OK.

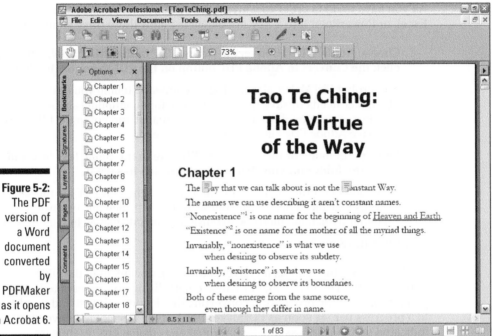

Figure 5-2:
The PDF
version of
a Word
document
converted
by
PDFMaker
as it opens
in Acrobat 6.

When the View Result in Acrobat option is turned on, PDFMaker converts the current Office document, displays the Save PDF File As dialog box, and then automatically launches Acrobat 6 (if it's not already running in the background) and displays the converted PDF file as the current document in the Acrobat Document window.

Converting and e-mailing PDF files

When converting an Office document to PDF, the PDFMaker offers you the option to automatically send the converted file as an attachment to a new e-mail message. You can use this option to quickly send a PDF version of an important Office document to a coworker or client who needs the information delivered in the cross-platform PDF format.

To convert the document currently open in Word, Excel, or PowerPoint into a PDF document and immediately send it off attached to a new e-mail message, follow these steps:

1. **In the Office application, choose Adobe PDF⇨Convert to Adobe PDF and E-mail or click the Convert to Adobe PDF and E-mail button (the second button) on the PDFMaker 6.0 toolbar.**

   If you haven't saved your Office document, Acrobat PDFMaker will prompt you to do so. After clicking Yes to save the current Office document, the Save PDF File As dialog box appears.

2. **Edit the filename of the converted PDF file in the Name text box and select the folder in which to save it on your hard drive.**

   If you don't edit the filename, PDFMaker gives the new PDF file the same name as its Office counterpart but with the .pdf filename extension. If you're using Office XP, the filename extension may not be displayed along with your title in the File Name text box, but PDF Files is automatically selected in the Save as Type list box below.

3. **Click the Save button to convert the file and then launch your e-mail program.**

4. **Fill in the e-mail addresses of the recipient(s) in the To and Cc text boxes, as required, and then describe the contents of the message in the Subject text box in the message header before writing a memo to the recipient(s) in the body of the message.**

5. **Click the Send button to send the e-mail message to the designated recipient(s), complete with the attached PDF document, and then return to your Microsoft Office program.**

Customizing the PDF conversion settings

PDFMaker enables you to change and customize the distilling settings used in any of your Office-to-PDF file conversions. To customize the distilling settings, you choose Adobe PDF⇨Change Conversion Settings from the Office application program's menu bar to open the Adobe PDFMaker.

Figure 5-3 shows this dialog box as it appears in Microsoft Word with its four tabs: Settings, Security, Word, and Bookmarks. Note that the Adobe PDFMaker dialog box that opens when you choose Adobe PDF⇨Change Conversion Settings from the Microsoft Excel or PowerPoint menus has only the two tabs: Settings and Security. A separate Bookmarks tab is unique to Microsoft Word and provides the ability to select specific headings and paragraph styles in your Word document that can be converted into bookmarks in the resulting PDF file. In addition, you won't find an application-specific tab (like the Word tab in Figure 5-3) when using Excel or PowerPoint. Application-specific options in those programs are either minimal enough to include in the Application Setting area of the Settings tab (as is the case with PowerPoint) or as a new menu option (as is the case with Excel) when using PDFMaker 6.

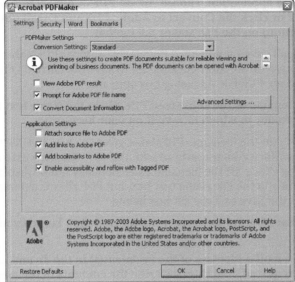

Figure 5-3:
Opening the
Adobe
PDFMaker
dialog box in
Microsoft
Word.

The Settings tab

The Settings tab of the Adobe PDFMaker dialog box enables you to change the Adobe PDF settings (now called *conversion settings* in PDFMaker). As when using Acrobat Distiller to create your PDFs, the default preset job option is Standard when you first open the Adobe PDFMaker dialog box. You can use the Conversion Settings drop-down list to select one of the other preset Adobe PDF Settings (PDFX1a, PDFX3, Press Quality, Smallest File Size, or Standard) or to select any of the custom Adobe PDF Settings that you create. In addition to being able to select different settings in the Conversion Settings drop-down list, you have a number of check boxes in the PDFMaker Settings and Application Settings areas on the Settings tab. The following gives a rundown on the options that appear whether you're using Microsoft Word, Excel, or PowerPoint:

✔ **PDFMaker Settings:** Select the View Adobe PDF Result check box to immediately view your converted PDF in Acrobat after distilling. Select the Prompt for Adobe PDF File Name check box to have the Save Adobe PDF File As dialog box open prior to converting your Word document. To convert the document-specific information (such as the Title, Subject, Author, and Keywords information found on the Summary tab of the document's Properties dialog box) to metadata in the new PDF file that can be indexed and searched (see Chapter 13 for information on searching), select the Convert Document Information check box. Note that the PDFMaker Settings area also includes an Advanced Settings button.

Clicking this button opens the Adobe PDF Settings dialog box in Acrobat 6 where you create customized Adobe Distiller conversion settings. This process is covered in detail in Chapter 4.

✔ **Application Settings:** Select the Attach Source File to Adobe PDF check box if you want to attach the Office source file as a comment in your converted PDF document. Select the Add Links to Adobe PDF check box to convert the hyperlinks in your Word document to Adobe PDF links. Select the Add Bookmarks to Adobe PDF check box to convert the headings and paragraph styles in a Word document to bookmarks in a PDF document. The Enable Accessibility and Reflow with Tagged PDF check box lets you create tagged PDF documents from the Word document structure.

To customize one of the preset Adobe PDF Settings and thereby create a new custom job option, select the preset that uses settings closest to the ones you want in the custom job option in the Conversion Settings drop-down list and then click the Advanced Settings button to open the Adobe PDF Settings dialog box for the selected preset.

The Adobe PDF Settings dialog box that PDFMaker opens in your Microsoft Office program contain the same tabs (General, Images, Fonts, Color, and PDF/X) with the same options as the Adobe PDF Settings dialog box that the Acrobat Distiller opens when you select its Settings⇨Edit Adobe PDF Settings menu command. As is true in the Acrobat Distiller, the particular values and settings that are selected on the individual tabs of the Adobe PDF Settings dialog box depend upon which preset you select when you open the dialog box with the PDFMaker's Advanced Settings button (refer to Chapter 4 for detailed information on how to modify these settings).

After customizing the settings on the tabs of the Adobe PDF Settings dialog box, you save these settings by clicking the Save As button and then naming the custom Conversion Settings. As with the Acrobat Distiller, any custom Conversion Settings you save are automatically added to the PDFMaker's Conversion Settings drop-down list as soon as you close the Adobe PDF Settings dialog box.

The Security tab

The Security tab in the Adobe PDFMaker dialog box contains options that enable you to password-protect the converted PDF file (so that only the people you give the password can open the file) and set the file permissions (which control how the document can be edited and whether or not it can be printed). The options on this tab are identical to the ones found in the Adobe PDF - Security dialog box (refer to Chapter 4 for details on how to go about setting the password and file permission options). Note that the Security tab options are exactly the same whether you are converting a Microsoft Word, Excel, or PowerPoint document to PDF.

The Word tab

The Word tab in the Adobe PDFMaker dialog box contains a bunch of check box options that enable you to control what Word-specific information is carried over to the new PDF documents you'll be generating. Figure 5-4 shows the Word tab as it appears when you open the Adobe PDFMaker dialog box in Microsoft Word.

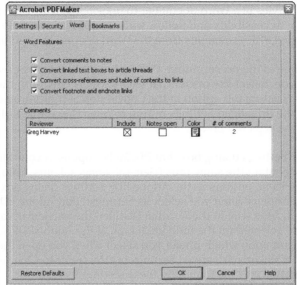

Figure 5-4: Examining the Word tab in the Adobe PDFMaker dialog box when using Microsoft Word.

The Word Features area on the Word tab contains the following settings for converting very specific word processing features into PDF equivalents:

- **Convert Comments to Notes:** Converts all comments added to the Word document into notes in the resulting PDF document.

- **Convert Linked Text Boxes to Article Threads:** Convert all notations made in the text boxes found in the Word document into articles that control the way the text is read in Acrobat 6 or Adobe Reader 6 (see Chapter 2 for more information).

- **Convert Cross-References and Table of Contents to Links:** Changes all cross-references and any table of contents found in the Word document into active hyperlinks in the resulting PDF document.

- **Convert Footnote and Endnote Links:** Converts all footnotes and endnotes in the Word document into active hyperlinks in the resulting PDF document.

The Comments area of the Word tab displays all the comments in the current Word document and lets you choose how they will be displayed in the converted PDF document. You can choose whether or not to include the comments, whether they appear open, and also specify a background color.

The Bookmarks tab

The Bookmarks tab (shown in Figure 5-5) is unique to the Word version of the Acrobat PDFMaker dialog box. Its options enable you to convert the headings and paragraph styles found in the original Word document into bookmarks in the resulting PDF document.

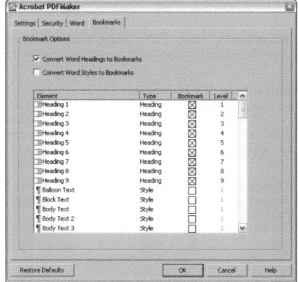

Figure 5-5: Examining the Bookmarks tab in the Word version of the Adobe PDFMaker dialog box.

The Bookmarks tab contains the following options:

✔ **Convert Word Headings to Bookmarks:** This option automatically converts all Word Heading styles used in the original document to bookmarks in the final PDF document. When this check box is selected (as it is by default), all Heading styles used in the document are selected in the list box below. To restrict bookmark conversion to just particular heading levels, deselect the check boxes for all the Heading styles you don't want used in this list.

✔ **Convert Word Styles to Bookmarks:** This option automatically converts all styles (not just the heading styles) used in the original Word document to bookmarks in the final PDF document. When you select this check box, the check boxes for all the styles used in your document are selected in list box below. To restrict bookmark conversion to just particular paragraph styles, deselect the check boxes for all the individual styles you don't want used in this list.

While there are no Excel-specific options on the Acrobat PDFMaker dialog box when you choose Adobe PDF⇨Change Conversion Settings in Microsoft Excel, there is an important new command on the Adobe PDF menu — Convert Entire Workbook. The default PDF conversion setting for an Excel document converts only the active worksheet. If you want to convert all the worksheets in your Excel workbook to Adobe PDF, choose this command.

The PowerPoint-specific application settings

The following PowerPoint-only options appear in the Settings tab on the Acrobat PDFMaker dialog box (shown in Figure 5-6) when you choose Adobe PDF⇨Change Conversion Settings in Microsoft PowerPoint:

- **Save Slide Transitions in Adobe PDF:** Ensures that the animated transitions setup in a PowerPoint presentation are carried over in the converted PDF file.

- **Convert Multimedia to PDF Multimedia:** Ensures that all multimedia elements in a PowerPoint presentation are converted to Adobe Multimedia in a PowerPoint-generated PDF file. Adobe Multimedia format adds interactive features to graphics, sounds, and movies that enhance their appearance in PDF documents. See Chapter 16 for more on this subject.

- **PDF Layout Based on PowerPoint Printer Settings:** Ensures that page layout in a PowerPoint-generated PDF file mirrors the printer settings specified in the PowerPoint presentation.

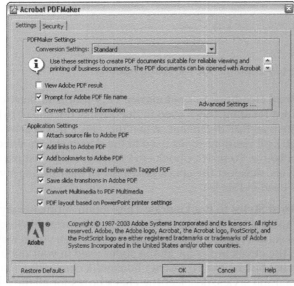

Figure 5-6: Examining the Application Settings for PowerPoint in the Acrobat PDFMaker dialog box.

Converting Office documents to PDF and sending them for review

The third option for creating a PDF file with PDFMaker enables you to create a PDF from an Office document and use the resulting PDF file to initiate a review cycle by sending it out to reviewers. To do so, follow these steps:

1. **Choose Adobe PDF⇨Convert to Adobe PDF and Send for Review in the Office application or click the Convert to Adobe PDF and Send for Review button on the PDFMaker 6.0 toolbar.**

   If you haven't saved your document, an Acrobat PDFMaker alert dialog box prompts you to do so. Click Yes. The Save Adobe PDF File As dialog box appears.

2. **Edit the filename of the converted PDF file in the Name text box and select the folder in which to save it on your hard drive.**

   If you don't edit the filename, PDFMaker gives the new PDF file the same name as its Office counterpart but with the .pdf filename extension. Note that by default, filename extensions aren't displayed in Windows XP.

3. **Click the Save button to close the Save Adobe PDF File As dialog box and start the conversion process.**

   When the PDFMaker finishes distilling your Office document, it opens the Send by E-mail for Review dialog box, as shown in Figure 5-7. Note that if you haven't entered a return e-mail address in Acrobat Preferences, you will be prompted to enter one prior to seeing the dialog box shown in Figure 5-7.

4. **Enter e-mail addresses of those you wish to send the PDF file to for review, a subject, and message in the appropriate text boxes.**

   The standard e-mail address text boxes (To, Cc, and Bcc) are provided. The Subject and Message to Reviewers text boxes have default entries that you can use or edit.

5. **Click the Send button to close the Send by E-mail for Review dialog box.**

   An alert from your e-mail client program appears, asking you to verify that you want to send an e-mail with the attached PDF file.

6. **Click the Send button (again) to send out the attached PDF file for review.**

The Send for Review dialog box, shown in Figure 5-7, also appears in Acrobat 6 when you choose File⇨Send by E-mail for Review. For a complete rundown on commenting and reviewing features in Acrobat 6 as well as the Acrobat Comments menu that appears in Microsoft Word, see Chapter 9.

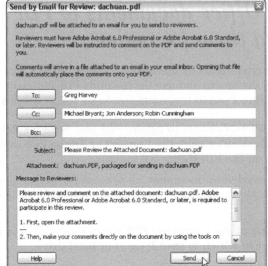

Figure 5-7:
Examining
the Send by
E-mail for
Review
dialog box.

You can add to the notes, links, and bookmarks that are carried over from the original Word document in the converted PDF document using the annotation features in Acrobat 6 — see Chapter 9 for details.

Converting Office X files on the Mac

If you're using Microsoft Office X for Mac OS X (and you have to because Acrobat 6 runs only on OS X), you have access to both the Convert to Adobe PDF and the Convert to Adobe PDF and E-mail buttons on the PDFMaker 6.0 toolbar in Word, Excel, and PowerPoint after you install Acrobat 6.0 on your computer. Note that although PDFMaker 6 does not support the review and commenting features found in the Windows version, you can use these buttons to convert Office documents to PDF files and e-mail them as you would using Office for Windows. You do not, however, have access to an Adobe PDF menu as you do in the Windows version of Office. This means that you have no way to change the conversion settings as described previously in this chapter. Mac users (I can hear you screaming at Adobe for Acrobat feature parity with your Windows brethren) can, however, choose Acrobat Distiller 6 preset Conversion Settings or any custom conversion settings you've created in the Print dialog box of your Office X program. To do so, follow these steps:

1. **With your Office X document open, choose File⇨Print or press ⌘+P to open the Print dialog box.**

2. **Select Adobe PDF on the Printer drop-down list.**

3. Select PDF Options on the drop-down list labeled Pages and Copies.

The PDF Options command is added to the list when you choose Adobe PDF as your printer. After selecting PDF Options, the Print dialog box changes to the one shown in Figure 5-8.

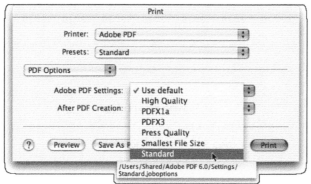

Figure 5-8: Selecting a preset or custom conversion setting when creating PDF files in Office X for Max OS X.

4. Click the Adobe PDF Setting drop-down list to select a preset Distiller Conversion Setting or one you've customized.

As shown in Figure 5-8, if you hover the mouse pointer over a conversion setting in this list, a screen tip displays the directory path for that conversion setting's location on your hard drive. You also have the option to choose Launch Nothing or Acrobat on the After PDF Creation drop-down list to specify whether or not you want to view your converted Office document PDF in Acrobat.

5. Click either the Save as PDF or Print button to open the Save to File dialog box.

If you want to see how your converted Office document is displayed in Acrobat, click the Preview button.

6. Type a filename in the Save As text box, choose a location for the finished PDF file (the default is your desktop), and click the Save button to convert your Office Document to PDF.

PDF files that are created from Office X documents do not retain their document structure tags. This means that those PDF files will not have the capability of being reflowed in Acrobat or Adobe Reader. For more on reflowing document text see, Chapter 2.

Chapter 6

Capturing Paper Documents

- -

In This Chapter

▶ Scanning paper documents into Acrobat 6

▶ Making scanned PDF documents editable and searchable

▶ Finding and correcting scanner foul-ups

▶ Converting previously scanned documents to PDF

▶ Using the Paper Capture Online service

- -

*A*crobat 6 makes it easy to turn your paper documents into PDF files that you can share with clients and coworkers via e-mail or post for viewing on your company's intranet or Web site on the Internet. Capturing paper documents as PDF files also provides a perfect way for you to electronically archive important documents such as contracts, reports, and financial statements.

Then, after you've scanned these documents in as PDF files, if you're a Windows user, you can use Acrobat's Paper Capture feature within Acrobat to turn them from graphic files to fully searchable text (if you're a Mac user, you do this using Adobe's free [for you] Paper Capture Online service). That way, even after you catalog the documents and store them on media, such as CD-ROM or removable disk media, you still retain the ability to search their text. As you find out in this chapter, all you need to turn almost any of your paper documents into PDF documents is a scanner connected to your computer and a little know-how about using the Acrobat 6 Paper Capture feature.

Scanning Paper Documents in Acrobat 6

To capture paper documents as PDF files, you first scan them using the import scan feature in Acrobat 6. The steps for doing this are quite straightforward:

1. **Turn on your scanner and position the first sheet of the document correctly on its glass.**

2. **Launch Acrobat 6, and if you want to add the pages you're about to scan to a particular PDF document, open that document in Acrobat.**

3. **Choose File➪Create PDF➪From Scanner or click the pop-up menu on the Create PDF Task button and select From Scanner.**

   The Create PDF From Scanner dialog box opens, as shown in Figure 6-1.

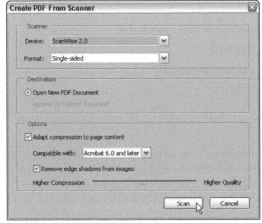

Figure 6-1:
Select the
scanner,
page format,
and
destination
in the
Create PDF
From
Scanner
dialog box.

4. **In the Scanner area of the dialog box, select the name of your scanner and the driver it uses (if the device listed is not the one you want to use, select its name and driver in the Device drop-down list) and indicate whether the device should scan one side (the default) or both sides of the paper.**

   Select Double-sided in the Format drop-down list if you need to scan both the front and back of the pages.

5. **If you have a PDF document open in Acrobat at the time you choose File➪Create PDF➪From Scanner, you have a choice in the Destination area of the Create PDF From Scanner dialog box between the Open New PDF Document option and the Append to Current Document option.**

   Note that if you have no PDF document currently open, the Append to Current Document radio button is grayed out. If a PDF document is currently open, Acrobat selects the Append to Current Document radio button by default, and you must remember to select the Open New PDF Document radio button if you want to avoid adding the scanned pages to the end of the current document.

6. **Click the Scan button.**

When you click the Scan button in the Create PDF From Scanner dialog box, the scanning software used by your particular brand of scanner opens its own window in which you can select the scanning settings and often preview the scanned page. Figure 6-2 shows the controls in the ScanWise window used by my Agfa scanner that opens when I click the Scan button in the Create PDF From Scanner dialog box.

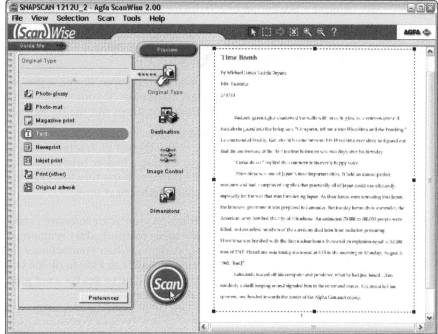

Figure 6-2:
Select the scanning settings with the software installed for your type of scanner.

When choosing the scanning settings, you want to select the lowest resolution quality for the type of document that stills gives you an acceptable image in the final PDF file. The reason for this is the higher the resolution, especially when dealing with color images, the larger the file, and at high resolutions with lots of colors, you can end up with an enormous document.

When selecting the scanning settings, keep these tips in mind:

✔ When scanning black-and-white images and text-only documents, you must set the resolution between 200 and 600 dpi (dots per inch). When scanning color images and text, you must select a range between 200 and 400 dpi. This is because the Paper Capture plug-in that recognizes the text in a scanned document and converts it to searchable and editable text can only process documents scanned in these ranges.

✔ For most documents, scanning at a resolution of 300 dpi produces the best paper captures. If, when using the Paper Capture plug-in, you find that the document contains many unrecognized words, or if the document has a lot of very small text (9 points or smaller), try scanning at a higher resolution (up to 600 dpi).

✔ Scan in black and white whenever possible.

✔ When scanning color or grayscale pages containing large type, try scanning at a resolution of 200 dpi for faster processing with Paper Capture.

✔ Avoid using dithering or halftone scanner settings. These improve the appearance of photographic images but make it difficult for the Paper Capture plug-in to recognize text.

✔ When scanning text printed on colored paper, increase the brightness and contrast by approximately 10 percent. If your scanner supports color filtering capability, select a filter that drops out the background color.

✔ If your scanner has a manual brightness control, use it to get the letters as clean as possible. If some of the thicker characters in the document are touching when scanned, try using a higher brightness setting and scanning again. If some of the thinner characters are too separated in the scan, try a lower brightness setting next time.

After selecting your scanning settings in your scan software (and previewing the page if your scan software offers this feature), start scanning the page by clicking the Scan button (or its equivalent). When your scanner finishes scanning the page, Acrobat displays an Acrobat Scan Plug-In dialog box (similar to the one shown in Figure 6-3) that prompts you to get the next page ready for scanning or to signal that you're done scanning.

Figure 6-3:
Click the
Next button
to scan the
next page
in the
document.

When this dialog box appears, you take one of the following three actions, depending upon what type of document you're scanning:

✔ If you're scanning a single-page document, click the Done button in this Acrobat Scan Plug-In dialog box.

✔ If you're scanning a double-sided document, turn the paper over in the scanner and then click the Next button.

✔ If you're scanning single-sided pages but your paper document contains multiple pages, replace the first page on the scanner with the second page and then click the Next button.

When you click the Done button, Acrobat closes the Acrobat Scan Plug-In dialog box and displays the page you just scanned in the Acrobat Document window. When you click the Next button, Acrobat closes the Acrobat Scan Plug-In dialog box and returns you to your scanning software, where you can start scanning the backside of the page or the next page by clicking its Scan button.

For a multipage document, you continue the process of clicking the Next button in the Acrobat Scan Plug-In dialog box, replacing the current page with the next page on the scanner, and then clicking the Scan button in your scanner software. When you finish scanning the last page in your document, click the Done button in the Acrobat Scan Plug-In dialog box to see the first page of your new PDF document displayed in Acrobat.

Making scanned documents searchable and editable

When you scan a document directly into a PDF file (as described in the preceding section), Acrobat captures all the text and graphics on each page as though they were all just one big graphic image. This is fine as far as it goes, except that it doesn't go very far because you can neither edit nor search the PDF document. (As far as Acrobat is concerned, the document doesn't contain any text to edit or search — it's just one humongous graphic). That's where the Paper Capture plug-in in Acrobat 6 for Windows comes into play: You can use it to make a scanned document into a PDF that you can either just search or both search and edit.

To use Paper Capture, all you have to do is choose Document⇨Paper Capture to open the Paper Capture dialog box (shown in Figure 6-4), select the page or pages to be processed (All Pages, Current Page, or From Page *x* to *y*), and then click the OK button; the Paper Capture utility does the rest. As it processes the page or pages in the document that you designated, a Paper Capture Plug-In alert dialog box keeps you informed of its progress in preparing and performing the page recognition. When Paper Capture finishes doing the page recognition, this alert dialog box disappears, and you can then save the changes to your PDF document with the File⇨Save command.

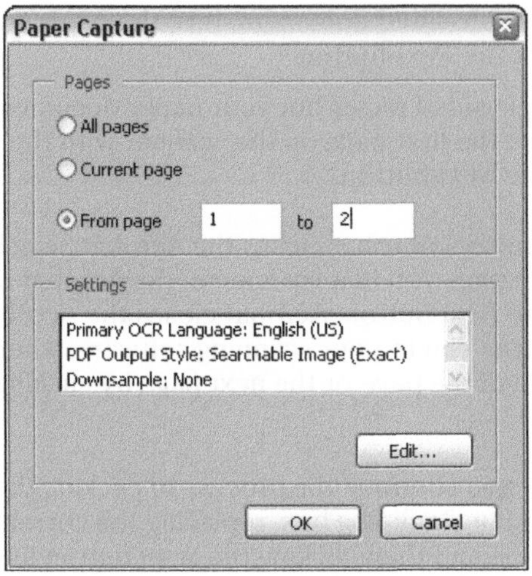

Figure 6-4:
Selecting
the pages to
process in
the Paper
Capture
dialog box.

When doing the page recognition in a PDF document, the Paper Capture plug-in offers you a choice between the following three Output Style options:

- ✔ **Searchable Image (Exact):** Select this option to make the text in the PDF document searchable but not editable (this is the default setting). This setting is the one to choose if you're processing a document that needs to be searchable but should never be edited in any way, such as an executed contract.

- ✔ **Searchable Image (Compact):** Select this option to make the text in the PDF document searchable but not editable and to compress its graphics. Use this setting if you're processing a document whose text requires searching without editing and that also contains a fair number of graphic images that need compressing. When you select this setting, Paper Capture applies JPEG compression to color images and ZIP compression to black-and-white images.

- ✔ **Formatted Text & Graphics:** Select this option to make the text in the PDF document both editable and searchable. Pick this setting if you not only want to be able to find text in the document but also possibly make editing changes to it.

To select a different output style setting, click the Edit button in the Paper Capture dialog box to open the Paper Capture Settings dialog box (as shown in Figure 6-5). This dialog box not only enables you to select a new output style in the PDF Output Style drop-down list, but also enables you to designate the primary language used in the text in the Primary OCR Language drop-down list (OCR stands for Optical Character Recognition, which is the kind of software that Paper Capture uses to recognize and convert text captured as a graphic into text that can be searched and edited).

Figure 6-5:
Selecting
options in
the Paper
Capture
Settings
dialog box.

If your PDF document contains graphic images, you can tell Paper Capture how much to compress the images by selecting the maximum resolution in the Downsample Images drop-down list. This menu offers you three options in addition to None (for no compression): Low (300 dpi), Medium (150 dpi), and High (72 dpi). The Low, Medium, and High options refer to the amount of compression applied to the images, and the values 300, 150, and 72 dpi (dots per inch) refer to their resolution and thus their quality. As always, the higher the amount of compression, the smaller the file size and the lower the image quality.

After processing the pages of your PDF document with the Paper Capture plug-in, use the Search feature (Ctrl+F on Windows and ⌘+F on the Mac) to search for words or phrases in the text to verify that it can be searched. If you used the Formatted Text & Graphics output style in doing the page recognition, you can select the TouchUp Text Tool by clicking its button on the Advanced Editing toolbar or by typing T, and then click the I-beam pointer in a line of text to select the line with a bounding box (see Chapter 10 for more on editing with this tool) to verify that you can edit the text as well. Always remember to choose File⇨Save to save the changes made to your document by processing with Paper Capture.

Correcting Paper Capture boo-boos

Although the OCR (Optical Character Recognition) software used by Paper Capture has become better and better over the years, it's still far from perfect. After processing a scanned PDF document using the Formatted Text & Graphics output style, you need to check your processed document for words that Paper Capture didn't recognize and therefore wasn't able to convert from bitmapped graphics into text characters.

To make this check and correct these OCR errors, follow these steps:

1. **Choose Document⇨Paper Capture⇨Find First OCR Suspect.**

   The program flags the first unrecognized word in the text by putting a gray rectangle around it and opens the Find Element dialog box. Acrobat shows a magnified view of the unrecognized word in the Find Element dialog box, as shown in Figure 6-6.

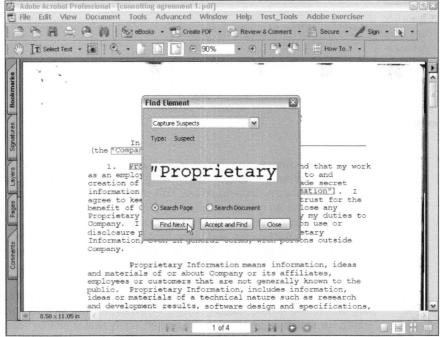

Figure 6-6:
Finding an unrecognized word in the processed text.

2. **Choose the TouchUp Text tool by clicking its button on the Advanced Editing toolbar.**

3. **In the Find Element dialog box, choose one of the following options:**

   • To accept the word displayed and convert it from a graphic into text and then continue to the next capture suspect, click the Accept and Find button.

   • To edit the suspect word directly in the Find Element dialog box, type over incorrect characters in the suspect word and then click the Accept and Find button and go to the next suspect.

   • To ignore an unrecognized word and not convert it to text, just click the Find Next button to move right on to the next suspect.

4. **Repeat Step 3 until you've checked and corrected all the unrecognized words in the processed document.**

   Note that if you choose Document➪Paper Capture➪Find All OCR Suspects, the program finds and highlights all suspect elements in the document without opening the Find Element dialog box. This allows you to individually choose which OCR suspect you'd like to edit.

5. **To edit one of the OCR Suspects in a document after choosing Find All OCR Suspects command, make sure the TouchUp Text tool is selected and double-click the desired element to open the Find Element dialog box.**

   The selected OCR Suspect appears in the Find Element dialog box. You can continue by repeating Step 3 or close the Find Element dialog box and repeat Step 5.

6. **Click the Close button in the lower-right corner of the Find Element dialog box to close it, and then choose File⇨Save to save your corrections to the PDF document.**

Importing Previously Scanned Documents into Acrobat

If you already have a scanned document or an electronic fax saved on your hard drive in a graphics format such as TIFF or BMP (the Tagged Information File Format and Bitmap format are most commonly used for saving scanned images), you can open the file in Acrobat 6 and then process its pages with the Paper Capture plug-in (as described in the previous section). Note that in order for the Paper Capture plug-in to render a searchable PDF document, the source document must be scanned at a resolution setting between 200 and 600 dpi. To open the scanned graphic file in Acrobat, follow these steps:

1. **Choose File⇨Create PDF⇨From File to display the Open dialog box.**

2. **Browse to the folder that contains the graphics file containing the scanned image and click its file icon.**

   If the graphics file is saved in a graphics format other than TIFF, select this file format in the Files of Type drop-down list (the Show drop-down list on the Mac) so that its file icon is displayed in the Open dialog box.

3. **Click the Open button.**

   The scanned graphic is displayed in the Document window in Acrobat.

4. **To save the graphics file as a PDF file, choose File⇨Save, and then edit the filename and the folder in which you want to save it (if desired) before clicking the Save button.**

5. **To make the text in the new PDF file searchable, choose Document⇨ Paper Capture⇨Start Capture.**

   The Paper Capture dialog box opens.

 6. **To modify the Paper Capture settings before using it to process the pages of your PDF document, click the Edit button to open the Paper Capture Settings dialog box. Otherwise, skip to Step 11.**

 7. **Select the language of the text in the Primary OCR Language drop-down list.**

 8. **In the PDF Output Style drop-down list, select one of the following:**

    - To be able to both search and edit the text, select the Formatted Text & Graphics option.

    - To make the document text searchable only, select the Searchable Image (Exact) option.

    - To make the text in a document containing many images searchable, select the Searchable Image (Compact) option instead.

 9. **To compress the graphics in the PDF document, select the amount of compression in the Downsample Images drop-down list.**

    Your choices are Low (300 dpi), Medium (150 dpi), or High (72 dpi).

 10. **Click OK to close the Paper Capture Settings dialog box and return to the Paper Capture dialog box.**

 11. **Click OK in the Paper Capture dialog box to begin the page processing.**

 12. **Choose File⇨Save a second time to save your changes.**

After processing the pages of a scanned image that you've saved as a PDF document with Paper Capture, if you used the Formatted Text & Graphics output style, you can locate and eliminate all OCR errors in the text by following the steps in the preceding section, "Correcting Paper Capture boo-boos."

Using the Paper Capture Online Service

Adobe's Paper Capture feature in Acrobat 6 is designed for individual or small office use. For the needs of larger businesses, Adobe provides their Create Adobe PDF Online service that enables you convert any type of business document to PDF. Company reports, printed archival materials, spreadsheets, calendars, and even entire Web sites are just a few of the types of documents that you can convert in order to take advantage of the universal file-sharing aspects of PDF. The service is subscription based (U.S. $9.99 per month or about U.S. $99 per year), but Adobe offers the service on a trial basis that allows you to create five PDF files free of charge.

You can go to Adobe's Web site and see what all the excitement is about by typing this URL into your favorite browser's Address text box:

```
http://createpdf.adobe.com
```

After you've subscribed to the service, you can then upload as many scanned files (of no more than 50 pages in length) as you want and process them online with Paper Capture as follows:

1. **Use your Web browser to go to** createpdf.adobe.com, **sign in by entering your username and password in the Adobe ID and Password text boxes, and then click the Login button.**

   The Create Adobe PDF page appears.

2. **Click the Choose a File graphic link to open the Create Adobe PDF Online - Select a File dialog box.**

   Note that you can also click the Submit a URL link in order to capture a Web page. A page appears where you specify which file to process.

3. **Click the Browse button to locate the desired file on your hard drive, click Choose, and then click the Continue button on Adobe's Select a File dialog box to open the Conversion Settings window shown in Figure 6-7.**

   Note that you can click the Supported File Types link to view a list of File types supported by the Create Adobe PDF Online service.

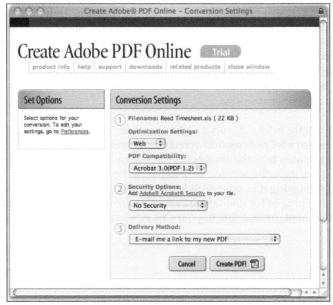

Figure 6-7: Choose conversion settings for online creation of a PDF document.

4. **Click the Optimization Settings drop-down list and choose either Web (the default), eBook, Screen, Print, or Press as the output conversion setting for your file.**

5. **Click the PDF Compatibility drop-down list to select either Acrobat 3.0 (PDF 1.2) (the default), Acrobat 4.0 (PDF 1.3), or Acrobat 5.0 (PDF 1.4) as the output compatibility setting for your file.**

6. **Choose a level of security for the converted PDF by clicking the Security Options drop-down list. The default is No Security.**

   You have the option of choosing two other basic levels of security: No Printing (40 bit) or No Printing (128 bit). You can further customize security settings for your converted PDF by clicking the Adobe Acrobat Security link above the Security Options drop-down list.

7. **Select the desired method for having the processed file returned to you in the Delivery Method drop-down list.**

   Your choices are No E-Mail, Download from Conversion History (which lets you archive PDF files at Adobe and download them as necessary from your Conversion History list), Wait for PDF Conversion in Browser, E-Mail Me a Link to My New PDF, or E-Mail Me My New PDF as an Attachment.

8. **Click the Create PDF button at the bottom of the window to upload your file and have it processed according to your wishes.**

Create Adobe PDF Online lets you create and save your own conversion settings, just as you would in Acrobat 6. To do so, click the Preferences link under the heading Set Options in the Conversion Settings window and select the new settings using the drop-down lists provided for various conversion settings in the Preferences window. Then click the OK button, enter a descriptive name for the new settings in the dialog box that appears, and click OK. Your new conversion settings will appear in the Optimization Settings drop-down list in the Conversion Settings window.

When the Create Adobe Acrobat Online service receives your uploaded document, it displays a Confirmation screen that gives you an identification number and that indicates how the processed file will be delivered to you. Depending upon your settings, the service then delivers the processed PDF file to you either by displaying it in your Web browser (assuming that you use one that supports the plug-in for displaying PDF files), in an e-mail message as a link or a file attachment, or as a link in your Conversion History list.

Chapter 7

Capturing Web Pages

*W*hen you first hear that Acrobat 6 can capture Web pages as PDF files, you may wonder why on Earth anyone in her right mind would want to do such a thing. After all, Web browsers are not only perfectly capable of displaying any and all Web pages in their native HTML (HyperText Markup Language) format, but they are also much more widespread than Acrobat and Adobe Reader. And, of course, this is true — as long as you're connected to the Internet. The moment you get disconnected from the Internet, all Web browser access to online content shuts off (unless your browser is capable of caching the pages on your hard drive and you know how to set this up).

In this chapter, you discover how easy it is to capture Web pages as PDF files that you can browse at any time on any computer equipped with a copy of Acrobat or Adobe Reader. Because the Web pages are PDF files, not only can you browse them when you don't have Internet access handy, but you can also annotate them and distribute them as you would any other PDF document. This makes internal Web site design reviews a real joy because it's easy to send the PDF versions of the Web pages to clients and coworkers for approval, as well as elicit feedback from them right on the pages if they're using Acrobat 6.

One of the best reasons for capturing a Web site in PDF format is to be able to browse its contents when you're traveling and at other times when you can't go online. This feature is also a godsend when you need to give a presentation or conduct a training session that involves the use of Web material because you still have access to the Web content (internal links and all), even if you lose your Internet connection or are not able for one reason or another to go online. When viewing Web pages in Acrobat or Adobe Reader, you can use the Full Screen view to get rid of all the distracting menus, toolbars, and so on (see Chapter 2 for details) because you will be using the site's own links and navigation controls to move from page to page. You control what page transitions are used and how to navigate from page to page in full-screen mode by opening the Preferences dialog box (Ctrl+K on Windows and ⌘+K on the Mac) and then clicking Full Screen in the list of preferences.

Opening Web Pages as PDF Files

To be able to capture Web pages (and even entire Web sites) as PDF files for viewing in Acrobat or Adobe Reader, all you need is Internet access, Acrobat 6, and the Web site's URL (Uniform Resource Locator). Before you can use Acrobat to capture Web pages, you must have your computer correctly configured for accessing the Internet. If you already get online with a popular Web browser, such as Microsoft Internet Explorer or Netscape Navigator, Acrobat should be able to detect these settings and use them for Web capture. If you find that you can't capture Web pages as described in this section, open the Internet Properties dialog box from within Acrobat by choosing Edit➪Preferences➪Internet Settings, and then seek help from your ISP (Internet service provider) or IP personnel in getting your Internet settings correctly configured in Acrobat.

The steps for capturing the pages are easy as can be:

1. **In Acrobat, choose File➪Create PDF➪From Web Page, or click the Create PDF button on the Tasks toolbar and choose From Web Page on the pop-up menu.**

   The Create PDF from Web Page dialog box appears, as shown in Figure 7-1.

2. **In the URL text box, type or paste in the URL address of the site whose Web pages are to be downloaded.**

   If you're converting a local HTML document to PDF (that is, one that's saved on your hard drive or local area network rather than on the Internet), click the Browse button. Then open the folder, select the document's file icon in the Select File to Open dialog box, and then click the Select button.

Figure 7-1:
Capturing
Web pages
as PDF files.

3. **In the Settings area of the Open Web Page dialog box, select the Get Entire Site radio button to capture all the Web pages on the site.**

   • To capture only the Web site's start page, leave the Get Only radio button selected with 1 in the level(s) spinner button text box to the immediate right.

   • To capture all the pages linked to the start page, increase the value in the level(s) text box to 2; to get all the pages linked to the pages linked to the start page, increase the level(s) value to 3, and so on.

   • To restrict the Web page capture to only pages found on the same Web site or on the same Web server, select the Stay on Same Path and the Stay on Same Server check boxes as well.

4. **Click the Create button to begin capturing the designated Web pages as PDF files.**

   If you select the Get Entire Site radio button, the Potentially Large Download Confirmation alert dialog box automatically appears, warning you that you may have bitten off more than your computer can chew. If you're sure that you have the patience (or a lightning-fast download connection), have sufficient hard drive space, and are not attempting to download the Library of Congress Web site, click the Yes button to proceed with the potentially large download of the entire site.

As soon as you click the Download button or the Yes button in the Potentially Large Download Confirmation alert dialog box, Acrobat begins downloading and converting the designated Web pages and displays the Download Status dialog box, which keeps you informed of the progress of the first part of the downloading process.

As the Web pages start arriving on your hard drive, the Download Status dialog box disappears as quickly as it appeared, and the first page of the Web site appears in Acrobat's Document pane. The Navigation pane with the Bookmarks palette selected is also automatically displayed in the Acrobat window. The Bookmarks palette illustrates the hierarchical relationship of the pages you downloaded (see Figure 7-2) as it continues to display the names of the pages on each level as they are successfully downloaded.

Figure 7-2:
Captured
Web pages
display their
linked
structure
in the
Bookmarks
palette.

If Acrobat is not able to download the complete contents of all the pages on
the levels you designated for download, it displays a dialog box called There
Were Errors that lists all the files that it could not find or otherwise successfully download. After reviewing this list of files, click the OK button in the
There Were Errors dialog box to close it.

After all the Web pages you asked for on a particular Web site are delivered to
your hard drive, you still need to save the pages as a single PDF file so that you
can access them in Acrobat or Adobe Reader without being connected to the
Internet. To do this, choose File⇨Save and then give the new PDF file a name,
select the folder in which you want to save it, and click the Save button.

Browsing captured Web pages in Acrobat or Adobe Reader

After you download Web pages and save them as PDF documents, you can
browse their contents in Acrobat 6 or Adobe Reader 6 just as you would any
other PDF file. You can go from page to page by clicking the page bookmarks
on the Bookmarks tab or the page thumbnails on the Thumbnails tab of the
Navigation pane, or you can use the buttons on the Navigation toolbar. (See

Chapter 2 for more specific information on all the ways to navigate a PDF document.)

Following Web links in Acrobat 6

In addition to using the normal navigation controls found in Acrobat 6 and Adobe Reader 6, because you're dealing with Web pages, you can use their own navigation controls, usually in the form of various navigation buttons and hyperlinks, to move from page to page. Be aware, however, that unless you've captured the entire Web site, you will often come upon buttons and links to pages that haven't yet been downloaded and aren't currently part of the PDF file. If your computer has access to the Internet at the time you're viewing the file, you can still follow its Web links and even download its Web pages and add them to the PDF document.

When browsing the file in Acrobat 6, you can tell when you're on a link to a page that you haven't downloaded as part of the PDF file because the program adds a plus sign (+) to the Hand-with-pointing-index-finger mouse pointer, and a ScreenTip showing the page's URL address appears. In Adobe Reader 6, the program adds a W (for Web) to the mouse pointer, along with the ScreenTip showing the page's URL.

The first time you click a link to a Web page that hasn't been captured in Acrobat 6, the program displays the Specify Weblink Behavior dialog box, as shown in Figure 7-3. To have Acrobat 6 download the Web page in Acrobat and add it to the current PDF file, leave the In Acrobat radio button selected and then click OK. To have Acrobat launch your Web browser to display the page there and, therefore, not add the Web page to your PDF document, select the In Web Browser radio button instead before clicking OK.

Note in Figure 7-3 that the Do Not Ask Again check box is automatically selected in the Specify Weblink Behavior dialog box. This means that the next time you click a link in the PDF file, Acrobat will either automatically download and display the page in Acrobat (if the In Acrobat option is selected) or in your Web browser (if the In Web Browser option is selected) without prompting you to decide between using the In Acrobat and In Web Browser option in the Specify Weblink Behavior dialog box.

If you want to be prompted each time you click a link to a page that hasn't yet been downloaded, deselect the Do Not Ask Again check box. Even if you don't deselect this check box, you can still switch between the In Acrobat and In Web Browser options by pressing the Shift key when you click a link (that's what the `When weblinks are clicked on in the future, the shift key will toggle the above selected behavior` message in the Specify Weblink Behavior dialog box is trying to tell you). So, for example, if you leave the In Acrobat radio button selected the first time you follow a hyperlink to have the page added to the PDF file in Acrobat, but decide at the next link that you only want to browse the page with your Web browser, you accomplish this by holding down the Shift key as you click that hyperlink.

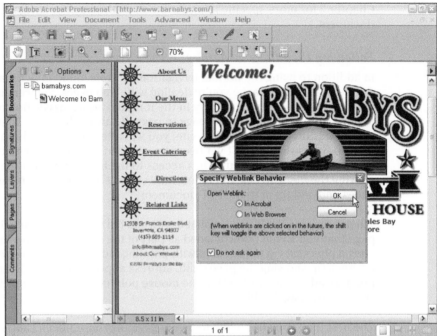

Figure 7-3:
Indicating
how to open
the linked
Web page.

Browsing Web links in Adobe Reader 6

When you follow Web links in a Web-captured PDF file with Adobe Reader 6, the program always opens the associated Web pages in your Web browser (only Acrobat 6 has the ability to capture Web pages and save them in PDF files). You can then surf the Web site by following its links as you would when browsing any other Web site.

Figure 7-4 shows you what happened when I clicked the About Us link (shown in Figure 7-3) in the Barnaby's PDF file after opening this file in Adobe Reader 6. Because Adobe Reader doesn't let you capture Web pages, it opens the About Barnaby's page in my Web browser, which just happens to be Internet Explorer 6.

Creating Web links in a standard PDF file

You can have Acrobat 6 convert all complete URL addresses (ones that follow the full format that includes http:// in the address) entered in a standard PDF file (one not created with the Web Capture feature) into active hyperlinks by choosing Advanced⇨Links⇨Create from URLs in Document. This opens the Create Web Links dialog box, as shown in Figure 7-5.

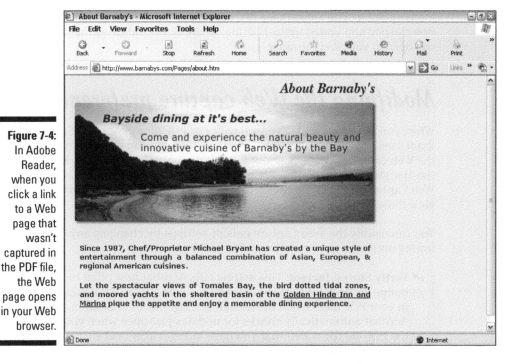

Figure 7-4:
In Adobe
Reader,
when you
click a link
to a Web
page that
wasn't
captured in
the PDF file,
the Web
page opens
in your Web
browser.

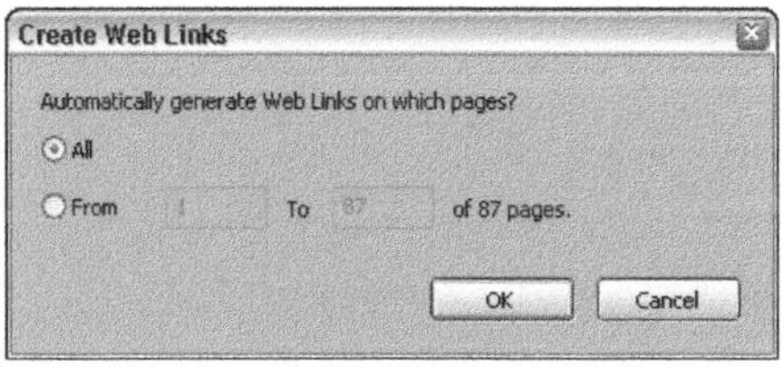

Figure 7-5:
Converting
URLs to live
Web links in
the Create
Web Links
dialog box.

To have Acrobat scan all the pages of the document for URLs to convert to live Web links, click the OK button. To have the program convert the URLs on just some of the pages in the PDF document, select the From radio button and enter the page number of the first and last page in the From and To text boxes, respectively.

After Acrobat 6 has converted the URLs on the specified pages of the PDF file to active links, you can follow the links by clicking them with the Hand-with-pointing-finger mouse pointer. Note that when following the Web links you add in this manner, Acrobat uses the Web link behavior that's in effect at that time. This is indicated by the icon that's added to the Hand-with-pointing-finger mouse pointer: The appearance of a plus sign (+) means the page will be downloaded and added to the PDF file, whereas a W indicates that the page will open in your Web browser.

Modifying the Web capture preferences

When you download and save Web pages as PDF files in Acrobat 6, the program uses a set of default capture settings that you can modify. To change the Web capture settings, choose Edit⇨Preferences or press Ctrl+K (⌘+K on the Mac) to open the Preferences dialog box, as shown in Figure 7-6. Click Web Capture in the scroll list on the left side of the Preferences dialog box to view those options.

You can modify the Web Capture default settings by changing any of the following options:

✔ **Verify Stored Images:** This setting tells Acrobat how often to check online for updates to the images on the Web pages that you've captured in your PDF files. When the default setting, Once Per Session, is selected, Acrobat automatically checks for updates just once when you first open the PDF file (provided that you have Internet access at that time). You can change this setting by selecting either Always (for continuous checking) or Never on its drop-down list.

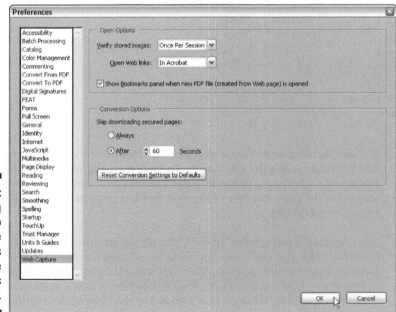

Figure 7-6:
Examining
the Web
Capture
options
in the
Preferences
dialog box.

✔ **Open Weblinks:** This setting indicates whether Acrobat should download and save new Web pages in Acrobat when you click their Web links or simply display the pages in your Web browser. Note that the Specify Weblink Behavior dialog box inherits the setting you select here as its default (which you can override by holding down the Shift key when you click a Web link).

✔ **Show Bookmarks Panel When New PDF File (Created from Web Page) Is Opened:** This check box tells Acrobat whether or not to display the Navigation pane with the Bookmarks palette selected when you first open a PDF file with the captured Web pages. Deselect this check box when you don't want to give up valuable viewing real estate in the Document window to the Navigation pane. Note that Acrobat creates bookmarks for the downloaded Web pages whether or not this check box is selected.

✔ **Skip Downloading Secured Pages:** The radio buttons under this heading indicate whether or not Acrobat should skip over the downloading of password-protected Web pages on the site you're capturing. Select the Always radio button to have the program immediately skip over all such pages. Select the After radio button and specify the number of seconds in the associated text box to have the program stop and prompt you for the site's password dialog box for the number of seconds specified, only to then automatically skip the downloading of that page and continue downloading other pages if you don't respond to the prompt.

✔ **Reset Conversion Settings to Defaults:** This button resets all the conversion settings to their original values (see the following section for information on changing the conversion settings).

Modifying the Web capture conversion settings

Before capturing Web pages from a Web site, you can modify the conversion settings that tell Acrobat how to treat their content in the new PDF file. To do this, click the Settings button on the bottom-right side of the Create PDF from Web Page dialog box. (To open the Create PDF from Web Page dialog box, choose File➪Create PDF➪From Web Page.) Clicking the Settings button opens the Conversion Settings dialog box, as shown in Figure 7-7.

The General tab is divided into two areas: File Type Settings and PDF Settings. In the File Type Settings area, you see a list box listing all the types of text and graphics files that are downloaded and converted in the new PDF file. The only settings that you can modify in this list are the HTML and Plain Text settings. When you click either one of these types, the Settings button to the right of the list box becomes active.

Figure 7-7:
Examining
the options
on the
General tab
of the
Web Page
Conversion
Settings
dialog box.

When you click the Settings button when HTML is selected in the list box, Acrobat opens an HTML Conversion Settings dialog box, where you can control the default layout, colors, and fonts displayed in the Web pages you capture. Don't mess with any of these settings if your purpose is to do a design review of the Web pages you're about to capture because these changes could prevent users from experiencing the pages as the designers intended.

The PDF Settings area in the Web Page Conversion Settings dialog box contains the following four check box options:

- ✔ **Create Bookmarks:** When selected, Acrobat automatically creates bookmarks for each Web page you download, using the page's title as the bookmark name. Note that if a page doesn't have a title, Acrobat uses the page's URL address as the bookmark name.

- ✔ **Create PDF Tags:** When selected, Acrobat creates and stores a hierarchical structure in the PDF file that tells special screen-reading software for the visually impaired how to sequence the various Web page elements for reading at large magnification. The support for screen readers is part of Acrobat 6's new group of Accessibility features designed to enhance the usability of the software for people with disabilities.

- ✔ **Place Headers and Footers on New Pages:** When selected, Acrobat creates page headers and footers that display the title of each Web page in the header at the top of the page and the URL of the page in the footer at the bottom.

- ✔ **Save Refresh Commands:** When selected, Acrobat saves a list of the URLs for all the pages captured in the PDF file that it can use to later check for updated content. You must have this conversion option selected when you capture Web pages if you want Acrobat to be able to automatically download new versions of the Web pages when it detects updated content (see the "Refreshing updated content" section, later in this chapter, for more on refreshing Web content).

Adding Web Pages to a PDF File

If the need arises, you can always add Web pages to an existing PDF file, whether or not that PDF document already contains captured Web pages. To capture Web pages and add them to the PDF currently displayed in the Acrobat Document window, choose Advanced⇨Web Capture⇨Append Web Page to open the Add To PDF From Web Page dialog box. Here, you enter the URL of the Web page you want to append and specify the number of page levels to include before clicking the Create button (this dialog box contains the same options as the Open Web Page dialog box — see the section, "Opening Web Pages as PDF Files," at the beginning of this chapter for details). When you click the Create button in the Add To PDF From Web Page dialog box, Acrobat downloads the specified pages, automatically adding them to the end of the PDF file.

Adding linked pages to a PDF file

Another way to add Web pages to a PDF file that contains captured Web content is through the Web links displayed in the Select Page Links to Download dialog box. For this method, you view all the Web links on a particular Web page in the PDF document, and then select the ones for the additional pages you want to append to the current PDF file as follows:

1. **In the Acrobat 6 Document window, display the Web page whose links you want to use for downloading new pages.**

2. **Choose Advanced⇨Web Capture⇨View Web Links.**

   The Select Page Links to Download dialog box opens, as shown in Figure 7-8.

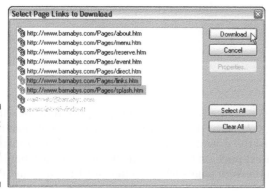

Figure 7-8:
Selecting
the URLs to
download.

3. **Click the URLs in this list for all the Web pages you want to add to the current PDF file.**

   To select multiple individual URLs, Ctrl+click them. To select a continuous range of URLs, click the first one and then Shift+click the last one in the range. To select all the URLs for downloading, click the Select All button.

4. **Click the Download button to add the Web pages for the selected URLs to the current PDF file.**

Note that if you don't want to select individual links and are sure you want to download and append all pages linked to the current Web page displayed in Acrobat 6, choose Advanced⇨Web Capture⇨Append All Links on Page.

Refreshing updated content

Some Web sites, especially those that cover current affairs or the news, frequently update the content of some or all of their pages. If your purpose in capturing Web pages is to keep up-to-date on the information offered by a site, you will need to refresh the pages on a regular basis to ensure that your file has the most recent content.

To refresh the content of the captured pages in your PDF file, choose Advanced⇨Web Capture⇨Refresh Pages. Doing this opens the Refresh Pages dialog box, as shown in Figure 7-9. Click the Refresh button to have Acrobat check all the pages in the Refresh Commands list for updates.

Figure 7-9: Checking Web pages for updated content with the Refresh Pages dialog box.

By default, the program compares the text of the captured pages with their counterparts online. If Acrobat detects any discrepancies between the two, it automatically updates the downloaded page in the PDF file by replacing it with a copy of the latest page on the Web site. If you want Acrobat to compare all elements on the Web pages when looking for the ones that need refreshing instead of just comparing the text, select the Compare All Page Components to Detect Changed Pages radio button in the Refresh Pages dialog box before you click the Refresh button.

If you want to exclude certain pages from the Refresh Command list, click the Edit Refresh Commands List button to open the Refresh Commands List dialog box. This dialog box lists all the pages marked for refreshing. To skip particular pages in the refresh operation, click the Clear All button and then select the URLs for all the pages you do want refreshed to highlight them before you click OK.

Keep in mind that you can't add new URLs to the list displayed in the Refresh Commands List dialog box: You can only tell Acrobat which ones to ignore when refreshing the pages. The only way to add a URL to the Refresh Commands list is to capture its Web page when the Save Refresh Commands check box option has been checked in the Web Page Conversion Settings dialog box.

Chapter 8

Printing PDF Files

· ·

· ·

*A*crobat may offer the promise of a paperless office, and PDF may be the quintessential electronic file format, but despite it all, you will find times when the one and only thing you want to do with the program is print out the PDF documents you open in it. In this chapter, you discover all the ways to print all or just part of a PDF file with your in-house printers, as well as how to customize the print settings to print selected pages and to accommodate the printing of oversized pages.

Printing PDF Files

Printing PDF documents in Acrobat 6 or Adobe Reader 6 is very similar to printing documents in any other Windows or Macintosh application program that you use.

Before you print a file, you can change the general print settings, such as the paper size or the printing orientation from the default of portrait mode to landscape mode. To change these settings, choose File⇔Page Setup in Acrobat or Adobe Reader or press Ctrl+Shift+P (⌘+Shift+P on the Mac) to open the Page Setup dialog box, modify the printing options as desired, and then click OK. The actual options and controls available in the Page Setup dialog box vary according to the actual printer selected as your default.

If you just need a printout of the document's pages using the standard Print options, follow these simple steps:

 1. **Choose File➪Print (in Acrobat or Adobe Reader) or press Ctrl+P (⌘+P on the Mac).**

    The Print dialog box opens, as shown in Figure 8-1.

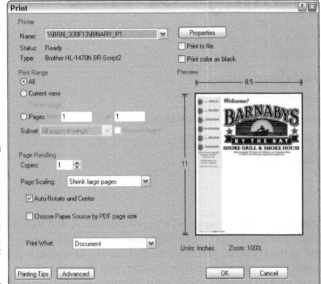

Figure 8-1:
Opening the
Print dialog
box in
Acrobat 6 to
print the
current PDF
document.

 2. **If you have more than one printer installed on your system, you can select a different printer to print the PDF document by selecting the name of the printer in the Name drop-down list (Windows) or by selecting a different printer on the Printer drop-down list (Mac).**

 3. **Specify which pages you want to print by doing one of the following:**

    • To print all the pages in the current PDF document, leave the All radio button selected.

    • To print just the area of a document that is currently visible in the Acrobat document window, select the Current View radio button.

    • To print only the page currently displayed in Acrobat or Adobe Reader, select the Current Page radio button.

    • To print a continuous range of pages in the document, select the Pages radio button and enter the first page to print in the From text box and the last page to print in the To text box.

    See Chapter 9 for details on adding notes and marking up text, and to find out how to summarize the comments in a document and save them in a separate file that you can print.

 4. **Click the OK button to begin printing the pages of your PDF file.**

In the upper-right corner of the Windows version of the Print dialog box, you find two check box options — Print to File and Print Color as Black:

✔ Select the Print to File option only when you want to create a file for a type of printer that you don't actually have available on your computer system. You can then send or take the print file to a computer that has the targeted printer connected to it but doesn't have the Acrobat or Adobe Reader program installed. When you drag the print file on the printer icon, it prints the PDF document with all the printing options you specified in Acrobat.

✔ Select the Print Color as Black option to change all non-white colors to black. This feature is useful when printing technical drawings that have lightly colored lines.

In the lower-left area of the Print dialog box you find the following Page Handling options:

✔ **Copies:** Type in the text box or click the spinner buttons to specify the number of copies of each page you want printed.

✔ **Page Scaling:** Reduces, enlarges, or divides pages when printing. The options on the drop-down list let you select various ways of scaling the printout of the current PDF document to the selected paper size in your printer. Choose None to have no scaling applied to a PDF printout or Fit to Paper to have Acrobat reduce or enlarge a PDF file to fit the paper size selected in the Page Setup dialog box. See the "Printing oversized documents" section, later in this chapter, for more on Acrobat's Page Scaling print features.

✔ **Auto-Rotate and Center:** Select this check box if you want the page orientation of the current PDF file to automatically match those specified in your printer properties.

✔ **Choose Paper Source by PDF Page Size:** Select this Windows-only check box to have the PDF page size determine which of your printer's paper trays to use rather than the Page Setup option. Use this feature in cases where a PDF file containing multiple page sizes is printed on a printer with different-sized output trays.

✔ **Print What:** Use the options on the drop-down list to specify which visible contents in a PDF to print. The Document option prints all visible contents and form fields, the Document and Comments option adds comments to the printout, and the Form Fields Only option prints out interactive form fields but no document contents.

✔ **Printing Tips:** Click this button to go online to Adobe's Web site for information on troubleshooting PDF printing problems.

Printing document layers

Acrobat 6 now supports document layers created in the AutoCAD and Microsoft Visio design programs. Those who create layered drawings in those programs can specify what layer content, such as watermarks or confidential information, must (or must not) be printed. They can then convert their documents to PDF, layers and all, to be viewed in Acrobat 6. If the resulting PDF file contains content that is not visible on the screen but should be printed (or vice versa), Acrobat 6 displays a warning message in the Print dialog box, as well as a preview of how the page will be printed.

You can use commands on the Options menu at the top of the Layers navigation tab to determine what specific layer content you want to print. To open the Layers tab, choose View⇔Navigation Tabs⇔Layers or just click the Layers tab on the left side of the Navigation pane. To view a document exactly as it will print, choose Apply Print Overrides on the Options menu, as shown in Figure 8-2. This option prints all layer content in the document, even if it is not visible in the Acrobat document pane.

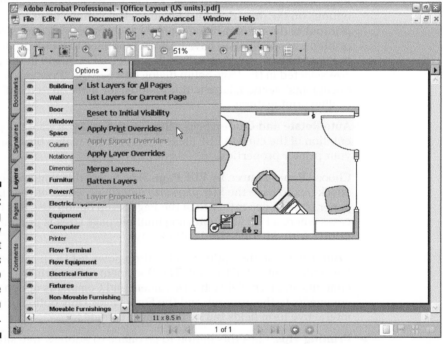

Figure 8-2: Choosing the Apply Print Overrides command to print all the layers in a document.

Playing with the PostScript options

If you have a PostScript printer, you can modify the PostScript options in the Advanced Print Setup dialog box in Acrobat or Adobe Reader. To open this dialog box, click the Advanced button in the Print dialog box. Use the Font and Resource Policy drop-down list to specify when fonts and resources are downloaded to your printer. Use the Print Method drop-down list to select the level of PostScript (2 or 3) best suited for your printer (some older laser printers don't understand levels of PostScript). When the Download Asian Fonts check box is selected, Acrobat downloads Asian Fonts used but not embedded in the PDF document to the laser printer if they are not already installed on it. Select the Save Printer Memory check box to have Acrobat download all the fonts for a given page before that page is printed to save on printer memory. Note that all options in the Advanced Print Setup dialog box display descriptive information in a scroll box below when you select an option.

You can also change print overrides for specific layers. To do so, follow these steps:

1. **Click the Layers tab in the Navigation pane to open the Layers palette and view the list of layers in the current PDF file.**

2. **Click a layer name in the Layers palette list to select a layer, and then choose Layer Properties on the Options menu at the top of the Navigation pane.**

   Alternatively, you can right-click the layer and choose Properties on the context menu to open the Layer Properties dialog box, as shown in Figure 8-3.

3. **Select the option you want from the Print drop-down list as follows:**

   • Select the Always Prints option to force the selected layer to print.

   • Select the Never Prints option to force the selected layer to not print.

   • Select the Prints When Visible option to force the layer to print only when it is visible in the document.

4. **Click OK to close the Layer Properties dialog box.**

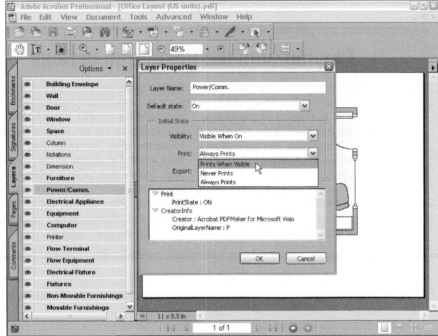

Figure 8-3: Choosing print override options for individual layers in a PDF document.

Printing selected pages

Sometimes, you don't need to print all the pages in a PDF document or even a continuous range of pages. If you're using Acrobat 6 or Adobe Reader 6, you can print individual, nonconsecutive pages in the document. To do this, you need to select the individual pages before you open the Print dialog box by following these steps:

1. **Click the Pages tab in the Navigation pane to bring its palette to the front. If the Navigation pane is closed, press F6 to open and select the Pages palette.**

2. **To see all the thumbnails for the pages you want to select for printing, you may need to switch to small thumbnails and widen the Navigation pane:**

    • To switch to small thumbnails, click the Options button at the top of the palette and then click Reduce Page Thumbnails near the bottom of its pop-up menu.

    • To widen the Navigation pane until all the thumbnails are displayed (or all the ones with pages you want to print), position the mouse pointer on the border between the Navigation and Document panes and then, when the mouse pointer becomes a double-headed arrow, drag the border to the right until the Navigation pane is wide enough to display all the thumbnails.

3. **Ctrl+click (⌘+click on the Macintosh) the thumbnails for all the individual pages you want to print to select them in the Thumbnail palette.**

4. **Choose File⇨Print or press Ctrl+P (⌘+P on the Mac).**

   The Print dialog box opens with the Selected Pages radio button selected, as shown in Figure 8-4.

5. **Click OK to begin printing only the selected pages in the PDF document.**

To print just a graphic on the page, click the Snapshot tool (G) on the Basic Tools toolbar and use it to draw a bounding box around the image. After selecting the image in this manner, right-click (Control+click on the Mac) to display the image's context menu and click the Print option to open the Print dialog box.

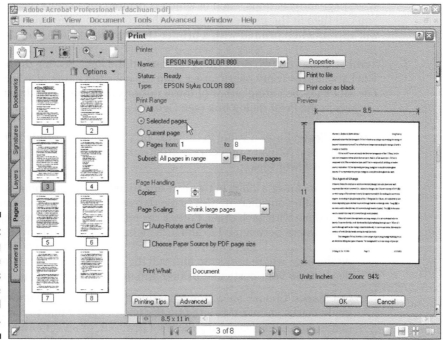

Figure 8-4:
Selecting
the
thumbnails
of the
individual
files to print.

Printing oversized documents

Some of the PDF documents that you want to print are too large to fit even the largest paper sizes that your printer can handle. As you can see in Figures 8-1 and 8-4, Acrobat handles this in the Print dialog box by automatically selecting the Shrink Large Pages on the Page Scaling drop-down list. This option automatically scales down the text and graphics on each page to fit the paper size selected for your printer.

When the Shrink Large Pages option is selected, the program automatically selects the Auto-Rotate and Center Pages check box option. When this option is selected, Acrobat routinely rotates PDF documents that are wider than the selected paper size, while at the same time centering the text and graphics that do fit. When this check box is selected in conjunction with the Shrink Oversized Pages to Paper Size option, Acrobat shrinks the text and graphics on each page so that they all fit and are centered on the page.

If you have a PostScript printer installed on your system, you can print oversized pages in your PDF documents using a method called *tiling*. When you print oversized pages by tiling, Acrobat or Adobe Reader divides each oversized page into sections, each of which is printed on a single page of paper. You can then fit the printed pages together to see how the oversized page will appear when printed with a printer that can handle the oversized paper.

Acrobat gives you two print tiling options on the Page Scaling drop-down list: Tile Large Pages (only pages larger than the selected paper size are tiled) and Tile All Pages. Selecting either of these options displays the following new settings in the Print dialog box (see Figure 8-5):

- **Tile Scale:** Enter a value in this text box to scale the printed PDF file onto tiles. A higher percentage creates more tiles, a lower percentage creates fewer tiles.

- **Overlap:** Enter a value in this text box to indicate the amount you want the printing on adjacent tiles to overlap each other so you can more easily align them with each other. Enter a decimal value for this overlap distance of anywhere between 0.125 and 0.25 inches. You need this overlap distance, because laser printers have to maintain a minimum of blank space on the page where they grab and pull the paper. The exact value you enter depends on your particular printer and the page size your tiles use.

- **Cut Marks:** Choose an option from this drop-down list to indicate which guide marks you want printed on the page. Select None to have no guides printed for cropping the tiled printout, or select either Western (the crosshatched registration marks universally used in North American and European printers) or Eastern style cut marks.

- **Labels:** Select this check box to print descriptive labels on each tile.

Figure 8-5:
Using the
Tiling
options in
the Print
Settings
dialog box
to print an
oversized
document.

Using the prepress printing settings

In addition to the standard printing options described in previous sections, the Print dialog box (refer to Figure 8-4) also contains an Advanced button that opens the Advanced Print Setup dialog box. These features are used only when preparing a PDF document for professional printing with high-end imagesetters. Don't mess with these prepress settings without the advice and consent of your favorite service bureau people.

When you click the name of any check box option in the Advanced Print Setup dialog box, Acrobat displays a brief description of that option in a text box at the bottom of the dialog box. Just be mindful that when clicking the name of an option to get a brief explanation of its function, you also end up either selecting or deselecting that check box. If you're just exploring the options to discover more about their use, be sure that you don't inadvertently select an option you don't really want to use.

Troubleshooting Printing Problems

You can click the Printing Tips button in the Print dialog box in Acrobat 6 and Adobe Reader 6 to go online to the Adobe Web site to get a slew of suggestions on how to troubleshoot the most common printing problems with Acrobat. This area of the Adobe support knowledge base is particularly helpful if you're having trouble printing a PDF file on a PostScript printer. The Web page includes instructions on how to enable the PostScript error handler for your printer, depending upon which operating system you're using (Windows or Macintosh) so you can track the specific errors that printing the PDF file is causing. It also contains a link to another page on the Adobe Web site that tells you what these PostScript errors really mean and gives you some suggestions on how to get around them.

Using PrintMe Internet Printing

Acrobat 6 offers support for the PrintMe Internet Printing service that enables you to print your PDF documents to any printer on the PrintMe Network or any fax machine in the world, which is a great convenience for globetrotters. To use the feature, just choose File⇨PrintMe Internet Printing. If you're not already signed up, the PrintMe Networks dialog box, shown in Figure 8-6, appears. Select the New Users radio button, and then click the Signup Now! button in to open the PrintMe New User Signup dialog box, shown in Figure 8-7, where you fill in the form and get a new user account.

Upon registering as a user with PrintMe Internet Printing, a PrintMe print driver is downloaded to your computer and you then follow the onscreen prompts to install the driver. After installation of the print driver, the PrintMe Networks dialog box (Figure 8-6) reappears, enabling you to log on to the network.

Figure 8-6:
Opening the
PrintMe
Networks
dialog box in
Acrobat 6 to
sign up for
an account.

To use PrintMe Internet Printing, follow these steps:

1. **Open the PDF document you want to print to a remote PrintMe printer or fax machine and choose File⇨PrintMe Internet Printing.**

   The PrintMe Networks dialog box opens (see Figure 8-8).

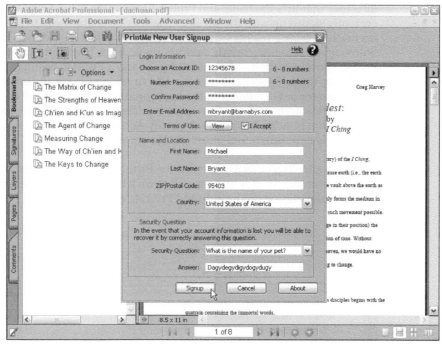

Figure 8-7:
The PrintMe
New User
Signup
dialog box.

2. **Enter a new name for the printed document in the Title text box (the current document title appears here by default) and then select either the Print All Pages or Pages options in the Page Range area. If you select Pages, enter a range of pages to print in the text boxes provided, and then enter the number of copies to print in the Copies text box.**

   By default, the My Favorites radio button is selected in the PrintMe To area.

3. **Choose a PrintMe destination or fax number from the Most Recent drop-down list that displays the last ten PrintMe destinations or fax numbers used.**

4. **To choose a new PrintMe printer or fax number, click the More button (black triangle) if it's not already selected when the dialog box opens.**

5. **Click the Printer radio button and then enter a new PrintMe destination in the PrintMe ID text box or the telephone number of the destination fax machine in the FAX# text box.**

6. **Click the PrintMe button to send your PDF document to the selected PrintMe enabled printer or fax machine.**

The PrintMe Networks dialog box also provides an Address Book used to store PrintMe destination Printer ID's and fax numbers as well as a searchable online directory that lists the name and Printer ID numbers of host printer locations currently signed up with the service. The service enables you to print to any fax machine whose telephone number you know. Click the Address Book button to access your PrintMe Address Book or the Find button to locate a PrintMe printer in their online directory. To add a PrintMe destination or fax number to the Address Book, choose Add to Address Book and enter a name for the printer or fax number in the appropriate text box as it will appear in your PrintMe Address Book. The entry is added to your Address Book when you click the PrintMe button. Click the My Account button to go online and view status and statistics of your PrintMe account.

Note that after selecting a printer in the PrintMe Networks dialog box, the Options button activates and provides you with additional printing options that vary depending on the selected PrintMe enabled printer.

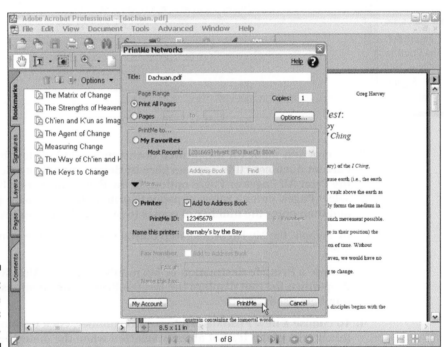

Figure 8-8:
The PrintMe
Networks
dialog box.

Part III
Reviewing, Editing, and Securing PDFs

The 5th Wave   By Rich Tennant

Here, boy.

MULTIMEDIA

In this part . . .

After you've converted your electronic and paper documents to PDF files, you're ready to explore the many Acrobat 6 features for reviewing, editing, organizing, and making them secure. Part III introduces all of these kinds of important, post-production features.

In Chapter 9, you find out how to use Acrobat 6 to annotate your PDF files so that coworkers and clients alike can review them online, and you can summarize their feedback. In the process, I introduce you to the new e-mail-based and browser-based review features in Acrobat 6. In Chapter 10, you discover the types of PDF document editing that you can perform in Acrobat 6. Chapter 11 introduces you to the ways to secure your PDF files from unwanted changes. It also gives you the lowdown on how to use digital signatures in Acrobat 6 to sign off on changes, as well as prevent future changes. Chapter 12 covers the ways you can repurpose the contents of your PDF files by extracting the text and graphics for uses with the other software programs you commonly use. Finally, Chapter 13 rounds out Part III by giving you vital information on how to catalog and archive your PDF files by building searchable PDF document collections that you can distribute on CD-ROM or on your company's network or intranet.

Chapter 9

Annotating PDF Files for Review

・・

In This Chapter

▶ Sending out PDF files for review

▶ Adding bookmarks to aid in document review

▶ Noting changes in the PDF document

▶ Giving audio comments and stamping the document

▶ Marking up and highlighting proposed changes in the document

▶ Attaching supplemental files to the PDF document

▶ Collecting and summarizing comments

・・

*O*ne of the most important groups of features in Acrobat 6 is the annotation features that enable you to mark up and add comments to a PDF document. These features facilitate the review process by enabling all the different people on a design team to give you their feedback in a consistent and timely manner. The annotation features in Acrobat 6 also assist in the approval process by enabling you to get feedback and eventually the final okay from clients and key personnel in-house.

In this chapter, you discover the many ways to send out a PDF document in order to initiate a review cycle. You also find out how to annotate a PDF document, including adding bookmarks to make it easier to navigate the document you're reviewing, as well as attaching comments (in many different formats, including text notes, sound notes, and attached files) and marking up text and graphics. You also become familiar with the ways to collect and summarize review comments for a particular PDF file in anticipation of making the final edits (as described in Chapter 10).

Sending Out PDF Files for Review in Windows

Acrobat is known for its arsenal of useful annotating tools, and Adobe continues to improve those tools, as you discover in later sections of this chapter.

What makes Acrobat 6 such a worthwhile upgrade is the addition of e-mail-based and browser-based reviewing. These new reviewing features, available to users of Acrobat 6 for Windows, streamline the initiation of a review cycle by allowing you to distribute a PDF review document either by e-mail *or* by posting the PDF file on a network (intranet or Internet) server and allowing participants to review it in a Web browser.

Here's how a typical Acrobat PDF review cycle works — the *initiator* of a review distributes a PDF document to reviewers, known as *participants,* who then use the Acrobat commenting tools to annotate the document for the edification of the review initiator. The initiator then reviews the reviews of the reviewers (sounds fun, right?). Acrobat enables you to set up either e-mail-based or browser-based reviews. When deciding which type of review to use, note that with e-mail-based reviews, participants don't need access to a shared server; with browser-based reviews, participants can see each others' comments on an ongoing basis.

Initiating an e-mail-based review

In an e-mail-based review, you (the review initiator) send an e-mail to each participant. Attached to this e-mail is a copy of the PDF document for review in the form of an FDF (Form Data Format) setup file that contains configuration settings for importing reviewer comments. FDF is an Adobe variation of PDF used to import and export form data in PDF documents. (For more on interactive forms in Acrobat, see Chapter 14.) The participants add comments to the PDF document copy, and then e-mail the comments back to you via the FDF setup file. When you open the attached FDF file, Acrobat opens your original PDF document and automatically imports participant comments and annotations for viewing in the original document. To get the ball rolling, make sure to save your PDF document in a convenient place on your hard drive so that the FDF setup file has no trouble finding it, and then follow these steps:

1. **Open the PDF document you want to send out for review and choose File⇨Send by E-mail for Review.**

   The Send by E-mail for Review dialog box appears, as shown in Figure 9-1.

   If you haven't specified an e-mail address in the Identity window of the Preferences dialog box in Acrobat 6, an alert dialog box appears, prompting you to enter an e-mail address where review comments will be sent. This e-mail address is added to your Acrobat preferences for future reviews. Enter your e-mail address and click OK.

2. **In the Send by E-mail for Review dialog box, enter participant addresses in the To, Cc (carbon copy), or Bcc (blind carbon copy) text boxes.**

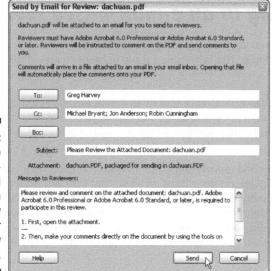

Figure 9-1:
Setting up
an e-mail-
based
review in
the Send by
E-mail for
Review
dialog box.

3. **Edit the default text in the Subject and Message to Reviewers text boxes as desired, and then click the Send button.**

   If your default e-mail client displays an alert dialog box, asking you to verify sending the e-mail, click the Send button again to distribute your PDF document to review participants.

E-mail attachments sent using the File⇨Send by E-mail for Review command are in FDF (Form Data Format). When a review participant opens this attachment, a copy of your original PDF file is opened in Acrobat, which the participant can then add comments to. When the review is finished, the participant sends the comments back to you by choosing File⇨Send Comments to Review Initiator or by clicking the Send Comments button on the Commenting toolbar. When you receive and open this FDF attachment, Acrobat opens your original PDF document and imports the participant's comments into the PDF document for viewing.

E-mail-based reviews can be initiated in the same manner described previously from applications other than Acrobat 6 that support the PDFMaker plug-in. These include Microsoft Office 2000 and XP (when using Acrobat 6 Standard or Professional), as well as AutoCAD, Microsoft Project, and Microsoft Visio (when using Acrobat 6 Professional only). Note that to initiate an e-mail-based review in those programs, you have to open the document you wish to send for review and choose Adobe PDF⇨Convert to Adobe PDF and Send for Review on the program's menu bar.

Participating in an e-mail-based review

The following list gives you some pointers on making a review cycle run smoothly, whether you're the initiator or a participant in an e-mail-based review:

- When you open the FDF attachment in an e-mail-based review, a Document Status message informs you that the document has been sent for review. You must be using either Acrobat 6 Professional or Standard versions to participate.

- When you're finished annotating a PDF file, save the file with your changes in a convenient place on your hard drive so that you can review the document without having to open the original e-mail attachment. This also provides a copy of the reviewed PDF in case you want to share the reviewed PDF file by e-mailing it to others (you're not allowed to enter additional e-mail addresses when you choose File⇨Send Comments to Review Initiator).

- If you want to send additional comments to the review initiator, open your saved version of the reviewed PDF file, edit or make additional comments, and choose File⇨Send Comments to Review Initiator again. The initiator will receive your revised PDF. (Note that any comments you deleted in the revised document will still appear in the initiator's version.) Initiators can use comment filtering and deletion features to keep things legible. See the section, "Managing reviews with the Review Tracker," later in this chapter.

- When you receive a participant's copy of the reviewed PDF file and open the FDF attachment, your original PDF document opens. If the original can't be found, you are prompted to browse for it.

- If you want to make changes to the original PDF document, save those changes under a different file name in order to preserve the original; otherwise, participant annotations may appear in the wrong places in the edited document.

- Use the Review Tracker (which is covered a little later in this chapter) to manage the annotations you collect in a review cycle, whether it is an e-mail-based review or a browser-based review.

Setting up a browser-based review

In a browser-based review, you can either upload a PDF document to a server or work with an existing document on a server. Like an e-mail-based review, the review initiator sends an e-mail to participants with an attached FDF

(Form Data Format) setup file that contains configuration settings for importing reviewer comments into the review PDF file. Reviewers must open this FDF attachment, as opposed to simply opening the PDF document posted on the server, in order to participate in a browser-based review. When a reviewer opens the FDF attachment, a copy of the PDF file is opened in their Web browser. Participants can then make annotations to the PDF document using tools on the Review and Comment toolbar that appears in their browser when the PDF file is opened. All participant comments are stored in the FDF setup file and imported into the shared PDF document for reviewing by everyone participating in the review cycle. Note that participants cannot edit or delete one another's comments, though they can reply to them, as you see in the next sections.

Looking at the Reviewing preferences for a browser-based review

In order to initiate a browser-based review, you have to first specify the type of server you're using and the location of the FDF setup file where all the participant comments are stored. Having this file accessible to all browser-based review participants is what allows everyone to view the ongoing review cycle in their Web browsers. You specify these settings in the Preferences dialog box in Acrobat 6. Choose Edit⇔Preferences or press Ctrl+K, and then click Reviewing in the list box on the left side of the Preferences dialog box to display the Reviewing options, as shown in Figure 9-2.

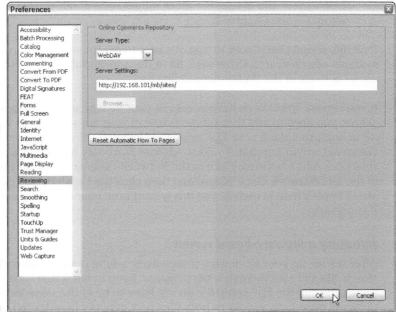

Figure 9-2: Specify reviewing preferences for a browser-based review in the Acrobat Preferences dialog box.

The following list describes the options found in the Reviewing options of the Preferences dialog box:

- ✔ **Server Type:** Use the Server Type drop-down list to define what type of server you're using to store the FDF setup file containing browser-based review annotations. Select the Database option if there is a database application server setup on your company intranet. Select the Network Folder option to upload your FDF setup file to a shared folder on your network. Select the Web Discussions option if you have access to a Microsoft Discussions server. Note that this type of server needs to be configured in Internet Explorer as well. Select the WebDAV (Web-based Distributed Authoring and Versioning) option, which is a special kind of server that allows users to collaboratively edit and manage files remotely, if you have access to a WebDAV server.

- ✔ **Server Settings:** Fill in the necessary directory path or (HTTP type) addresses in the Server Settings text box, which activates when you make a selection on the Server Type drop-down list.

- ✔ **Browse:** If you select Network Folder as your Server Type, the Browse button activates so that you can locate the shared folder you want to use in a browser-based review. Remember that all participants need access to this folder in order to participate in the review.

- ✔ **Reset Automatic How To Pages:** Click this button to ensure that the How To window will display topics that are appropriate to the type of review cycle you define. For more information about getting help in Acrobat 6, see Chapter 3.

If all this sounds like Greek to you, it's best to get these settings from your systems administrator. Otherwise, fill in the appropriate information and click OK to close the Preferences dialog box.

If you choose WebDAV or have access to your own or someone else's Web server, you need to add that server as one of your network places in Windows XP in order to upload your PDF using the Upload for Browser-Based Review command within Acrobat. To do so, choose Start➪My Network Places, and then click Add a Network Place in the Network Tasks area. Follow the prompts in the Add Network Place Wizard and then click the Finish button. Don't be afraid to seek help in completing this wizard from your systems administrator if necessary.

Initiating a browser-based review

After setting up your Reviewing preferences, you're ready to upload the PDF review file and specify review participants. Keep in mind that though the PDF review file and the FDF setup file do not have to be in the same location, participants must have access to both files on a network in order to review the

PDF document. Also note that you should wait until you've uploaded a PDF for review to make any initial comments. If you don't, any comments you make to a PDF file prior to uploading will be embedded in the PDF document and you won't be able to further edit them. To upload your PDF document and initiate a browser-based review, follow these steps:

1. **Open the PDF review document in Acrobat 6 and choose File⇨Upload for Browser-Based Review.**

2. **In the Upload for Review dialog box that appears, click My Network and locate the folder in which you want to store the PDF review file.**

   Make sure that all participants have access to this network location.

3. **Click the Upload button to copy the PDF review document.**

   When your PDF file finishes uploading, the Start Browser-Based Review dialog box appears, as shown in Figure 9-3.

Figure 9-3:
Setting up a browser-based review in the Start Browser-Based Review dialog box.

4. **In the Start Browser-Based Review dialog box, enter participant addresses in the To, Cc, or Bcc text boxes.**

5. **Edit the default text in the Subject and Message to Reviewers text boxes and click the Send button.**

   If your default e-mail client displays an alert dialog box asking you to verify sending the e-mail, click the Send button again to send an e-mail message to participants that specifies the location of the PDF review file.

If the PDF file you want to have reviewed already exists on a server, you can initiate a browser-based review as well as invite new participants to the review cycle by first navigating to the file and opening it in your browser. The Review and Comment Tasks button appears in your browser window; from its pop-up menu, choose Invite Others to Review This Document to open the Start Browser-Based Review dialog box, where you enter participant addresses before clicking the Send button. You can also use this same command in Acrobat 6 during an e-mail-based review to invite more participants to review your PDF document.

Participating in a browser-based review

When participants open the FDF setup file attached to their invitation e-mail, a copy of the PDF review document is opened in their browser. In addition to the basic Adobe Reader tool set displayed in the browser window, you also get the Review and Comment Tasks button, shown in Figure 9-4, that allows you to annotate the PDF in your browser. The following list gives you some pointers on making a review cycle run smoothly, whether you're the initiator or a participant in a browser-based review:

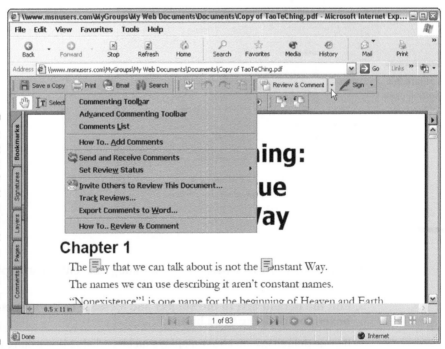

Figure 9-4:
Acrobat displays the PDF review document and the Review and Comment Tasks button with its pop-up menu commands in your browser.

✔ You must use Acrobat 6 Professional or Standard versions to participate in a browser-based review.

✔ You must open the FDF file attached to your invitation e-mail in order to participate in a browser-based review.

✔ To annotate a PDF file, use the tools and commands on the Review and Comment Tasks button because the menu commands in this case are browser-specific. The Review and Comment Tasks button also contains commands for displaying the Commenting and Advanced Commenting toolbars. Like all tool bars in Acrobat, these can be displayed as either floating or docked.

✔ In order to be able to see other participant's comments, your Reviewing preferences must match those of the review initiator. If you can't see other people's comments, request the correct server settings from the review initiator and make sure you have access to that location.

✔ To view updated annotations from other participants or to enable others to view your recent contributions, choose Send and Receive Comments on the Review and Comment Tasks pop-up menu.

✔ When you're finished adding annotations to a PDF review document, you can change the status of your review to completed to communicate that fact to the review initiator and other participants. You complete a review by choosing Review and Comment⇨Set Review Status⇨Completed from the Review and Comment Tasks button pop-up menu.

✔ If you'd like to perform your review in Acrobat rather than your Web browser, click the Save and Work Offline button on the Commenting toolbar.

✔ If at anytime you've stopped adding annotations to a PDF review document and want to continue the process, either reopen the FDF attachment in your original e-mail invitation or, if you've saved the document to work offline, open it in Acrobat and choose File⇨Go Back Online. This command reopens the PDF document in your browser and uploads your comments.

✔ Use the Review Tracker to manage the annotations you collect in a review cycle, whether it is an e-mail-based review or a browser-based review. See the next section for details.

Managing reviews with the Review Tracker

The Review Tracker is a handy new feature that helps the review initiator organize participant comments, communicate with participants, and keep track of ongoing or completed review cycles, whether they are e-mail-based or browser-based reviews. To open the Review Tracker, shown in Figure 9-5, choose Track Reviews on the Review and Comment Tasks button pop-up menu, or choose Open Review Tracker on the Options pop-up menu at the top of the Comments palette in the Navigation pane.

Figure 9-5:
The Review
Tracker,
displayed in
the How To
window, lets
you manage
e-mail-
based or
browser-
based
reviews.

As you can see in Figure 9-5, the Review Tracker has two pop-up menus, Show and Manage, as well as two list boxes, one on top of the other. The Show pop-up menu lets you specify which reviews are displayed in the top list box. Choose either All, Active, Completed, Sent, or Received. Note that displayed reviews are categorized as either e-mail-based or browser-based. Attached Expand (+) and Collapse (–) buttons on these categories, when clicked, display or hide individual review document names. Clicking a review document name in the review list displays that review's status information in the list box directly below.

Clicking the Open button displays the review document in either Acrobat, if it's an e-mail-based review, or in your Web browser, if it's a browser-based review. Clicking the Remove button deletes the review from the Review Tracker.

The Manage pop-up menu enables you to communicate with participants associated with the selected review and contains the following options:

- ✔ **E-mail All Reviewers:** Used to send an e-mail message to all reviewers associated with the selected review.

- ✔ **Send Review Reminder:** Used to send a gentle (or otherwise) reminder to those participants who might be lagging in their rate of review contribution.

✔ **Invite More Reviewers:** Used to liven up the party, especially if you find yourself using the Send Review Reminder command a little too often.

✔ **Go Back Online:** Activates when you select a browser-based review in the Review Tracker list. This command, surprisingly enough, enables you to go back online and refresh the selected browser-based review for those who might be online at the very moment you decide to change the review status.

The Review Tracker also has the standard How To window navigation buttons at the top of the pane — How To, Home, Back, Forward, and Hide. Just don't click the Home button and expect to be able to click the Back button to redisplay the Review Tracker. In order to reopen the Review Tracker, you have to use the Review and Comment Tasks button or the Options command on the Comments palette in the Navigation pane.

The Ins and Outs of Bookmarks

Bookmarks are the links that appear on the Bookmarks palette in the Navigation pane in a PDF document. They are most often used to take you directly to different sections within the document. Bookmarks can take you to different pages in the document or even different views of a page. Bookmarks can also link you to different documents (PDF and non-PDF) on your computer, as well as to Web pages on the Internet. All of these functions make bookmarks perfect for providing review participants with a quick means of navigating to annotations and markups you make in a PDF document review cycle. As if this weren't enough, bookmarks can also perform certain actions in the PDF document, such as submitting a form's data, playing a sound or movie, or selecting a particular menu item. (See Chapters 14 and 16 for information on working with PDF forms and adding interactivity to PDF files.)

To use a bookmark to jump to a particular page or page view, to open a new document or Web page, or to execute a command or perform a specified action, all you have to do is click the name or icon of the bookmark in the Bookmarks palette in the Navigation pane. If you want, you can have Acrobat automatically close the Navigation pane whenever you click a bookmark by selecting the Hide After Use setting on the Options pop-up menu at the top of the Navigation pane. This option is particularly useful for bookmarks that open pages in the document that are displayed in the Fit Width or Fit Visible page views and require maximum screen area for legibility.

Generating automated bookmarks

When you use the PDFMaker plug-in to convert documents created with Microsoft Word for Windows to PDF, you can specify that the document heading and other styles, cross-references, and footnotes automatically be converted into bookmarks in the final PDF file (see Chapter 5 for details). Also, when capturing Web pages, Acrobat can automatically generate bookmarks for each page that you capture (see Chapter 7 for details).

When the Add Bookmarks to Adobe PDF option is selected during conversion, the bookmarks automatically generated from Word documents with the PDFMaker 6.0 and from Web pages in Acrobat 6 are saved as a special type called *tagged* bookmarks. Tagged bookmarks keep track of the underlying structure of the document (such as heading levels and paragraph styles in Word documents and HTML tags in Web pages) by tagging these elements.

You can use the elements stored in any tagged PDF document or captured Web page to automatically generate bookmarks for any particular element in the document. (For details on creating a tagged PDF file or converting a non-tagged PDF file, see Chapter 15.) To generate automatic bookmarks for a tagged file, click the Options pop-up menu on the Bookmarks palette and then click New Bookmarks from Structure on the menu to open the Structure Elements dialog box, as shown in Figure 9-6. Note that the New Bookmarks from Structure menu item is grayed out if the PDF document you're working with isn't tagged.

Figure 9-6:
Selecting the
elements to
automatically
bookmark
in the
Structure
Elements
dialog box.

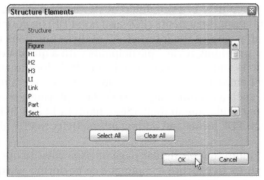

To have Acrobat generate bookmarks for particular elements in the PDF document, you then select the names of the elements for which you want the bookmarks generated (Ctrl+click on Windows or Control+click on the Mac to select multiple elements) in the Structure Elements dialog box before you click OK. Acrobat then goes through the document, identifying the tags for the selected elements and generating bookmarks for each of them.

Figure 9-7 illustrates how this works. In this figure, you see a group of four automatically generated bookmarks created from the Figure tag in the original tagged PDF document. As you can see, when Acrobat generates these tags, it gives them the name of the tagged element used to create them (which in this case just happened to be Figure). These four Figure tags are automatically nested under a generic bookmark named Untitled. All that remains to do is to rename these bookmarks to something a little bit more descriptive, such as Table of Figures for the Untitled bookmark, Cover for the first Figure bookmark, Title Page for the second, Half Title Page for the third, and Copyright for the fourth and last bookmark. (See the "Editing bookmarks" section, later in this chapter, for details on how to rename bookmarks.)

Creating manual bookmarks

Although the automated methods are by far the fastest ways to generate bookmarks, they are by no means the only ways to add bookmarks. You can also manually add bookmarks to any PDF multipage document that you've opened in Acrobat 6. Each bookmark that you add to a PDF document has two parts: the bookmark link and the bookmark destination. The bookmark link consists of a page icon followed by the name of the bookmark in the Bookmarks palette, and the bookmark destination is the page, page view, new document, or Web page that is displayed or the action that is executed when you click the bookmark link.

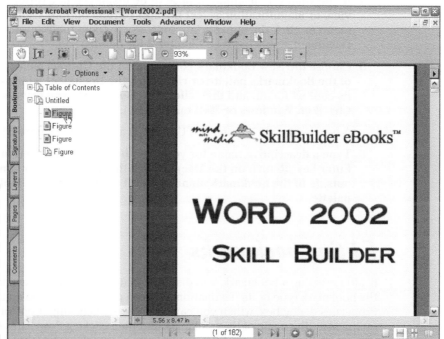

Figure 9-7:
The bookmarks generated for the Figure element in a tagged PDF document.

Making bookmarks to go to pages in the document

When you create a new bookmark to another page in the same PDF document, Acrobat records not only the page but also the page view and the magnification setting in effect as part of the bookmark's destination. This means that the most productive way to create manual bookmarks is to first navigate to the destination page *and* make any desired change to the page view and/or magnification settings *before* you begin creating the bookmark. Although you can designate the destination page as part of the process of creating the new bookmark, going to the page and setting things up beforehand just makes the process all the easier and more efficient.

With this tip in mind, the steps for manually creating a bookmark to a new page in the same document are as follows:

1. **Launch Acrobat and then open the PDF document to which you want to add bookmarks.**

2. **If necessary, open the Navigation pane by pressing F6 and click the Bookmarks tab to display its palette on top.**

3. **Using the buttons on the Navigation toolbar or navigation buttons on the Document window status bar, go to the destination page in the document for the first bookmark.**

4. **If you want the destination page to be displayed in a different page view or magnification, select the appropriate options from the View menu or click the appropriate buttons on Zoom toolbar and the Document status bar (see Chapter 2 for details).**

5. **Choose the New Bookmark command on the Options menu at the top of the Bookmarks palette or right-click the Document window to open its context menu, and then click New Bookmark (you can also press Ctrl+B on Windows or ⌘+B on the Mac).**

   A new bookmark icon named Untitled is added (see Figure 9-8).

6. **Type a descriptive name for your new bookmark and then press the Enter key (Return on the Mac) or click the mouse pointer somewhere outside of the bookmark name to add it to the list in the Bookmarks palette.**

Editing bookmarks

If, after creating a bookmark, you discover that you need to make changes to the bookmark type or its destination, you can do this in the Bookmark Properties dialog box, which you can open by right-clicking (Control+clicking on the Mac) the name of the bookmark and then clicking Properties on its context menu. You can also edit the appearance of a bookmark in this dialog box.

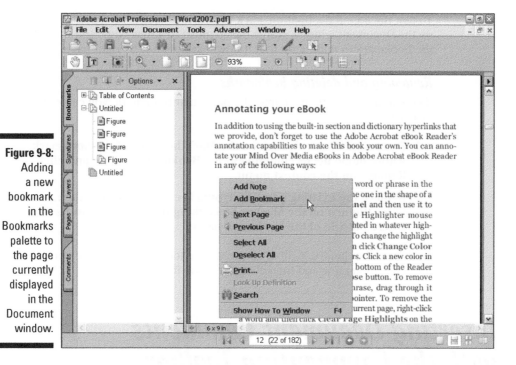

Figure 9-8:
Adding
a new
bookmark
in the
Bookmarks
palette to
the page
currently
displayed
in the
Document
window.

To change the text color of the bookmark as it appears in the Bookmarks palette, click Appearance tab and then the Color button to select a new color in the color palette. To change the text style of the bookmark, click the new style (Bold, Italic, or Bold & Italic) on the Style drop-down list. To assign your new color and/or text style to the bookmark, click the Close button in the Bookmark Properties dialog box.

Changing the page destination for a bookmark

If you find that you've linked a bookmark that goes to the wrong page, you can easily edit just its destination by taking these few steps:

1. **Using the buttons on the Navigation toolbar or navigation buttons on the Document window status bar, go to the correct destination page in the document for the bookmark.**

2. **Right-click (Control+click on the Mac) the name of the bookmark whose destination needs editing in the Bookmarks palette and click Set Destination on the context menu.**

3. **Click Yes in the alert dialog box that asks you if you're certain that you want to make this change.**

To test the edited destination, click the buttons on the Navigation toolbar or on the Document window status bar to move to a new page, and then click the bookmark to make sure that it now takes you to the right page.

Renaming and deleting bookmarks

If you aren't happy with a name of a particular bookmark, you can rename it in a snap:

1. **Right-click (Control+click on the Mac) the name of the bookmark whose name needs changing in the Bookmarks palette and click Rename on the context menu.**

2. **Replace the existing name by typing the new name and then pressing Enter (Return on the Mac) or by clicking the mouse pointer somewhere outside of the bookmark name.**

To delete a bookmark, right-click (Control+click on the Mac) the bookmark in the Navigation pane and then click Delete on its context menu.

Inserting Document Comments with the Commenting Toolbar

In its original state, the Commenting toolbar displays the buttons for four tools — Note, Indicate Text Edits, Stamp tool, and Highlight Text — that you can use to annotate your PDF document, as well as the Show button that is used to display or hide (also known as filtering) comments in your PDF document. (For more on filtering comments see the "Showing and hiding comments" section, later in this chapter.) Three of the tool buttons, Indicate Text Edits, Stamp tool, and Highlight Text, contain pop-up menus that you can click to display additional features for the selected tool.

When you click the pop-up menu button on the Indicate Text Edits tool, it displays options for marking up edited text selections. Figure 9-9 shows the options provided on this menu. You normally use this group of commands in conjunction with the Indicate Text Edits tool to perform various markups on selected text in PDF document you're reviewing for the benefit of other review participants. These self-explanatory options include Insert Text at Cursor, Replace Selected Text, Highlight Selected Text, Add Note to Selected Text, Cross Out Text for Deletion, and Highlight Selected Text, among others.

When you click the pop-up menu button on the Stamp tool, it displays all the options for using the electronic rubber stamp feature in Acrobat 6. See the "Using the Stamp tool" section, later in this chapter, for more information.

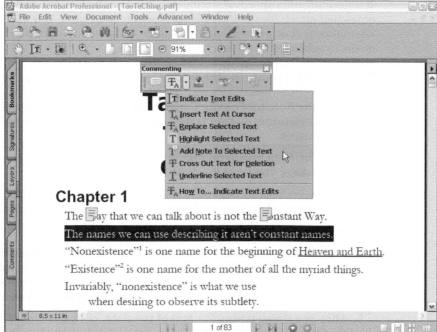

Figure 9-9:
The
Indicating
Text Edits
pop-up
menu on the
Commenting
toolbar.

When you click the pop-up menu button on the Highlight tool, it displays different highlighting tools — Cross-Out Text tool and the Underline Text tool, in addition to the standard Highlighter tool. You usually use this group of tools to draw attention to text in the PDF document you're reviewing that needs some type of editing (normally deletion, when you use the Cross-Out Text tool) or emphasizing (when you use the Underline Text tool). See the "Hitting the highlights" section, later in this chapter, for details.

Note that Acrobat saves all notations that you add with Commenting and Advanced Commenting tools on a distinct and invisible top layer of the PDF document, keeping them separate from the PDF document text and graphics underneath. This makes it possible for you to import comments from other reviewers and add them to the PDF document, as well as to summarize all comments made in the document and export them as a separate file. For a description of all Comment and Advanced Comment tools, see Chapter 3.

Using the Note tool

The notes that you can add when reviewing a PDF file run the gamut of hidden comments (identified by a note icon), simple text displayed at all times in the document, audio comments that you listen to, and predefined stamps indicating approval, confidentiality, and the like. You can even add notes that attach files to the PDF document (useful when you want to include alternative text or graphics that should be considered as possible replacements or additions).

To add a hidden comment with the Note tool, follow these steps:

1. **Click the Note tool on the Commenting toolbar or type S if the single-key accelerators feature is turned on in the Acrobat General Preferences.**

2. **Click the Note mouse pointer at the place on the page in the PDF document where you want the Note icon to appear.**

   When you click this pointer, Acrobat opens a comment box that shows your name and the current date on the colored (yellow by default) title bar.

3. **Type the text of the note in the comment box.**

4. **If the text of your note is short, you can resize the comment box to better suit the amount of text by positioning the mouse pointer in the sizing box in the lower-right corner and dragging the outline of the box with the arrowhead pointer until it's the shape and size you want.**

5. **After you finish typing the text of the note, click the Close button in the upper-left corner of the comment dialog box to close it. You can also double-click the Note icon to close its comment box.**

After you click the Close button in the comment box, only the Note icon appears on the page, as shown in Figure 9-10. To open the note's comment box to read its text, select the Hand tool by pressing H and double-click the Note icon, or right-click the icon (Control+click on the Mac), and then select Open Pop-up Note on its context menu. You can leave a comment box open next to its Note icon on the page by clicking outside of the box rather than clicking its Close button.

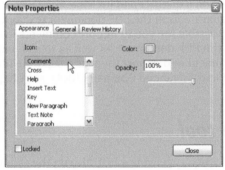

Figure 9-10: Changing note settings in the Note Properties dialog box.

You can move notes by dragging their Note icons or their comment boxes (if they're open) with either the Hand tool or the Note tool. Simply drag the arrowhead pointer to the desired position on the page (usually off the text that you're commenting on) and then release the mouse button. To move a note back to its original position, right-click (Control+click on the Mac) its Note icon and click Reset Pop-up Note Location on its context menu. To delete a hidden comment, choose Delete on the context menu.

You can also change the color and icons used when you add your comments with the Note tool. This is a good feature to use when many people will be adding comments to the same PDF. By having the reviewers select individual colors and icons, you can tell at a glance which notes belong to which reviewers. To select a new color and/or icon for your notes, follow these steps:

1. **Add your first note (by following the preceding steps).**

2. **Right-click the Note icon (Control+click on the Mac), and then choose Properties on the context menu.**

   The Note Properties dialog box appears (refer to Figure 9-10).

3. **To select a new Note icon, select it in the Icon list box.**

4. **To select a new color for the Note icon, click the Color button and then click a new color in the palette.**

   Note that you can also increase or decrease the opacity of the Note icon by entering either a percentage number in the Opacity text box or moving the slider button right for less opacity or left for more opacity.

5. **To change the author or subject for the note, click the General tab and enter a new name in the Author text box or a new subject in the Subject text box.**

6. **Click Close to put your changes into effect.**

Roll me over and line me up

You can have Acrobat automatically open a note's comments box to display its text when you position the mouse pointer on the Note icon. To do so, open the Preferences dialog box by pressing Ctrl+K (⌘+K on the Mac), and then click Commenting in the list box. Then select the Automatically Open Pop-ups on Mouse Rollover check box in the Viewing Comments section. You can also have Acrobat automatically display connecting lines between Note icons and its pop-up window when you rollover the Note icon by selecting the Show Lines Connecting Markups to Their Pop-ups on Mouse Rollover check box.

When you close the Note Properties dialog box, Acrobat changes the current comment to suit the new icon and/or color settings. All notes that you subsequently create will use the new note settings. Be aware, however, that the icons for notes previously added are unaffected by your changes to these settings (you would have to delete and then re-create them to have all your notes reflect the new color and icon settings). Also keep in mind that changes you make in the Author or Subject text boxes of the Note Properties dialog box affect only the particular note selected at that time.

Acrobat 6 uses your Windows Identity or Log-in name as the default entry in the Author text box for Notes. If your Windows Log-in name differs from your Acrobat Identity (entered in the Identity Preferences dialog box), you can choose your Acrobat Identity for all subsequent notes you create with the Note tool. To do so, open the Preferences dialog box (Ctrl+K on Windows, ⌘+K on the Mac), click Commenting in the list box, and then deselect the Always Use Log-in Name for Author name check box in the Making Comments Preferences area.

You can also change the font and font size for text used in the comments you create with the Note tool, as well as the opacity of the comment box (by decreasing it, you can see more of the text and graphics underneath) in the Viewing Comments area of the Commenting Preferences dialog box. Note that changes you make in the Font and Font Size drop-down lists affect only new comments created with the Note tool. The same holds true for any new setting you select with the Opacity text box or slider.

Using the Stamp tool

You can use the Stamp tool to imprint the document with a predefined graphic mark that mimics real-world rubber ink stamps used to indicate the status of the document, such as Draft, As Is, Confidential, or Final. When you use one of these marks, you can also add a hidden comment to it, just like you do when creating a comment with the Note tool. Acrobat comes with a wide variety of ready-made stamps that you can use (which are organized into different categories). You can also add your own marks to these collections.

Don't confuse adding a stamp to the PDF document you're reviewing with digitally signing a PDF document. When you stamp a document, you're simply adding another, more graphic form of notation to the document. When you digitally sign a document, however, you're actually using a secure method for identifying yourself as the signatory (see Chapter 11 for details on the process involved in digitally signing a document). Use stamps when you want to call attention to the current state of the PDF document or add a very visible review comment, such as red-flagging a change with, of all things, a *red flag*. Digitally sign the PDF document when you're ready to freeze it and prevent all further changes to it.

To add a stamp to a PDF document, take these steps:

1. **Click the Stamp tool on the Commenting toolbar.**

2. **Click the Stamp tool mouse pointer at the place on the page in the PDF document where you want the stamp's imprint to appear.**

   When you click the Stamp tool mouse pointer, Acrobat inserts the last-used stamp at the place you click (this is the Approved mark when you first begin using this feature in Acrobat).

3. **If you want to use a different stamp, click the mark that you just added to the document to select it (you can tell it's selected because a bounding box with sizing handles at the corners appears), and then click the Stamp tool pop-up menu to select another stamp.**

The Stamp tool pop-up menu and submenus contain all the built-in stamps available in Acrobat 6. These are divided into three categories: Dynamic, Sign Here, and Standard Business. Dynamic stamps like the Approved stamp, shown in Figure 9-11, automatically display author, time, and date information, as opposed to Standard Business like the For Public Release stamp shown selected on Stamp tool pop-up menu in the figure, which has no additional dynamic information. The Sign Here category provides a number of stamps used to highlight digital signature areas, much like the Sign Here Post-It notes you may have seen attached to paper documents from your accountant or lawyer.

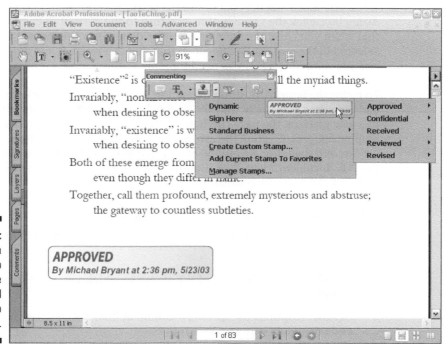

Figure 9-11:
Choosing a new stamp on the Stamp tool pop-up menus.

As mentioned earlier, you can attach hidden comments to stamps (see the following section to find out how) and also specify properties for those comments. To change properties for comments made with the Stamp tool, right-click a stamp imprint in the current document and choose Properties on the context menu to open the Stamp Properties dialog box. The following is a rundown of the options you find there:

✔ **Appearance tab:** To change the color used in the title bar of any comment box that you attach to a stamp, click the Pop-up Color button and then click the new color in the palette. To decrease or increase the opacity of the stamp imprint so that you can see more or less of the document background, enter a percentage number in the Opacity text box or move the slider button to the left to decrease the opacity or to the right to increase the opacity of the stamp imprint.

✔ **General tab:** To change the author associated with the stamp, click the Author text box and then edit the name. To change the subject of the stamp, click the Subject text box and edit the default text. Note that Acrobat 6 uses your Windows Identity or Log-in name as the default entry in the Author text box for stamps. To use your Acrobat Identity instead for all subsequent notes you create with the Stamp tool, see the instructions at the end of the previous section, "Using the Note tool."

✔ **Review History tab:** Contains a list box that displays any changes in status for the selected comment.

When you finish making changes to the settings in the Stamp Properties dialog box, click the Close button to return to the current document. Note that when you close the Stamp Properties dialog box, the imprint is still selected in the current document so that you can resize it and move it to a new place on the page if you need to.

To resize the imprint, position the mouse pointer on one of the sizing handles and then drag diagonally with the double-headed pointer. To move the imprint to a new place on the page (perhaps to the side or above related text or graphic images), position the arrowhead pointer somewhere within its bounding box and then drag its outline and drop it in place. To delete a stamp from the PDF document, right-click (Control+click on the Mac) the Stamp's imprint and click Delete on its context menu.

Adding a hidden comment to a stamp imprint

If you want to add a hidden text comment to the imprint of a stamp, you can do so by following these steps:

1. **Double-click the imprint of the stamp to which you want to add the comment.**

   Acrobat responds by opening a comment box, just like the ones used to add comments with the Note tool.

Getting your hidden comments added and seen

When using stamps to annotate a PDF document, you may want to make a couple of changes to the Comments Preferences — one that will help you remember to add hidden comments and the other to let you and your reviewers know that hidden comments are attached to particular stamp imprints. To have Acrobat automatically open a blank comment box whenever you add a new stamp imprint, open the Commenting section of the Preferences dialog box (by pressing Ctrl+K on Windows or ⌘+K on the Mac, and then clicking Commenting in the list box on the left), and then select the Automatically Open Comment Pop-ups for Comments Other Than Notes check box in the Pop-up Open Behavior section. To have the program automatically display the comment boxes you add to stamp imprints whenever you position the mouse over them, select the Automatically Open Pop-Ups on Mouse Over check box in the Viewing Comments section (note that selecting this check box option affects hidden comments added with the Notes tool, as well as those added with the Stamps tool).

2. **Type the text of your comment in the open comment box.**

3. **To resize the comment box so it better fits the text you entered, drag the sizing box in the lower-right corner diagonally until it's the right shape and size.**

4. **To move the comment box so that its title bar doesn't obscure the stamp's imprint, drag the comment box by its title bar.**

5. **When you finish making changes to the comment box, click its Close button to make the box and its note disappear. You can also double-click a stamp imprint to toggle between hiding and displaying its attached comment.**

Adding custom marks to your own stamp category

You can create your own marks in graphics programs, such as Adobe Illustrator or Adobe Photoshop, and then use them as stamps in Acrobat 6. To do this, convert the graphic image you want to use as a stamp to either a JPEG, GIF, or bitmap file. You can also convert Illustrator and Photoshop files saved in their native format (AI or PSD).

After you have the mark saved, follow these steps to make it available as a stamp in Acrobat 6:

1. **Choose Tools⇨Commenting⇨Stamp Tool⇨Create Custom Stamp or simply click Create Custom Stamp on the Stamp tool pop-up menu.**

   The Create Stamp dialog box opens.

2. Click the Select button to open the Select dialog box.

3. Click the Browse button, and in the Open dialog box that appears, locate the desired graphic and click the Select button to return to the Select dialog box.

4. Click OK to close the Select dialog box and return to the Create Stamp dialog box.

5. Enter the name you want to give the stamp (something with the company name or a description of the mark) in the Name text box, enter a name in the Category drop-down list box or select a previously created custom category, and then click the OK button.

After you add a custom graphic as a new stamp, its category, name, and thumbnail appear on the Stamp tool pop-up menu as well as the Acrobat menu bar, and you can start using it in the PDF documents you're reviewing as you would any of the other built-in stamps. After clicking the Stamp tool, select your new custom imprint on the Stamp tool submenus and then click the Stamp tool mouse pointer at the location in the current PDF document where you want the stamp to appear. If you want to delete a custom stamp you've created, choose Manage Stamps on the Stamp tool pop-up menu, and in the Manage Stamps dialog box that appears, select the custom stamp for deletion by choosing its category and name in the drop-down lists before clicking the Delete button. When you're finished deleting custom stamps, click the OK button to close the Manage Stamps dialog box. Note that you can also invoke the Create Stamps dialog box by clicking the Create button in the Manage Stamps dialog box.

Hitting the highlights

Acrobat includes three text-only markup tools: Highlighter tool, Cross-Out Text tool, and Underline Text tool:

- **Highlighter tool:** Highlights text in a color (yellow by default) just like the highlighting pens you used to mark key words and phrases to remember in your text books.

- **Cross-Out Text tool:** Indicates words and phrases that should be deleted from the text. (Acrobat puts a line through the text just like they do in voter pamphlets to show what provisions of a referendum will be removed from a statute.)

- **Underline Text tool:** Underscores the importance of text.

Figure 9-12 shows you examples of three types of text markup: highlighting in the title, underlining in the first-paragraph text at the top of the first column, and crossing-out in the title at the top of the second column.

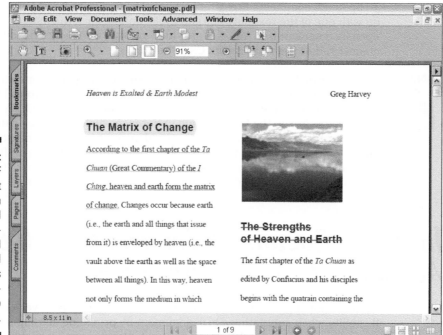

Figure 9-12:
A PDF document with highlighted text, cross-out text, and underlined text, thanks to the text-only markup tools.

As with the graphics markup tools, when you mark up text with the text-only tools, Acrobat automatically adds hidden comment boxes to the markups. To have the comment boxes contain a copy of all the text that you've marked with the text-only markup tool, open the Acrobat Preferences dialog box by choosing Edit⇨Preferences or pressing Ctrl+K (⌘+K on Mac), click Commenting in the list box, and then select the Copy Selected Text into Highlight, Cross-Out, and Underline Comment Pop-Ups check box in the Making Comment section before clicking OK to close the Preferences dialog box. You can then annotate this comment text or replace it with the corrections you'd like to see made.

The text-only tools all work the same way: After you click the desired text-only markup tool, you drag the I-beam mouse pointer through all the text you want to highlight, cross-out, or underscore. Each text-only markup tool has the same Properties dialog box as the graphics markup tools (Note and Stamp) where you can edit the Color, Opacity, Author, Subject, and Review History of created markups. To access these options, right-click the marked-up text and choose Properties on the context menu to open the associated Properties dialog box.

To delete the highlighting, strikeout, or underlining made to words or phrases in the PDF document, right-click (Control+click on the Mac) the marked-up text and then click Delete on its context menu.

To open the comments box attached to the words or phrases you've marked up with one of the text-only markup tools, double-click the marked-up text to open its comment box. You can also hide an open comment box in this manner rather than clicking its Close button.

Remember that you can have Acrobat automatically open a comment box each time you mark up text with one of the text-only markup tools by selecting the Automatically Open Comment Pop-Ups for Comments Other Than Notes check box in the Commenting Preferences dialog box. You can also have Acrobat automatically display a hidden comment when you position the mouse on the marked-up text by selecting the Automatically Open Pop-Ups on Mouse Rollover check box as well. For details, see the sidebar, "Getting your hidden comments added and seen," earlier in this chapter.

Inserting Document Comments with the Advanced Commenting Toolbar

Options that appear on the Advanced Commenting toolbar give you a lot of flexibility when annotating a PDF document by providing markup tools that go way beyond the standard note, text edit, stamps, and highlighting features found on the Commenting toolbar. You can use the Rectangle tool and its many built-in variations to create drawn shapes used to highlight text or graphics that you want to call attention to with an attached comment. The Text Box tool creates static annotations that always appear in a document rather than hidden comments made with the Note tool. The Pencil tool draws free-hand shapes around document elements you want to call attention to with an attached comment. You can even attach sound files or other document files using the Attach Sound tool and Attach File tool. The following sections give the particulars on these useful markup tools. To get an overview of the Advanced Commenting toolbar, see Chapter 3.

Using the Text Box tool

You use the Text Box tool to create comments in the PDF document that are always visible. Because free-text comments are always displayed, you need to position them in margin areas or places where they won't obscure document text or graphics text underneath.

To create a comment with the Text Box tool, follow these steps:

1. **Click the Text Box tool on the Advanced Commenting toolbar or press X if the single-key accelerator feature is turned on.**

   (See Chapter 3 to find out how to enable single-key accelerators.)

2. **Click the I-beam mouse pointer or draw a marquee at the place on the page in the PDF document where you want the text of the comment to appear.**

   When you click or draw a marquee with this pointer, Acrobat opens a yellow bounding box (which appears dotted on some monitors) in which you type the note.

3. **Type the text of the free-text note in the note's bounding box.**

   As you type a note in a bounding box you created by drawing a marquee with the I-beam pointer, Acrobat automatically breaks the lines of text to fit within the width of the bounding box and expands its height.

4. **When you finish typing the text of the free-text note, click the Hand tool and then click outside of the note's bounding box.**

   Acrobat displays your free-text note in a box.

If you create a bounding box by simply clicking an area in your document with the I-beam pointer, you must make the first line break in your text note by pressing Enter (Return on the Mac) in order for Acrobat to make subsequent automatic line breaks. Otherwise, you end up typing a never-ending line of text that expands the width of the bounding box right off the page!

To resize the Text Box note to make all of its text visible or to eliminate excess white space around the note text, position the Hand tool somewhere on the note and then click the arrowhead pointer to display the sizing handles at the four corners of the free-text note box. Next, position the pointer on one of the sizing handles and drag the double-headed pointer diagonally until the outline of the note box is the shape and size you need. Click outside the note box to deselect the sizing handles.

To move a free-text note, click within its note box to display the sizing handles and then, with the arrowhead mouse pointer inside the box, drag the outline to a new position on the page before releasing the mouse button. To delete a free-text note from the PDF document, right-click (Control+click on the Mac) the note text or its bounding box, and then click Delete on its context menu.

As with comments added with the Note tool, you can change the default settings for the free-text notes you create with the Text Box tool. Right-click the text box and select Properties on its context menu to open the Text Box Properties dialog box, as shown in Figure 9-13. As you can see, the setting options in this dialog box enable you to change the Appearance, General settings, and display Review History by clicking the appropriate tab.

On the Appearance tab, select a border style in the Style drop-down list. Your choices are Solid or six different dashed-line styles. To make the border of the text box thicker, increase the value in the Thickness text box. To remove the border entirely from text box, set this value down to 0. To change the color of the box border, click the Border Color button and then click a new color on the palette. To decrease or increase the opacity of the text box so that you can see more or less of the document background, enter a percentage number in the Opacity text box or move the slider button to the left to decrease the opacity or to the right to increase the opacity of the text box. To add a background color to the text box, click the Fill Color button and click the background color from its color palette (but for heaven's sake, don't select a background color on this palette that's so dark that you can't read the note text).

Figure 9-13: Changing the appearance of a text box in the Text Box Properties dialog box.

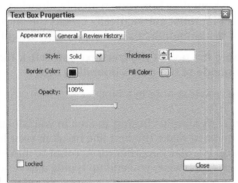

The options on the General and Review History tabs are exactly the same as those for the other markup tools (Note, Stamp, and Indicate Text). Change the author or subject of a comment attached to a Text Box on the General tab or display changes of status to the Text Box comment on the Review History tab. When you finish making changes in the Text Box Properties dialog box, click Close to see the effects of your changes on the currently selected text box.

Using the Attach Sound tool

You use the Attach Sound tool to record a sound note or select an audio file that is played back when the user double-clicks the Sound Note icon. Note that your computer must have a microphone in order to record your own sound notes and add them to your PDF document.

To record a sound note for playback in your PDF document, follow these steps:

1. **Click the Attach Sound tool on the Advanced Commenting toolbar pop-up menu.**

2. **Click the Speaker mouse pointer at the place on the page in the PDF document where you want the Sound Note icon to appear.**

   When you click this pointer, Acrobat opens a Sound Recorder dialog box.

3. **To record the sound note, click the Record button and speak into your computer's microphone.**

   When you finish recording, click the Stop button (see Figure 9-14). To play the note before adding it to your document, click the Play button (which replaces the Stop button).

Figure 9-14:
Recording a sound note.

4. **Click OK in the Sound Recorder dialog box.**

   The Sound Recorder dialog box closes, and the Sound Attachment Properties dialog box opens.

5. **Click the Appearance tab and select an icon for the sound attachment — either Ear, Microphone, or Sound (speaker) in the Icon list box.**

   Click the Color button and select a new color for the sound attachment icon on the color palette that appears. Increase or decrease the opacity of the sound attachment icon by typing in a new percentage number in the Opacity text box or using the slider button.

6. **Click the General tab and edit the default text in the Author, Subject, and Description text boxes.**

   Text entered in the Description text box identifies the sound file when you position the mouse pointer over its attached sound icon.

7. **Click the Review History tab to view any recent changes to the status of the attached sound during a review cycle. When you're finished changing Sound Attachment properties, click Close to exit the dialog box.**

You can also select a prerecorded sound file to play back when the Sound Attachment is played. To select a prerecorded sound file, click the Browse button in the Sound Recorder dialog box to open the Select Sound File dialog box. Click the folder that contains the desired sound file, click the sound file icon, and then click the Select button.

To play a sound note that you've added to a PDF document, double-click its Sound Note icon with the Hand tool or right-click (Control+click on Mac) its icon and then click Play File on the context menu.

Using the File Attachment tool

You can use the File Attachment tool to attach or append another file (not necessarily saved as a PDF) to the PDF document you're reviewing. You can use this feature to attach new copy and graphics that you'd like to see replace particular text passages and images in the PDF file. You can also use this tool to attach a memo or some other text document that outlines the review steps or special instructions to the design or review team.

Don't use this feature to attach files saved in other file formats besides PDF unless you're sure that each reviewer has the software necessary to open it installed on his or her computer. Of course, the way to be sure that each and everyone concerned will be able to open and evaluate all the files you attach to a PDF document under review is to save them as PDF files before you attach them.

To attach a file to the PDF file you're reviewing, follow these steps:

1. **Click the Attach File tool on the Advanced Commenting toolbar or press Shift+J until its icon (the one with the pushpin) is selected.**

2. **Click the Pushpin pointer at the place in the PDF document's text or graphics where you want the File Attachment icon (a paper clip by default) to appear, indicating to other reviewers that a file has been attached.**

   Acrobat responds by opening the Select File to Attach dialog box.

3. **Open the folder and select the icon for the file that you want to attach to the current PDF document, and then click the Select button.**

   The File Attachment Properties dialog box opens.

4. **Change the properties of the file attachment as follows:**

   • To select a new icon besides the default paper clip, click the Appearance tab and choose an item in the Icon list box.

   • To change the color of the File Attachment icon, click the Color button and then click the new color in the palette.

   • To increase or decrease the opacity of the file attachment icon, type in a new percentage number in the Opacity text box or use the slider button.

   • To modify the ToolTip description that appears when the user positions the mouse over the File Attachment icon, click the General tab and replace the filename in the Description text box. Acrobat automatically displays the filename as the ToolTip if you don't modify this text box.

- To change the author or subject associated with this file attachment, click the Author or Subject text box and edit the default text that appears there.

5. **Click the Close button to close the File Attachment Properties dialog box.**

As soon as you close the File Attachment Properties dialog box, you see the File Attachment icon (a paper clip unless you changed it) at the place you clicked in the document. To move this icon, drag it with the arrowhead pointer. To display the ToolTip with the name of the attached file (or some other description if you modified the Description text box), position the arrowhead mouse pointer over the File Attachment icon.

To open the attached file, double-click its File Attachment icon, or right-click (Control+click on the Mac) the icon and then click Open File on the context menu. Acrobat responds by displaying an Open Attachment alert dialog box, warning you about possible dangers in opening the file. When you click the Open button in the alert dialog box, Acrobat then goes ahead and opens the file.

If the attached file is a PDF document, Acrobat opens it and makes it the current document (you can then return to the original PDF document by selecting its name at the bottom of the Windows menu). If the attached file is saved in some other file format, your computer's operating system launches the program that created the file (provided that it can be identified and that the program is installed on the computer), opening it in a new window. You can then return to the original PDF document by clicking its program icon on the Windows taskbar or clicking the Application icon on the OS X Dock.

To remove an attached file from the PDF document, right-click the File Attachment icon (Control+click on the Mac) and then click Delete on its context menu. To save the attached file on your hard drive before you delete it, click Save Embedded File to Disk on its context menu, select the folder in which you want it saved, and click the Save button.

Mark it well

The graphic markup tools (Pencil and Rectangle) found on the Advanced Commenting toolbar enable you to mark up elements that need changing in the PDF document you're reviewing. When you use these graphic markup tools to call attention to particular passages of text and graphics, you can add hidden notes (like you can do when using the Stamp and Note tools) that explain the type of changes you'd like to see made to the elements you've marked.

All the graphic tools work in a similar manner and share the same Appearance, General, and Review History properties as associated with Commenting toolbar markup tools. The Pencil tool comes with its own Pencil Eraser tool (just like a real pencil!), and the Rectangle tool is actually one of seven shape tools found on its pop-up menu. Which of these tools you select varies according to the kind of document elements you want to mark up:

- **Pencil tool:** Draws freehand shapes around text and graphics.

- **Rectangle tool:** Draws rectangular and square boxes around text and graphics. Hold down the Shift key to constrain the shape to a square as you draw with this tool.

- **Oval tool:** Draws a circle or oval around text and graphics. Hold down the Shift key to constrain the shape to a perfect circle as you draw with this tool.

- **Arrow tool:** Draws arrows that point to a specific document element.

- **Line tool:** Adds a line to text or graphics (often referred to as adding a rule). Hold down the Shift key to constrain the shape to a straight line and drag left and right for a horizontal rule, up and down for a vertical rule, and diagonally for a rule on the bias at 45 degrees.

- **Cloud tool:** Draws a nice puffy cloud around text or graphic elements you want to call attention to. Using this tool greatly enhances the cuteness quotient of your reviewing contribution.

- **Polygon tool:** Draws a closed multisegment polygon shape around a document element.

- **Polygon Line tool:** Draws an open multisegment polygon shape around a document element.

To use one of these tools to mark up a PDF document, follow these general steps:

1. **To use the Pencil tool, click its button on the Advanced Commenting toolbar or press N. To use one of the other markup tools, press Shift+D until its icon (rectangle for the Rectangle tool, oval for the Oval tool, diagonal line for the Line tool, and so on) is selected.**

2. **Position the cross-hair mouse pointer near the text or graphic that you want to mark up, and then drag to draw the line or shape made by the tool to call attention to it.**

   When using the Pencil tool, you can draw a freehand line or enclosing shape. When using the Square, Circle, or Line tool, remember that you can constrain the shape or line by holding down the Shift key. When using the Cloud or Polygon tools, click the point where you want to start drawing and drag to draw a line. When you want to change direction, click again to start a new line in the same manner. Continue clicking and dragging until you've either enclosed the desired document element with a final click at your starting point, or in the case of the Polygon Line tool, make a final click to end your drawing. Note that you can cancel or complete a drawing at any time during the process by right-clicking and selecting either Cancel or Complete on the context menu.

3. **Release the mouse button when you finish drawing the desired line or shape with the selected tool.**

When you release the mouse button, Acrobat lays the graphic down on the page. To select the markup graphic to resize it, move it, or change its graphic settings, select the Hand tool by pressing H, and then click the line or shape with the arrowhead pointer. If the graphic is a shape made with any tool other than the Line tool, Acrobat encloses it in a bounding box with sizing handles at the corners. If the graphic is a rule made with the Line tool, the program selects the line with sizing handles at either end. To move a markup graphic, drag its outline with the arrowhead pointer and then drop it in its new position. To resize it, drag one of its sizing buttons.

Remember that you can have Acrobat automatically open a comment box each time you add a markup graphic by selecting the Automatically Open Comment Pop-ups for Comments Other Than Notes check box in the Pop-up Behavior area of the Commenting Preferences dialog box. You can also have Acrobat automatically display a hidden comment when you position the mouse on the markup graphic by selecting the Automatically Open Pop-ups on Mouse Rollover check box as well. For details, see the sidebar, "Getting your hidden comments added and seen," earlier in this chapter.

Spelling it out

Acrobat includes a spell check feature that you can use to catch typos you make in the comments that you add to a PDF document. You can use this feature to catch and eliminate all those embarrassing spelling errors before you send your comments out to someone else on the review team.

To spell-check the text in all comments in the document (along with all text in any form fields you've added), go to the first page of the document, choose Edit⇨Check Spelling⇨In Comments and Form Fields, or press F7 to open the Check Spelling dialog box (shown in Figure 9-15), and then click the Start button.

Acrobat will then flag the first unknown word it encounters in either the form fields or the comments in the document, and you can then take one of the following steps:

✔ To replace the flagged word with one of the suggested corrections listed in the Suggestions list box, click the correction and then click the Change button.

✔ To replace the flagged term with the selected correction in all instances in the other form fields and comments in the document, click the Change All button.

✔ To ignore the flagged word, click the Ignore button.

✔ To ignore the flagged word in all the other form fields and comments in the document, click the Ignore All button.

✔ To add the word to the dictionary, click the Add button.

When Acrobat finishes checking the spelling in the last form field or comment on the last page of the document, it automatically returns to the first page and displays the message `Spell Check Complete` in the Check Spelling dialog box. You can then click the Done button to close the Check Spelling dialog box.

Figure 9-15:
Spell-checking the comments made in a PDF document.

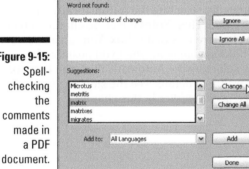

If you want to have Acrobat spell-check a passage in the document text, use the Highlight tool to highlight the text to be spell-checked, which is then automatically added to a hidden comment box. Run the spell check feature and use it to correct all the misspellings in the text's comment box. You can then use the corrected text stored in the comment box when making the corrections during the final editing phase (see Chapter 10 for details on editing). Note that in order for the process described previously to work in Acrobat 6, you need to make sure that the Copy Selected Text into Highlight, Cross-Out, and Underline Comment Pop-ups check box is selected in the Commenting section of the Preferences dialog box. To check if this feature is selected, choose Edit➪Preferences or press Ctrl+K (⌘+K on Mac) and click Commenting in the list box on the left side of the Preferences dialog box.

Viewing Comments in a PDF Document

With Acrobat's new and highly efficient E-mail-Based Review and Browser-Based Review features, it's likely that you'll eventually find yourself viewing a PDF document with a whole bunch of annotations, especially if you're a review initiator. Fortunately, Acrobat provides a number of great tools to help you make sense of all the notes and scribbles you and others have contributed to a PDF review document. These Comment tools let you easily summarize, filter, navigate, search, and even delete all annotations from a PDF document with the click of a button. The following sections familiarize you with the great comment features in Acrobat 6, so that you can approach any PDF review document without trepidation, no matter how many review participants are involved.

Summing up

After you've received reviewers' comments in a PDF document, whether e-mail or browser-based, you can use the Summarize feature to create a summary report that lists all the different types of comments attached to a PDF document. This convenient feature lets you sort comments and specify a page layout in order to generate a printable comment synopsis. The summary is a separate PDF document that can be printed directly in Acrobat or saved and distributed to others for viewing and printing. To generate a summary report, follow these steps:

1. **Choose Document⇨Summarize Comments.**

   The Summarize Options dialog box appears, as shown in Figure 9-16.

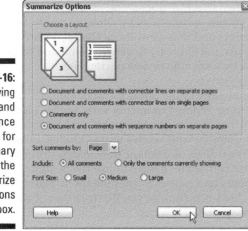

Figure 9-16: Specifying layout and appearance options for a summary in the Summarize Options dialog box.

2. **Click one of the radio buttons in the Choose a Layout section of the Summarize Options dialog box to specify how the summary will appear onscreen or when printed.**

   As you can see in Figure 9-16, in addition to having a lengthy description of the page layout attached to each radio button, you also get a graphic depiction of the selected page layout in the area above when you click a radio button.

3. **Choose a comment sort order for the summary by clicking the Sort Comments By drop-down list and choosing either Author, Date, Page, or Type.**

4. **Select one of the Include radio buttons, either All Comments, which displays all comments whether they are hidden or not in summary, or Only the Comments Currently Showing, which keeps hidden comments hidden in the summary.**

5. **Choose a Font Size radio button, either Small, Medium, or Large, to specify the size of displayed text in the summary.**

6. **Click OK to close the Summarize Options dialog box and generate the summary report.**

Acrobat generates the summary report in a separate PDF document that it displays in the Document window using the Fit Width view. You can then save and print this summary file.

Showing and hiding comments

The Show menu button, located at the end of the Commenting toolbar, contains a large variety of options for displaying and hiding (also known as *filtering*) review comments attached to a PDF document, as shown in Figure 9-17. Filtering makes it easier to review annotations by allowing you to temporarily hide certain types of comments and only view those that you want to work with. For example, you can use the Show by Reviewer command to display only those comments made by a specific review participant.

Note that the first time you use any of the Show menu commands in Acrobat 6, you may get a largely esoteric Hiding Comments with Replies alert dialog box telling you that Filtering does not apply to individual replies and that when you have a comment with replies that is hidden, all of its replies are hidden as well, regardless of whether they match the criteria for being hidden or not. The gist is that you'll have to use the Search Comments feature to find these comments and replies if you hide them. Select the Don't Show This Message Again check box (unless you like this sort of abuse) and then click OK to close the alert dialog box.

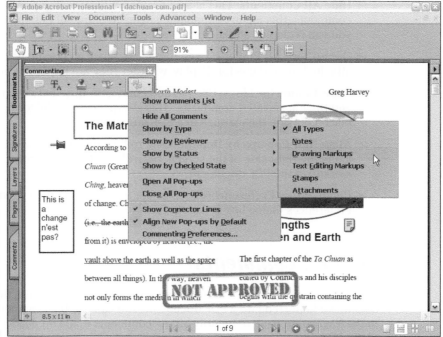

Figure 9-17:
Selecting
the types of
comments
that you
want
displayed in
the PDF file.

To begin filtering a PDF review document, simply click the Show menu button
on the Commenting toolbar and select a command on its menu or submenus.
In Figure 9-17, I'm choosing Show⇨Show by Type⇨Drawing Markups. This
command displays only those comments in the PDF document that were made
with either the Pencil tool or the Rectangle tool. As the figure shows, in addition to displaying only Drawing Markups, you can also choose to display All
Types of comments, only Notes, only Text Editing Markups, only Stamps, or
only Attachments on the Show by Type submenu. Other filtering criteria on
the menu include Show by Reviewer, where you can choose all participants or
a specific participant, Show by Status, which gives you the option of displaying comments that have been Accepted, Rejected, Cancelled, or Completed
(you can also choose All Status or None), and Show by Checked State, which
displays only those comments that you've marked Checked or Unchecked.
These markups are for the use of the review initiator only and don't appear
to other review participants.

The following list describes other commands that appear on the Show menu
that you can use to filter comments in a PDF document:

✔ **Show Comments List:** Used to open the Comments palette in the
Navigation pane.

✔ **Hide All Comments:** This is a no-brainer. When you temporarily hide all comments, this menu command changes to Show All Comments so that you can redisplay all those you've hidden.

✔ **Open/Close All Pop-ups:** Used to open or close all pop-up comments attached to markups for display, whether they are hidden or not.

✔ **Show Connector Lines:** Used to add connector lines between markups and their associated comments. This is especially useful for comments placed outside the margins of a PDF document.

✔ **Align New Pop-ups by Default:** Used to line up new pop-up comments along the right side of the screen, regardless of the location of its markup in the PDF document.

✔ **Commenting Preferences:** Used to open the Commenting window in the Preferences dialog box in Acrobat 6.

Finding comments

Acrobat provides a couple of methods for locating the comments that you've added and imported into a PDF document: You can use the Comments palette in the Navigation pane to identify all the comments made on particular pages of the PDF document, or you can use the Search Comments button in the Comments palette button bar to search comments for particular words or phrases. Figure 9-18 shows the Comments palette selected in the Navigation pane, as well as the Search PDF pane displayed on the right side of the screen where you enter the text to search for in the text of the comments added to the PDF document. The Search PDF pane is displayed by clicking the Search Comments button shown in the figure. Note that the Comments palette, because of its expanded button bar and greater content, is the only Navigation pane that displays horizontally rather than vertically. Unlike the other Navigation panes (Bookmarks, Pages, and so on), if the Navigation pane is open when you select the Comments palette, you can close the Navigation pane by clicking its Close button while leaving the Comments palette open, thus giving your document more horizontal viewing space. If the Navigation pane is closed when you select the Comments palette, it remains closed.

Locating comments in the Comments palette

To use the Comments palette to locate and select a particular comment in the document, follow these steps:

1. **Click the Comments tab on the Navigation pane or choose View⇨ Navigations tabs⇨Comments to display the Comments palette.**

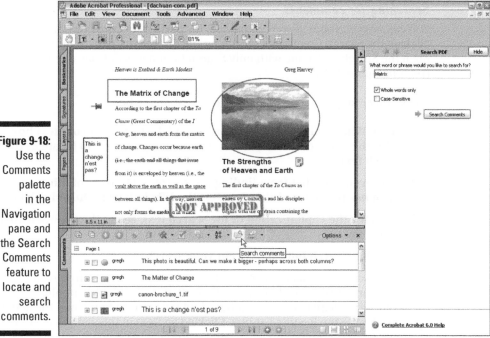

Figure 9-18:
Use the
Comments
palette
in the
Navigation
pane and
the Search
Comments
feature to
locate and
search
comments.

2. **To choose a different sort order for the comments, select one of the options on the Sort By pop-up menu: Type, Author, Date Last Modified, Color, Checkmark Status, or Status by Person.**

   By default, Acrobat sorts the comments in the Comments palette by page.

3. **Click the Expand button (a plus sign on Windows and triangle pointing right on the Mac) for the page, comment type, author, or date modified (depending upon how the list in the Comments palette is sorted) that you think contains the comment or comments you want to find.**

4. **Click the icon for the comment you want selected in the expanded list of comments on that page.**

When you click a comment in the Comments palette, Acrobat displays the page and the comment markup in the Document pane. Because the comment you selected in the Comments palette is also selected in the PDF document, if you want to change its setting, you can then open its Properties dialog box by right-clicking the markup and choosing Properties on the context menu. To open its comment box, however, you still have to double-click the selected text or icon. Note that you can also edit a comment directly in the Comments palette without opening the comment box attached to the markup in the PDF document.

Searching for comments

You can have Acrobat search comments for particular words or phrases by clicking the Search Comments button on the Comments palette button bar to open the Search PDF pane with only Search Comments options displayed (refer to Figure 9-18).

Follow these steps in using the Find Comment dialog box:

1. **In the What Word or Phrase Would You Like to Search For? text box, enter the word or phrase in the comment(s) you want to locate as the search text.**

2. **To prevent Acrobat from finding the search text inside of other words (as in *her* in the word *there*), select the Whole Words Only check box.**

3. **To match the capitalization of the search text, select the Case-Sensitive check box.**

4. **Click the Search button to begin your search.**

   After Acrobat scans the PDF document, it displays the search result in the Search PDF pane, letting you know that it's finished searching for your term, displaying the number of total instances found and the actual result(s) in the Results list box. Clicking an item in this list selects not only the icon or markup associated with the search result comment text in the PDF document, but also the associated comment in the Comments palette.

5. **If no results appear after a search, click the New Search button to start the process over.**

6. **When you finish searching the comments in the PDF document, click the Done button or the Hide button in the Search PDF pane.**

Note that you can enter the name of an author (as it appears on the title bar of the comment boxes) in the What Word or Phrase Would You Like to Search For? text box to use the Search Comments feature to locate and select comments made by a single reviewer.

Don't confuse searching for comments in a PDF document with searching for text in the document. You use the regular Edit⇨Search command to search for words or phrases in the general text of the document. You use the Search Comments button in the Comments palette to search for words or phrases only within the comments that you've added or imported into the PDF document.

Removing all comments

After you've made all the required editing changes (as explained in Chapter 10), you can remove all the comments and various markings from the original PDF document by opening the Comments palette, selecting all the comments listed, and then clicking the Delete the Selected Comment button on the Comments palette button bar. To select all comments, make sure all comments are collapsed by clicking their Collapse buttons (minus sign in Windows, triangle pointing down on the Mac), click the top comment group in the Comments pane, and then Shift+click the remaining comment groups. Note that Acrobat does not display an alert dialog box asking for your confirmation before removing all the comments in the current PDF document. You can, however, restore them by choosing Edit⇨Undo Multiple Deletes or by pressing Ctrl+Z (⌘+Z on the Mac).

Before you make your edits and remove all the comments, use the File⇨Save As command and rename the file to make a copy of the PDF document with all its comments. That way, you always have a copy of the original file with all the reviewers' feedback.

Chapter 10

Editing PDF Files

· ·

· ·

*T*he text- and graphics-editing tools included in Acrobat 6 are designed to enable you to do last-minute touchups to your PDF document. As you will soon discover, they are simply not robust enough for heavy editing needs. If, in the course of the document review cycle (described in detail in Chapter 9), you discover that your PDF document requires major text or graphics revisions and/or changes to the document layout or structure, you may have to make these changes in the original documents with their native application programs and then re-convert them to PDF for final review in Acrobat.

In this chapter, you find out how to use the Acrobat 6 editing tools to make various kinds of editing changes and corrections to your PDF document. These changes can include correcting errors in lines of text, modifying text attributes, and repositioning graphics, as well as inserting, rearranging, deleting, cropping, and renumbering the document pages. You also find out how to edit your PDF documents by creating articles for determining the flow of text that spans columns and pages and guiding readers through their online reading experience of the document. Finally, you discover the wonderful world of batch processing that enables you to automate routine editing sequences, such as removing all file attachments or saving the text in the Rich Text Format (RTF) used by word processors, and perform them on several PDF documents at one time.

Touching Up the Text and Graphics

You use the TouchUp tools on the Editing toolbar to make last-minute changes to the text and graphics in your PDF document. Acrobat includes two TouchUp tools that share a single button: the TouchUp Text tool (T) that you can use to do text corrections in individual lines of text in a PDF file, and the TouchUp Object tool (Shift+T) that you can use to reposition graphics.

The single-key accelerator feature that allows keyboard shortcuts, such as pressing T to select the TouchUp Text tool, is not turned on by default in Acrobat 6. To enable single-key accelerators, choose Edit➪Preferences or press Ctrk+K (⌘+K on Mac) to open the Preferences dialog box, click General in the list box on the left to display the general options, and then select the Use Single-Key Accelerators to Access Tools check box. Finally, click OK to enable your settings. After turning on this feature, when you point to an editing tool button on the Acrobat 6 toolbars, a screen tip displays the name of the tool, as well as the key that can be pressed to quickly select the tool.

Using the TouchUp Text tool to edit text

You use the TouchUp Text tool much like the mouse cursor in a word processing program. You can either select the text containing the characters you want to edit or simply insert the cursor into the text and edit text on either side of the cursor. Thanks to Acrobat 6 support of document structure tags, you can now make much larger text selections than previously possible. The Acrobat 6 TouchUp Text tool lets you make text selections based on a heading or paragraph style tag present in the original document you converted to PDF — hopefully, a document created in an RTF (Rich Text Format) word processing program like Microsoft Word that adds these structure tags automatically. (See Chapter 1 for more on document structure tags in PDFs.) The end result is that clicking on text in a PDF document with the TouchUp Text tool displays a bounding box (also referred to as a *container*) around the text, based on its underlying document structure. You can then select any or all text within the bounding box. For example, if the text you click has tags that define it as Normal paragraph style, a bounding box appears around the whole paragraph, indicating that you can select any part or the entire paragraph for editing. This is great progress for a program that until recently only allowed you to select one line of text at a time for editing.

When you select the TouchUp Text tool on the Advanced Editing toolbar, the mouse pointer changes to an I-beam. Click the I-beam on a line or block of text where you need to make your first edit. When you click, Acrobat encloses the text in a bounding box defined by the underlying document structure tag, as shown in Figure 10-1. You can select any or all the text within the bounding box by dragging the I-beam through the desired text.

Figure 10-1:
Selecting
text within a
document
structure
bounding
box to make
edits with
the TouchUp
Text tool.

To make editing changes to the surrounding characters when you insert the
I-beam into text, use one of the following techniques:

✔ To insert new characters at the insertion point, just type the characters.

✔ To delete characters to the immediate right of the insertion point, press
the Delete key.

✔ To delete characters to the immediate left of the insertion point, press
the Backspace key.

✔ To restore characters deleted in error or remove ones incorrectly
inserted, press Ctrl+Z (⌘+Z on the Mac), your good ol' trusty Undo key.
Note that Acrobat 6 now supports multiple levels of undo.

To make editing changes to text you've selected by dragging the I-beam
cursor, use one of the following techniques:

✔ To replace the text you've selected with new text, just begin typing.

✔ To delete selected text, press the Delete key or right-click the text selection and choose Delete on the context menu.

Editing text from the context menu

When text is selected, you can also edit it using the options available on its context menu. To open selected text's context menu, right-click (Control+click on the Mac) the text with the TouchUp Text tool. The context menu includes the following options:

- ✔ **Cut:** Removes selected text from the PDF document and adds it to the Clipboard.

- ✔ **Copy:** Copies selected text to the Clipboard.

- ✔ **Paste:** Inserts text stored in the Clipboard into selected text or onto the current document page if no text is selected.

- ✔ **Delete:** Removes selected text.

- ✔ **Select All:** Selects all text within a bounding box on the current document page.

- ✔ **Select None:** Deselects all text within a bounding box on the current document page.

- ✔ **Create/Delete Artifact:** Designates or deletes text or an object in a PDF as either a Page (such as printing crop marks), Pagination (such as page numbers), or Layout (such as dividing lines between columns of text or footnotes) Artifact that may or may not be included in the document when it is repurposed in another format. For example, you may want printer's marks on a PDF that will be printed, but not on the same PDF repurposed as a Web page.

- ✔ **Insert:** Inserts various formatting elements into your text selection that improve the flow of text when you right-click and choose the desired element on the Insert submenu. Options available are: Line Break, Soft Hyphen (that is, one that disappears when the word doesn't break across two lines), Non-Breaking Space (a space that keeps hyphenated words together on the same line at all times), and Em Dash (a longer-than-usual dash usually equal to the width of the letter M in the selected text that does permit line breaks across words).

When you finish editing text, click the Hand tool to ensure that you don't inadvertently select other lines of text and do unintentional editing to them. Just be aware that you can't use your good ol' H keystroke shortcut to select the Hand tool because this only succeeds in typing the letter *h* in the line!

Remember that some PDF files use the restrictions in the Changes Allowed security option to prevent anyone from making further editing changes. When this option is in effect in your document, you can't get the TouchUp Text tool to select any text in the PDF document no matter how hard you click.

Modifying text attributes

Provided that you have the font (or someone's been nice enough to have embedded it in the PDF document for you), you can modify the attributes of the characters that you highlight with the insertion point in text selected with the TouchUp Text tool. Note that if your system doesn't have the font and it hasn't been embedded, Acrobat displays a nice little alert dialog box saying, `Warning. You cannot edit text in this font`.

After selecting text within a bounding box, right-click and choose Properties on the context menu to open the TouchUp Properties dialog box with the Text tab already selected, as shown in Figure 10-2. This dialog box contains the following attribute options that you can change:

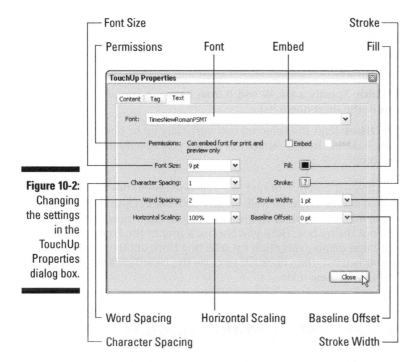

Figure 10-2:
Changing the settings in the TouchUp Properties dialog box.

✔ **Font:** Specify a new font for the selected text from the Font drop-down list.

✔ **Embed:** Embed the font displayed in the Font drop-down list and, if desired, its subset fonts (Italic, Bold, and so on) in the PDF document.

Note that the default Permissions, Can Embed Font for Print and Preview Only, appear in the area to the left of the Embed button. This setting allows you to embed or unembed a font and its subsets. Permissions settings may differ depending on the security put in place by the author of the PDF document. See Chapter 11 for more on PDF file security settings.

- ✓ **Font Size:** Specify a new font size for the selected text in the Font Size drop-down list.

- ✓ **Character Spacing (also known as *tracking*):** Uniformly adjust the spacing between more than two characters selected in the text by the amount you specify in this drop-down list box.

- ✓ **Word Spacing:** Uniformly adjust the spacing between two or more words selected in the text by the value (in thousandths of an em space) you specify in this drop-down list box.

- ✓ **Horizontal Scaling:** Horizontally compress or expand the selected text by the percentage you enter in this drop-down list box.

- ✓ **Fill:** Specify a new fill color (interior color) for the selected font on the color palette.

- ✓ **Stroke:** Pick a new stroke color (outline color) for the selected font on the color palette.

- ✓ **Stroke Width:** Specify a stroke width from between 1point and 4 point thickness in the drop-down list.

- ✓ **Baseline Offset:** Shift the selected text vertically up or down in relation to the text baseline by the number of points you specify in this drop-down list box.

In addition to allowing you to edit text in a PDF document, the TouchUp Text tool also lets you add new text as well. Simply Ctrl+click (Option+click on Mac) the area in a PDF document where you want to enter new text to open the New Text Font dialog box. Here you choose a font in the Font drop-down list, choose the text display direction by selecting Horizontal or Vertical in the Mode drop-down list, then click OK to close the New Text Font dialog box and begin typing your new text.

Touching up your graphic images

You can use the TouchUp Object tool to select graphic images or other objects that have been embedded in a PDF document. This tool uses an arrowhead with a tiny square icon. You can switch between selecting the TouchUp Text tool and the TouchUp Object tool from the Advanced Editing toolbar by pressing Shift+T. As you hold the Shift key and press T, the arrowhead icon used by the TouchUp Object tool and outlined T icon used by the TouchUp Text tool toggle between one another on the toolbar.

To select a graphic with the TouchUp Object tool, you simply click it with the arrowhead pointer. After a graphic is selected (indicated by a gray bounding box around the image or object — there are no sizing handles because you can't resize graphics in Acrobat), you can then reposition it by dragging its outline to the new position before you release the mouse button. You can also nudge a selected graphic image with the arrow keys: Just press the ←, →, ↑, and ↓ keys to move the graphic by small increments until it's in the desired position.

To select more than one graphic image or object on the page at the same time, Shift+click each object. To select a group of graphic images or objects on the page, drag the TouchUp Object tool to draw a bounding box around all the graphics to select them all together.

When you're trying to move charts and graphs embedded on the document page (especially those originally generated in a spreadsheet program like Microsoft Excel), drag a bounding box around the entire chart to ensure that you select all the components (such charts are actually composed of a whole bunch of individual graphic objects) before you attempt to reposition it on the document page.

Using the layout grid in repositioning graphics

Acrobat has a layout grid that you can use to help you in repositioning graphic images. To turn on the display of the layout grid in the PDF document, choose View➪Grid or press Ctrl+U (⌘+U on the Mac).

When working with the layout grid, you can modify the default grid settings in the Units & Guides section of the Preferences dialog box by pressing Ctrl+K (⌘+K on the Mac) and then clicking Units and Guides in the list box on the left. The Layout Grid section of the dialog box contains a number of grid options that you can change:

- ✔ By default, Acrobat subdivides each of the major grid squares into three divisions across and three down, making a total of nine little subdivisions. To increase the number of squares in each of the major grid squares, increase the value in the Subdivisions text box.

- ✔ To offset the layout grid in relation to the top and left margin of the page, enter a value in the Grid Offset from Left Edge and the Grid Offset from Top Edge text boxes.

- ✔ By default, Acrobat makes each major grid square one-inch square with one inch between their vertical lines and one inch between their horizontal lines. To make the major grid squares larger so that there are fewer, farther apart, increase the values in the Width Between Lines and Height Between Lines text boxes. To make the grid squares smaller so that there are more, closer together, decrease the values in these text boxes. Note, however, that if you decrease the values in these text boxes too much, Acrobat is no longer able to subdivide the square using the value entered in the Subdivisions text box.

✔ By default, Acrobat colors the lines in the layout grid blue. To select a new color for all grid lines, click the Grid Line Color button and then click the desired color in the color palette.

Editing graphic images from the context menu

When a graphic is selected, you can also edit it using the options available on its context menu. To open a graphic's context menu, right-click (Control+click on the Mac) the image with the TouchUp Object tool. These context menu options include many of the same options as the context menu for selected text (see the "Modifying text attributes" section for the complete list). The following items on the context menu for selected graphics differ from the context menu for selected text:

✔ **Delete:** Removes the selected image and places it in the Recycle Bin (Trash on the Mac).

✔ **Delete Clip:** Removes any objects that are *clipping* the selected image (that is, cutting off part of the image in some way). This feature is grayed-out if no clipping occurs in the current document.

✔ **Select All:** Selects all graphic objects on the current document page.

✔ **Select None:** Deselects all graphic objects on the current document page.

✔ **Edit Image:** Opens the selected graphic in the default image-editing program. When a graphic object is selected, this option changes to Edit Object, and choosing it opens the object in the default page/object editing program. When multiple graphic objects are selected, this option becomes Edit Objects. When no graphic images are selected, this option becomes Edit Page, and choosing it opens the object in the default page/object editing program as well.

When you choose the Edit Image/Object(s)/Page option, Acrobat attempts to launch the program specified as the image editor or the page/object editor in the TouchUp section of the Preferences dialog box and open the selected image or graphic object in the application for editing. If Acrobat cannot launch the specified program, its displays an alert dialog box that informs you of this fact.

To specify a new program as the default image editor or the page/object editor, press Ctrl+K (⌘+K) to open the Preferences dialog box. Then click TouchUp in the list box on the left. To select a new image editor, such as Photoshop 7.0, click the Choose Image Editor button. The Choose Image Editor dialog box appears; open the folder that contains the application, select its program icon, and click the Open button. To select a new page/object editor, such as Illustrator 10, click the Choose Page/Object Editor button. In the Choose Page/Object Editor dialog box, open the folder that contains this application, select its program icon, and click the Open button.

When using programs like Photoshop 7.0 and Illustrator 10 as your image editing and graphics object editing programs, respectively, you can make your changes in the programs launched from Acrobat 6 with the Edit Image or Edit Object command, and then, when you save your editing changes to the image or graphic in these programs, they are automatically updated in your PDF document.

Figure 10-3 illustrates this relationship. Here, you see the editing changes I made to the photo image of the Tibetan countryside in Photoshop 7.0 (launched by right-clicking the photo in the PDF document and then clicking Edit Image on the context menu) saved not only in Photoshop 7.0 shown in the foreground but also automatically saved in the PDF document in the background.

Figure 10-3: Edits saved to an image in Photoshop 7.0 are automatically updated in the PDF document.

Page-Editing Practices

Acrobat makes it easy for you to perform a number of routine page edits on one or more pages of a PDF document. Possible page edits can include rotating and cropping the pages, replacing pages from another PDF document, inserting a new page, deleting pages, and reordering the pages in the document, as well as assigning page numbers. You find all the commands to make these types of page edits on the Options pop-up menu at the top of the Pages palette in the Navigation pane.

When you're using the Pages palette to navigate or edit pages, you can display more thumbnails of the pages in this palette by selecting the Reduce Page Thumbnails option at the bottom of the Pages palette Options pop-up menu. You can also increase the number of thumbnails visible by dragging the border between the Navigation and Document panes with the double-headed arrow to the right to make the pane wider.

Rotating pages

Sometimes, you end up dealing with a PDF document that contains one or more sections whose pages need to be reoriented (perhaps switched from portrait to landscape mode) to better suit their text and graphics. To rotate pages in a PDF document, you select the Rotate Pages command on the Pages palette Options pop-up menu or choose Document⇨Pages⇨Rotate on the menu bar. (Don't confuse this command with the Rotate View command found on the View menu, which rotates all the pages in the current PDF document for viewing.) When you choose Rotate Pages, Acrobat displays the Rotate Pages dialog box, as shown in Figure 10-4.

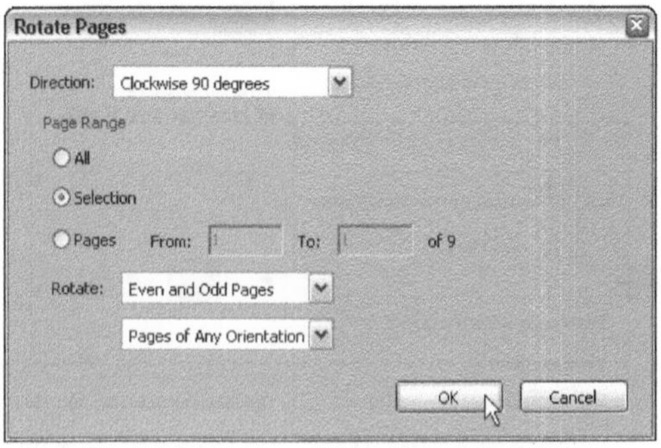

Figure 10-4:
Rotating some pages in the PDF document in the Rotate Pages dialog box.

Rotate Pages

Direction: Clockwise 90 degrees

Page Range

○ All
◉ Selection
○ Pages   From: 1   To: 1   of 9

Rotate: Even and Odd Pages
         Pages of Any Orientation

OK   Cancel

You can select from the following options in the Rotate Pages dialog box to change the orientation of the desired page or pages:

- ✔ **Direction:** Choose to rotate the image Clockwise 90 degrees, Counterclockwise 90 degrees, or 180 degrees.

- ✔ **Page Range:** Determine which pages to rotate: Select the All radio button to rotate all pages, the Selection radio button to rotate only the page(s) selected in the Pages palette, or the Pages radio button to rotate the range you specify in the From and To text boxes.

- ✔ **Rotate:** Limit what type of pages in the designated page range to rotate with these two drop-down lists. You can choose Even and Odd Pages, Even Pages Only, or Odd Pages Only from the top drop-down list. From the bottom drop-down list, you can select Pages of Any Orientation, Landscape Pages, or Portrait Pages.

Cropping pages

On occasion, you may find that you need to crop one or more pages whose overall page dimensions conflict with the others in the PDF document. Acrobat offers two methods for doing this: You can crop pages in the Crop Pages dialog box, where you must specify the values of the crop margins, or with the Crop tool on the Editing toolbar, where you draw the crop marks right on the page.

To open the Crop Pages dialog box, select the Crop Pages command on the Pages palette Options pop-up menu or choose Document➪Pages➪Crop on the menu bar. When you do this, Acrobat displays the Crop Pages dialog box, as shown in Figure 10-5.

You can then select from the following options in the Crop Pages dialog box to resize the desired page or pages:

- ✔ **Page Display:** Specify different types of clipping paths for the cropping operation in this drop-down list: Crop Box (defines display and printing by the Crop tool), Bleed Box (defines, for professional printing, where a bleed area is included to allow for paper trimming or folding), Trim Box (defines the finished dimension of the page after cropping), or Art Box (defines page contents that include white space).

  Note that each page display option is defined by a different color box in the page preview of the Crop Pages dialog box. Selecting the Show All Boxes check box displays all defined display options in preview. Deselecting this check box displays each display option individually when selected in the Page Display drop-down list.

✓ **Crop Margins:** Specify how much to cut off the page from the top, left, right, and bottom margins by typing a number in the associated text boxes or by using the toggle buttons. Select the Remove White Margins check box to have Acrobat figure out the crop margins by removing all the white space around the text and graphics on the specified pages. Click the Set to Zero button to restore all margin values to zero. Click the Revert to Selection button to use the dimensions of the previously used cropping rectangle. Select a measuring unit (Inches is the default) in the Set Values drop-down list.

✓ **Page Range:** Determine which pages you want to crop. Select the All radio button to crop all pages, the Selection radio button to crop only the page(s) selected in the Pages palette or the Pages radio to crop the range you specify in the From and To text boxes.

✓ **Crop:** Limit what type of pages are cropped in the selected range by choosing Even and Odd Pages, Odd Pages Only, or Even Pages Only.

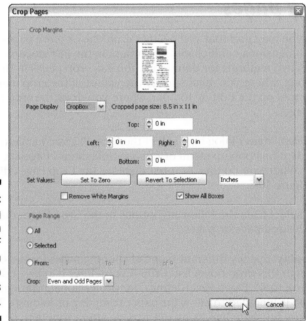

Figure 10-5:
Cropping
a page in
the PDF
document in
the Crop
Pages
dialog box.

To use the Crop tool to do the cropping, follow these steps:

1. **Click the Actual Size button on the Viewing toolbar and, if necessary, the Single Page button on the status bar of the Document pane.**

2. **Click the Crop tool on the Advanced Editing toolbar.**

3. **Use the cross-hair mouse pointer to draw a bounding box that marks out the approximate cropping margins and then release the mouse button.**

   Acrobat responds by placing sizing handles at the four corners of the bounding box.

4. **If necessary, use the double-arrow mouse pointer on the edges or corners of the cropping bounding box to adjust the crop margins.**

5. **Double-click the arrowhead pointer somewhere within the bounding box.**

   The Crop Pages dialog box (refer to Figure 10-5) opens.

6. **If necessary, adjust the values in the Top, Left, Right, and Bottom text boxes in the Crop Margins section of the dialog box.**

7. **If you want to crop more than just the current page in the document, specify the page range in the Page Range section of the Crop Pages dialog box.**

8. **Click OK to crop the page(s) to the specified crop margins.**

Replacing pages from other PDF files

Every now and then in editing a PDF document, you come across a situation where you need to replace just certain pages in the file. Keep in mind when you're replacing an original page with an updated version that only the text and graphics on the original page are replaced by those on the updated page. All interactive elements associated with the original page remain and carry over to the updated page (this could potentially cause problems if the links carried over from the original page no longer match up with buttons or linked text in the updated version).

As with cropping pages, Acrobat offers you two different ways to replace a page or pages in a PDF document. In the first method, you open just the document, select the page or pages to be replaced, and then use the Replace Pages command to specify the PDF document (which doesn't have to be open) and the page or pages in it to replace the selected pages. In the second method, you use a variation of drag-and-drop, where you drag a thumbnail of the replacement page from its Pages palette onto the page it's replacing in its Pages palette (of course, to do this, you must have both documents open, tiled side by side, with both of their Pages palettes selected).

Use the first method when you're sure (without looking) which pages in what PDF document to use as the replacements for the currently selected pages. Use the second method when you want to have a visual check as you make the replacements in your PDF document. The steps for using the first method with the Replace Pages command are as follows:

1. **Open the document that has the page or pages that need replacing in Acrobat 6; make sure that all changes are saved in the file.**

   If you're not sure if the changes have been saved, choose File➪Save.

2. **Open the Pages palette in the Navigation pane and select the thumbnail(s) of the page or pages that need replacing (Shift+click to select multiple pages).**

3. **Select Replace Pages on the Options menu at the top of the Pages palette.**

   The Select File with New Pages dialog box opens.

4. **Open the folder and select the file icon of the PDF document that contains the replacement pages, and then click the Select button.**

   The Replace Pages dialog box opens.

5. **Check the page numbers that appear in the Replace Pages and To text boxes in the Original section of the dialog box to make sure that they represent the one(s) you mean to replace.**

6. **Enter the page number of the first page of the replacement range in the With Pages text box.**

   Acrobat replaces the same number of pages from the replacement PDF as are designated in the Replace Pages range.

7. **Click the OK button.**

   The Acrobat alert dialog box appears, asking you to confirm the replacements. Click the Yes button to make the replacements.

Be aware that you can't use the Undo command to undo a replacement that's gone wrong. If you mess up, choose File➪Revert to reopen the original PDF document with all of its pages intact (and send me a thank-you for reminding you to save the document in Step 1).

To replace pages by dragging and dropping them in place, follow these steps:

1. **Open both PDF documents: the one with the pages to be replaced and the one with the replacement pages.**

   In both documents, click the Fit Width button on the Zoom toolbar and click the Pages tab if the Pages palette is not displayed in the Navigation pane.

2. **Choose Window➪Tile➪Vertically or press Ctrl+Shift+L (⌘+Shift+L on the Mac).**

3. **In the window with the page or pages to be replaced, scroll the Navigation pane so that the thumbnail of the first page to be replaced is visible.**

4. **In the window with the replacement page or pages, select the thumbnails of the replacement page or pages (starting with the first replacement page).**

   Shift+click or drag a bounding box around the thumbnails to select a series of pages.

5. **Drag the arrowhead mouse pointer from the Pages palette with the selected replacement thumbnail(s) to the Pages palette with the pages to be replaced.**

6. **Position the mouse pointer over the number at the bottom of the first thumbnail to be replaced and then release the mouse button.**

   You can tell when you've reached the right spot because the number and the page thumbnail become highlighted, along with any subsequent pages in the palette that are to be replaced. As soon as you release the mouse button, Acrobat makes whatever page replacements are necessary to bring in all the pages you selected before dragging.

As with the first method, if you discover that you replaced the wrong pages, choose the File➪Revert command to put the pages back where they were.

Replacing and adding PDF pages through Acrobat can result in a not-so-obvious problem involving files that have font subsets.

When you insert or replace pages containing those fonts, Acrobat automatically includes all the font subsets in the resulting file. If you do a lot of inserting and replacing, you can end up with a lot of redundant font subsets that can't be removed from the file. Mild to severe bloat can happen, depending on how may subsets are involved.

To cure this problem, choose Advanced➪PDF Optimizer. On the PDF Optimizer dialog box that appears, click the Fonts tab, use the Move buttons to unembed any redundant font subset, and then click OK to optimize your PDF file.

Inserting and deleting pages

Instead of replacing pages, you may just find that you need to insert a new page or group of pages in the PDF document. When inserting new pages, you can choose between similar methods as when replacing pages. You can insert all the pages from an unopened PDF file using the Insert Pages command, or you can use the side-by-side, drag-and-drop method to insert one or more individual pages. The big difference between these two insertion methods is that in the dialog box method, you must insert all the pages from the incoming PDF file. In the drag-and-drop method, you can insert a single page or a limited group of pages.

Follow these steps to insert all the pages in a single PDF file:

1. **Open the document in which you want to insert the new pages; make sure that all your changes are saved.**

   If you're not sure if the changes have been saved, choose File⇨Save.

2. **Choose Insert Pages on the Options menu at the top of the Pages palette.**

   The Select File to Insert dialog box opens.

3. **Open the folder and select the file icon of the PDF document with the pages you want to insert, and then click the Select button.**

   The Insert Pages dialog box opens.

4. **In the Page area, click one of the following radio buttons:**

   • **First:** Inserts the pages at the beginning of the PDF document, either before or after the first page.

   • **Last:** Inserts the pages at the end of the file, either before or after the last page.

   • **Page:** Inserts the pages either before or after the page number designated in the associated text box.

   By default, Acrobat inserts the pages after the page you specify in the Page portion of the Insert Pages dialog box. To have the pages inserted in front instead, select Before on the Location drop-down list.

5. **Click the OK button to have Acrobat insert the pages from the selected file.**

To use the drag-and-drop method for inserting one or more pages in a document, you use the same setup as described in the preceding section, "Replacing pages from other PDF files." Place the two documents in Fit Width view side by side with both their Pages palettes displayed. Then select the thumbnail of the page or pages to be inserted and drag them to Pages palette of the document in which copies are to be placed.

The only difference between this method and replacing pages with drag-and-drop is that you position the mouse pointer *in between* the thumbnails at the place where you want the newly inserted pages to appear (and never on a thumbnail's page number). You can tell you've hit the right spot because an insertion bar (like the one shown in Figure 10-6) appears in the Pages palette to let you know where the copies of the incoming pages are about to be inserted. You also notice that a plus sign appears at the arrowhead pointer, indicating that copies of the pages will be inserted as soon as you release the mouse button.

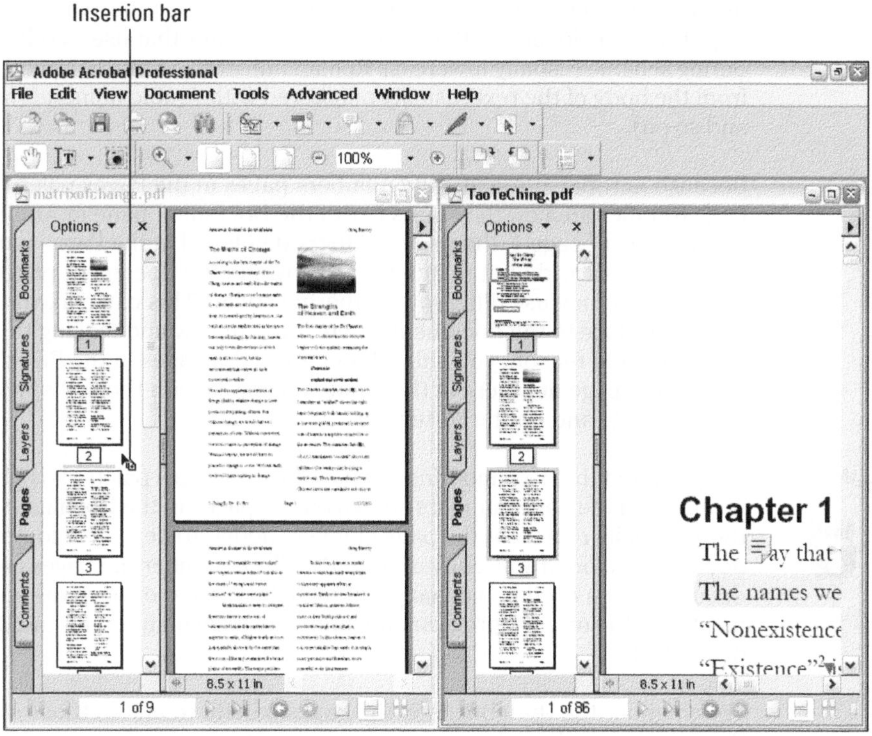

Insertion bar

Figure 10-6:
Inserting a
page by
dropping its
thumbnail in
the new
document's
Pages
palette.

Reordering the pages

You can rearrange the order of the pages in a PDF document just by relocating their page thumbnails in the Pages palette. Just drag the page thumbnail to its new place in the Pages palette and drop it into place when its insertion bar appears either ahead of the thumbnail of the page it is to proceed in the document or immediately after the thumbnail of the page it is to trail.

Keep in mind that when you're reordering pages, you can move a range of pages at a time by selecting a series of thumbnails with the Shift+click method before you drag them to their new position in the Pages palette.

Renumbering the thumbnail pages

You can use Acrobat's Page Numbering feature to renumber the pages in the Pages palette to match the page numbers shown on the pages of the document in the Document window. You need to do this, for example, when you're dealing with a PDF document that contains front matter that uses a different numbering scheme (usually lowercase Roman numerals as in i, ii, iii, and so on) from the body of the text (usually numbered with Arabic numerals as in 1, 2, 3, and so on).

Because Acrobat automatically numbers pages in the Pages palette and in the Page Number area on the status bar of the Document pane in Arabic numerals, starting at page 1, the page numbers displayed in the Pages palette and on the status bar do not match those shown in the document pages themselves when they use different numbering styles. This can make it harder to find your place in the document when doing review and making touchup edits. For that reason, you should renumber the pages in the PDF document so that the page numbers in the document agree with those displayed in the Pages palette and on the status bar.

Keep in mind that renumbering the pages in the Pages palette has absolutely no effect on the page numbers shown on the pages in the Document pane, as these actually represent the page numbers added to header or footer of the document before it was converted to PDF. To renumber the pages of a PDF document, you need to manually edit them in Acrobat or open the source document with the original program, updating the page numbering, and then re-distill the file.

To renumber the thumbnails in the Pages palette to match those shown on the pages of the PDF document, take these steps:

1. **Select Number Pages on the Options menu at the top of the Pages palette.**

   The Page Numbering dialog box opens, as shown in Figure 10-7.

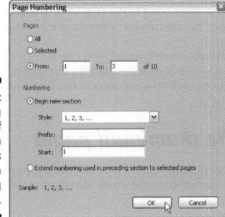

Figure 10-7:
Renumbering
sections of
pages with
the options
in the Page
Numbering
dialog box.

2. **Choose how you want to renumber the pages.**

   To renumber all the pages in the document, click the All radio button. To renumber only the pages that you've selected in the Pages palette, leave the Selected radio button chosen. To renumber a specific range of pages, select the From radio button and then enter the first page number in the From text box and the last page number in the To text box.

   To change the numbering style for the specified range, leave the Begin New Section radio button selected. To continue numbering when a range of pages is specified, click the Extend Numbering Used in Preceding Section to Selected Pages radio button.

3. **When you're beginning a new numbering section, select the numbering style on the Style drop-down list, specify any prefix to be used in the number (for example, 2- when you want the numbers to appear as 2-1, 2-2, 2-3, and so on) in the Prefix text box, and enter the beginning number in the Start text box if the section numbering begins at a number higher than 1.**

4. **Click OK to renumber the pages as specified.**

Adding Headers and Footers to a PDF Document

Acrobat 6 provides a new feature that enables you to add header and footer information (such as document title, date, time, or page numbers) to the top and bottom margins in a PDF document. This feature is especially useful when editing PDF documents that weren't created using PDFMaker 6.0, which has the ability to convert header and footer information from the original document. See Chapter 5 for more on creating PDF files with PDFMaker 6.0.

To add a header or footer to your PDF document, follow these steps:

1. **Choose Document➪Add Headers & Footers.**

   The Add Headers & Footers dialog box opens, as shown in Figure 10-8.

2. **Click the Header or Footer tab, depending on which element you want to add to your PDF document.**

   The procedure is the same for either option.

3. **Click in one of the three alignment boxes (on the left, center, or right at the top of the dialog box) to specify where the header/footer information is displayed in the PDF document.**

   Note that these boxes correspond to the Align buttons and can be selected via these buttons as well.

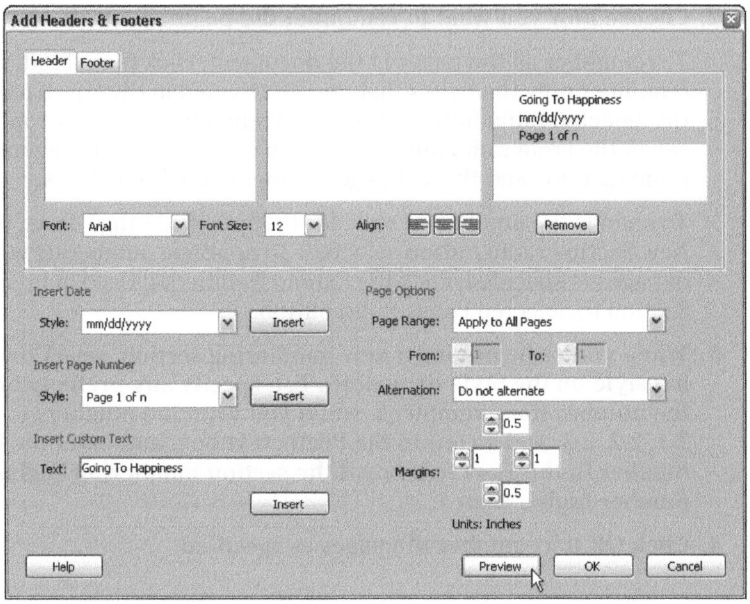

Figure 10-8:
Setting up
headers and
footers in
the Add
Headers &
Footers
dialog box.

4. **Choose a font and font size in the appropriate drop-down list.**

5. **Choose a date style in the Style drop-down list in the Insert Date section of the dialog box and click the Insert button to insert the date in a header/footer.**

6. **Choose a page number style in the Style drop-down list in the Insert Page Number section of the dialog box and click the Insert button to insert page numbers in a header/footer.**

7. **Enter text in the Text box in the Insert Custom Text section of the dialog box and click the Insert button to insert your own text in a header/footer.**

8. **Select from the options in the Page Options area of the Add Headers & Footers dialog box as follows:**

   • **Page Range:** Select Apply to All Pages or Apply to Page Range in the drop-down list to specify on which pages the header/footer appears. If you select Apply to Page Range, specify the page range in the From and To text boxes below.

   • **Alternation:** Choose either Even Pages Only or Odd Pages Only in the drop-down list to specify the display of the header/footer on even or odd pages or choose Do Not Alternate to bypass this feature.

   • **Margins:** Specify white space around the header/footer either by clicking the spinner buttons or by entering values in the text boxes in the Margins area.

9. **When you're finished setting up a header/footer, click the Preview button to preview your header/footer and then click OK to return to the Add Headers & Footers dialog box.**

10. **Click OK to insert your new header or footer.**

Headers and footers can be edited in a number of ways by selecting their Date, Page Number, or Custom Text elements in the alignment boxes in which they appear and then using the Remove and Insert buttons. For example, to change the position of a header/footer element, select the Date, Page Number, or Custom text element in the alignment box that it appears in, and then click the appropriate Align button to change its position. To delete a selected element, click the Remove button. After deleting an unwanted header/footer element, you can then create new ones by specifying Date, Page Number, or Custom Text parameters and using the Insert and Align buttons to position them in the header/footer.

You can Undo and Redo headers and footers created in a single session, meaning any you've created before clicking OK to close the Add Headers & Footers dialog box, by choosing Edit⇨Undo Headers/Footers or Edit⇨Redo Headers/Footers. If you created headers or footers at different times, you can repeat these commands to Undo or Redo headers/footers from previous Task sessions.

Adding Watermarks and Backgrounds to PDF Documents

Acrobat 6 now supports document layers created in AutoCAD or Microsoft Visio (see the "Editing Document Layers in a PDF File" section, later in this chapter). One of the benefits of this new functionality is the ability to add watermarks and background images to a PDF document. Just remember that you can't edit watermarks and background layers in Acrobat 6 as you can with AutoCAD or Visio layers.

A watermark in the non-digital world is a faint image impressed on paper during manufacture that appears when the paper is held up to the light, such as the company logo you see on fine manuscript paper. They are also used as a security measure, such as the word "Sample" across a photo that makes it difficult to reproduce, or the authenticating images you find on traveler's checks and the like. In Acrobat 6, watermarks are placed in a layer on top of the displayed page. Background images are the color, texture, or pattern placed in a layer behind the displayed page. Note that an image must be converted to PDF in order for it to be used as a watermark or background in Acrobat 6. For more on creating PDF files from graphic formats, see Chapter 4.

To add a watermark or background image to a PDF document, follow these steps:

1. **Choose Document⇨Add Watermark & Background.**

   The Add Watermark & Background dialog box appears, as shown in Figure 10-9.

2. **Choose the desired page element in the Type area by clicking either the Add a Background (Appears Behind the Page) or the Add a Watermark (Appears on Top of the Page) radio button.**

   Note that the settings in this dialog box are the same for both water-marks and backgrounds.

3. **Select one or both viewing options in the Type area.**

   To display the watermark/background when viewing the PDF document on your computer screen, select the Show When Displaying On Screen check box. To display the watermark/background when the PDF docu-ment is printed, select the Show When Printing check box.

4. **Click the Browse button in the Source Page area to locate the PDF document you want to use for your background or watermark.**

   If the source PDF is a multi-page document, use the Page Number text box to identify which page you want to select as your source.

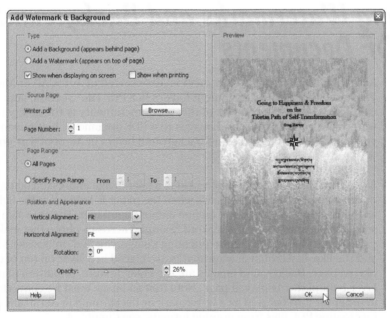

Figure 10-9:
Setting up a water-mark or background in the Add Water-mark & Background dialog box.

5. **Click the All Pages radio button in the Page Range area to have the watermark/background appear on all the pages in your document.**

   If you want to be choosier, click the Specify Page Range radio button and then enter a range of pages in the From and To text boxes.

6. **From the Vertical Alignment drop-down list in the Position and Appearance area, choose Top, Center, Bottom, or Fit to specify the vertical placement of your watermark/background on the page.**

   Note that all changes made in the Position and Appearance are displayed in the Preview window on the right side of the Add Watermark & Background dialog box.

7. **From the Horizontal Alignment drop-down list in the Position and Appearance area, choose Left, Center, Right, or Fit to specify the horizontal placement of your watermark/background on the page.**

8. **Click the Rotation spinner button to rotate the watermark/background on the page; use the Opacity slider button or enter a percentage value in the text box to increase or decrease the opacity of the watermark/background.**

   The preview window really helps with these two options.

9. **When you're finished tweaking your watermark/background, click OK to close the Add Watermark & Background dialog box and view your changes in the current PDF document.**

You can remove or restore deleted watermarks and backgrounds by choosing Edit➪Undo Background or Undo Add Watermark to remove a watermark/background. Choose Edit➪Redo Add Background or Add Watermark to restore a deleted watermark/background.

Adding Articles to a PDF Document

Although Acrobat's editing features do not enable you to physically restructure the layout of the text in a PDF document in any way, its Articles feature does enable you to restructure the online reading experience. As an essential part of the Accessibility features included in Acrobat 6, articles are designed to make the reading of long, disjointed sections of text, especially those set in newspaper columns that span pages, a smooth experience in Acrobat 6 or Adobe Reader 6.

Articles accomplish this by breaking up sections of text into discrete blocks that are displayed in sequence as you click the Hand pointer, requiring no scrolling and no resetting of the page view. This eliminates the need for you to interrupt your reading experience with any type of scrolling or any other kind of page manipulation in order to get to the following section of text, a common experience in normal online reading where when you reach the end of one column, you must reset the page by scrolling back up (and often over) to continue reading at the top of the next column.

Defining articles

To add articles to a PDF document you're editing, you divide a section of text into blocks by enclosing them in a series of boxes (invisible to the user when he or she reads the article) that control the sequence in which the text blocks are displayed in the Document pane. This sequence of boxes creates a navigation path through the text formally known as an *article thread*. You use the Article tool on the Editing toolbar in Acrobat 6 to draw the succession of boxes that create the article thread and define its order.

To define a new article in a PDF document, follow these steps:

1. **Open the PDF document to which you want to add an article.**

2. **If the Navigation pane is open, press F6 to close it.**

3. **If the page view is not in Fit Page and Continuous page mode, click the Fit Page button on the Zoom toolbar and the Continuous button on the status bar of the Document pane.**

4. **Click the Article tool button (the one with a serpentine arrow icon) on the Advanced Editing toolbar, and then drag the cross-hair pointer to draw a bounding box that encloses the first block of text in the article (including all the text up to any excluded element, such as a figure you don't want included or the end of the column).**

5. **After you have the first text block outlined in the bounding box, release the mouse button to add the first article box.**

   This article box is labeled 1-1 at the top with sizing handles around the perimeter and a continuation tab (with a plus sign) at the bottom (see Figure 10-10). Note that the mouse pointer changes from a cross-hair to the Article pointer (with a serpentine arrow).

6. **Scroll the page as required to position the Article pointer in the upper-left corner of the next block of text to be added to the article, and then drag the pointer to draw a bounding box around its text. Release the mouse button.**

   The second article box, which is labeled 1-2, is created (see Figure 10-11).

7. **Repeat Steps 4 through 6, adding as many article boxes as are required to define the reading path of the article.**

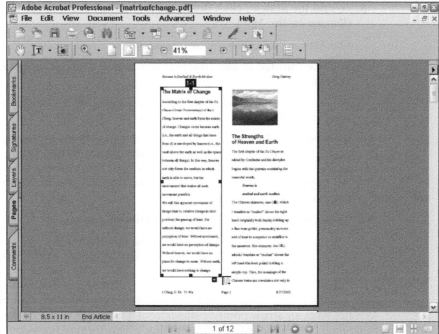

Figure 10-10:
Defining the
first article
box in the
article with
the Article
tool.

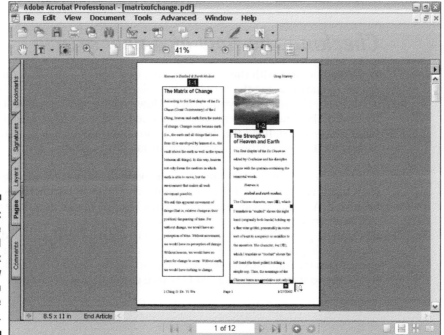

Figure 10-11:
Defining the
second
article box
in the new
article with
the Article
pointer.

8. **To end the article, click the Hand tool (H) or press the Enter key (Return on the Mac).**

   The Article Properties dialog box opens.

9. **Replace Untitled in the Title text box with a descriptive name for the article.**

   This name is displayed in the Articles palette that enables users to select the articles they want to read — see Chapter 2 for details.

10. **If you want, add a brief description of the contents of the new article in the Subject text box, the name of the author in the Author text box, and key terms, separated by commas, that describe the contents in the Keywords text box (terms that you can use in searching the PDF document).**

11. **Click OK to close the Article Properties dialog box.**

    If you pressed the Enter key (Return on the Mac) to end the article, click the Hand tool or press H to select the Hand pointer, which hides all the article boxes in the article.

Note that as soon as you select the Hand tool after defining a new article, Acrobat adds an arrow pointing down from a crossbar to the back of the Hand icon (which looks like a tattoo to me). This form of the Hand icon appears whenever a user positions the Hand pointer over an article that you've defined in a PDF document.

Checking the flow of a new article

This Hand pointer with the arrow pointing down from a crossbar enables the reader to start reading the article at any place he or she chooses. You can use it to check the flow of your article. However, because you're currently at the end of the new article you've just defined, you need to go back to the place where you defined the first article box before you click it, so that you can check the flow of the entire article from start to finish.

Before you click this pointer and start checking the flow of the article, you may want to adjust the default fit-visible zoom magnification setting that's currently in effect in Acrobat, because all articles in a PDF document apply the default fit-visible zoom magnification setting to any article that you're reading. To change this setting, press Ctrl+K (⌘+K on the Mac) to open the Preferences dialog box, click Page Display in the list box on the left, and enter an appropriate percentage value in the Max Fit Visible Zoom text box at the bottom of the dialog box (this starts out at a whopping 800%) before clicking OK.

To check the flow of the article, click the Hand pointer with the arrow pointing down from a crossbar somewhere in the text of the first article box, and then continue to click the Hand pointer (which loses the crossbar while retaining the downward-pointing arrow) to view in succession each portion of every article box in the article. Acrobat lets you know when you've reached the end of the article (the last visible portion of the last article box) by adding a crossbar at the bottom of the downward-pointing arrow on the Hand pointer. When you click this Hand pointer, Acrobat returns you to the top of the article, and the page resumes the magnification setting currently in effect in the Document window (as shown in the Magnification text box on the Zoom toolbar).

Editing Document Layers in a PDF File

Now that Acrobat 6 supports document layers created in programs such as AutoCAD, Microsoft Visio, and Microsoft Project, you may one day find yourself staring at a PDF document with the new Layers palette overflowing with layers, just like the one shown in Figure 10-12. Fortunately, Acrobat makes it a breeze to select, move, edit, delete, and even merge and flatten document layers. Note that you can *view* document layers in either the Standard or Professional versions of Acrobat 6. If you want to *edit* document layers, you must have Acrobat 6 Professional version.

The good news is that Acrobat treats visible text and graphic objects on document layers in exactly the same way as regular objects in PDF documents. This means that even though a portion or even a whole object may reside on different document layers, Acrobat views the object as a single item for selection and editing. Because of this seamless view of document layers, you can apply the same tools and editing techniques to document layer objects that have been described in previous sections of this chapter. For example, you can use the TouchUp Object tool to select, move, or edit a layer object. Figure 10-12 shows the selection of all the visible chair components in the drawing using TouchUp Object tool, even though some of the furniture is drawn on different layers.

You might occasionally encounter a locked layer in a PDF document. You'll know because a padlock icon appears next to a layers name in the Layers palette in the Navigation pane. These layers were locked by the author of the original AutoCAD, Visio, or Project document and are visible for informational purposes only. You can edit the Layer name in these cases by right-clicking the layer in the Layers palette and choosing Properties on the context menu. In the Layer Properties dialog box, enter a new name in the Layer Name text box and click OK.

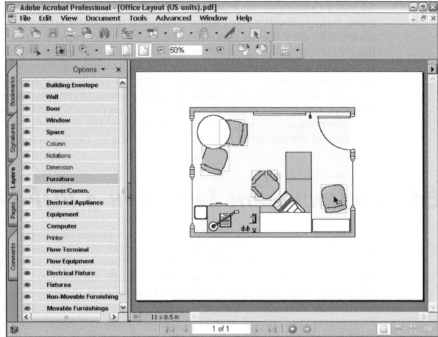

Figure 10-12:
Selecting
layer
objects with
the TouchUp
Object tool.

Flattening PDF layers

When you flatten PDF layers, you remove any layers that aren't visible and consolidate the rest into one layer. You might use this technique if you want to freeze a drawing or project at a certain stage of development in order to archive a non-editable version. To do so, follow these steps:

1. **Choose File⇨Save As to open the Save As dialog box.**

2. **Locate a folder destination in the Save In drop-down list and enter a new name for your flattened PDF document in the File Name text box.**

   It is very important that you change the name of this file because flattening the layers in a PDF document *cannot* be undone.

3. **When you've saved the PDF file under a new name, click the Layers tab on the Navigation pane and choose Flatten Layers on the Options menu at the top of the Layers palette.**

   A Warning dialog box appears, stating `This operation cannot be undone. Would you like to proceed?`

4. **Click Yes to close the Warning dialog box and flatten the document layers.**

The proof of your flattening action is exhibited in the Layers palette, which is now completely empty.

Merging PDF layers

When you merge PDF layers, you consolidate one or more layers into another single layer. The layer properties of this *target* layer specified by the author of the original document prior to conversion to PDF are applied to the merged layers. Like flattening layers, merging layers cannot be undone. For this reason, you should always work with a copy of the original PDF saved under a different name, unless you're absolutely confident about your merging and flattening desires. To merge one or more document layers into another, follow these steps:

1. **Click the Layers tab on the Navigation pane to display the Layers palette.**

2. **Choose Merge Layers on the Options pop-up menu at the top of the Layers palette.**

   The Merge Layers dialog box appears, as shown in Figure 10-13.

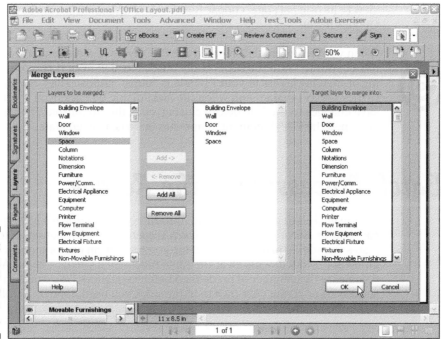

Figure 10-13: Selecting individual layers to merge into a single layer.

3. **In the Layers To Be Merged list box on the left, select the layers you want to merge.**

   To make multiple selections, Ctrl+click (⌘+click on Mac) each layer name, and then click the Add button to move the selected layers to the middle list box.

   You can remove layers from the middle list box by selecting a layer name and clicking the Remove button.

4. **Click the Add All button to select all layers for merging and move them into the middle list box or click the Remove All button to delete all the layers selected for merging in the middle list box.**

5. **In the Target Layer to Merge Into list box, select the single layer you wish to merge the selected layers into.**

6. **Click OK to close the Merge Layers dialog box, and then click Yes to close the Warning dialog box and merge your selected PDF layers.**

After you've merged PDF layers and display the Layers palette in the Navigation pane, you'll notice that the target layer still appears in the Layers palette list, but the merged layers do not. To view the target layer by itself, click all the Show/Hide Layer buttons (the eye icon) attached to all layers but your target layer. When the target layer is the only layer showing, notice that it displays all the elements of the merged layers in addition to its own. To restore the layer view to its original state, choose Reset to Initial Visibility on the Layers palette Options menu.

When you've flattened or merged the PDF layers in a document, you do have *one* chance to undo the supposedly undoable. If your first response to flattening or merging layers in your PDF file is "oops!" choose File⇨Close or press Ctrl+W (⌘+W on Mac) and when the alert dialog box asks you if you want to save changes to the PDF before closing, click the No button. The next time you open the PDF document, it appears in its last saved state.

Batch Processing to the Rescue

For the final editing topic, I want to introduce you to Acrobat's batch-processing capabilities. *Batch processing* (or *batch sequencing* as Acrobat refers to it) automates the editing process by enabling you to perform one or more actions on a group of PDF documents all at the same time. When you first install Acrobat 6, it comes with a number of predefined batch sequences. You can then edit these sequences or create your own to fit the work you need done by Acrobat.

The key to successful batch processing is setting up an input folder in which you've moved all the PDF documents that need processing with a particular batch sequence and, if you're going to run a sequence that makes changes to the PDF documents, setting up another output folder to hold all the processed files (which you specify as part of the batch sequence).

Editing batch sequences

You can run, edit, or create new batch sequences from the Batch Sequences dialog box (shown in Figure 10-14) that you open by choosing Advanced⇨ Batch Processing. To run a batch sequence from this dialog box, click its name in the list box and then click the Run Sequence button.

Figure 10-14:
Running a batch sequence in the Batch Sequences dialog box.

To edit an existing batch sequence, click the name of the sequence in the list box and then click the Edit Sequence button to open the Batch Edit Sequence dialog box (shown later in Figure 10-15). From this dialog box, you can change the sequence of commands executed when you run the sequence with the Select Commands button, change which files are processed by the sequence from the Run Commands On drop-down list, and change where processed files are located in the Select Output Location drop-down list. For details on using these options, refer to the series of steps on creating a new batch sequence in the following section (the steps for using these controls are identical for editing and creating batch sequences).

Creating new batch sequences

To create a new batch sequence, you open the Batch Sequences dialog box (refer to Figure 10-14) by choosing Advanced⇨Batch Processing. Then follow these steps:

1. **Click the New Sequence button in the Batch Sequences dialog box.**

   The Name Sequence dialog box opens.

2. **Enter a descriptive name for the new batch sequence and then click OK.**

   The Batch Edit Sequence dialog box opens, showing the name of your batch sequence in the title bar (see Figure 10-15).

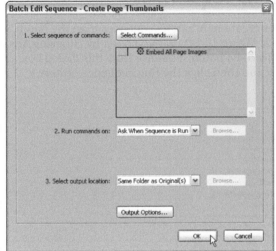

Figure 10-15: Building a sequence in the Batch Edit Sequence dialog box.

3. **Click the Select Commands button.**

   This opens the Edit Sequence dialog box, shown in Figure 10-16, where you define all the commands that the batch sequence is to process in the order in which they are to be executed.

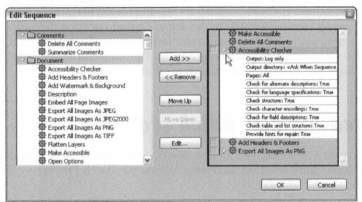

Figure 10-16: Selecting menu commands for a sequence in the Edit Sequence dialog box.

4. **Scroll through the list box on the left until you find the category (Comments, Document, JavaScript, or Page) and the name of the first command you want executed; select the command and click the Add button to add its name to the list box on the right.**

5. **Repeat Step 4, adding any additional commands to be executed as part of the batch sequence in the order in which they are to occur.**

   When you finish adding the commands in the sequence to the list box on the right, check them over. Note in Figure 10-16 that some added menu items have an attached expand button (white triangle) that when clicked displays current settings for that menu command. Double-clicking one of these menu items opens its associated properties dialog box enabling you to change settings.

6. **If you find any mistakes in the sequence, use the Move Up and Move Down buttons to rearrange the sequence, and then click OK.**

   The Edit Sequence dialog box closes, and you return to the Batch Edit Sequence dialog box.

7. **By default, all new batch sequences prompt you to specify the files for batch processing by selecting the Ask When Sequence Is Run option on the Run Commands On drop-down list.**

   Here are some additional options you can choose from the Run Commands On drop-down list:

   - To have the batch sequence run on all files that you designate, select the Selected Files option.

   - To have all the files in a designated folder processed, select the Selected Folder option.

   - To have all the files open at the time you run the sequence processed, select the Files Open in Acrobat option.

   If you select the Selected Files or Selected Folder option on the Run Commands On drop-down list, its Browse button becomes active.

8. **Click the Browse button to open the Select Files to Process or the Browse for Folder dialog box.**

   In the case of the Select Files to Process dialog box, open the folder containing the files you want included, select all their file icons to add their names to the File Name text box, and click the Select button. In the case of the Browse for Folder dialog box, select the name of the folder on your hard drive, and then click OK.

9. **If you select the Selected Folder option in Step 7, the Source File Options button becomes active. Click this button to open the Source File Options dialog box, where you specify what file types in addition to PDF files to process.**

By default, the check boxes for all file types — AutoCAD, BMP, CompuServe GIF, JPEG, JPEG2000, Microsoft Office, Microsoft Project, Microsoft Visio, PCX, PNG, PostScript/EPS, and TIFF — are selected. To eliminate a file type, click its name to deselect it before clicking OK.

10. **By default, all new batch sequences put all the processed files in the same folder by selecting the Same Folder as Original(s) option on the Select Output Location drop-down list. To change the default output location, choose another option from the Select Output Location drop-down list:**

    • To have the batch sequence prompt you for where to put the processed files at the time of the batch sequence, select the Ask When Sequence Is Run option.

    • To have the sequence put the files in a specified folder, select the Specific Folder option. When you select the Specific Folder option, the Browse button activates so you can specify an output folder in the Browse for Folder dialog box.

    • If you don't want changes saved in the processed files, select the Don't Save Changes option.

11. **Click the Output Options button to open the Output Options dialog box, shown in Figure 10-17, where you can specify the file naming that is to be applied to the processed files and the file format in which the processed files are to be saved.**

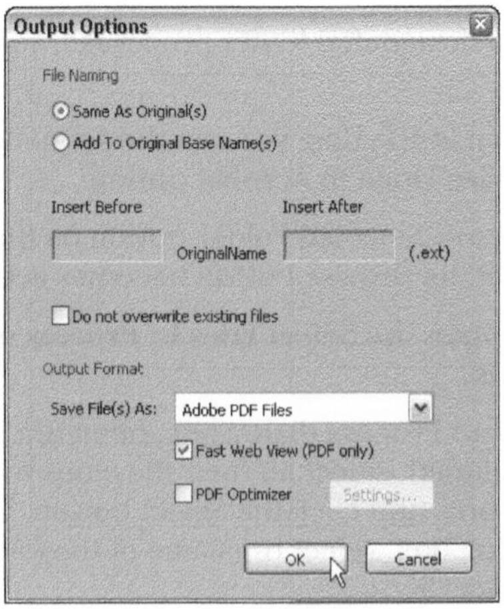

Figure 10-17: Specifying the file naming and output format in the Output Options dialog box.

12. **By default, Acrobat saves changes to the processed files with the same filenames in the Adobe PDF file format. If you want Acrobat to save the changes with a different filename, choose one of the following options:**

- To have the filenames changed in processing, select the Add to Original Base Name(s) radio button, and then enter characters as a prefix to the filename in the Insert Before text box and/or characters to be appended as a filename extension in the Insert After text box.

- To prevent Acrobat from overwriting any filenames, select the Do Not Overwrite Existing Files check box.

13. **To have Acrobat save the processed files in another file format besides Adobe PDF, select one of the supported file formats in the Save File(s) As drop-down list. After changing all the file naming and format options that you want modified, click OK.**

    The Output Options dialog box closes, and you return to the Batch Edit Sequence dialog box.

14. **Check your command sequence along with your Run Commands On and Select Output Location settings. If everything looks okay, click the OK button.**

    The Batch Edit Sequence dialog box closes, and you return to the Batch Sequences dialog box, where the name of your new batch sequence now appears selected in the list box. All batch sequences are run from the Batch Sequences dialog box.

15. **To run the new batch sequence and test it out (preferably on copies of your PDF files, just in case something goes wrong), click the Run Sequence button. To close the Batch Sequences dialog box without running the new batch process, click the Close button instead.**

You can share the batch sequences you create for Acrobat with others who use Acrobat 6. Batch sequences that you create are saved as special sequence files using the title name you give them as the filename (with a .sequ file extension on Windows) and are stored in a folder called ENU on your Windows hard drive. Here is the directory path for Windows users: C:\Programs\Acrobat 6.0\Acrobat\Sequences\ENU. Macintosh users go to: Macintosh HD\Library\Acrobat User Data\Sequences.

When you send copies of your sequence files to coworkers, they must be sure to put them in the ENU folder on Windows machines or the Sequences folder on Mac OS X computers. When they do, the names of the batch sequences you share appear in the list in the Batch Sequences dialog box in Acrobat 6 on their computers as though they created the batch sequences themselves.

If you use Acrobat for Windows, you might want to create a batch sequence that uses the Make Accessible plug-in to convert a bunch of regular PDF files to tagged PDF files so that they can take advantage of the Acrobat 6 and Adobe Reader 6 Accessibility features (especially the Reflow button on the Viewing toolbar — see Chapter 2 for details).

Chapter 11

Securing PDF Files

· ·

· ·

*A*crobat 6 offers different types and different levels of security that you can apply to PDF documents. At the most basic level, you can password-protect your documents so that only associates who know the password can open the files for viewing, editing, and printing. You can further set file permissions that restrict the kind of user actions that can be performed on the PDF documents without access to a second password. You can also use the Certificate Security Digital Signatures feature to digitally sign a document and to verify the signatures and integrity of PDF files that you receive as part of your document review cycle. Finally, you can add the ultimate in security by encrypting your PDF documents using the Certificate Security feature, so that they can be shared only with a list of trusted associates. In this chapter, you find out all about the different ways to protect your PDF documents from unwarranted and unwanted access and editing.

Protecting PDF Files

You can password-protect the opening and editing of PDF documents at the time you first distill them (as part of their Security Settings — see Chapter 4 for details) or at anytime thereafter in Acrobat 6. When you set the security settings, you can choose between two different levels of encryption:

 ✔ **40-bit RC4:** Used for PDF files created when you set the encryption level to 40-bit RC4 (Acrobat 3.x, 4.x)

 ✔ **128-bit RC4:** Used when you set the encryption level to 128-bit RC4 (Acrobat 5.x, 6.0)

40-bit RC4 encryption offers a lower level of file security but is compatible with Acrobat 3 and Acrobat 4. 128-bit RC4 offers a higher level of security (it's a lot harder to hack into) but is compatible only with Acrobat 5 and Acrobat 6. If you'll be sharing secured PDF documents with coworkers who haven't yet upgraded to Acrobat 5 or 6, you'll have to content yourself with the less-secure, 40-bit RC4 encryption. However, if you're dealing with highly sensitive, "for-your-eyes-only" material, you may want to upgrade everybody to Acrobat 6 as soon as possible, so that you can start taking advantage of the more secure 128-bit RC4 encryption.

Checking a document's security settings

You can check the security settings in effect for any PDF document you open in Acrobat 6 or Adobe Reader 6 (of course, you can tell immediately if the file requires a user password because you must supply this password before you can open the document in Acrobat or Adobe Reader). To check the security settings in effect, you choose Document⇨Security⇨Display Restrictions and Security.

When you select this command in Acrobat, the program opens a Document Properties dialog box with the security settings showing, where you can both review and change the settings. When you select this command in Adobe Reader (choose File⇨Document Properties and click Security in the list box to display the security settings), the program simply lists all the settings in effect.

The security settings in the Document Properties dialog box contain the Security Method drop-down list that shows you the type of security in effect. This list can contain one of these three options:

 ✔ **No Security:** The document uses no protection at all.

 ✔ **Password Security:** The document uses a user password and/or master password and possibly restricts the type of edits.

 ✔ **Certificate Security:** The document is encrypted so that only trusted associates with digital certification can open and change it.

Beneath the Security Method drop-down list, you find a Document Restrictions Summary area that lists all the security options in effect. To the right of the Security Method drop-down list, you find the Change Settings button that enables you to change the security settings when either the Password Security or the Certificate Security option is selected in the Security Method drop-down list.

Securing files with low or high encryption

If you want to secure a PDF file that currently uses no security with the less-secure, 40-bit RC4 level of encryption (compatible with versions 3 and 4 of Acrobat and Adobe Reader), or with the more secure, 128-bit RC4 level of encryption (compatible only with version 5 and 6 of Acrobat and Adobe Reader), follow these steps in Acrobat 6:

1. **Choose Document⇨Security⇨Display Restrictions and Security.**

   The Document Properties dialog box opens, as shown in Figure 11-1.

2. **Select Password Security from the Security Method drop-down list, as shown in the figure.**

   The Password Security - Settings dialog box opens, as shown in Figure 11-2.

3. **From the Compatibility drop-down list, select either Acrobat 3.0 and Later or Acrobat 6.0 and Later.**

   If you select Acrobat 3.0 and Later, the Encryption Level automatically changes to Low (40-bit RC4).

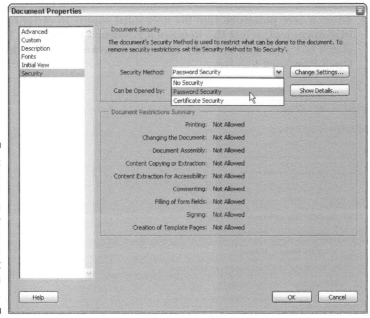

Figure 11-1:
Selecting
Password
Security as
the security
method
in the
Document
Properties
dialog box.

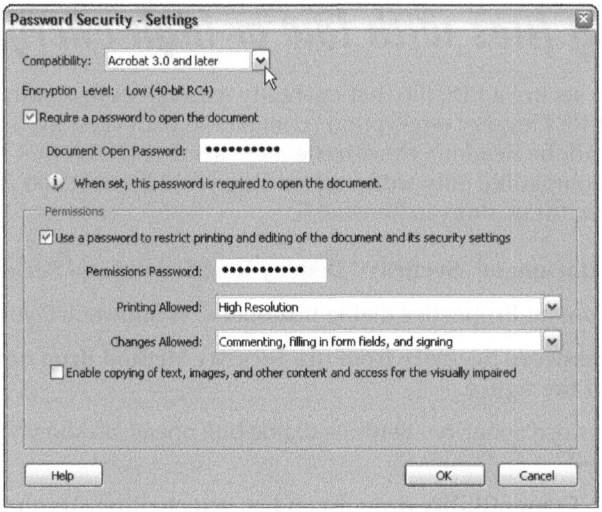

Figure 11-2:
Setting the
security
options for
40-bit RC4
encryption
in the
Password
Security -
Settings
dialog box.

If you select Acrobat 5.0 or 6.0 and Later, the Encryption Level automatically changes to High (128-bit RC4). When you select this higher level of encryption, the options in the Permissions area of the Standard Security dialog box change, as shown in Figure 11-3.

4. **To set a user password that the user must supply in order to open the PDF document, select the Require a Password to Open the Document check box and then carefully enter the password in the Document Open Password text box.**

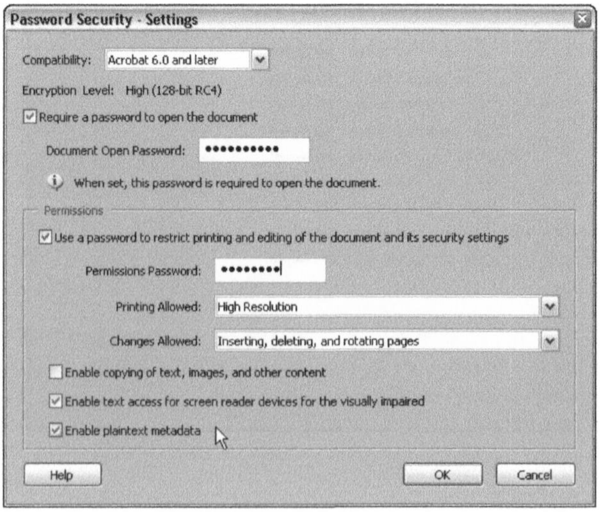

Figure 11-3:
Setting the
security
options for
128-bit RC4
encryption
in the
Password
Security -
Settings
dialog box.

5. **To set a master password that the user must supply in order to change the user password, allow printing, or modify the file permissions, select the Use a Password to Restrict Printing and Editing of the Document and Its Security Settings check box and then carefully enter the password in the Permissions Password text box.**

   This password must be different from the one you entered in the Document Open Password text box, if you followed Step 4.

6. **In the Printing Allowed drop-down list, choose the editing permissions you wish to put into effect (the default is None).**

   If you selected the low (40-bit RC4) encryption level, your choices are either None or High Resolution.

   If you selected the high (128-bit RC4) encryption level, your choices are None, Low Resolution (150 dpi), or High Resolution.

7. **In the Changes Allowed drop-down list, choose the editing permissions you wish to put into effect (the default is None).**

   Your choices are None; Filling in Form Fields and Signing; Commenting, Filling in Form Fields, and Signing; and Any Except Extracting Pages.

8. **If you selected high (128-bit RC4) encryption, the Enable Text Access for Screen Reader Devices for the Visually Impaired is selected by default, while the Enable Copying of Text, Images, and Other Content and the Enable Plaintext Metadata check boxes are not selected, thus preventing user access to these options. To enable these options, select the appropriate check box.**

   Note that the last check box in the Password Security - Settings dialog box that allows the ability to make changes to plaintext metadata is only available when you choose Acrobat 6.0 and Later in the Compatibility drop-down list.

9. **Click OK.**

   If you set a user password, reenter your password in the Password dialog box that appears, asking you to confirm the password to open the document, and then click OK.

10. **If you set a master password, reenter this password in the Password dialog box that appears next, asking you to confirm the password to change security options in the document, and then click OK.**

11. **Click the Close button in the Document Properties dialog box.**

12. **Choose File⇨Save to save your security settings as part of the PDF file.**

Note that if you mess up when attempting to confirm a user or master password in Steps 9 or 10, Acrobat displays an alert dialog box informing you of this fact and telling you that you have to try reentering the original password to confirm it. If you are unable to confirm the password successfully (no doubt because you didn't enter the password you had intended originally), you must revisit the Document Open Password or the Permissions Password text box, completely clearing out its contents and reenter the intended password.

After saving your security settings to the PDF document and closing the file, thereafter you or whomever you send the PDF document to must be able to accurately enter the user password assigned to the file in order to open it. Further, you must be able to successfully enter the master password you assigned the file if you ever need to change the user password or modify the file permissions.

Signing Off Digital Style

The Certificate Security option in the Security Method drop-down list in the Document Properties dialog box enables you to digitally sign a PDF document or to verify that a digital signature in a PDF document is valid. Certificate Security is what is known in the trade as a *signature handler* that uses a private/public key (also known as PPK) system. In this system, each digital signature is associated with a profile that contains both a *private key* and a *public key*.

The private key in your profile is a password-protected number that enables you to digitally sign a PDF document. The public key, which is embedded within your digital signature, enables others who review the document in Acrobat to verify that your signature is valid. Because others must have access to your public key in order to verify your signature, Acrobat puts your public key in what's called a *certificate* that is shared. The Certificate Security uses what is known as a *direct trust* system for sharing certificates, because it doesn't use a third-party agent (like VeriSign) to do this.

Everything you never wanted to know about Certificate Security

In Certificate Security, the private key encrypts a checksum that is stored with your signature when you sign a PDF document. The public key decrypts this checksum when anyone verifies the signature (by making sure that the checksum checks out). In case you're the least bit interested, Certificate Security uses the RSA algorithm for generating private/public key pairs and the X.509 standard for certificates.

Setting up your profile

The first step to be able to use Certificate Security for digitally signing PDF documents is to set up your Digital ID. Your Digital ID contains your password, along with basic information about your role. You can set up multiple profiles for yourself if you digitally sign documents in different roles.

To create a new user profile, follow these steps:

1. **Choose Advanced⇨Manage Digital IDs⇨My Digital ID Files⇨Select My Digital ID File.**

   The Select My Digital ID dialog box opens.

2. **Click the New Digital ID File button.**

   The Create Self-Signed Digital ID dialog box appears, as shown in Figure 11-4.

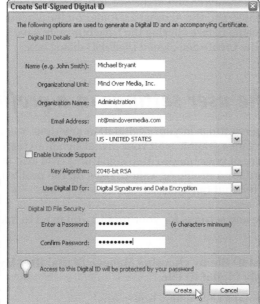

Figure 11-4: Selecting a password in the Create Self-Signed Digital ID dialog box.

3. **Edit the Name, Organization Unit, Organization Name, E-mail Address, and Country/Region text boxes, if necessary (only the Name text box must be filled in), in the Digital ID Details section of the dialog box.**

   Note the profile name that appears in the Name text box is the name that appears in the Signatures palette in Acrobat 6 and is used in the naming of the Self-Signed Digital ID filename. If you select the Enable

Unicode Support check box, Acrobat displays additional text boxes for entering Unicode values for extended characters next to the ASCII versions you just entered.

4. **Select an RSA algorithm (either 1024-bit or 2048-bit) in the Key Algorithm drop-down list, and then select a purpose for your Digital ID in the Use Digital ID For drop-down list.**

   Note that 2048-bit offers more security, but 1024-bit is more compatible with current encryption technologies. Your choices are Digital Signatures, Data Encryption, or the default Digital Signatures and Data Encryption.

5. **Click in the Enter a Password text box and enter a password of six characters or more.**

6. **Press Tab to jump to the Confirm Password text box and then reenter the password.**

7. **Click the Create button to open the New Self-Sign Digital ID File dialog box.**

   By default, Acrobat names the new profile file by combining the profile name with the .pfx file extension in the Security folder within the Acrobat 6.0 folder in Windows, and the Acrobat 6.0 folder on the Macintosh. If you wish, edit the filename before clicking the Save button to save the new profile and close the Create Self-Signed Digital ID dialog box.

Modifying the user settings in a profile

You can modify the user settings in your Digital ID at any time. You might, for instance, want to associate a graphic with your digital signature (especially one that is actually a picture of your handwritten signature). You also might need to change the password for a profile or want to back up the profile file or change the password timeout options.

Before you can change any settings for your profile, you need to take these steps:

1. **Open your Digital ID file by choosing Manage Digital IDs⇨My Digital ID Files⇨Select My Digital ID File.**

   The Select My Digital ID File dialog box opens.

2. **Select the filename of your user Digital ID in the Digital ID File drop-down list, enter your password in User Password text box, and click the OK button.**

   Acrobat automatically opens your Digital ID file.

3. **Choose Manage Digital IDs⇨My Digital ID Files⇨My Digital ID File Settings to open your Digital ID File Settings dialog box.**

After you've opened your Digital ID file and have your Digital ID File Settings dialog box open, you're ready to make any of the changes outlined in the following sections.

Making a backup of your Digital ID

You should always make a backup copy of each Digital ID that you create so that if the original file saved in the Acrobat folder (Acrobat 6.0 on the Mac) ever becomes corrupted, you can use the backup to both sign documents and verify other people's signatures. To make a backup of your Digital ID, click the Export button in the Digital ID File Settings dialog box for your Digital ID. Then in the Data Exchange File - Export Options dialog box, select the Save the Data to a File radio button in the Export Options area. Click the Next button to open the Export Data As dialog box, select the folder in the Save In drop-down list (preferably on another hard drive, if you have more than one drive on your system or are connected to a network), and click the Save button. Acrobat then displays Certificate Security - Alert dialog box, indicating in which folder you've successfully backed up your Digital ID file.

Changing your password settings

You can change the password you assigned to your Digital ID, or you can change your password timeout settings (that is, how often you're prompted for a password when working with a PDF document that you've signed). Note that changing your password has no noticeable effect on your digital signature.

To change your password, follow these steps:

1. **Click the Change Password button in the Digital ID File Settings dialog box for your Digital ID.**

2. **Click in the Old Password text box and enter your current password.**

3. **Click in the New Password text box and enter the new password you want to set.**

4. **Click in the Confirm Password text box and reenter the new password.**

5. **Click the OK button.**

   An alert dialog box appears, telling you that your password has been successfully changed.

By default, Acrobat prompts you for your password each time you digitally sign a PDF document. If you don't ever want to be prompted for your password when signing off on a bunch of PDF files, or you want the program to prompt again only after a certain time period has elapsed, you can change these password options as follows:

1. **Click Password Settings button in the Digital ID File Settings dialog box for your Digital ID.**

2. **To not be prompted for your password when signing, deselect the Require Password to Access When Signing check box.**

3. **To select a time period before being prompted for your password, select the After radio button (the default is Always), and then choose a timeout setting on the After drop-down list.**

   The settings on this list include a fair number of timeout intervals between 30 seconds and 24 hours.

4. **Enter your password in the Enter Password (Needed to Apply the Change) text box.**

5. **Click OK.**

   An alert dialog box appears, telling you that your password timeout has been successfully changed.

If you change the password and password time period settings for your Digital ID, don't forget to replace all backed-up versions of your Digital ID (the .apd file) with the new version that contains your updated password settings. Should you forget to do this and ever have to rely upon a backup of your Digital ID, you'll have to be able to reproduce your old password in order to log in and sign documents with it.

Adding a graphic to your signature in a signature appearance

Although they're called digital signatures, they don't look anything like signatures you're used to seeing on documents, unless you add a picture of your handwritten signature. If you have an image of your handwritten signature or a particular picture that you'd like to use as your identifying mark, and the image is saved as a PDF file, you can add it by creating a signature appearance as outlined in the following steps:

1. **Choose Edit➪Preferences or press Ctrl+K (⌘+K on the Mac) to open the Preferences dialog box in Acrobat. Click Digital Signatures in the list box on the left side of the Preferences dialog box to display the Digital Signatures options.**

2. **Click the New button.**

   The Configure Signature Appearance dialog box appears, as shown in Figure 11-5.

3. **Click the Title text box and enter a descriptive name for the new signature appearance you're creating.**

4. **Select the Imported Graphic radio button.**

5. **Click the PDF File button.**

   The Select Picture dialog box opens.

6. **Click the Browse button to display the Open dialog box, where you open the folder and click the icon of the PDF file that contains the graphic of your handwritten signature, and then click the Select button to close the Open dialog box and return to the Select Picture dialog box.**

Figure 11-5:
Importing a graphic image to use in your digital signature.

7. **Check that you've selected the correct image in the Sample area in the Select Picture dialog box, and then click the OK button.**

   The Select Picture dialog box closes, and you return to the Configure Signature Appearance dialog box.

8. **Check the preview of your digital signature in the Preview area. To remove various pieces of information from the signature display, de-select their check boxes in the Configure Text area of the dialog box.**

   Keep your eye on the Preview area as you remove individual items.

9. **When you have the digital signature looking the way you want it to appear in the PDF document, click the OK button to close the Configure Signature Appearance dialog box, and then click the Close button in the Digital ID File Settings dialog box.**

Palm handheld users take note

If you have a Palm handheld connected to your computer, you can use the Palm (TM) Organizer button (no longer grayed-out when Acrobat detects graphic files on the device) in the Configure Signature Appearance dialog box to select a version of your handwritten signature as the graphic to be used in your digital signature in Acrobat. You can create this picture of your handwritten signature by writing with your stylus on the Palm screen and then saving the handwriting as a graphics file on your device. When you click the Palm Organizer button, you can then select the graphics file with your hand-written signature in the Palm Organizer drop-down list, which appears to the immediate right of the button.

Signing a PDF document

After you've set up your Digital ID, you're ready to use it to digitally sign off on PDF documents. In digitally signing a PDF document, you add a special signature form field to the document that contains the mark and signing information that you want displayed (see Chapter 14 for more on form fields in PDF documents). The first time a document is signed by you or one of your coworkers, Acrobat saves the PDF file with the signature in a special append-only form. Every time someone digitally signs the document after that, Acrobat saves a new version of the file to which his or her editing changes and signature are appended.

Keep in mind that when you're viewing a PDF document with multiple signatures, you're looking at the latest version of the document with all changes since the first time it was signed. If you want, you can view the original version of the signed document side by side with the most current version by selecting the signatory in the Signatures palette and then selecting View Signed Version in the Options pop-up menu. You can also compare the changes between the original signed version and the current document (by selecting Compare Signed Version to Current Version on the same Signatures palette Options pop-up menu).

If you ever decide that you should manually save a PDF document that's been digitally signed, don't use the File⇨Save command to do it. Use instead the File⇨Save As command to save a copy of the PDF document under a new file-name. If you use File⇨Save to save a signed PDF document, you automatically invalidate all the signatures in it.

Adding a visible or invisible signature to a PDF document

When signing a document, you can sign it invisibly so that no signature form field appears in the PDF document, or you can sign it so that all your signature information appears (as designated in the Configure Signature Appearance dialog box), including any graphic that you've selected.

To sign a document, take these steps:

1. **Open your Digital ID file by choosing Advanced⇨Manage Digital IDs⇨My Digital ID Files⇨Select My Digital ID File.**

   The Select My Digital ID File dialog box opens.

2. **Select the filename of your user Digital ID in the Digital ID File drop-down list, enter your password in User Password text box, and click the OK button.**

3. **Choose Document⇨Digital Signatures⇨Sign this Document or, if the Sign Task button is open on the Tasks toolbar, click it and choose Sign This Document on the pop-up menu.**

   If the Alert - Document Is Not Certified dialog box appears, you are given the opportunity to add a Certifying Signature to the document, which will be invalidated if unauthorized changes are made. To specify this added security feature, click the Certify Document button and follow the prompts; otherwise, click the Continue Signing button to open the Sign Document dialog box.

4. **Select the Create a New Invisible Signature radio button, and then click Next to open the Apply Signature to Document dialog box.**

   Alternatively, if you wish to sign the PDF document with a visible signature, select the Create a New Signature Field to Sign radio button, click Next, and then draw a signature field in the PDF document by dragging the mouse in the area you want to sign.

5. **If you want to add the reason for signing the document, your location, or contact information to the signature information (that can be viewed in the Signatures palette), click the Show Options button to expand the Apply Signature to Document dialog box, so that it includes the fields shown in Figure 11-6.**

6. **To include the reason for signing the document as part of the signature information, select the reason from the Reason for Signing Document drop-down list (such as I Am Approving This Document or I Am the Author of This Document).**

   Note that you can edit the reason you select by clicking the insertion point in the text and then inserting or deleting text as needed.

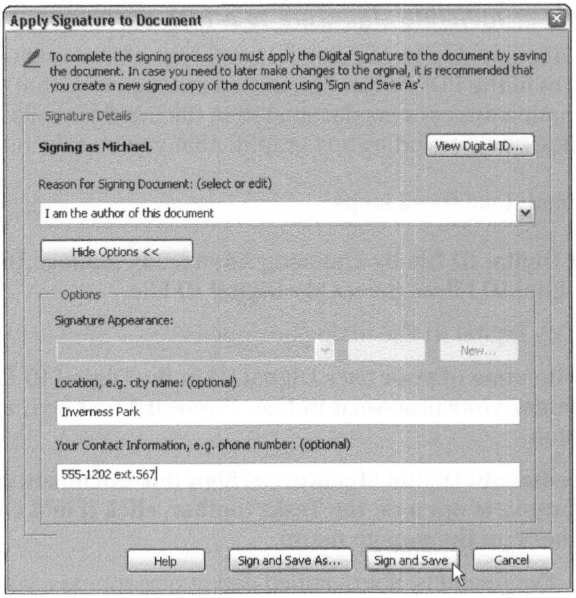

Figure 11-6:
Specifying
information
for an
invisible
signature
in the
expanded
Self-Sign
Security -
Sign
Document
dialog box.

Apply Signature to Document

To complete the signing process you must apply the Digital Signature to the document by saving the document. In case you need to later make changes to the orginal, it is recommended that you create a new signed copy of the document using 'Sign and Save As'.

Signature Details

Signing as Michael.   [View Digital ID...]

Reason for Signing Document: (select or edit)

[I am the author of this document]

[Hide Options <<]

Options

Signature Appearance:

[ ] [ ] [New...]

Location, e.g. city name: (optional)

[Inverness Park]

Your Contact Information, e.g. phone number: (optional)

[555-1202 ext.567]

[Help]   [Sign and Save As...]   [Sign and Save]   [Cancel]

7. **If you wish to save your location as part of the digital signature information, click in the Location text box and enter your current location (as in Chicago or Corporate Headquarters).**

8. **If you wish to include contact information, such as your telephone number, so that coworkers can contact you if they need your certificate in order to verify your digital signature, click in the Your Contact Information text box and enter that information there.**

9. **If you're using a visible signature, by default, Acrobat selects Standard Text as the Signature Appearance. To preview how this signature field will appear in the document, click the Preview button.**

   If you wish to select a new appearance for your signature field, select its name in the Signature Appearance drop-down list. To create a new signature appearance, click the New button. To edit the appearance you selected in the drop-down list, click the Edit button, which replaces the Preview button when you select an appearance you created.

   See the "Adding a graphic to your signature in a signature appearance" section, earlier in this chapter, for details on creating or editing signature appearances.

10. **Click the Sign and Save button to save your changes and signature in the document in its current location with the same filename.**

    Alternatively, click the Sign and Save As button to open the Save As dialog box, where you can modify the file's location and/or save it under a new filename.

After you click the Sign and Save button in the Apply Signature to Document dialog box (to save the file with the same name) or the Save button in the Save As dialog box (to save the file in a new location or with a new filename), Acrobat saves the PDF document with your signature and then displays a Certificate Security - Alert dialog box, informing you that you have successfully signed the document.

After you click OK to close this dialog box, you can verify that you've signed the document (if you used an invisible signature) by opening the Signatures palette by clicking the Signatures tab on the Navigation pane (if the palette isn't already displayed in the Navigation pane). To display the detailed information you added to your signature (including the reason, location, and contact information), click the Expand button (the plus sign on Windows and the triangle pointing right on the Mac) to expand the signature information.

If you used a visible signature to sign the document, after you click OK to close the alert dialog box, you can see your signature right on the document page. Figure 11-7 shows a PDF document with my digital signature (using a custom signature appearance that incorporates a facsimile of my handwritten signature). Note that the Signatures palette shown in this figure displays a list of the detailed signature information that also appears (much smaller) in the signature field to the right of the facsimile of my handwritten signature.

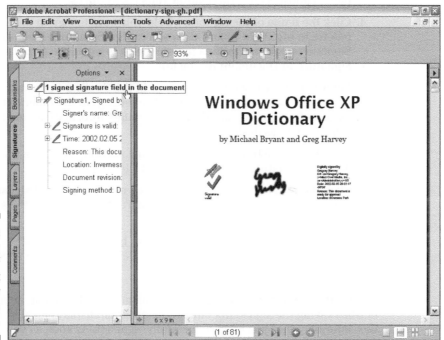

Figure 11-7:
Viewing the PDF document with a new signature field.

You can always review the signatory information for a particular signature in its Signature Properties dialog box. You can open this dialog box for a visible signature by right-clicking (Control+clicking on the Mac) the signature field and then clicking Properties on the context menu. You can also open this dialog box (for an invisible or visible signature) by selecting the signatory's name in the Signatures palette and then selecting Properties at the bottom of the Options pop-up menu.

Signing a PDF document using a predefined signature field

You can also digitally sign a PDF document by using a signature form field that's already been added to it (see Chapter 14 for details on how to add signature form fields to a PDF document). To sign a document in a predefined signature form field, you follow these steps:

1. **Open your Digital ID file by choosing Advanced⇨Manage Digital IDs⇨My Digital ID Files⇨Select My Digital ID File.**

   The Select My Digital ID File dialog box opens.

2. **Select the filename of your user Digital ID in the Digital ID File drop-down list, enter your password in User Password text box, and click the OK button.**

3. **If the Signatures palette isn't open and selected in the Navigation pane, choose View⇨Navigation Tabs⇨Signatures.**

4. **Click the name of the signature field you want to sign in the Signatures palette to highlight it, and then select Sign Signature Field on the Signatures palette Options pop-up menu to open the Apply Signature to Document dialog box.**

5. **Enter your user Digital ID password in the Confirm Password text box if necessary, and then modify the settings in the other options (Reason for Signing, Location, Your Contact Information, and Signature Appearance) as desired.**

   Refer to Steps 5 through 10 in preceding section, "Adding a visible or invisible signature to a PDF document," for details.

6. **Click the Sign and Save button to save your changes and signature in the selected signature field in its current location with the same filename.**

   Alternatively, click the Sign and Save As button to open the Save As dialog box, where you can modify the file's location and/or save it under a new filename.

As with the other methods of digitally signing a PDF document, after Acrobat finishes saving the signed document, the program displays an alert dialog box, informing that you have successfully signed it. As soon as you click the

OK button to close the alert dialog box, you can see your signature in the signature form field. Figure 11-8 shows you a PDF document after I signed a signature form field beneath the book title and byline.

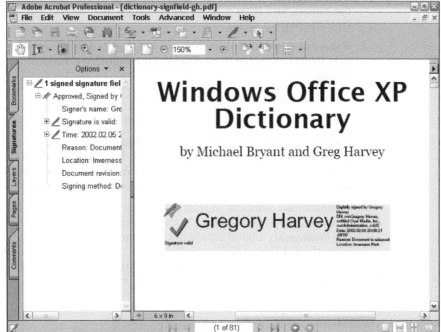

Figure 11-8:
Viewing
a PDF
document
with a
digitally
signed
signature
form field.

Validating digital signatures

Whenever you add your own signature to a PDF document, Acrobat automatically uses your user Digital ID information to verify your signature as valid (indicated by the green check mark and the text *Signature Valid* underneath it). When you receive a document that has been signed by other people, their signatures will not automatically be recognized as valid when you open the PDF file.

You can then validate their signatures. As part of this process, you need to get in contact with the signatory and verify that one or both of the two so-called fingerprint numbers stored in the public key attached to the signature in your PDF document match the fingerprint numbers in the signatory's public key stored as part of his or her certificate attributes on his or her hard drive. (The two fingerprints are made up of a combination of letters and numbers that make your software serial number look short; the first is called the MD5 Fingerprint, and the second is called the SHA-1 Fingerprint.)

To validate a signature in a PDF document that you have open, follow these steps:

1. **Open the Signatures palette and select the name of the unknown signatory you want to validate (indicated by a blue question mark before the name), and then select Validate Signature on the Signature palette Options pop-up menu.**

2. **If the unknown signatory has not been added to your list of trusted certificates, Acrobat next displays the Signature Validation Status dialog box.**

3. **Click the Signature Properties button.**

   The Signature Properties dialog box appears, as shown in Figure 11-9.

4. **Use the contact information (if listed) to get a hold of the signatory (preferably by telephone) to verify the MD5 and/or the SHA-1 Fingerprint numbers listed at the bottom of the Certificate Attributes dialog box. Click the Show Certificate button to view these numbers.**

   To find these numbers to read off to you, the signatory must choose Advanced➪Manage Digital IDs➪My Digital ID, select their Digital ID in the Manage My Digital IDs dialog box, and click the Settings button to open the Set Digital ID Usage dialog box. The signatory then clicks the Show Certificate Details button to open the Certificate Attributes dialog box and view their MD5 and SHA-1 Fingerprint numbers.

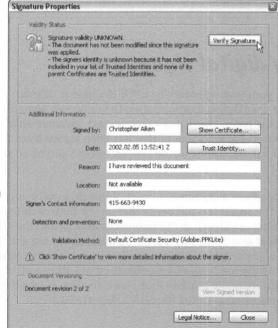

Figure 11-9:
Verifying
fingerprint
numbers
in the
Certificate
Attributes
dialog box.

5. **If the fingerprint numbers on your screen match the numbers given to you over the phone, click the Trust Identity button.**

   The Certificate Security-Alert dialog box opens, telling you that Trusting Certificates directly from a document is unwise.

6. **Click OK to close the Alert box and open the Import Contact Settings dialog box.**

7. **Click the Import button and then click OK in the Import Complete dialog box to add the person to your list of trusted certificates and to validate the selected signature in the PDF document.**

You can quickly validate individual signatures for the people you've added to your Trusted Certificates list (see the following section, "Adding certificates to your Trusted Certificates list") by simply double-clicking their signature fields. Acrobat will quickly search your list and, upon finding the person's certificate, display a Signature Validation Status alert dialog box, informing you that the signature is valid. You can also use this technique on your own signatures in the event that they show up as unknown signatures when you reopen the PDF document, even when your Digital ID file is open. To update all the signatures in your PDF at one time, simply choose Document⇨Digital Signatures⇨ Validate All Signatures in Document, or select the Validate All Signatures in Document option on the Signatures palette Options pop-up menu.

Exchanging certificates with associates

You can simplify the process of validating signatures in the PDF files you review by having all the review team members exchange copies of their Self-Sign Security certificates. Acrobat makes this easy by adding an export function to the Manage Trusted Identities dialog box. To open this dialog box, choose Advanced⇨Manage Digital IDs⇨Trusted Identities. Select your Digital ID from the list box in the Manage Trusted Identities dialog box and click the Export button to open the Data Exchange File - Export Options dialog box. Two radio buttons appear in the Export options section. The first is the E-mail the Data to Someone radio button that you can select to send a copy of your certificate to team members in a new e-mail message. The second is the Save the Data to File radio button that you can use to make a copy of the certificate file that others can import into their Trusted Certificates list. (For example, you can use this option if you and your coworkers are on the same network and share access to certain folders.)

When you select the Save the Data to a File radio button, Acrobat opens an Export Data As dialog box, where you can designate the drive and folder on which the copy of your certificate is saved (saved in a special Acrobat Self-Sign key file format that uses a .fdf file extension) when you click the Save button. When you select the E-mail the Data to Someone radio button, Acrobat opens the Compose E-mail dialog box, as shown in Figure 11-10.

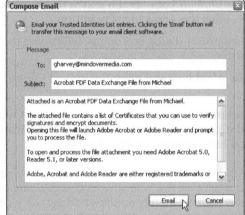

Figure 11-10:
Sending
your
certificate
via an
e-mail
message.

To send the e-mail, fill in the recipient's e-mail address in the To text box, make any necessary changes in the default text provided in the message window, and click the E-mail button. Acrobat transfers the information into your e-mail client in order to send your certificate data to someone else.

Figure 11-11 shows you the typical e-mail message that the recipient receives when you click the E-mail button. Note that this e-mail not only attaches a copy of your Self-Sign Security certificate file, but also instructs the recipient that opening the attached file will automatically launch Acrobat 6 and prompt the recipient to process the file (by validating those lovely fingerprint numbers).

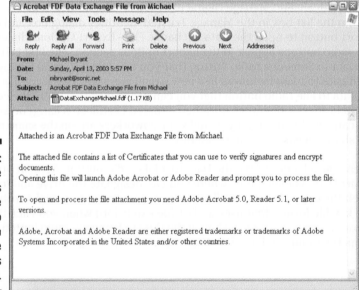

Figure 11-11:
Reading the
instructions
in the
message to
which a
Certificate
data file is
attached.

Adding certificates to your Trusted Certificates list

The way that you add the certificates that you receive to your Trusted Certificates list depends upon how you receive them. If you receive an e-mail message with a certificate attached, you can launch Acrobat, validate the certificate, and add the certificate to your Trusted Certificates list all by simply opening the certificate file attached to the message in your e-mail program (in most programs, you open an attachment by double-clicking the file attachment icon).

When Acrobat launches, it displays the Data Exchange File - Import Contact dialog box. To add the certificate to your list, click the Set Contact Trust button to open the Import Contact Settings dialog box (shown in Figure 11-12). The Trust Signatures Created with this Certificate check box is selected by default. Click the Import button to import the certificate data and create a Digital ID certificate that will appear in your Trusted Identities list.

If you have access to someone's Self-Sign Security certificate file on your computer system, you can add it to your Trusted Certificates list by clicking the Import from File button in the Trusted Certificates portion of your User Settings dialog box. To do this, follow these steps:

1. **Choose Advanced⇨Manage Digital IDs⇨Trusted Identities to open the Manage Trusted Identities dialog box.**

2. **Click the Add Contacts button to open the Select Contacts to Add dialog box, and then click the Browse for Certificates button.**

3. **Locate the certificate exchange file you want to import in the Locate Certificate File dialog box, and then click the Open button.**

   The selected certificate data file appears in the upper list box of the Select Contacts to Add dialog box.

4. **Click the Add to Contacts List button to display the certificate exchange file in the Contacts to Add list box below; then click OK.**

5. **Click OK to close the alert dialog box and return to your Manage Trusted Identities dialog box, where you see the name of the person you just added to your Trusted Identities list.**

6. **Click the Close button to close the Manage Trusted Identities dialog box.**

Comparing signed documents

As I mention earlier in this chapter, each time a person digitally signs a PDF document that already has one signature, Acrobat saves the changes and signature of each subsequent signatory in a special appended version of the file. You can then compare the various versions to note what changes, if any, each signatory made.

Acrobat notes when a PDF document that you've sent out for subsequent signatures comes back to you with changes by adding a Document Was Modified item to the Signatures palette. You can then display the details of the modifications by clicking the Expand button (with the plus sign on Windows and the triangle pointing to the right on the Mac). Note that the detailed change items shown in the expanded list are purely informational and do not perform as bookmarks.

To have Acrobat do a side-by-side comparison of the versions to let you visually compare the changes, select View Signed Version on the Signatures palette Options pop-up menu. Acrobat then displays the original version of the PDF file and the most current version in a Document pane. To compare the files side by side, choose Window⇨Tile⇨Vertically, as shown in Figure 11-12. You can then scroll through the pages, visually noting the differences. When you're finished checking the changes, close the original version on the left by clicking its document window's Close button and maximize the latest version on the right by clicking its document window's Maximize button.

If you would prefer, you can have Acrobat do a page-by-page comparison and locate all the changes between the latest signed version and the original. To do this, select Compare Signed Version to Current Document on the Signatures palette Options pop-up menu. Acrobat then performs a page-by-page comparison and creates a second PDF document containing only the pages that have changed. These changed pages are displayed side by side.

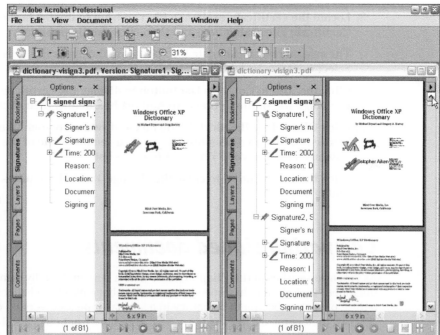

Figure 11-12:
Comparing
different
signed
versions
of the
same PDF
document.

When you have finished comparing these pages, you can close this newly created document by pressing Ctrl+W (⌘+W). You can then save it in its own PDF file by clicking the Yes button in the alert dialog box that asks you if you want to save the changes before closing. If you have no further need for this comparison PDF file, you can click the No button to abandon the comparison document and just return to the most up-to-date signed version of the PDF document.

Encrypting PDF Files

The last and most secure type of security that you can add to your PDF documents employs the Certificate Security system that you use to digitally sign documents, along with the list of Trusted Certificates in your user Digital ID file. When you encrypt a PDF document with Certificate Security, no one has access to the document other than those you specifically designate as recipients, and you can designate as recipients only those persons who are already on your Trusted Certificates list.

The steps for encrypting a PDF document with Certificate Security are as follows:

1. **Choose Document⇨Security⇨Encrypt for Certain Identities Using Certificates.**

   The Restrict Opening and Editing to Certain Identities dialog box opens.

2. **In the Identity Directories list box, click the name of the person you want to add to the Recipients list box below, and then click the Add to Recipient List button.**

3. **Click the name of the newly added recipient to highlight it in the Recipients list box.**

4. **Click the Set Recipient Permissions button.**

   By default, Acrobat grants the recipient full access to the PDF document whose user permissions include general editing, commenting and form field authoring privileges, the ability to print the document at any print resolution, and full copying and extraction privileges.

5. **To restrict the recipient's user permissions in some way, click the Restrict Printing and Editing of the Document and Its Security Settings button.**

6. **Limit the permissions by deselecting the Enable Text Access for Screen Reader Devices for the Visually Impaired check box and/or the Enable Copying of Text, Images and Other Content check box and/or by selecting new options in the Changes Allowed and Printing Allowed drop-down lists before you click OK.**

7. **Repeat Steps 3 through 6 (as they apply) to add your other recipients from the Identity Directories list box and set their user permissions in the Recipients list box.**

8. **After you've added all the recipients and set their user permissions, click the OK button.**

   If the Certificate Security - Alert box appears, telling you that settings will not be applied until you save your PDF document, click OK. You can also opt to not show this dialog box in the future by selecting the Do Not Show This Message Again check box before you click OK.

9. **Choose File⇨Save to save the Certificate Security encryption settings for the current document.**

   Alternatively, choose File⇨Save As and edit the filename and/or folder location of the encrypted document before clicking the Save button.

After you save your PDF file encrypted with Certificate Security, you can distribute copies to all the people you added to the Recipients list. When someone on the list tries to open the encrypted file, Acrobat displays the Select My Digital ID File dialog box, where the user selects his or her user Digital ID and enters his or her user password. When the user clicks the OK button to close the Select My Digital ID file dialog box, Acrobat checks the user's public key against the certificate information (specifically the MD5 and SHA-1 fingerprints) in the encrypted file. When Acrobat finds they match, it then opens the PDF document. The user then has access to the opened document according to user permissions that you set. To check these permissions, the user can right-click (Control+click on the Mac) the Document Encrypted key that now appears on the Document pane Status bar (a locked padlock on the left of the Status bar), select Document Security on the context menu, and then click the Security Settings button in the Document Properties dialog box.

If someone not on the Recipients list attempts to open a PDF document that's encrypted with Certificate Security, upon logging in, he or she will receive the Certificate Security - Alert dialog box with the message `You do not have access rights to this encrypted document`. When the user clicks OK to clear this dialog box, the document will fail to open.

Chapter 12

Extracting Text and Graphics from PDF Files

*A*crobat 6 is a great tool for distributing PDF documents for review and annotation. But as you know if you read any of the sections in Chapter 10 on editing, Acrobat is not so great for making any but the most simple of editing changes, and when it comes to changes in the basic design and layout, you can just forget it. This means that you have to rely on the native applications (such as your word processing, spreadsheet, page layout, and image editing programs) for making significant edits to the content and structure of PDF documents.

This is fine if you have access to the original files from which the PDF document was distilled, but what about the times when you can't find or never had the original electronic documents in their native file formats? In those situations, you need to rely on Acrobat's extraction features to take out the contents and as much structure as possible from the original PDF files and save them in file formats that other more edit-friendly software programs can handle.

In this chapter, you explore the various ways in Acrobat 6 for repurposing your PDF documents by pulling out the PDF file text, specific text elements, and graphics, and saving them in file formats that other popular editing programs can open.

You can choose three basic methods when extracting content from your PDF files:

- ✔ Copying and pasting discrete sections of text and selected graphics by using the Windows or Mac OS Clipboard or dragging and dropping between open windows.
- ✔ Saving the text in the entire PDF file in a completely new file format by using the File⇨Save As menu command.
- ✔ Exporting all the graphic images in the PDF file to separate graphics files in a new graphics file format compatible with your layout or image editing programs by using the Advanced⇨Export All Images menu command.

Extracting Blocks of Text

Before you can copy sections of text in a PDF document to the Clipboard or another open document, you need to select the text in the PDF document. To select text in a PDF document, you use two of the three different tools found on the Selection toolbar, which is attached to the Basic toolbar:

- ✔ **Select Text tool (V):** Use this tool to select lines or columns of text by dragging through them.
- ✔ **Select Table tool (Shift+V):** Use this tool to select a table or block of text with its formatting by drawing a bounding box around the table or text block.

You can also use the TouchUp Text tool (press T to select this tool) to select a block of text defined by its underlying document structure tags, such as whole headings or whole paragraphs. True to its name, this tool should be used only when you need to extract small amounts of text from a PDF document. Like the text selection tools on the Basic toolbar, text selected with the TouchUp Text tool can be copied, deleted, edited, and placed in other program documents. To find out everything about the TouchUp Text tool, see Chapter 10.

When you use the Select Text tool to select lines or columns of text in a PDF document, you can then copy the selected text to the Clipboard by choosing Edit⇨Copy or by pressing Ctrl+C (⌘+C on the Mac). After you've copied the text to the Clipboard, you can switch to a document open in another program and then paste the copied text into the file by using that program's Edit⇨Paste command or by pressing Ctrl+V (⌘+V on the Mac).

Using drag-and-drop to copy text

Instead of copying and pasting to and from the Clipboard, you can just drag the selected text from the PDF file open in an Acrobat window to a new document open in another program window. Figures 12-1 and 12-2 illustrate how this method works.

In Figure 12-1, in the PDF document open in the Acrobat program window on the right, I dragged the Select Text tool through the lines with the title and the first paragraph of text to select it. Then I dragged this text selection to the new document window open in Microsoft Word on the left by positioning the arrowhead mouse pointer (with the outline of the text selection) at the very beginning of the blank document. Figure 12-2 shows what happened when I released the mouse button to drop the text selection into place in the new Word document. (Note that in order to see both the Acrobat and Word program windows in Windows XP, you need to right-click the Windows taskbar and choose Tile Windows Vertically on the context menu.)

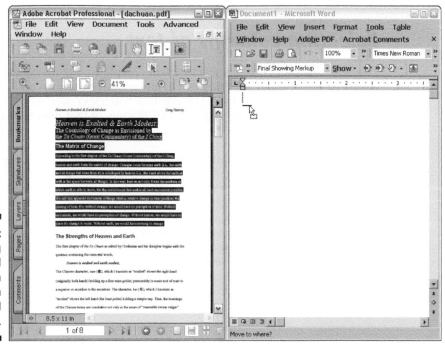

Figure 12-1: Dragging selected text from a PDF file to a new Word document.

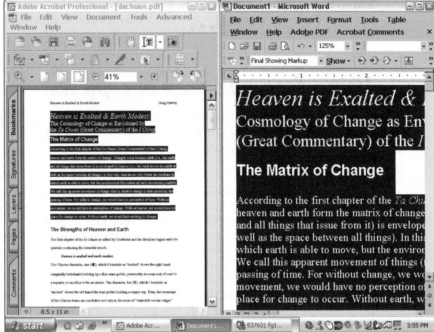

Figure 12-2:
The Word
document
window
after
dropping the
selected
text into
place.

Selecting columns of text

The Select Text tool enables you to select complete columns of text without having to worry about selecting text in any adjacent columns on the page that you don't want to include. Use this tool when you need to copy all or part of columns on a single page of a PDF document that uses newspaper columns.

To select a column of text with the Select Text tool, you simply drag the I-beam pointer from the top-left corner of a column of text in a diagonal direction toward the bottom-right corner of the column of text and release the mouse button.

Figure 12-3 shows a page of a PDF document set in two newspaper columns. In this figure, I have used the Select Text tool to select all the text in the right-hand column. The selected text is now available for copying to the Clipboard or dragging to a document in another program window.

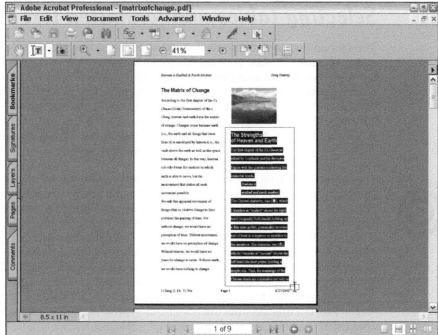

Figure 12-3:
Using the Select Text tool to select only the second column of text in a PDF document.

If you're working with a lot of text in a PDF document, you can configure the Hand tool in Acrobat 6 to automatically function as the Select Text tool when you hover it over text in a PDF document. Choose Edit⇨Preferences or press Ctrl+K (⌘+K on Mac) to open the Preferences dialog box. Click General in the list box on the left to display the General Preferences options, and then select the Enable Text Selection for the Hand tool check box. You can enter values (measured in picas) in the Text Selection Margin Size and Column Selection Margin Size text boxes to specify how much white space around text or columns to allow before the Hand tool transforms into the Text Selection tool and vice versa.

Looking up a word

The Select Text tool in Acrobat 6 comes with a look-up feature that is very handy (especially if you're blessed with broadband always-on Internet access). When you select a single word in a PDF document with the Select Text tool and then right-click to open the context menu, you find the Look Up "selected word"

command. Choose this command to go online to Dictionary.com and instantly look up the definition of your selected word on that Web site. Of course, if you've only got dial-up access to the Web, it's probably quicker to use the old-fashioned method — grab your ol' copy of Webster's and look the word up yourself.

Selecting tables and formatted text

The second text tool on the Basic toolbar is called the Select Table tool, and as its name implies, you use this tool when you want to copy text set in a table or to copy text along with its formatting (including font, font size, text color, alignment, line spacing, and indents when saving in an RTF — Rich Text Format — file format). To use the Select Table tool, you use its cross-hair mouse pointer to draw a bounding box around a table or lines of text that you want to select. As soon as you release the mouse button, Acrobat encloses the selected text or table in a heavy blue outline.

The Select Table tool can make table selections based on a PDF document's underlying document structure tags. To find out if you're working with a tagged PDF document, right-click the page with the Select Table tool to see if the Select Table Uses Document Tags command is activated (the PDF file is tagged) or grayed-out (the PDF file is untagged) on the context menu. Acrobat automatically selects this command when you open a tagged PDF document. If you're working with a tagged PDF document, you can simply click with the Select Table tool to select a table or lines of text formatted as a table. For more on document structure tags, see Chapter 1. To see how PDFMaker 6.0 creates tagged PDF documents from Microsoft Office programs, take a look at Chapter 5.

When Acrobat identifies a text selection as a table, it maintains the structure of the table by preserving the layout of the data in rows and columns of cells. If you then save the table data in the RTF file format for use in a word-processed document, the table maintains this layout in the new document. If you save the table data in the CSV (Comma Separated Values) text file format, which is the default format selected by Acrobat, the program maintains the table structure by separating the data items with commas and hard returns. This creates what is often called a *comma delimited text file* that most database and spreadsheet programs can convert easily into their own native file formats.

Saving a table or formatted text in a new file

Unlike when you select text with the Select Text tool, after you highlight a table or blocks of text with the Select Table tool, you can not only copy it to the Clipboard but also save the selection into a new file format. To do this, you right-click (Control+click on the Mac) the text or table selection and then click Save Selected Table As on the context menu to open the Acrobat Save As dialog box, where you specify the folder, filename, and type of file format in which to save the selection.

Select the Rich Text Format when you want to open the table or formatted text in a word processor such as Microsoft Word. Stay with the Comma Separated Values (*.csv) default file format when you're saving a table of data and you want to be able to import that data into a spreadsheet program (such as Microsoft Excel) or a database program (such as FileMaker Pro).

Copying PDF tables into word processors and spreadsheets

The Select Table tool makes it a joy to copy tables from PDF files into word-processed documents or spreadsheets. Figures 12-4 and 12-5 illustrate what happens when you drag a table selected with the Select Table tool into a new Word document (Figure 12-4) and into a blank worksheet in a new Excel workbook (Figure 12-5).

As you can see in Figure 12-4, Microsoft Word automatically recognizes and preserves the table structure by creating a new Word table. Even more importantly, Word has maintained the number formatting as well (indicated by the dollar signs, commas, percent signs, and parentheses for the negative values).

In Figure 12-5, you see that Excel also has no problem recognizing and correctly interpreting the layout and formatting of the table data. It immediately inserted the incoming table data into the correct worksheet cells, while maintaining the correct cell formatting. (By the way, in case you aren't yet an Excel user, if you see #### symbols in the new worksheet, these symbols merely indicate that the column isn't wide enough to display the values in that cell — these are not error indicators and are easily disposed of by widening the column.)

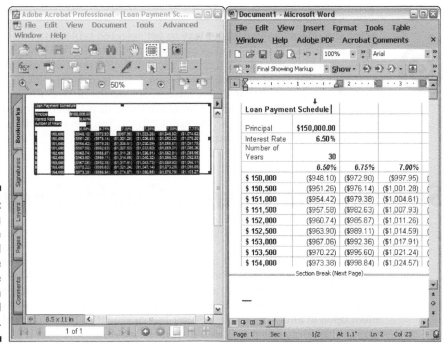

Figure 12-4: Dragging a table selected with the Select Table tool to a new Word document.

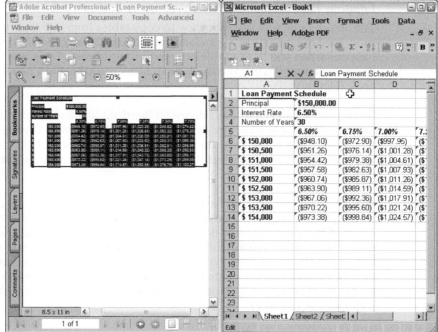

Figure 12-5:
Dragging a table selected with the Select Table tool into a new Excel workbook.

Acrobat 6 offers an even easier way to get selected table data into a spreadsheet program. (This method assumes that you already have a CSV-compliant spreadsheet program like Microsoft Excel installed on your computer.) Select a table in a PDF document with the Select Table tool, right-click to open the context menu, and choose Open Table in Spreadsheet. Your CSV-compliant spreadsheet program (and all of them are these days) opens a document with your table data imported into the spreadsheet. You can then edit and save your table data in that program's document format.

Selecting and Copying Graphic Images

You use the Select Image tool, located at the bottom of the Selection toolbar menu on the Basic toolbar, to select individual graphic images for copying. When you choose the Select Image tool, the mouse pointer becomes a cross-hair that you use to draw a bounding box around the graphic. After you've enclosed the entire graphic (and you don't have to worry if your marquee is a little larger than the image borders), you can copy the graphic to a new document open in another program either by copying it to the Clipboard (Edit⇨ Copy) or by dragging it to a new document window. Note that if your PDF document is tagged, you can simply click an image with the Select Image tool to select a graphic object.

Keep in mind that when you copy images to the Clipboard, Acrobat uses the graphics resolution of your monitor and that set for the Clipboard by your computer's operating system, rather than the resolution of the images as saved in the PDF document (which could well be a lot higher than either of the two). Also, be aware that all images you copy into the Clipboard are automatically converted onto the Clipboard as pixels, even if they are saved as vector (or line) graphics in the PDF file.

Exporting Images in Various Graphics Formats

To save all the graphic images in the current PDF document, choose Advanced⇨Export All Images. The Export All Images As dialog box appears, enabling you to save the images in one of four different file formats that you select from the Save As Type drop-down list:

- ✔ **JPEG (Joint Photographic Experts Group):** Choose this file format for true color compressed images.

- ✔ **PNG (Portable Network Graphics):** Choose this file format for compressed bitmap images.

- ✔ **TIFF (Tagged Image File Format):** Choose this file format for compressed bitmap images using both text and graphics. (TIFF is usually the format used to store the paper pages you scan.)

- ✔ **JPEG2000 (Joint Photographic Experts Group):** Choose this file format, a newer version of JPEG that utilizes state of the art wavelet compression, for even truer color compressed images.

After you select a graphics file format from the Save As Type drop-down list, select the drive and folder where you want the images saved. As soon as you click the Save button, the program goes through the current document and saves all the images in separate graphics files in the selected folder in the designated graphics file format.

Acrobat names these new graphics files by adding sequential numbers (starting with 0001) to the filename of the original PDF document (and tacking on the filename extensions .jpg for JPEG, .png for PNG, .tif for TIFF, and .jpf for JPEG2000 files in Windows). You can rename these numerical files with descriptive, more meaningful filenames either in Windows or the Mac OS or after opening them in an image editing program, such Adobe Photoshop 7.0.

If you want to save a single image as its own individual file, select the image with the Select Image tool, right-click, and choose Save Image As on its context menu. In the Save Image As dialog box that appears, choose a location for your new image file on the Save In drop-down list, enter a name for the file in the File Name text box and click Save. Because you can only select either bitmap (.bmp) or JPEG (.jpg) as a file type in the Save As Type drop-down list of this dialog box, use this method to quickly create an image file that you can open, edit, and save in a number of different image file formats in your favorite image editing program.

Saving Entire PDF Files in a New File Format

Copying and pasting and dragging and dropping are fine as long as you need to work with only portions of text in the PDF document. In those situations where you need to repurpose all the text in a PDF file, you simply use the File⇨Save As command. In the Save As dialog box that appears, select the appropriate file format in the Save as Type drop-down list, and then click the Save button.

Saving PDF files as text files

When saving PDF files as text files for use with text editors and word processing software, you have a choice between saving the PDF document in a Plain Text or an RTF. Select Plain Text when your only concern is getting the raw text into a more editable format. Select the RTF format whenever you want to preserve not only the document text but also as much formatting as possible. Always select the RTF file type when saving the text of PDF documents that you intend to edit with Microsoft Word.

Keep in mind that although RTF attempts to preserve much formatting from the PDF document, it is far from flawless, and in most cases you will end up having to do extensive reformatting in the resulting Word document. On those occasions, perhaps you can content yourself with the fact that you didn't have to retype any of the text. Of course, if your PDF document is tagged, as would be the case for any PDF created using PDFMaker 6.0, all document formatting will be preserved when you import the PDF text into a word processor. See Chapter 5 for more on creating tagged PDF documents in Microsoft Office programs.

Saving PDF files as HTML files

Acrobat 6 now enables you to save your PDF files in the HTML (HyperText Markup Language) file format, in essence turning them into Web pages. In Acrobat 5, you needed to download and install an Acrobat plug-in to have this functionality. Right out of the box, Acrobat 6 lets you choose between saving your PDF document in various versions of the HTML file format and in the newer XML (Extensible Markup Language) file format, which is used by many Web sites to improve Web page layout and interactivity. To save a PDF document in a Web format, choose File⇨Save As, and in the Save As dialog box, click the Save As Type drop-down list to select an HTML or XML file format to convert your PDF document to, enter a name for your new file in the File Name text box, choose a drive and folder location for your saved file in the Save In drop-down list, and click the Save button.

Chapter 13

Cataloging and Distributing PDF Files

*A*s you continue on your journey toward the goal of a truly paperless office, your collections of PDF files will undoubtedly grow exponentially. To keep on top of this burgeoning mountain of electronic information, you can start cataloging your PDF documents by organizing them into discrete collections and creating indexes that make the collection fast and easy to search. Catalogs provide a perfect way to archive the PDF files that are no longer in current use but contain valuable information that you may need to find and reuse at anytime in the future.

In this chapter, you discover the ins and outs of creating, maintaining, and searching PDF document collections. In addition, you pick up some pointers on how to package and distribute your collections for archiving or for general use on your network.

Cataloging 101

Cataloging your PDF files entails two basic steps: organizing your PDF files into a document collection ready for indexing, and then building the index. The indexes that you build for your collection are what make it possible to search for information across all the PDF files it contains and are also responsible for speeding up the search significantly.

Optimizing PDF files for indexing

When creating a collection you want to make searchable across a network, especially in a cross-platform environment (that is, one that networks both Windows and Mac machines) or a network with older DOS Windows machines (pre-Windows XP), you should consider renaming the files using the so-called eight-dot-three file naming convention (no more than eight characters for the main filename with no spaces, a period, and a three-character filename extension). Also, make sure that all PDF files in the collection use the .pdf filename extension (necessary on the Windows platform). Finally, you can optimize indexing and speed up searches by splitting long documents up into smaller files, each of which contains a chapter or major section.

Creating the PDF document collection

The keys to creating a successful PDF document collection are organizing the files and preparing them for indexing. To organize the files, you copy or move them all into a single folder. (You can organize files into subfolders within this folder, if necessary.) Before copying or moving the files into the collection folder, make sure that you're using only final versions of the PDF documents, which contain all necessary bookmarks, links, and form fields, and for which you've completed editorial review and made the final touch-up edits as well.

In preparing the files for indexing, you should make sure that you've added the title, subject, author, and keywords metadata for each PDF document, and in the case of documents that require a user password to open, you must remove the password, because Acrobat 6 cannot catalog PDF files that are password-protected.

Checking and editing the metadata

To check a PDF document's metadata and, if necessary, add this information, take these steps:

1. **Launch Acrobat 6 and then open the PDF file whose metadata you want to check.**

2. **Choose File⇨Document Properties or press Ctrl+D (⌘+D on the Mac); in the Document Properties dialog box, click Description in the list box.**

   The Description options for the file appear, as shown in Figure 13-1.

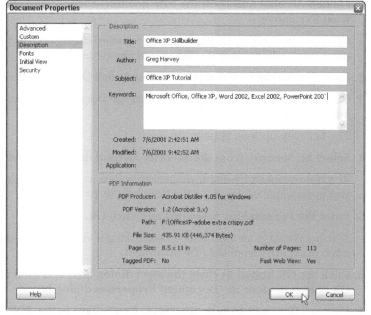

Figure 13-1:
Entering the
title, author,
subject, and
keywords
metadata
for a PDF
document.

3. **Add to or edit the Title, Author, Subject, and Keywords text boxes as needed to make it easier to identify and find the document later.**

4. **Click OK to close the Document Properties dialog box.**

5. **Choose File⇔Save to save any changes you made to the document's metadata.**

Removing password protection and checking the extraction file permissions

Because Acrobat can't search password-protected files, you must remove the Password Security from all files in the collection. If you've read Chapter 11, you know that Acrobat 6 gives you the option of using two different password protections on a PDF document. The Document Open Password restricts the opening of the document, and the Permissions password restricts the ability to print, edit, or make changes to security settings, as defined by the author in the Permissions section of the Password Security - Settings dialog box.

To be able to remove Password Security from a PDF document, you not only need to have access to the Document Open password (or you can't open it) but you also need to have access to the Permissions password (or you can't get rid of the security permissions). Assuming that you're armed with both passwords, follow these steps to remove the user password:

1. **Launch Acrobat and open the PDF document whose password you want to remove.**

   Acrobat responds by displaying the Password dialog box, in which you must successfully enter the Document Open password.

2. **Enter the Document Open password and click OK to open the document.**

3. **Choose File⇨Document Properties; in the Document Properties dialog box, click Security in the list box.**

   The Security options appear.

4. **Select No Security from the Security Method drop-down list.**

   Acrobat responds by displaying another Password dialog box, where you must successfully enter the Permissions password.

5. **Enter the Permissions password and click OK.**

   Acrobat displays an alert dialog box, asking if you're sure you want to remove security from the PDF document.

6. **Click the OK button to close the alert dialog box, and then click the OK button to close the Document Properties dialog box.**

7. **Choose File⇨Save to save your security changes to the PDF document.**

Building an index for your collection

After you've prepared your document collection, you're ready to build the index for it. When you create the index, you specify the folder that contains the PDF document collection (this is also the folder in which the index file and its support folder must reside). You also can specify up to a maximum of 500 words that you want excluded from the index (such as *a, an, the, and, or,* and the like) and have numbers excluded from the index to speed up your searches. Words that you exclude from an index are called *stop words.* Keep in mind that while specifying stop words does give you a smaller and more efficient index (estimated at between 10 and 15 percent smaller), it also prevents you and other users from searching the collection for phrases that include these stop words (such as "in the matter of Smith and James").

To build a new index, follow these steps:

1. **Launch Acrobat and choose Advanced⇨Catalog.**

   (You don't have to have any of the files in the PDF document collection open at the time you do this.) The Catalog dialog box opens.

2. **Click the New Index button in the Catalog dialog box.**

   The Index Definition dialog box opens, as shown in Figure 13-2.

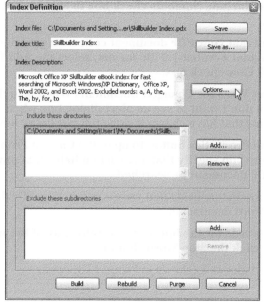

Figure 13-2:
Specifying
what folder
to include in
a new index
in the Index
Definition
dialog box.

3. **Enter a descriptive title that clearly and concisely identifies the new index in the Index Title text box.**

4. **Click in the Index Description list box and enter a complete description of the index.**

   This description can include the stop words, search options supported, and the kinds of documents indexed.

5. **Click the Add button to the right of the Include These Directories list box; in the Browse for Folder dialog box, select the folder that contains your PDF document collection and click OK.**

6. **To specifically exclude any subfolders that reside within the folder that contains your PDF document collection (the one whose directory path is now listed in the Include These Directories list box), click the Add button to the right of the Exclude These Subdirectories list box, select the subfolders of the folder you selected in Step 5, and click OK.**

   Repeat this step for any other subfolders that need to be excluded. (Actually, you should be able to skip this step entirely, because the folder that contains your PDF document collection ideally shouldn't have any other folders in it.)

7. **To further configure your index definition, click the Options button.**

   The Options dialog box opens.

8. **Select the Do Not Include Numbers check box to exclude numbers from the index.**

9. **In the rare event that your PDF document collection contains PDF files saved in the original Acrobat 1.0 file format, select the Add IDs to Acrobat 1.0 PDF Files check box.**

10. **Select the Do Not Warn for Changed Documents When Searching check box if you don't want to see an alert dialog box when you search documents that have changed since the last index build.**

11. **Click the Custom Properties button to open the Custom Properties dialog box, where you specify that any custom fields that have been added to the PDF document be searched.**

    These include any custom fields that were converted by PDFMaker 6.0 from Microsoft Word documents.

12. **To specify stop words for the index or to disable any of the word search options, click the Stop Words button.**

    The Stop Words dialog box (shown in Figure 13-3) opens.

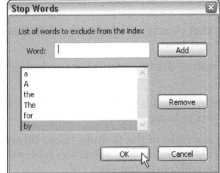

Figure 13-3: Specifying stop words in the Stop Words dialog box.

13. **To specify a stop word that is not included in the index, enter a term in the Word text box and click the Add button.**

    Repeat this step until you've added all the stop words you don't want indexed.

14. **Click OK to close the Stop Words dialog box and return to the Options dialog box.**

15. **Click the Tags button to specify which document structure tags (if the PDF Document is tagged) can be used as search criteria in the Tags dialog box.**

    See Chapter 1 for more about tagged PDF files.

16. **Click OK to close the Options dialog box and return to the New Index Definition dialog box.**

17. **Check over the fields in the New Definition dialog box and, if everything looks okay, click the Build button.**

    The Save Index File dialog box opens.

18. **If you want, replace the generic filename** index.pdx **in the File Name (Name on the Mac) text box with a more descriptive filename, and then click the Save button.**

    When editing the filename, be sure that you don't select a new folder in which to save the file (it must be in the same folder as your PDF document collection) and, in Windows, don't remove the .pdx extension (for Portable Document Index) that identifies it as a special Acrobat index file.

Acrobat responds by displaying the Catalog dialog box that keeps you informed of its progress as it builds the new index. When the Progress bar reaches 100% and the program finishes building the index, you can then click the Close button to close the Catalog dialog box and return to the Acrobat program, where you can start using the index in searching the files in the PDF document collection. Note that when Acrobat builds an index, it not only creates a new index file (with the .pdx filename extension on Windows), but also creates a new support folder using the same filename as the index file.

All settings specified in the Options dialog box (Steps 7 through 15 in the preceding step list) apply only to the currently opened index file. If you want to apply any or all of these options globally to every catalog index you create, choose Edit➪Preferences and click Catalog in the list box to display the Catalog Preferences options. You can then specify global settings for index file creation, using the same options found in the Options dialog box.

Rebuilding an index

If you modify a PDF document collection for which you've created an index by removing or adding files to the collection, you must rebuild the index in order to have Acrobat search its entire contents. Before you rebuild an index for a collection from which you have removed some PDF files, you need to purge the index. When you do this, Acrobat actually removes the files no longer part of the collection from the index, rather than just marking them as invalid. Purging them from the index streamlines it considerably and makes searching it as fast as possible.

To purge and then rebuild an index, follow these steps:

1. **Choose Advanced⇨Catalog; in the Catalog dialog box that appears, click the Open Index button.**

   The Open Index File dialog box appears.

2. **Select the folder that contains the PDF document collection and the index file, and then click the index file icon (the one with the .pdx file extension in Windows) before you click the Open button.**

   The Open Index File dialog box closes, and the Index Definition dialog box appears.

3. **Click the Purge button at the bottom of the Index Definition dialog box.**

   Acrobat responds by opening the Catalog dialog box that displays the status of your index purge operation with a progress bar. When the purge operation is finished, you are informed of that fact in the list box below the progress bar.

4. **To rebuild the purged index, click the Open Index button again, click the index file icon, and then click the Open button.**

   Once again, the Open Index File dialog box closes, and the Index Definition dialog box appears.

5. **Click the Rebuild button to rebuild the index using only the PDF files left after the purge.**

6. **After Acrobat finishes rebuilding the index, click the Close button to close the Catalog dialog box.**

After you've finished purging and rebuilding an index, you can then immediately start using it in the searches you perform on the PDF document collection. Although not specifically noted in the preceding steps, keep in mind that prior to clicking the Rebuild button, you can click the Options button to modify stop words or change the other number and document element search options, as discussed earlier in this chapter in the section, "Building an index for your collection."

If you use only one particular index that you built when searching a particular PDF document, you can associate the index file with the PDF file. That way, Acrobat automatically mounts the index so you're ready to search the document with it every time you open the PDF document in Acrobat. To do this, choose File⇨Document Properties and click Advanced in the list box to display the Advanced Document Properties options. In the PDF Setting area, click the Browse button to locate and select the index file you want to associate with the current PDF document. Click Open to select the index file and return to the Document Preferences dialog box. The directory path for the index file now appears in the Search Index text box. Click OK to close the Document Preferences dialog box.

Searching a Collection

After you've created the indexes you need to search your PDF document collections, you can use the Search feature in Acrobat 6 or Adobe Reader 6 to quickly locate key terms and phrases. Keep in mind that when you use the Search feature, Acrobat is searching for the occurrence of your terms in any of the indexed documents included in the PDF document collection. Therefore, along with specifying the search terms, you need to specify which index should be used in doing the search.

In order to be able to search collections in Adobe Reader 6 (as opposed to Acrobat 6), you must download the Full version of the program from Adobe's Web site. The Basic version lacks the ability to search PDF files.

When specifying the search terms, you can use wildcard characters. Use the asterisk (*) to indicate any number of missing characters and the question mark (?) for single missing characters. You can also use the following Boolean operators:

- ✔ **NOT:** Excludes documents in the collection that contain a certain word or phrase, such as NOT "Chicago". You can also use the NOT operator by entering the ! (exclamation point) in front of the term to be excluded.

- ✔ **AND:** Narrows the search to documents that contain both terms, such as "Chicago" AND "New York". When you use the AND operator, Acrobat matches a document only when it contains both terms.

- ✔ **OR:** Expands the search to include documents that include either search term, such as "Chicago" OR "St. Louis". When you use the OR operator, Acrobat matches any document that contains one or the other term.

When specifying a search term, you can also include any of the following word search options:

- ✔ **Whole Words Only:** Limits matches to occurrences of the whole words specified in the search words or phrases.

- ✔ **Case Sensitive:** Limits matches in a search to the words in the document collection that exhibit a strict upper- and lowercase correspondence to the term for which you're searching.

- ✔ **Proximity:** Ignores any matches unless one instance of the search term occurs within three pages of another instance of it in the documents included in the PDF document collection. For example, if you search for the phrase customer satisfaction guaranteed, Acrobat will show matches only when this phrase occurs more than once in the document and at least two occurrences are within three pages of each other.

✔ **Stemming:** Enables the Word Assistant preview (that you can use to refine searches — see the "Refining your search" section, later in this chapter) and expands matches in a search to words in the document collection that use the same word stem (so that occurrences of *foremost*, *foreman*, and *foresee* in the collection all match when you specify *fore* as the search term).

✔ **Search in Bookmarks:** Expands matches in a search to occurrences in the PDF document bookmarks.

✔ **Search in Comments:** Expands matches in a search to occurrences in the PDF document comments.

The steps for finding terms or phrases in a PDF document collection with the Search feature are as follows:

1. **Choose Edit⇨Search, or press Ctrl+Shift+F (⌘+Shift+F on the Mac) to open the Search PDF pane.**

   The Search PDF pane opens, as shown in Figure 13-4.

2. **Click the Use Advanced Search Options link at the bottom of the Search PDF pane and from the Look In drop-down list, choose Select Index.**

   The Index Selection dialog box opens, as shown in Figure 13-5.

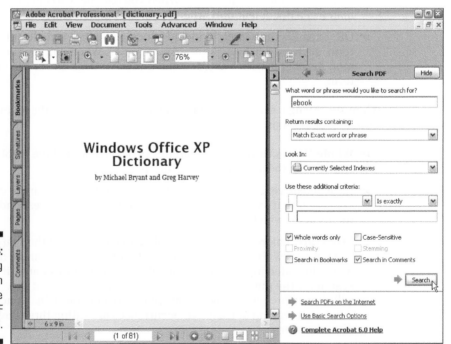

Figure 13-4: Specifying the search terms in the Search PDF pane.

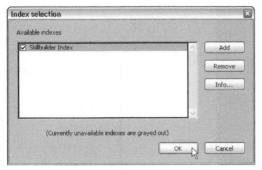

Figure 13-5:
Specifying
the index to
use in the
Index
Selection
dialog box.

3. **If the index you want to use is not listed in the Available Indexes list box, click the Add button, open the folder with the PDF document collection you want to search, click the index file icon, and then click the Open button.**

   The Select Index dialog box closes, and you return to the Index Selection dialog box.

4. **Select the index you want to use for your search; deselect any index(es) you don't want to use for your search. After you have selected only the index(es) you want to use in the search, click OK.**

   The Index Selection dialog box closes, and you return to the Search PDF pane.

5. **Enter the search term(s) or phrase in the What Word or Phrase Would You Like to Search For? text box.**

   Remember that you can use wildcard characters for characters of which you're uncertain in the search term or phrase.

6. **Choose a search criterion (Match Exact Word or Phrase, Match Any of the Words, Match All of the Words, or Boolean Query) in the Return Results Containing drop-down list.**

7. **Select any of the search options (Whole Words Only, Case Sensitive, Proximity, Stemming, Search in Bookmarks, and Search in Comments) that you want to apply.**

8. **Click the Search button to have Acrobat search the designated index or indexes.**

   The results are displayed in the Search Results dialog box, as shown in Figure 13-6.

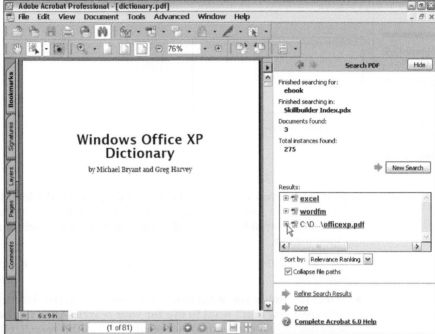

Figure 13-6:
Checking over the result PDF documents ranked by matches in the Search PDF pane.

Viewing the search results

When Acrobat finishes doing the search (which it completes very quickly, except in the cases of huge document collections), it displays all matching files and ranks them in order of relevance in the Results list box (refer to Figure 13-6). Relevance Ranking is the default setting in the Sort By drop-down list. You can change the sort order of the Results list box by selecting Date Modified, Filename, or Location from the Sort By drop-down list.

To have Acrobat open a document in the Results list and show you the first occurrence of the search term, click the Expand button (plus sign on Windows, triangle pointing right on Mac) to display a list of occurrences of the search term as they appear in the PDF document. Acrobat creates hyperlinks out of all search terms in the Results list box. If you hover the mouse pointer over a search term, a screen tip appears, indicating the page number that the term appears on in the selected PDF document. Clicking a search term opens the PDF document in the document pane and highlights the occurrence of search term on the page in the selected PDF document.

You can close the Search PDF pane, which, like all How To panes, takes up a third of your screen, so that you can more easily view the matches highlighted in the selected document. To redisplay the Search PDF pane, press Ctrl+F (⌘+F on Mac), or you can use the Search Result commands on the

Acrobat menu bar. Choose Edit⇨Search Results and choose either Next Document, Next Result, Previous Result, or Previous Document on the sub-menu. The keyboard shortcuts are listed on this submenu.

Refining your search

Sometimes, your first search for a particular term results in too many match-ing files pulled from the PDF document collection, and you find that you need to refine your search further narrow the search results. To do this, follow these steps:

1. **Click the Refine Search Results link near the bottom of the Search PDF pane to display Advanced Search options in the Search PDF pane.**

   Note that when you refine your search in this manner, the options you choose are applied to the previous search results.

2. **Replace or further refine the search term in the Search Within the Previous Results For text box.**

3. **Select a new option, if desired, in the Return Results Containing drop-down list, and then select or deselect the Whole Words Only, Case-Sensitive, Proximity, or Stemming check boxes to further refine your search criteria.**

4. **Click the Refine Search Results button to begin your new search.**

The Advanced Search options that appear in the Use These Additional Criteria section of the Search PDF pane provide a means of using metadata and date filtering as search criteria. These powerful search options are cov-ered in the next section.

By default, Acrobat displays its Basic Search options when you choose Edit⇨Search or press Ctrl+F (⌘+F on Mac) to initiate a search. The Advanced Search options are displayed only when you choose Refine Search Results in the Search PDF pane after performing a basic search. To have Acrobat display the Advanced Search options rather than the Basic Search options in the Search PDF pane when you initiate a search, choose Edit⇨Preferences or press Ctrl+K (⌘+K on Mac) to open the Preferences dialog box. Click Search in the list box to display the Search options. Select the Always Use Advanced Search Options check box, and then click OK to close the Preferences dialog box. Note that when you choose this option, you won't have access to the Basic Search options until you turn off this feature by deselecting the check box in the Search section of the Preferences dialog box.

Adding document information (metadata) and date filtering to your searches

Earlier in this chapter, in the "Creating the PDF document collection" section, I go through a big thing about recording your metadata in the Document Summary dialog box in the Title, Subject, Author, and Keywords text boxes. Acrobat doesn't automatically include document information (otherwise known as *metadata*) as part of the search. Nor does it include an equally powerful search feature called *date filtering* (which enables you to match documents in a collection that were created or modified within a range of dates). As described previously, you get these options only if you choose to refine your Basic Search or choose to have these Advanced options displayed by default in the Search PDF pane when you initiate a search.

Figure 13-7 shows you the Advanced Search options in the Search PDF pane and an example of the type of options provided in the Use These Additional Criteria area. As you can see, you can now search for the metadata that you so assiduously entered for each PDF document in the collection (at my gentle insistence), as well as the aforementioned date filtering technique, all in the same search. To add metadata and date filtering to your search criteria, follow these steps:

Figure 13-7:
Setting up
metadata
and date
filtering
criteria
in the
Advanced
Search
options
palette of
the Search
PDF pane.

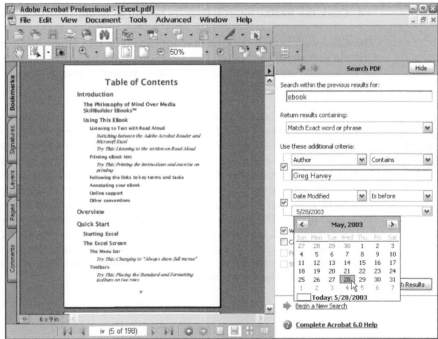

1. **From the drop-down list on the left under Use These Additional Criteria, select the metadata criteria (Title, Subject, Author, and Keywords) you wish to search for.**

   In addition to Document Properties information (metadata), you can also choose Filename, Bookmarks, Comments, JPEG Images, and XMP Metadata (a format that makes it easier to share metadata between documents created in different Adobe programs) as search criteria from the Use These Additional Criteria drop-down lists.

2. **From the drop-down list on the right under Use These Additional Criteria, select either Contains or Does Not Contain.**

3. **Enter the words or names to search for in text box below the Use These Additional Criteria drop-down lists.**

4. **To add date filtering, choose either Date Modified or Date Created from the Use These Additional Criteria drop-down list.**

   Refer to Figure 13-7.

5. **From the drop-down list to the right, select Is Exactly, Is Before, Is After, or Is Not.**

6. **Click the drop-down list below the date criteria drop-down lists and select a date on the calendar that appears.**

   After you click a date, the calendar closes and the date appears in the drop-down list box.

By adding the date filtering fields (Created or Modified After or Before) in the Use These Additional Criteria area, you can also refine a search by the approximate date the particular PDF files in the collection were originally created and/or modified. This makes it possible to find a document that shares essentially the same metadata as others in the collection but was created or last modified on a particular date.

Distributing PDF Document Collections

After you've established your PDF document collections, you can make them available to your coworkers in a couple of ways. One of the most popular methods is to back up one or more of the collections (depending upon the number of PDF files they contain) on CD-ROMs that you can send out or make available for use from a central archive. Another method available to users whose computers are part of a company-wide network is to copy the PDF document collections onto a volume on the network server and share that volume with all the users who need to access its information.

The biggest potential problem with making PDF document collections available on a network is that together they can eat up a lot of disk space, depending upon how many PDF files they contain. Of course, this isn't a problem when you distribute collections on individual CD-ROMs, although it does mean that you have to be smart about how you classify and categorize the collections on each CD-ROM because they can only be mounted and searched individually. This means that you can't peruse the various collection folders at one time as you can when they're all located together on a shared volume of a network.

You may wonder about making PDF document collections available from a corporate intranet or Internet Web site. Unfortunately, as of now, the only way to make PDF document collections searchable on Web servers is with the Adobe PDF iFilter, a free downloadable DLL (Dynamic Link Library) that enables searching PDF files using Microsoft's specifications for filtering text. Of course, this is no solution if your company doesn't happen to use a version of the Microsoft Internet Information Server and Microsoft Index Server (both of which have to be in place for the PDF iFilter to work). For more information on the Adobe iFilter and to download it, go to the following Web address:

```
www.adobe.com/support/downloads
```

Part IV

PDFs as Electronic Documents

The 5th Wave   By Rich Tennant

DAD ADDS MULTIMEDIA SOUND AND GRAPHICS TO THE TRADITIONAL CAMPFIRE GHOST STORY.

In this part . . .

Part of the allure of Adobe's Portable Document Format is its promise to reduce the amount of paper documents in the office by replacing them with fully functional electronic counterparts. This part of the book covers the major electronic forms of PDF files, interactive forms, eBooks, and online presentations you will encounter more and more in your work.

In Chapter 14, you find out all about creating and using electronic PDF forms, including collecting their data from Web sites on the company's intranet and the Internet. Chapter 15 introduces you to the world of Acrobat eBooks using PDF documents designed specifically, and sometimes exclusively, for online reading. Finally, in Chapter 16, you find out how you can turn PDF files into multimedia presentations by adding audio and video elements to be viewed in Acrobat 6 and Adobe Reader 6.

Chapter 14

Creating Interactive Forms

*F*illing out forms is a way of life in the Information Age. These everyday documents come in all shapes and sizes and are perfect candidates for conversion in Acrobat 6 (Professional version only), where they take advantage of the fixed layout, portability, editing, and import/export features of Adobe PDF. The results are interactive electronic forms that are cross-platform and easily distributed over a computer network. The ability to create and modify electronic forms with Acrobat 6 is arguably the greatest thing since sliced bread, especially for those who rely on a company intranet or the World Wide Web to gather and distribute crucial information.

This chapter introduces you to *form fields,* the main components used to create an interactive PDF form. In the process, you find out about the various types of form fields and the way they define and add interactivity to a form. You also discover how to format and modify fields, use them to build a form from scratch, and create forms that automatically calculate entered data. Finally, you find out how to use Acrobat 6's import/export feature and submit your form online so that it can be distributed and used to gather data.

Introducing Form Fields

The term *electronic form* is used to describe forms that can be distributed over a computer network (including a company intranet or the Internet). In the old days (before PDF), to create an electronic form, you either scanned an existing paper form into a graphics-editing program or built one from scratch using a word processor or page layout program. Recipients could view these electronic forms only if they had the proper software and the forms were not interactive, meaning that you still had to print one and fill it out with a pen or pencil. At that point, your form wasn't electronic anymore.

What makes Acrobat 6 so fantastic is that, in addition to creating PDF forms by scanning existing forms or developing them right in the program, it also lets you produce truly interactive and portable forms that can be filled out on a computer screen and submitted over a computer network. This amazing feat is accomplished through the magic of form fields.

Although some of you might think of *fields* as those places that keep disappearing to accommodate urban sprawl, for the purpose of PDF forms, *fields* are containers for specific types of information and interactive elements. For example, the Name box on a form, where you put — you guessed it — your name, is a *text field*. An example of an interactive element field is a *check box* or *list box* that makes it easier for a user to fill out a form by selecting rather than entering data. (To find out all about the different types of form fields, see the "Getting Acquainted with Form Field Tools" section, later in this chapter.) Adding different types of fields to a PDF document enables you to distribute it online, and users can fill it out in the comfort of their own computer desktop.

Adding Fields to Forms

Although creating a simple interactive form from scratch in Acrobat 6 is certainly possible (see the "Creating form field tables" section, later in this chapter), most people find that what they really want is to add interactivity to a form that is already set up. For example, say that in the past you've paid big bucks to a graphic designer for a logo and spent even more to print reams of forms with your new logo on them. However, now you want people to fill out your forms online to save trees (and money). To do so, you just need to convert your form to PDF and then add the necessary form fields. (See Chapter 15 for details on creating PDF files from a variety of popular Windows and Macintosh graphics and page layout programs.)

Acrobat 6 (Professional version only) provides seven different form field tools (Button tool, Check Box tool, Combo Box tool, List Box tool, Radio Button tool, Text Field tool, and Digital Signature Field tool) used to create interactive form fields, and each is covered in later sections of this chapter. The tools are grouped together on the Forms toolbar that you open by choosing Advanced Editing⇨Forms⇨Show Forms Toolbar. The Forms toolbar appears in its undocked (floating) state, which makes it easy to access when you're building an interactive form. For more about the Forms toolbar, see the "Getting Acquainted with Form Field Tools" section, later in this chapter.

Figure 14-1 shows an order form I created in Microsoft Excel and then converted to PDF (see Chapter 5 for details on converting MS Office documents to Acrobat files). Like most forms, this example uses numerous cells (such as the Name and Date cells) for writing information in. You need to add fields to these areas so that users can enter data on-screen in the finished product. Fields that you enter text or numbers into are called *text fields*. Naturally, you create these types of fields in a form with the Acrobat Text Field tool.

After you convert your form to PDF and open it in Acrobat 6, use the following steps to add text fields to the form:

1. Click the Text Field Tool button on the Forms toolbar or press F to select the Text Field tool.

(Note that you can display the Forms toolbar, shown in Figure 14-1, by choosing Tools⇨Advanced Editing⇨Forms⇨Show Forms Toolbar.) The cursor turns into a cross-hair pointer, which you use to draw square or rectangular shapes for your fields.

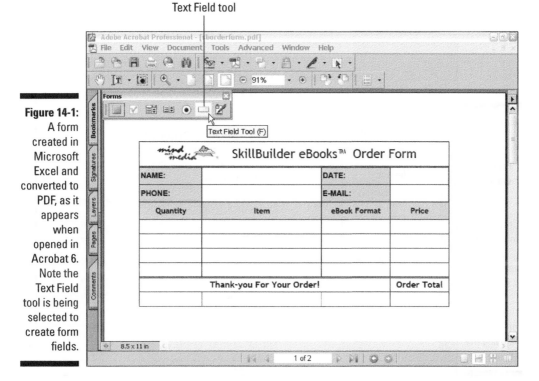

Figure 14-1: A form created in Microsoft Excel and converted to PDF, as it appears when opened in Acrobat 6. Note the Text Field tool is being selected to create form fields.

2. **Drag the Text Field tool pointer to draw a box in the desired field area of your PDF form and release the mouse button.**

   The Text Field Properties dialog box (shown in Figure 14-2) opens.

3. **On the General tab of the Text Field Properties dialog box, type a name for the field in the Name text box, and then enter a short description or instruction in the ToolTip text box, if desired.**

   The ToolTip is the message that appears when a user hovers the mouse over the form field.

4. **Choose options for the text field from the tabs provided.**

   Field options for all the form tools are covered in detail in the section "Selecting Form Field Options," later in this chapter.

5. **Click OK to close the Text Field Properties dialog box.**

   The field box appears in your document in editing mode, that is, outlined in bold red with its name in the middle of the box.

Form field

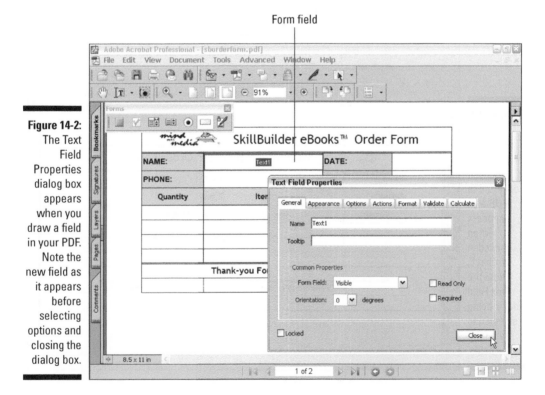

Figure 14-2: The Text Field Properties dialog box appears when you draw a field in your PDF. Note the new field as it appears before selecting options and closing the dialog box.

Presto, you've added a text form field to your PDF document! Here are some important characteristics of your new form field:

- ✔ Unselected fields are colored black but turn bright red when you click the mouse to select them.

- ✔ Sizing handles appear on a selected field box to facilitate resizing.

- ✔ To edit a field's name or change options, double-click the field to open its Field Properties dialog box.

- ✔ To delete a field, select the field and press the Delete key.

Each form field tool creates its own unique form field type — one that can only be selected and edited with the form field tool that created it. For example, you can't select and edit a radio button form field (created with the Radio Button tool) with the Text Field tool. When you have a number of different of form field types in a PDF document, use the Select Object tool (Tools⇨Advanced Editing⇨Select Object Tool), which can not only select any one of the seven form field types, but also let you access their specific options by right-clicking a form field and choosing Properties on the context menu. This is much easier than switching back and forth between different form field tools for selection and editing.

When drawing a text field box with the Text Field tool's cross-hair pointer, make sure to keep the lines of the box inside the boundaries of the cell or line you've chosen in your PDF form. This ensures that when a person is filling out the form, his or her data won't overflow those boundaries.

Move those fields!

You can move, resize, and align form fields in numerous ways after you add a few to your form. Here are the basic techniques that you can apply to one or more fields:

- ✔ **To move:** Click a field and drag it to a new location. To make more precise movements, select a field and nudge it with the arrow keys. You can apply these same techniques to multiple field selections. Select multiple fields by holding down the Shift key while making your selections. The first selected field turns red, and subsequent selections are outlined in blue. Note that multiple field selections can be non-contiguous. After you've made your selections, release the Shift key and drag the selections to another location or nudge them with the arrow keys.

  When using the mouse to move multiple fields, you can constrain field movement to a horizontal or vertical direction by pressing the Shift key after you've started to drag the selected group of fields. To center single and multiple field selections on a page, right-click the field selection and choose Center and select Vertically, Horizontally, or Both on the Center submenu.

✔ **To resize:** Position the mouse pointer on any of the sizing handles that appear on a selected field. When the mouse pointer turns to a double-headed arrow, drag in the direction of the arrows to change the size of a form field. To resize a single field or multiple field selections in smaller increments, hold down the Shift key while pressing the arrow keys. You can also resize multiple fields by first right-clicking the field selection and then choosing Size and selecting Height, Width, or Both on the Size submenu. These commands resize all selected fields to the respective height, width, or both of the first selected field.

✔ **To align:** Select the field that you want other form fields to align with first and then select the fields you want to align. To align all selected fields with the respective border of the first field selected, right-click the field selection and choose Align and select Left, Right, Top, or Bottom on the Align submenu. Choosing Vertical or Horizontal from this menu aligns the selected fields along the vertical or horizontal axis of the first selected field. See the "Looking at the Layout Grid" section, later in this chapter, to find out about Acrobat 6's best feature for keeping fields straight.

Duplicating form fields

At some point, you may need to create a whole bunch of fields that have the same attributes or properties — such as a group of check boxes or radio buttons. You can streamline this process by duplicating fields. After you've configured the size and properties of the field you want to duplicate, select it, hold down the Ctrl key (the Option key on the Mac), and drag the field to a new location, using the marquee lines that appear as a guide. Repeat this process until you've created the desired number of fields. If you have mega amounts of fields to duplicate, you can use the same method on multiple field selections, which doubles the number of selected fields. Note that all fields created in this manner have the same name, which is perfect for radio buttons (see the "Understanding the Options tab" section, later in this chapter).

To copy and paste fields using key commands, select a desired field for duplication and press Ctrl+C (⌘+C on the Mac) to copy the field to the Clipboard. Then press Ctrl+V (⌘+V on the Mac) to paste the field into your PDF. Note that you can copy and paste multiple field selections in this manner and that pasted items will appear centered on the PDF page.

If you need to duplicate form fields in a multi-page PDF document, right-click the desired form field(s) and choose Duplicate on the context menu to open the Duplicate Fields dialog box. Here you can choose to duplicate the selected form field(s) on all pages in your document by clicking the All radio button, or click the From radio button and select a range of pages in a PDF document on which to duplicate the selected form field(s).

Getting Acquainted with Form Field Tools

As mentioned earlier in this chapter, Acrobat provides seven form field tools for adding interactive elements to an online form. The tools are grouped together on the Forms toolbar that you open by choosing Advanced Editing⇨Forms⇨Show Forms Toolbar. Figure 14-3 shows the Forms toolbar in its undocked (floating) state. Each form field tool has its own associated Properties dialog box containing various options that appear on tabs. These options are described in detail in the next section, "Selecting Form Field Options."

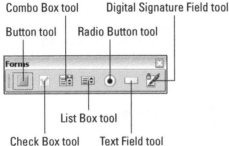

Figure 14-3: The Forms toolbar contains individual form field tools.

Combo Box tool   Digital Signature Field tool
Button tool   Radio Button tool
List Box tool
Check Box tool   Text Field tool

The following list gives you a run-down on the seven form field tools that define the type of information you want to collect and add interactivity to your form:

✔ **Button tool:** Used to create a button that performs an action in a form, such as a Reset button that erases previously entered information so you can start over, or a Submit button that sends the form information to a network server. In addition, buttons can play sounds and movies, open files, or download Web pages from the Internet. Acrobat 6 also lets you automatically create JavaScript button rollovers. These types of buttons change appearance when the cursor is hovered or *rolled over* the button.

✔ **Check Box tool:** Used to make multiple selections from a list of items. Check boxes were used extensively in old-fashioned paper forms and usually followed the instruction, "Check all that apply."

✔ **Combo Box tool:** So called because it functions as a combination text field/list box, enabling the user to either pick an item from a list or enter custom text in a field, with the added advantage of saving space on a form by presenting the items in a drop-down list.

✔ **List Box tool:** For a long list of items to present in your form, a list box is a good solution because it has scroll bars that allow the user to scroll through the list to select an item.

✔ **Radio Button tool:** Used when only one item from a list can be selected. For example, you can use a radio button to have users indicate whether they're male or female or to specify which credit card they want to use to pay for an online transaction.

✔ **Text Field tool:** Used for entering text and numbers, such as a person's e-mail address or birth date. You can set up text fields to format and limit the type of information entered in them as well as to perform calculations. You can also attach JavaScript actions and data validation to text fields.

✔ **Digital Signature Field tool:** Used to enable the user to digitally sign a document. Like hand-written signatures, digital signatures represent the user's identity and his or her approval or acceptance of a document. They have the added advantage of storing information about the signer and the exact state of the PDF form when it was signed.

Selecting Form Field Options

The Properties dialog box associated with each form field tool displays up to seven different tabs of options, depending on which tool you choose when adding a field to your PDF form. Field options govern characteristics, such as the way a field appears in a form, the format and type of data that can be entered in the field, actions that you attach to a field (such as playing a sound or movie), and also the types of calculations performed on data entered in a field.

To edit field options, double-click the field with the Select Object tool or the form field tool that created the field to open its associated Properties dialog box, and then click the desired tab. The separate tabs and options (in all their copiousness) are described in the following sections.

Jawing about General tab options

The options on the General tab are applicable to every field type and are used to specify the identity of the field and select common display and function properties. Figure 14-4 shows the General tab of the Button Properties dialog box, which shows the same options you find on the General tab regardless of which field type properties dialog box is opened. Note that after selecting General options (or any other field option for that matter), you must click Close to close the Field Properties dialog box, and then click the Hand tool on the Basic Tools toolbar or press H in order to view your changes.

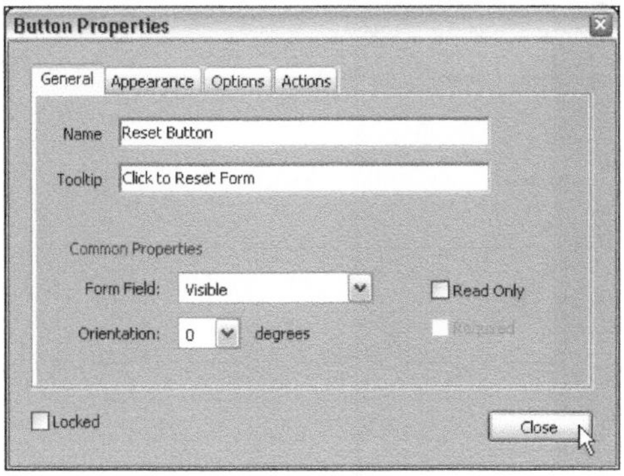

Figure 14-4:
The options
on the
General tab
apply to all
form field
tools in the
Properties
dialog box.

The following list describes the options found in the labeled areas of the
General tab:

- ✔ **Name:** Enter a descriptive name for a form field in this text box. When
  you create a form field, it is given an incremental default name, such as
  Button1, Button2, and so on.

- ✔ **ToolTip:** Enter a descriptive name or short instruction in this text box;
  this text appears as a ToolTip when the user hovers the mouse pointer
  over the form field element.

- ✔ **Common Properties:** These miscellaneous options apply to all field
  types. Select the Read Only check box to specify text fields that cannot
  be modified by a user. Select the Required check box to specify that a
  field must be filled in before form data can be submitted. Use the Form
  Field drop-down list to select whether a field is Visible, Hidden, Visible
  but Doesn't Print, or Hidden but Printable. The Orientation drop-down
  list lets you choose the text orientation in 90-degree increments for text
  that is either entered in a text field, selected in a combo or list box, or
  used as a button label. The Orientation option also applies to graphic
  icons used as button labels. To restrict any future changes to the selected
  form field, select the Locked check box in the lower left corner of the
  General tab.

Applying Appearance tab options

The options on the Appearance tab (shown for Text Field Properties in
Figure 14-5) are applicable to every field type and are used to specify the way
a field is displayed in a PDF form. Note that to apply appearance options (or
any other field option for that matter) to a selected form field, you first click
Close to close the Properties dialog box, and then click the Hand tool on the
Basic Tools toolbar or press H in order to view your changes.

Figure 14-5:
The options
on the
Appearance
tab of the
Field
Properties
dialog box.

The following list describes the options found in the labeled areas of the
Appearance tab that you can use to change the way a form field is displayed
in a PDF form:

- ✔ **Borders and Colors:** Provides options for setting the border and background of a field. Click the Border Color or the Fill Color buttons and
  choose from the color palette (Windows) or the color picker dialog box
  (Mac OS) that appears. From the Line Thickness drop-down list, select
  Thin, Medium, or Thick border lines; from the Line Style drop-down list,
  select Solid, Dashed, Beveled, Inset, or Underlined border line styles.

- ✔ **Text:** Provides options for setting the color, font, and font size of text as
  it appears when either typed in a text or signature field or displayed in a
  button label, combo box, or list box. Click the Text Color box to select
  from the color palette (Windows) or the color picker dialog box (Mac
  OS) that appears. Click the Font or Font Size drop-down list to make font
  selections. The Font option is not available for check boxes and radio
  buttons; however, Font Size and Text Color options do affect the dot in
  the middle of a selected radio button or the check mark that appears in
  a selected check box.

You can apply appearance changes to multiple form fields, even if they are
different field types. Hold down the Shift key and click to select multiple fields,
and then double-click one of the selected fields to open the Field Properties
dialog box. The Appearance tab is always displayed, and on occasion, the
Option tab appears as well. Sometimes a particular field property differs
among the selected fields. In these instances, the option either appears
blank, in which case you can't select the option, or contains a grayed-out
check or question mark, which allows you to apply the setting to all selected
form fields or keep their existing properties so they can be edited separately.

Understanding the Options tab

In general, these field options set the degree or appearance of interactive features for a given field type. For example, you can use them to define a list in a combo box or set the shape of the check mark when the user selects a check box field. Commands that appear on the Options tab differ, depending on which form field tool is used to create the form field. The one exception is the Digital Signature field type, which does not display the Options tab when selected.

Because field options are contextual, the following list describes the commands that appear on the Options tab when you create a specific field type:

✓ **Button field options:** These field type options, shown in Figure 14-6, add visual enhancements to a button field by defining button display and creating actions associated with mouse movement. Note that these actions affect only the button's appearance, as opposed to the more advanced special effects actions discussed in the "Interacting with the Actions tab" section, later in this chapter. Here's a rundown of the options:

 • **Layout drop-down list:** Lets you choose whether a button will display the text entered in the Label field, or a graphic icon chosen in the icon area, or a combination of the two placed in various layouts combinations (Icon Top, Text Bottom or Text Top, Icon Bottom, and so on). Click the Advanced button to specify how an icon is scaled to fit within a button in the Icon Placement dialog box. To select a button graphic, click the Choose Icon button to open the Select Icon dialog box, and click the Browse button to locate a suitable graphic on your hard drive in the Open dialog box that appears.

 • **Behavior drop-down list:** Lets you choose how a button reacts when you click it with the mouse. Choose Invert to invert the colors in the button, None to cause no change in a button's appearance, Push to use the elements defined in the State list box that displays mouse actions, and Outline to highlight the button field border. The standard mouse behaviors for button actions are Up (when the user releases the mouse button), Down (when the user clicks the mouse button), and Rollover (when the user hovers the mouse pointer over an object). See Chapter 16 to find out how to apply this feature.

✓ **Check box and radio button field options:** The commands that appear on the Options tab when you use the Check Box tool or Radio Button tool to create a form field are identical. Here's a rundown:

 • **Check Box Style drop-down list:** Choose from a list of six different check mark styles that include the traditional Check, as well as Circle, Cross, Diamond, Square, and Star. The selected check style appears when the user clicks a check box in your form.

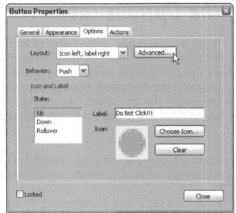

Figure 14-6:
The Options
tab of the
Button
Properties
dialog box
when the
Button tool
is used to
create a
form field.

- **Button Style drop-down list:** When you use the Radio Button tool to create a field, the same options appear that are described in the preceding bullet. The selected style shape appears as an icon in the center of the radio button.

- **Check Box/Button Is Checked By Default check box:** Specify that the radio button or check box will appear selected by default in your PDF form. The Radio Button Options also include the Buttons with the Same Name and Value Are Selected in Unison check box. While I can't think of a reason for this option, it's nice to know it's there, should the need arise. . . .

- **Export Value text box:** Enter a value that will be exported to a CGI application in order to identify that the check box or radio button has been selected in a form. See the "Exporting CGI values" sidebar, later in this chapter.

✔ **Combo box and list box field options:** The commands that appear on the Options tab when you use the Combo Box tool or List Box tool to create form fields are nearly identical. These options are used to define and configure the lists you want to appear in a combo or list box field:

- **Item text box:** Type an item for your list in this text box and then click the Add button to display it in the Item list box.

- **Item list box:** Use this list box to arrange the order of items in a combo or list box. You can delete an item in the list by selecting it and clicking the Delete button. To change the order of an item, select it and click the Up or Down button to move the item up or down in the list. To have an item appear as the default choice in a combo or list box, select the item in the Item List and click Close.

- **Sort Items:** To sort the list first numerically (if numbered items are present), and then alphabetically, select the Sort Items check box.

- **Editable check box:** The Combo Box field type provides an option that allows a user to edit or enter custom text in its list. Select the Allow User to Enter Custom Text check box to activate this feature.

- **Check Spelling check box:** Used to allow spell checking in the custom text field of a combo box.

- **Commit Selected Value Immediately check box:** Used to save the value as soon as the user selects it in a combo or list box. Note that this feature is deactivated if the Multiple Selection check box is selected.

- **Multiple Selection check box:** Select this option to allow a user to select multiple items in a list box field.

- **Export Value text box:** Enter a value that will be exported to a CGI application in order to identify a user's selection in a combo or list box. See the "Exporting CGI values" sidebar, later in this chapter.

✔ **Text field options:** Commands that appear on the Options tab when you use the Text Field tool enables you to configure the text that a user enters in a form text field. Here are your options:

- **Alignment drop-down list:** Choose Left, Center, or Right to specify the alignment of the text entered by a user.

- **Default Value:** Enter text in this field when you want to display a suggested default value in a text field.

- **Multi-line check box:** Select this option to create a text box with more than one line.

- **Scroll Long Text check box:** Select this option to allow text box scrolling in a multiline text field to compensate for text entered that extends beyond the boundaries of the text field.

- **Allow Rich Text Formatting check box:** Select this option to specify that text entered in a text form field can be formatted in RTF (such as applying Bold or Italic formatting).

- **Limit Of check box:** Limit the number of characters that can be entered in the field by selecting this check box and entering a number from 1 to 32,000 in the Characters field.

- **Password check box:** Select this option to specify that text entered in the field will be displayed as a series of asterisks so that it can't be read.

- **Field Is Used for File Selection check box:** Select this option to have a file submitted along with the form by entering a file path as the field's value. This feature requires JavaScript, which is covered in the next section.

- **Check Spelling check box:** Select this option to allow spell checking on the text entered in a text field.

- **Comb Of check box:** Select this option and enter a value in the Characters field to create a text field with characters spread out evenly across the text field, such as a name field that provides a single box for each character entered.

Interacting with the Actions tab

You can apply the commands on the Actions tab to every field type created by the seven form field tools in Acrobat. They allow you to choose from a list of different mouse behaviors and then associate those behaviors with a variety of actions that are built into Acrobat 6. You might, for example, attach a Sound action to the Mouse Up behavior so that a sound plays when the user clicks a field item in a form.

Figure 14-7 shows the Actions tab of the Button Properties dialog box. The following list defines the mouse behaviors you encounter in the Select Trigger list box:

✔ **Mouse Up:** The mouse button is released.

✔ **Mouse Down:** The mouse button is clicked.

✔ **Mouse Enter:** The mouse pointer moves into the field boundaries.

✔ **Mouse Exit:** The mouse pointer moves out of the field boundaries.

✔ **On Focus:** Using either the mouse pointer or key tabbing to move into the field boundaries.

✔ **On Blur:** Using either the mouse pointer or key tabbing to move out of the field boundaries.

Attaching an action to a form field

Use the following steps to attach an action to a selected form field:

1. **Right-click the form field with the Button Tool and choose Properties to open the Button Properties dialog box; click the Actions tab.**

2. **Select a mouse behavior in the Select Trigger list box.**

3. **Select an action in the Select Action drop-down list.**

   The Select Action drop-down list (shown in Figure 14-8) contains sixteen built-in actions provided in Acrobat 6. Each selected action displays a specific editing dialog box. These actions and corresponding editing features are described in detail in the following section, "Taking in the Action."

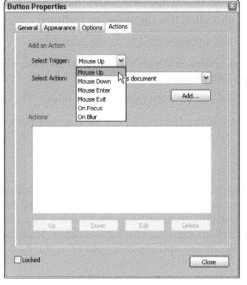

Figure 14-7:
The mouse
options on
the Select
Trigger
drop-down
list on the
Actions tab
of the
Button
Properties
dialog box.

4. **Choose options for your selected action and click OK to close the editing box.**

   The selected action appears in the Actions list box on the Actions tab of the selected field type Properties dialog box.

5. **Repeat Steps 2 through 4 to add more actions to this list.**

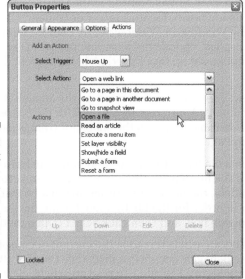

Figure 14-8:
The Select
Action drop-
down list,
where
Acrobat 6's
built-in
actions are
displayed.

6. **If you need to rearrange the order of the actions, select an action in the Actions list box and click the Up or Down buttons.**

   Note: Actions in this list are executed from top to bottom.

7. **To edit or replace an action that you've added to the list, select the action and click the Edit button.**

   The Edit dialog box associated with that action opens.

8. **To delete an action from the list, select the action and click the Delete button.**

Taking in the Action

The separate editing dialog boxes associated with a selected action appear automatically the first time you add an action to the Actions list box. To edit an action at a later date, select the action in the Action list box and click the Edit button in the Properties dialog box. The following list describes the actions and corresponding editing options that appear in the Add an Action dialog box:

- **Go to a Page in This Document:** To go to a page in the current PDF document specified in the Go to a Page in This Document dialog box. Choose the Use Page Number radio button, enter a page number, and select a Zoom setting in the Zoom drop-down list. If you've created a link destination in the current document, choose the Use Named Destination radio button, and then click the Browse button to select that destination. See Chapter 15 for more on creating hyperlinks in a PDF document.

- **Go to a Page in Another Document:** To go to a specified page in another document. Click the Browse button in the Go to a Page in Another Document dialog box to locate a target document, choose New Window, Existing Window, or Window Set by User Preference in the Open In drop-down list, choose the page number and Zoom settings, or if desired, a destination set up by a hyperlink in the current document, in the Options area.

- **Go to Snapshot View:** To go to a view created by the Snapshot tool in the current PDF document. After creating a view with the Snapshot tool on the Basic toolbar, Acrobat converts the snapshot (that is saved to the Clipboard) as a Go to Page destination.

- **Open a File:** To open a file when the associated mouse behavior occurs in a field. Note that if the file is not a PDF (which will open automatically in the user's PDF reader), the file's native program must be installed on the user's computer in order for the file to open. Locate the file in the Select File to Open dialog box, and then click Select (Open on the Mac).

- **Read Article:** To follow an article thread in the current document when the associated mouse behavior occurs in a field. (See Chapter 10 to find out about creating articles in a PDF file.) To read an article, click the Select Article button and choose from the list of articles residing in the current document before clicking OK to close the Select Article dialog box.

Exporting CGI values

When a form is submitted to a server on the World Wide Web, it is processed by a CGI (Common Gateway Interface). This method requires a script that tells the server to process the form by handing it off to a separate program, in this case a database, which stores the form data and makes it available for redistribution over the network.

You can define CGI export values for Check Box, List Box, Combo Box, and Radio Button field types. Note that you need to define an export value in the Options tab of the Properties dialog box associated with a selected field tool only if both of the following are true: The form data will be collected on a network or Web server, and the data is different from the item designated by the form field (or the form field is a radio button).

Here's how these rules apply to form field types that can export CGI values:

✔ **Check Box:** Use the default export value *Yes,* which tells the CGI application that the check box has been checked.

✔ **List and Combo Box:** The item selected in a combo or list box is usually used as the export value. Enter a value in the Options tab of the Field Properties dialog box only if you want the value to be different from the item listed. For example, a user chooses AZ from a list of abbreviated state names, but you need to export the value "Arizona" to match that field in a database on the server.

✔ **Radio Button:** A radio button by itself can use the default export value *Yes* to indicate it has been selected. If the radio buttons are related — for example, you've presented users with a series of radio buttons to indicate their yearly income among several ranges — the radio buttons must have the same field name but different export values so that the correct values will be collected in the database.

✔ **Execute a Menu Item:** To select a specified menu command when the associated mouse behavior occurs in a field. Select a menu command in the Menu Item Selection dialog box.

✔ **Set Layer Visibility:** To change the target layer states when the associated mouse behavior occurs in a field. Acrobat automatically sets the target layer visibility to that of the current layer. See Chapter 10 for more on layer visibility in a PDF document.

✔ **Show/Hide a Field:** To show or hide a field when the associated mouse behavior occurs in a field. Choose either the Show or Hide radio button in the Show/Hide Field dialog box. Note that to toggle between showing and hiding a field, you must associate one or the other state with the Mouse Up and Mouse Down behaviors in the Select Trigger list box.

✔ **Submit a Form:** To send all form field data to a specified URL for collection. For more about submitting and resetting forms, see the next section, "Adding Submit and Reset buttons."

✔ **Reset a Form:** To clear previously entered data from form fields. You can select/deselect which fields are reset in a form by clicking to add or remove the check marks next to a form field in the Select Fields to Reset list box on the Reset Form dialog box. Click the Select All button to choose all the form fields listed or the Deselect All button to remove the check marks from all form fields listed. When you're finished selecting fields, click OK.

✔ **Import Form Data:** To import form data stored on a server. This action is typically used to fill in forms with often-used data, such as the address of a company. Locate a file that contains form data in the Select File Containing Form Data dialog box. When the form data file is listed in the Actions list box (and only if you're familiar with JavaScript), click the Edit button to open the JavaScript Edit dialog box, which is a basic script editor for writing a JavaScript. See the "Importing/exporting form data" section, at the end of this chapter.

✔ **Run a JavaScript:** To run a custom JavaScript when the associated mouse behavior occurs in a field. You write scripts in the JavaScript Edit window — a basic scripting tool that appears when you click the Add button after selecting this action, or when you select the action in the list box and click the Edit button. The Go To button in the JavaScript Editor lets you jump to a specific line in the written code for editing purposes.

✔ **Play Media:** To play a QuickTime or AVI movie that has been linked to the PDF document. (See Chapter 16 for the lowdown on adding movies to a PDF file.) After movies are linked to a PDF, choose a movie in the Select Movie dialog box. The selected movie will play when the associated mouse behavior occurs in a field. Note that this action comes in two flavors on the Select Action drop-down list: Acrobat 5 Compatible and Acrobat 6 Compatible. The latter provides support for Acrobat 6's enhanced media features.

✔ **Play a Sound:** To play a specified sound file when the associated mouse behavior occurs in a field. Locate a sound file in the Select Sound File dialog box and click the Select button. Acrobat 6 embeds the sound in a cross-platform format that will play in Windows and Mac OS. In Mac OS, you can add QuickTime, System 7, AIFF, Sound Mover (FSSD), or WAV format sound files. In Windows, you can add AIF or WAV files. Note that selected sound files must be uncompressed in order for Acrobat to embed them in a PDF form.

✔ **Open a Web Link:** To download a Web page from the Internet. Enter or paste a URL address in the Edit URL dialog box and click OK. Note that besides the `http` network protocol used for Web pages, you can also use the `ftp` and `mailto` protocols when defining this action link. See Chapter 7 for more on capturing Web pages.

You can greatly enhance form field interactivity by using custom JavaScript actions. You can find out a great deal about writing your own scripts as well as find sources for numerous ready-made JavaScripts that perform a wide variety of actions in the "Acrobat JavaScript Scripting Guide" PDF document. If you are a seasoned programmer, see the "Acrobat JavaScript Scripting Reference" PDF that provides an in-depth reference to objects and classes defined specifically for Adobe PDF forms. Both documents are available on the Adobe Systems Web site:

```
http://partners.adobe.com/asn/acrobat/docs.jsp#javascript
```

As a general rule, you should attach JavaScripts that execute special-effect actions or major changes (such as playing a sound or movie, submitting the form, or downloading a page from the World Wide Web) to the Mouse Up behavior. This allows users a last chance to change their minds about executing an action by moving the mouse away from a form field before releasing the mouse button. If the action is attached to the Mouse Down behavior, the action executes the moment the mouse is clicked.

Adding Submit and Reset buttons

Reset and Submit buttons on a form perform two basic form field actions that are important features to use when setting up an interactive form that will be submitted over a network. The following steps show you how to add these components to a form.

To add a Reset button, follow these steps:

1. **Select the Button tool on the Forms toolbar and use its cross-hair pointer to add a form field to your PDF form document in the area you want your Reset button to appear.**

   See the "Adding Fields to Forms" section, earlier in this chapter, for details.

2. **In the Button Properties dialog box, click the Actions tab, select the Mouse Up behavior in the Select Trigger drop-down list, choose Reset a Form in the Select Action drop-down list, and then click the Add button.**

   The Reset a Form dialog box appears, as shown in Figure 14-9. By default, all fields are selected in the Select Fields to Reset list box, as indicated by the check marks next to each field name.

3. **Deselect any fields you don't want to include when the user clicks the Reset button. To deselect all fields and make individual selections, click the Deselect All button and select individual fields in the list box.**

4. **Click OK to accept your choices and close the Reset a Form dialog box.**

5. **Click Close to close the Button Properties dialog box.**

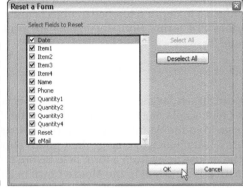

Figure 14-9:
Editing the
Reset a
Form action
type in the
Reset a
Form dialog
box.

To view and test your Reset button, click the Hand tool on the Basic Tools toolbar or press H, and then enter data in the various fields of the form before you click the Reset button.

Follow these steps to add a Submit button:

1. **Select the Button tool on the Forms toolbar and use its cross-hair pointer to add a form field to your PDF form document in the area you want your Submit button to appear.**

    See the "Adding Fields to Forms" section, earlier in this chapter, for details.

2. **In the Button Properties dialog box, click the Actions tab, select the Mouse Up behavior in the Select Trigger drop-down list, choose Submit a Form in the Select Action drop-down list, and then click the Add button.**

3. **Type a URL for the destination server in the Enter a URL for This Link text box, as shown in Figure 14-10.**

4. **Click one of the four radio buttons and select options in the Export Format area. Form data can be exported in four different formats:**

    • **FDF (Form Data Format):** Exports data as an FDF file and allows you to include field data, comments, and incremental changes to the PDF. The incremental changes feature sends data, such as a digital signature, in a format that can be easily read and stored by the server application. (See the "Importing/exporting form data" section, later in this chapter, for more on this file format.)

    • **HTML:** Form data is exported as an HTML file.

- **XFDF:** Exports as an Adobe XML/FDF variant file and allows you to also send field data and annotations (comments).

- **Complete Document (PDF):** Sends the entire PDF form, rather than just the field data. This option is useful for preserving written digital signatures in a PDF form. Note that you must use Acrobat 6 Professional or Standard versions to send an entire PDF form. Adobe Reader users can only submit FDF data from a form.

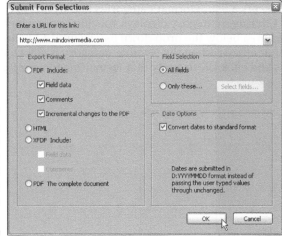

Figure 14-10:
Options that appear on the Submit Form Selections dialog box.

5. **In the Field Selection area, select which fields to export.**

   Click the All Fields radio button to export data in every form field. If you choose the Only These radio button, click the Select Fields button to open the Field Selection dialog box. Choose which fields to include or exclude by selecting or deselecting the check box next to a field name and clicking the Include Selected or Exclude Selected radio buttons. To export selected form fields, even if they contain no data, select the Include Empty Fields check box. To select all or deselect all the fields in the Select Fields to Submit list box, use the appropriate button to the right of the list box. Click OK after making your selections.

6. **If you want to export all the dates entered in your form, regardless of how they are entered, select the Convert Dates to Standard Format check box in the Date Options area.**

7. **Click OK to accept your choices and close the Submit Form Selections dialog box.**

8. **Click OK to close the Button Properties dialog box.**

To view and test your Submit button, click the Hand tool on the Basic Tools toolbar or press H, and then enter data in the fields of the form before you click the Submit button.

Getting familiar with the Format tab

The commands on the Format tab are applicable only to Combo Box and Text field types. The same can be said of the Validate and Calculate tabs as well. These format options enable you to specify a particular numerical format for data entered in the form field. For example, you can create a text field for entering a Social Security number that must contain nine numbers and automatically places dashes after the third and fifth numbers.

The Format tab presents a list of format categories in the Select Format Category list box. Clicking a category displays specific options for that category in the Options area below the drop-down list. Figure 14-11 shows the Number Options that appear when the Number category is selected. Choose formatting options and click OK to apply that formatting to your form field.

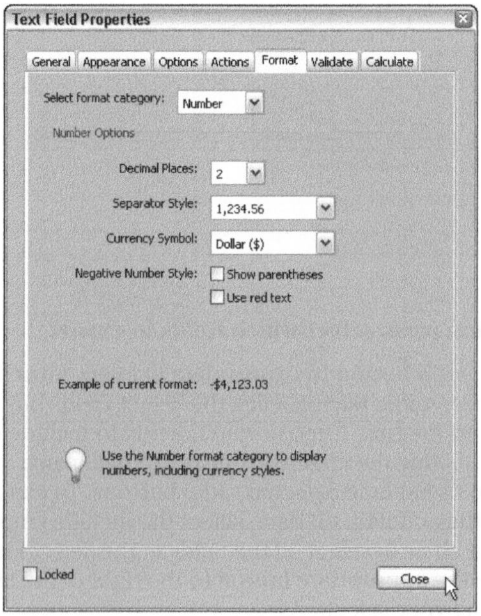

Figure 14-11:
The Format tab on the Field Properties dialog box appears when you select Text or Combo box field types.

The following list describes the categories and options provided on the Format tab:

- **None:** The default setting that specifies that no formatting is applied to data entered in a field.

- **Number:** Type a number in the Decimal Places field or click the attached spinner buttons to set the number of decimal places for the number entered in the text field. Use the Separator Style drop-down list to select a comma and decimal separators preference. Use the Currency Symbol drop-down list to select from a wide variety of foreign currency symbols. Select how negative numbers appear in a field by selecting the Show Parentheses or Use Red Text check box. (If neither check box is selected, negative numbers appear with a minus sign before the number.)

✔ **Percentage:** Automatically displays the percent symbol with numbers entered in a Text or Combo Box type field. Type a number in the Decimal Places field or click the attached spinner buttons to set the number of decimal places. Click the arrow on the Separator to select a comma and decimal separators preference. The sample area provides a preview of your selected percentage options.

✔ **Date:** Choose from a wide variety of date-only or date and time formats (choose the Time category for time-only formats) in the Date Options list box. The sample area below the Date options list box displays the format style of a selected formatting code. For example, selecting the formatting code m/d/yy in the Date Options list displays its format style as 4/19/03. When you're familiar with these simple date and time formatting codes, you can select Custom at the bottom of the Date Options list box and create custom date and time formats in the text box provided.

✔ **Time:** Choose from four time formats provided in the Time Options list or choose Custom to create your own. View the time format style for the selected time formatting code in the sample area below the list box.

✔ **Special:** Choose from the list of five options that appear in the Special Options list: Zip Code, Zip Code+4, Phone Number, Social Security Number, or Arbitrary Mask, which is used to specify the types of characters a user can enter in any given position and how the data displays in a text field.

✔ **Custom:** Provides a means of using JavaScript to format text or apply keystroke validation to text entered in a field. (See the next section to find out about field validation.) Click the Edit button next to either the Custom Format Script or Custom Keystroke Script area to open the JavaScript Edit window. If you're familiar with JavaScript language, you can write your own or copy and paste a predefined JavaScript in the script editing window. Click OK to close the JavaScript Edit window. The keystroke or formatting script appears in its proper Custom Options area. Note that you can use the arrow keys to view the script, but you can't edit it.

Viewing the Validate tab

Like the Format and Calculate tabs, options on the Validate tab apply only to Combo box and Text field types. You use these commands to restrict data entry in a field to a specific range, such as a dollar amount less than or equal to $1,000. Note that in order to specify a data range, the selected form field must be formatted with either the Number or Percentage category on the Formatting tab of the field type Properties dialog box.

You can accomplish more sophisticated validation, such as restricting data to specific values and characters, through the use of JavaScript. You might, for example, want to limit a date entry to only the years between 1950 and 2000 or allow a password that only contains three letters and four numbers separated by a dash.

To set a data range or attach a JavaScript to validate a field, click one of the radio buttons on the Validate tab:

- **Field Value Is Not Validated:** The default state. This radio button is selected automatically if a field does not use number or percentage formats (selected on the Format tab). Otherwise, click this option if you don't want validation applied to data entered in a field.

- **Field Value Is In Range:** Provides two text boxes in which to define upper- and lower-range parameters, as shown in Figure 14-12. Type a number in the From or To field to specify limits on a data range.

- **Run Custom Validation Script:** Click the Edit button to open the JavaScript Edit window. If you're familiar with JavaScript language, you can write your own or copy and paste a predefined JavaScript in the script editing window. Click OK to close the JavaScript Edit window. The validation script appears in a preview box below the Run Custom Validation Script radio button. Note that you can use the arrow keys to view the script, but you can't edit it.

Figure 14-12: Defining data-range parameters for a field on the Validate tab of the Field Properties dialog box.

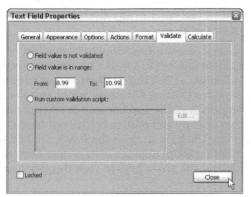

Cruising the Calculate tab

Like its Format and Validate tab brethren, options on the Calculate tab apply only to Combo box and Text field types. You use these commands to perform mathematical calculations on data entered in two or more form fields and display the result in another field. This feature is often used in an interactive order form where the product of an item's quantity and price is automatically displayed in a total field. In addition, it's possible to perform more advanced calculations using JavaScript.

To define the fields in a form that will perform calculations or attach a JavaScript calculation to a field, select one of the three radio buttons on the Calculate tab:

- ✔ **Value Is Not Calculated:** The default state. Select this option if you don't want to perform a calculation on data entered in a field.

- ✔ **Value Is the <Operation> of the Following Fields:** Provides a drop-down list of five operations: sum (+), product (×), average, minimum, and maximum. Select an operation option and then click the Pick button to open the Field Selection dialog box, which displays a list of fields in your form. Select a field's check box in the Select Fields for Calculation list box. You can select more than one field at a time, and you can select or deselect all the fields by clicking the appropriate button. When you're finished selecting fields, click the OK button.

- ✔ **Custom Calculation Script:** Click the Edit button to open the JavaScript Edit window. If you're familiar with JavaScript language, you can write your own or copy and paste a predefined JavaScript in the script editing window. Click OK to close the JavaScript Edit window. The calculation script appears in a preview box below the Custom Calculation Script radio button. Note that you can use the arrow keys to view the script, but you can't edit it.

By default, field calculations are performed in the same order as the form field's tab order — that is, the order in which the fields are selected when the user presses the Tab key (see the "Tabbing through a form" section, later in this chapter). This is not always a good idea, especially if your form contains multiple calculations where the result of one calculation depends on the result of another calculation. To override the default, set your own calculation order by choosing Advanced⇨Forms⇨Set Field Calculation Order to open the Calculated Fields dialog box. Select fields in the window and use the Up and Down buttons to arrange their calculation order, and then click OK to save your changes.

Sizing up the Selection Change tab

The Selection Change tab provides you with the means to execute JavaScript actions when making a selection in the List Box field type.

To use this feature, click one of the two radio buttons on the Selection Change tab:

- **Do Nothing:** Use this option if you don't want to run a JavaScript action when a user makes a list box selection.

- **Execute This Script:** Use this option to attach an action, and then click the Edit button to open the JavaScript Edit window. If you're familiar with JavaScript language, you can write your own or copy and paste a predefined JavaScript in the script editing window. Click OK to close the JavaScript Edit window. The JavaScript appears in a preview box on the Selection Change tab. Note that you can use the arrow keys to view the script, but you can't edit it.

Singling out the Signed tab

Options on the Signed tab apply only to the Signature field type. Its commands enable you to specify actions that occur in a form when data is entered into a blank signature field. You add signature fields to a form in the same manner as you do other form fields by using the Digital Signature tool. (See the "Adding Fields to Forms" section, earlier in this chapter, if you need a refresher.) The Digital Signature tool creates a blank signature field that can be filled out as part of completing a form. (To find out all about digital signatures, see Chapter 11.)

To configure a blank signature field, click one of the three radio buttons on the Signed tab:

- **Nothing Happens When Signed:** Use this default option if you don't want any actions to occur to data entered in a field.

- **Mark as Read-Only:** Provides a means of locking portions of a form at the time it is signed off in the signature field, in essence "freezing" the form at that moment in time. Select one of three items on the drop-down list: All Fields, All Fields Except These, and Just These Fields. If you select either of the latter two options, click the Pick button to open the Field Selection dialog box, where you choose the fields you want to render as read-only. Pick a field by selecting the check box next to the field name in the Mark Fields as Read Only list box. When you're finished adding fields, click the OK button.

- **This Script Executes When the Signature Field Is Signed:** Click this radio button to execute a specific JavaScript action when data is entered in a signature field. Click the Edit button to open the JavaScript Edit window. If you're familiar with JavaScript language, you can write your own or copy and paste a predefined JavaScript in the script editing window. Click OK to close the JavaScript Edit window. The action script appears in a preview box below the radio button. Note that you can use the arrow keys to view the script, but you can't edit it.

Looking at the Layout Grid

Acrobat 6 provides a wealth of tools that make the process of laying out and modifying form fields quick and easy. One of these tools is the Layout Grid — a non-printing, customizable on-screen grid that provides guidelines for drawing field boxes with the seven form field tools. To show or hide the Layout Grid, choose View➪Grid or press Ctrl+U (⌘+U on the Mac). The best part of the Layout Grid, however, is its Snap to Grid feature, which causes field boundaries to snap to gridlines when they're being drawn, as shown in Figure 14-13. To turn this feature on or off, choose View➪Snap to Grid or press Ctrl+Shift+U (⌘+Shift+U on the Mac). Note that because these two features are discrete, the Snap to Grid feature will still work even if the Layout Grid is hidden and vice versa. A check mark next to either command's name on the menu bar lets you know the feature is turned on.

Setting Layout Grid preferences

Layout Grid preferences let you specify a grid's spacing, position on a page, subdividing lines, and color. Choose Edit➪Preferences or press Ctrl+K (⌘+K on the Mac) to open the Preferences dialog box, and then click Units & Guides in the list box to display the options shown in Figure 14-14. The following options are found in the Layout Grid area:

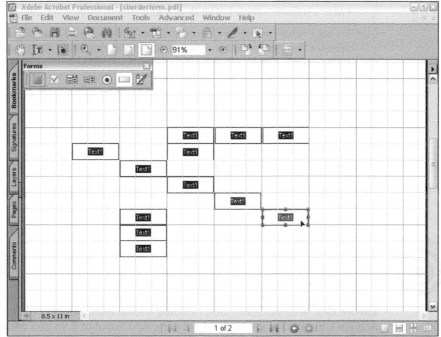

Figure 14-13:
Drawing
form fields
using the
Layout Grid
with its
Snap to Grid
feature
turned on.

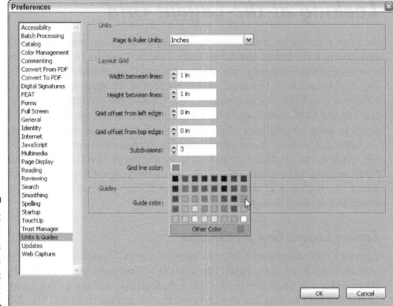

Figure 14-14:
Layout Grid
options
in the
Preferences
dialog box.

✔ To specify the space between major gridlines, click the spinner buttons or enter a measurement in the Width and Height between Lines text boxes.

✔ To offset the Layout Grid from the top-left corner of the page, click the spinner buttons or enter a measurement in the Grid Offset from the Left Edge or Grid Offset from the Top Edge text boxes.

✔ To display a specified number of subdividing lines between major gridlines, click the spinner buttons or enter a number in the Subdivisions text box.

✔ To specify the color of the gridlines, click the Grid Line Color button and select the desired color on the color palette (Windows) or the color picker dialog box (Mac) that appears.

When you're finished selecting Layout Grid preferences, click OK to apply your changes and close the Preferences dialog box.

You'll probably find that the Layout Grid isn't really very useful for adding fields to ready-made forms that you've scanned into Acrobat 6 because its gridlines will rarely match the cells that are already drawn in your paper form. In these cases, use the Align commands (see the "Move those fields!" section) to keep your fields straight. Where it really makes sense to use the Layout Grid is in designing and building a form from scratch. Here's a quick and easy method of getting a blank page into Acrobat 6 so you can use the

Layout Grid to custom build a form: Open a new blank document in Microsoft Word (Windows or Mac) and click the Convert to PDF button on the PDFMaker 6.0 toolbar. You can open the resulting blank PDF in Acrobat 6, configure and display the Layout Grid, and then start cranking out a form of your own design. For more on converting Microsoft Office documents to PDF, see Chapter 5.

Creating form field tables

Building a table of form fields is a snap. The fields can be all the same type or different types, and the methods for creating a table vary slightly, depending on which case is true. To create a table made up of form fields that are all the same type, follow these steps:

1. **Add a form field to your PDF in the area you want to serve as the corner of your table.**

   See the "Adding Fields to Forms" section, at the beginning of this chapter, for details.

2. **Hold down the Ctrl key (the Option key on the Mac) and draw a marquee around the single field to select it.**

   If you're selecting one field only, it's just as easy to click the field to select it. Using the Ctrl key (Option key on Mac) is better for selecting multiple fields and ensures you won't create one big form field when what you really want is to make a multiple selection.

3. **Choose Advanced⇨Forms⇨Fields⇨Create Multiple Copies or right-click the selected field and choose Create Multiple Copies on the context menu.**

   The Create Multiple Copies of Fields dialog box appears, as shown in Figure 14-15.

4. **Specify the layout for your form field table by choosing options in the following areas of the Create Multiple Copies of Fields dialog box:**

   - **Number of Fields:** Use the spinner buttons or enter a value in the Copy Selected Fields Down or Copy Selected Fields Across text fields. If the Preview check box in the lower left corner of the dialog box is selected, all changes made in this dialog box are displayed for preview in the current document behind the dialog box.

   - **Overall Size (All Fields):** Use the spinner buttons or enter a value in the Change Width or Change Height text fields to alter the size of the fields in your table. The default values in these fields reflect the size of the original field selected in the current document.

   - **Overall Position (All Fields):** To move the entire table in the current document to a new position, click the Up, Left, Right, or Down buttons.

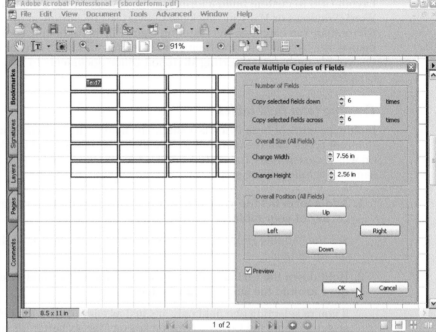

Figure 14-15:
Specifying
and
previewing
the layout of
a form field
table in
the Create
Multiple
Copies
of Fields
dialog box.

5. **When you're finished selecting options, click OK to close the Create Multiple Copies of Fields dialog box and view your form table in the current document.**

To create a table made up of different field types, you need to vary the preceding steps slightly. Instead of creating a single field (as in Step 2), you need to create an initial row or column of different field types that will serve as a basis not only for the number of rows or columns that appear in your table but also for how the different field types will occur in the table. After establishing that, you then individually select and copy each field type in the Create Multiple Copies of Fields dialog box using the Copy Selected Fields Down or Across options, depending on the original location (at the head of a column or beginning of a row) of the selected field in the current document.

Creating fields for tables in the manner just described is not the same as duplicating form fields (see the "Duplicating form fields" section, earlier in this chapter). In this process, you give each field a unique name, which allows a higher degree of individual editing choices. Therefore, it's not the method to use if you want to create a group of related radio buttons that must have the same name. See the "Understanding the Options tab" section, earlier in this chapter, for more on creating radio buttons.

When your form is in the development stage and you're beginning to accumulate a number of fields, it's a good idea to take advantage of the Fields palette. Choose View➪Navigation Tabs➪Fields to display the Fields palette, as shown in Figure 14-16. The Fields palette is a floating navigation pane that provides a hierarchical, icon view of the fields in a PDF. It allows you to remotely select, rename, delete, edit the properties of, and more importantly, lock/unlock a field. Locked fields can't be moved or edited, which comes in handy when you've gotten a number of fields just where you want them but are still fiddling with others in the form. To access these commands, right-click (Control+click on the Mac) a field icon in the Fields palette and choose the desired command from the context menu that appears. To lock/unlock a field, choose Properties on the context menu and select or deselect the Locked check box in the Properties dialog box that appears.

What to do with all these fields?

As you go merrily along stacking up form fields and bringing your PDF form design to fruition, you'll want to know some of the handy features Acrobat 6 provides to ready your form for distribution over a company intranet or the World Wide Web. In the following sections, you find out all about the features that make an interactive form top-notch.

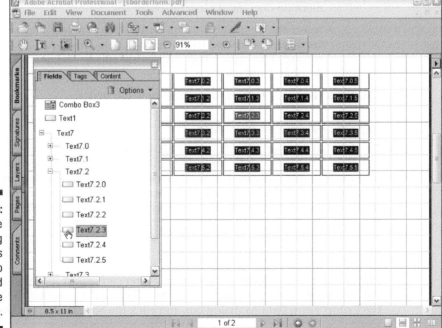

Figure 14-16: Using the floating Fields palette to view and navigate form fields.

Tabbing through a form

A form's tabbing order is the order in which the user selects fields when he or she presses the Tab key. This order is initiated when you add the first field and continues from there as you add fields to a form. Now if you know this ahead of time and are keeping track of the way you want the form filled out as you add fields, everything will work out fine. If you're like the rest of us, you'll probably have to set the tabbing order after you've finished adding fields to your form. Here's how:

1. **Click the Pages tab on the Navigation pane to open the Pages palette and select the page containing the form fields you wish to set tabbing order for.**

2. **Choose Page Properties on the Options menu at the top of the Navigation pane; in the Page Properties dialog box that appears, click the Tab Order tab.**

3. **Select from the options on the Tab Order tab as follows:**

   - Select the Use Row Order radio button to tab through rows from top to bottom and right to left.

   - Select the Use Column Order radio button to tab through columns from left to right and top to bottom.

   - Select the Use Document Structure radio button to use the document structure tree in a tagged PDF document. (See Chapter 1 for more on document structure tags.)

   - Select the Unspecified radio button (for compatibility with earlier versions of Acrobat) to tab through rows first and annotations second. This option is chosen by default for documents created in Acrobat 4 and earlier.

4. **Click the Close button to set your new tab order.**

Importing/exporting form data

The Acrobat 6 Import/Export feature allows you to move data in and out of a PDF form. That data can be imported into another PDF form or archived in a file format that is optimized to save space. When you export data from your form, Acrobat creates an FDF (Forms Data Format) file. This file contains only the data found in a form's fields, so it's much smaller in size than the original PDF form. After converted to FDF, any other PDF can import that data, as long as its field names match those of the original form. Field names that don't match are ignored in the import process.

After you have your form up and running, you can export its data by choosing Advanced⇨Forms⇨Export Forms Data. Type a file name for the FDF file in the Export Form Data As dialog box and click the Save button. To import data from an FDF file, choose Advanced➪Forms➪Import Forms Data and then, in the Select File Containing Form Data dialog box, locate the file and click Select (Open on the Mac).

Keep in mind that importing and exporting field data is not the same as collecting and distributing form data through a browser on the World Wide Web. FDF files can reside on a network server, and users can access them on a company intranet, and you can even e-mail the FDF files to others to perform import/export functions right on their computers. In order to collect your form data and distribute it over the Web, you need to use a CGI script written specifically for the form you want to use. If you're not familiar with coding CGI scripts, you'll have to leave it to the IT administrator of your company or Internet service provider's Web server. See the "Exporting CGI values" sidebar, earlier in this chapter, for more information.

Acrobat 6 also allows you to import data from a tab-delineated text file into a PDF form. This type of file is a text table that you create by placing a tab between each entry to create table rows. The first row serves as columnar field headings for the table and is filled with names that correspond to the field names found in your PDF form. Subsequent rows correspond to the data to be entered in those form fields. You can create this text file in a word processor such as Microsoft Word, but I find it easier to create the data table in Microsoft Excel and then save it as a tab-delineated text file in that program.

Chapter 15

Building and Publishing eBooks

*I*f you've browsed any of your favorite online bookstores lately, you've probably noticed the burgeoning presence of eBooks for sale. Like it or not, eBooks are definitely the wave of the future, and while they'll never replace a nice, cuddly printed book, they do have distinct advantages that ensure their future widespread use. Portability and ease of navigation are just two of the many advantages eBooks have over traditional books, and as I've mentioned throughout this book, these are areas where the Adobe PDF really shines.

In this chapter, you discover all the ways that Acrobat 6 allows you to build a better eBook. You see how easy it is to design and create a PDF file specifically for the eBook market. You also find out how to add interactivity to an eBook and create the kind of graphically rich page layouts that are only possible using Adobe PDF. More importantly, you discover how to create tagged PDF files that allow Acrobat eBooks to at last be viewed on handheld devices running Palm OS or Microsoft Pocket PC software. Finally, you find out how to package and distribute your eBooks and, in the process, ready yourself to catch the next big wave in digital publishing.

But First, a Little eBook History . . .

The origins of eBook technology are directly descended from SGML (Standard Generalized Markup Language), the grandmother of all markup languages. This venerable document structuring language (developed in 1986), along with its offspring HTML (HyperText Markup Language) and the more recent and dynamic XML (Extensible Markup Language), are responsible for the billions of Web pages floating around the Internet today.

Markup languages like HTML use *tags* to define the structure and function of a document, in this case, a Web page that allows two remarkable features: The document content can be *reflowed,* meaning the reading order of the text is preserved no matter what screen size it is being viewed on, *and* it can contain hyperlinks.

To see an example of reflowed text, just crank up your favorite Web browser, visit your favorite Web site, and use the browser's text zoom feature to shrink or enlarge the text. Even though the text gets bigger or smaller, the reading structure of the Web page remains the same. This is accomplished through the use of tags that define the order of a document's headings, paragraphs, fonts, graphics, and other elements. The "link" tag, on the other hand, is what makes hyperlinks possible, and the ability to click a hyperlink to navigate from one document to the next is what makes the World Wide Web interactive.

Reflowing text and creating hyperlinks were the main reasons HTML was used early on in the development of eBooks. These features engendered two of the biggest advantages eBooks have over printed books. Because text could reflow, the entire content of a book could be viewed on a screen as small as a handheld computing device, allowing you to carry dozens of books in the palm of your hand. The use of hyperlinks in eBooks is just as compelling. You only need to imagine the difference between clicking a Table of Contents heading and having the beginning of a chapter appear instantly in an eBook reader, and using the traditional look-up-and-thumb-through-pages technique required for printed books. The only drawback to using HTML as a development tool for eBooks is that, like Web pages, they cannot be as graphically rich or as precisely laid out as printed books, which from a reading experience standpoint, is an innate expectation eBook users bring to the party.

Acrobat PDF files, on the other hand, rely on PostScript (see Chapter 1 for more on the origins of PDF), which is a page-layout language invented by Adobe specifically to create both electronic and printed documents that preserve the look and feel of their original counterparts. In versions prior to Acrobat 5 and 6, the problem with the standard PDF file as an eBook was that because it emphasized page layout, reflowing text was impossible. This fact relegated Acrobat eBook viewing to computer screens and laptops. Handheld devices as PDF viewers were never an option in the early stages of the Adobe Acrobat eBook development game. All that has changed with the release of Acrobat 6. Adobe has integrated the structure and navigational advantages of markup language with the "just like a printed book" reading experience of PDF. Acrobat 6's ability to create tagged PDF files offers the best of both worlds when it comes to designing and developing an eBook.

Designing eBooks for Different Devices

You design Adobe Acrobat eBooks in a word processor or page layout program and then convert their documents to PDF. You can then perform any last-minute tweaks in Acrobat, such as adjusting text flow or linking multimedia objects, and then view your final product in the Adobe Acrobat eBook Reader on your computer, laptop, or on a Palm OS or Microsoft Pocket PC handheld device. (See Chapter 2 to find out how to use Adobe's eBook Reader program.) Note that Acrobat 6 and Adobe Reader 6 now support the purchase and down-loading of eBooks. As of this writing, Adobe plans to discontinue the Acrobat eBook Reader, though users of that program can continue to purchase and download eBooks as long as current eBook distributors support that program.

PDF files come in three document structure flavors — unstructured, structured, and tagged. Structured PDF files enable you to convert or *repurpose* a PDF for another format, such as RTF (Rich Text Format), while retaining much of the original page layout and reading structure. Tagged PDF files have the highest degree of success in retaining their original formatting when converting to RTF and are also able to reflow text, which is not the case with unstructured or structured PDF files. For the purpose of creating eBooks, then, you should always use tagged PDF files, because they offer the most flexibility when it comes to viewing the final product on the greatest number of viewing devices.

To get more information about PDF file types, choose Help⇨Complete Acrobat 6.0 Help and see "Building flexibility into Adobe PDF files" on page 368 of the online Adobe Acrobat Help.

The following programs allow you to convert their documents to tagged PDF files in order to build an eBook:

- ✔ FrameMaker SGML 6.0 (Windows and Mac OS)
- ✔ FrameMaker 7.0 (Windows and Mac OS)
- ✔ PageMaker 7.0 (Windows and Mac OS)
- ✔ InDesign 2.0 (Windows and Mac OS)
- ✔ Microsoft Office (Windows 2000 and XP only)

Adobe Reader 6 and Acrobat 6 were developed to provide a means of viewing PDF eBooks on a computer screen or laptop. Because of their size, computer screens are well suited to display graphically rich page layouts that re-create the reading experience of a printed book. For designing these types of eBooks, page layout programs (PageMaker, InDesign, or FrameMaker) are the best tools to use. In addition to allowing complex page layouts, their ability to create tagged PDF files adds a higher degree of accessibility for visually challenged users viewing PDF files in either Adobe Reader or Acrobat.

Graphic size and page layout are definitely restricted by the screen size of hand-held devices, so it's better to develop eBooks that you want to view on those devices in Microsoft Word, which is text-based and has Acrobat 6 features built in that enable you to create tagged PDF files with the click of a button. (See Chapter 5 for more on creating PDF files in Microsoft Office programs.)

Here are a few considerations to take into account in order to optimize eBooks designed for Palm OS or Microsoft Pocket PC handheld devices:

- ✔ **Graphics:** With handheld device screen resolutions running between 320 x 320 for Palm OS devices and 320 x 240 for Pocket PC devices, graphics must be optimized for the target screen size if they're used at all. Note that while the majority of Pocket PC and newer Palm devices in use have color screens, many more older Palm devices are out there right now without color. You could consider preparing your graphics in grayscale (thus creating a smaller file) for this reason. For more on optimizing graphics for eBooks, see Chapter 4 as well as the "Designing Library and Cover Graphics" section, later in this chapter.

- ✔ **Fonts:** Use the common Base 14 system fonts that are installed on your computer. These typefaces have been optimized for on-screen viewing and produce the best results when viewed on a handheld device.

- ✔ **Paragraphs:** Separate paragraphs with an additional hard carriage return for clearer visibility on the Palm handheld screen.

- ✔ **Conversion settings:** For grayscale Palm handheld devices, Adobe suggests some slight changes to the eBook job option in the Acrobat Distiller. You can get the specifics on creating a custom job option for these handheld devices at:

  `http://studio.adobe.com/learn/tips/acr5acropalm/main.html`

Adobe currently offers three free versions of Adobe Reader for hand-held devices that support Palm OS, Pocket PC, or Symbian OS (which runs on Nokia Communicator devices). You can get information and download these products at:

`www.adobe.com/products/acrobat/readstep2.html`

The Acrobat Readers are applications that are installed on their respective handheld devices and are designed to accommodate their specific screen characteristics. In addition to the reader software, the PocketPC and Symbian OS versions includes a Windows desktop application for preparing and transferring a PDF to a user's handheld device. The Palm OS reader includes a desktop application for both Macintosh and Windows and a HotSync conduit. To handle synchronization, the Pocket PC version includes the ActiveSync filter, which has an added feature that attempts to create tags from untagged PDF files prior to uploading them to the Pocket PC handheld device.

Turning Out Tagged PDF Files

As I mention earlier in this chapter, a number of programs enable you to create a tagged PDF file. They do this either by exporting tags during the process of creating a PDF or, in the case of Microsoft Office programs, by converting them using the PDFMaker 6.0 plug-in. You can find out all about converting Office documents to tagged PDF files in Chapter 5. Keep in mind that if you're designing an eBook with little or no graphics for display on a handheld device, Microsoft Word is the tool of choice. On the other hand, if your goal is to create a beautifully stylized eBook for viewing in Acrobat 6, Adobe Reader 6, or Acrobat eBook Reader 2.2, then PageMaker, InDesign, or FrameMaker is the best bet.

Perfecting your eBook in PageMaker

Authoring programs that export their tags to PDF perform a vital function when developing Acrobat eBooks. They allow you to complete nearly all the mechanical and structural work on your eBook before you send it upstream to Acrobat 6. After your eBook is converted to PDF, you'll find that Acrobat's functional but limited editing toolset is best suited for fine-tuning the graphic and interactive elements of your PDF file. Take an eBook table of contents for an example. Creating a table of contents (TOC) with more than a handful of headings in Acrobat is a tedious proposition (to put it mildly), especially compared to automatically generating an exportable, tagged, table of contents in PageMaker. The following sections take you through the process of preparing your eBook content so that 99 percent of your work is finished by the time you export it, tags and all, to Acrobat 6.

Setting up your eBook document

The following list provides a number of important tips to utilize that will ensure high-quality output when you convert your eBook to tagged PDF. Some of the items deal with conversion settings that you specify in Acrobat Distiller prior to exporting your eBook document to PDF. (See Chapter 4 to find out about selecting Distiller options.)

- When creating eBook content in PageMaker or any other layout program, make sure to set up a smaller page size so that your text won't be distorted when rendered in the smaller screen area provided by your eBook reader of choice. A 6-x-9-inch page dimension with ½- or ¾-inch margins all around translates well to desktop and laptop screen resolutions.

- Target output resolution should be 300 dpi or better to ensure clear, crisp text when the file is downsampled and compressed during the PDF conversion process.

✔ Try to use your system's Base 14 fonts in your eBook document. Otherwise, choose fonts that have strong serifs and strokes. If these font properties are too delicate, they'll distort and cause reading difficulty when displayed in the Adobe Reader or Acrobat. In addition, be sure to embed those fonts you decide to use in the converted PDF. You can experiment with the readability of a chosen font by converting a test document to PDF and viewing it in Acrobat or Adobe Reader using a variety of magnifications and CoolType settings. You might also check for differences when viewing the eBook on a CRT or LCD computer screen.

✔ The minimum font size for body text should be 12 points. Use at least 2 points of leading. If you want to spread out your text, select a wider tracking value for your chosen font rather than using character kerning. Tracking can be applied globally and produces more significant visual enhancement than kerning, which also bulks up the size of your file.

✔ When creating paragraph heading styles in PageMaker, make sure you specify their inclusion in your table of contents by clicking the Include in Table of Contents check box in the Paragraph Specifications dialog box. You can open this dialog box by selecting the heading text in your document and choosing Type⇨Paragraph or pressing Ctrl+M (⌘+M on the Mac). You can also access this dialog box while editing styles. Choose Type⇨Define Styles, select a heading style in the Style list box, click the Edit button to open the Style Options dialog box, and finally, click the Para button.

Figure 15-1 shows the first page of my eBook example using the document setup parameters I just described. I used ½-inch margins all around with the exception of the ¾-inch margin on the bottom of the page to accommodate page numbers. The font is 12 point Georgia, using 2.4 points of leading for body text and up to 3 points for bulleted and numbered lists.

Generating a TOC

You can create a table of contents from those heading styles that are marked for inclusion in your PageMaker publication. The TOC can reside in the same document as your eBook body or in a separate publication for use with PageMaker's Book utility. I cover both methods in the following steps for creating a table of contents with hyperlink tags that can be exported to Acrobat.

To create a table of contents in the same publication as your eBook body, follow these steps:

1. **In PageMaker, select the first page in your publication and choose Utilities⇨Create TOC.**

   The Table of Contents dialog box, shown in Figure 15-2, appears.

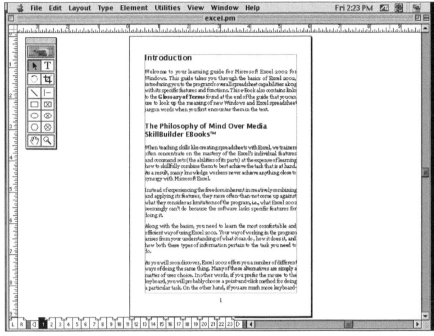

Figure 15-1:
The first page of my SkillBuilder eBook body section.

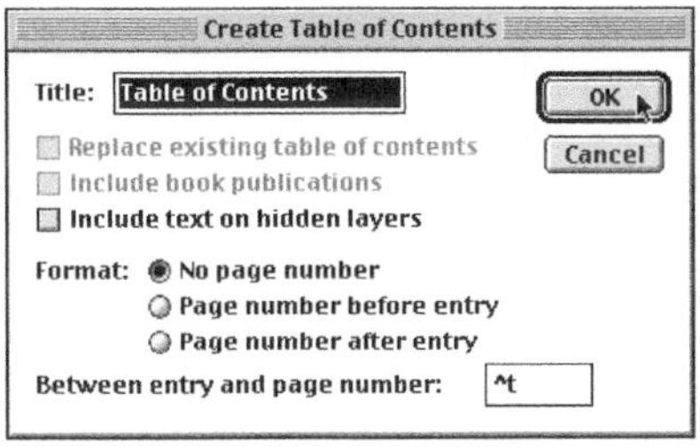

Figure 15-2:
The Create Table of Contents dialog box.

2. **Type a new title or accept the default "Table of Contents" title in the text box provided and select one of the radio buttons in the Format area to specify the appearance and position of page numbers in the TOC.**

   You can also specify a special character to appear between the entry and the page number (a tab space is the default) here.

3. **Click OK to generate your table of contents story.**

   A *story* in PageMaker terms is an independent text object with unique formatting that can be positioned anywhere in a page layout.

   The mouse pointer changes to the story flow cursor. Now you need to create empty pages in which to flow your TOC story.

4. **Choose Layout➪Insert Pages and enter the desired number of empty pages you want inserted, select Before the Current Page from the drop-down list, and click the Insert button.**

5. **Go to the first of your newly inserted pages and click to flow your TOC story onto the empty pages from there.**

To create a table of contents in a separate publication from your eBook body, follow these steps:

1. **Create a new document from your eBook template containing the desired number of pages for your TOC and then save and name the publication.**

2. **Choose Utilities➪Book.**

The Book Publication List dialog box opens, as shown in Figure 15-3. This dialog box is used to specify the order of the publications you want to include in your book. Your current TOC document appears in the Book List on the right side of the dialog box.

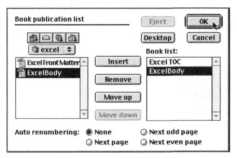

Figure 15-3: Define the order of your eBook sections in the Book Publication List dialog box.

3. **In the list on the left, locate the documents you want to include and add them to the Book List by clicking the Insert button located between the two lists. Click OK to save your changes.**

You can remove files and change the order of files in the list using the appropriate buttons. In Figure 15-3, I've added the body publication to the Book List after the TOC publication.

4. **Choose Utilities➪Create TOC.**

The Table of Contents dialog box opens.

5. **Type a new title or accept the default "Table of Contents" title in the text box provided and select one of the radio buttons in the Format area to specify the appearance and position of page numbers in the TOC.**

You can also specify a special character to appear between the entry and the page number (a tab space is the default) here.

Note that when you're creating a TOC from a document listed in a book publication, the Include Book Publications check box is automatically selected, as opposed to being grayed-out as in Figure 15-2.

6. **Click OK to generate your table of contents story; then go to the first page of your TOC publication and flow your TOC story from there.**

Your brand-new table of contents contains tagged hyperlink entries that will produce accurate bookmarks and page references in your eBook when converted to PDF and viewed in Acrobat. You can check your links in PageMaker by selecting the Hand tool on the floating toolbox. The links appear in blue outline in Layout view, as shown in Figure 15-4, and you can click the hyperlinks in order to test their accuracy.

PageMaker inserts a text marker in front of every entry in the placed table of contents story in order to create hyperlink tags that will function when exported to tagged PDF. These text markers are visible only in story editor, (PageMaker's text editing window) and if they are removed, the links will not operate. For this reason, if you are editing a TOC entry, be very careful not to press the Delete key when the insertion point is directly in front of a TOC entry or page-number reference, because this will remove the text marker from the publication. Your only recourse in such an event is to either close and reopen the document without saving (if you haven't saved the changes already) or regenerate the TOC.

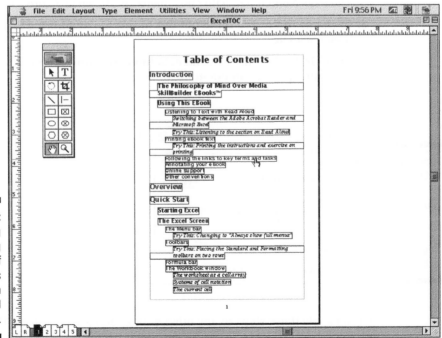

Figure 15-4:
Displaying and testing table of contents links with the Hand tool.

You can make text edits to your TOC entries (heeding the warning in the preceding paragraph), but if you decide to add any new entries in either the TOC or the body of your eBook, you will have to regenerate a new TOC to create links for those entries that will export to tagged PDF.

Using mixed page-numbering schemes

The main reason for using PageMaker's Book utility to combine separate sections of your eBook is that doing so enables you to create different numbering schemes for those parts. A typical example is the way printed books use Roman numerals for their front matter (copyright, title, acknowledgment, and table of contents pages) and Arabic numerals for the body. Some books will also use different number formats for their appendixes and index. PageMaker allows you to renumber pages in a single publication but not change their format, which works well for many types of publications. As an eBook publisher, though, it's nice to know you can add these little details to re-create the look and feel of printed books.

To apply a different number format to one of your eBook publications, follow these steps:

1. **Open the publication you want to reformat in PageMaker.**

2. **Choose File⇨Document Setup, and in the Document Setup dialog box, click the Numbers button.**

   The Page Numbering dialog box opens, as shown in Figure 15-5.

3. **Click one of the five radio buttons to select a numbering format and then click OK.**

4. **Click OK to close the Document Setup dialog box and view your newly formatted page numbers in the document.**

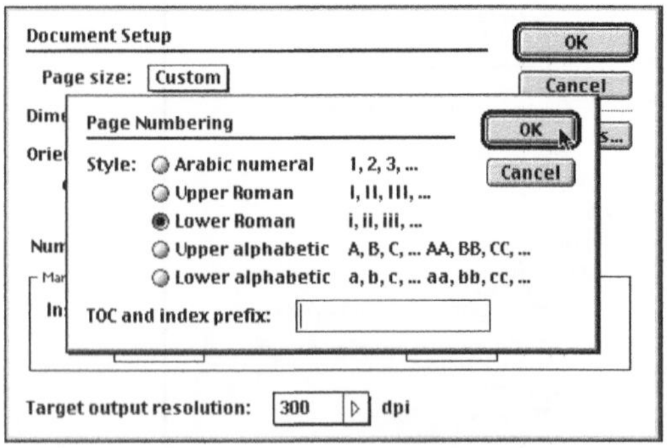

Figure 15-5:
Choose a page-numbering format for your PageMaker publication.

Document Setup   OK

Page size: Custom   Cancel

Dim | **Page Numbering**   OK

Orie | Style: ○ Arabic numeral   1, 2, 3, …   Cancel
| ○ Upper Roman   I, II, III, …
| ● Lower Roman   i, ii, iii, …

Num | ○ Upper alphabetic   A, B, C, … AA, BB, CC, …
| ○ Lower alphabetic   a, b, c, … aa, bb, cc, …

In | TOC and index prefix: [   ]

Target output resolution: [300] ▷ dpi

You can apply these steps to any other eBook sections as desired. The beauty of the PageMaker Book utility is that it compiles your eBook sections in the order in which they appear in the Book List and, at the same time, preserves all your links when you export the eBook to PDF.

Creating a tagged PDF file

When you're satisfied with the look and feel of your eBook, your final step is to export the publication and its tags to PDF. The following steps show you how to export your PageMaker publication to PDF, which can then be opened up in Acrobat 6 for final adjustments prior to distributing your eBook:

1. **In PageMaker, open the publication you want to export to PDF.**

   Note that if you've compiled your PageMaker publications into a book, you need to open the first publication in your Book List. This should be some element of the front matter, such as the table of contents. The Book utility takes care of sending the parts of your book in their correct order to Acrobat 6.

2. **Choose File⇨Export⇨Adobe PDF.**

   Acrobat takes a few moments to configure itself for this task and then opens the PDF Options dialog box, shown in Figure 15-6.

3. **Select options in the PDF Options dialog box.**

   See the next section for details on specifying options that pertain to eBooks when exporting them to tagged PDF in PageMaker.

4. **Click the Export button to send your publication to Acrobat 6.**

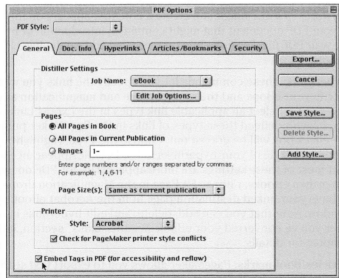

Figure 15-6: Specifying options for your eBook export in the PDF Options dialog box. Note that the Embed Tags in PDF check box is checked.

Specifying PDF options for eBooks

The PDF Options dialog box in PageMaker contains five tabs of options for configuring the way your eBook publication is exported to Adobe tagged PDF. Many of the options add functionalities that are specific to electronic publishing, such as setting up document information metadata that can be used as search criteria. The printing options don't really apply to eBooks, because they will most likely stay in their electronic form. The following list describes these tabs and their options:

- **General:** Make sure to select the Embed Tags in PDF (for Accessibility and Reflow) check box. This is the only way to specify that your eBook be converted to tagged PDF. To use a preconfigured Distiller job option, select from the Job Name drop-down list. Click the Edit Job Options button to make changes to the selected job. To find out more about Distiller job options, see Chapter 4.

  Choose one of the appropriate radio buttons in the Pages area to either export all the pages in a Book publication, all the pages in the current single publication, or a range or ranges of pages in the current publication. Select Same as Current Publication from the Paper Size(s) drop-down list to send the optimized PageMaker document settings you specified for your eBook to PDF. If you created separate document settings, choose Apply Settings of Each Publication. Leave the Style as Acrobat and the Check for PageMaker Printer Style Conflicts check boxes selected, which are the default settings; these options don't affect your eBook.

- **Doc. Info:** Information entered in the Doc. Info tab appears as metadata in the document properties of the tagged PDF file. For this reason, it can also be used as search criteria. You can specify the author, title, subject, and keywords of a document and create a note that appears on the first page of your PDF document that might contain an introduction or instructions for your PDF file. For more info on searching and cataloging a PDF file, see Chapter 13.

- **Hyperlinks:** These commands let you specify the links you want to activate in your eBook and their appearance and magnification after conversion to PDF. Select all applicable link types in the Export Links area. If you haven't defined these types of links in the PageMaker publication, the check box will be grayed out. Choose the Type, Highlight, Width, Color, and Style of your hyperlinks in the Default Appearance area. Note that most of these settings are more appropriate for PDF documents other than eBooks. Choose Fit Page in the Magnification drop-down list to have your linked destination page fit in the Acrobat eBook Reader window. Note that you can add, delete, and edit hyperlinks in Acrobat 6 after you've converted your eBook. See the "Links" section, later in this chapter, for details.

- **Articles/Bookmarks:** PageMaker allows you to export text stories as PDF articles. It automatically finds these when you use the export command, and you can also define your own within the PageMaker story by clicking the Define button in the Articles area. (For details on PDF articles, see Chapter 10.) If you've created index or table of contents links in your publication, you can convert these to PDF bookmarks by selecting the appropriate check box in the Bookmarks area. Select the Fit Page setting from the Magnification drop-down list to have your bookmarked destination page fit in the Acrobat eBook Reader window.

✔ **Security:** You can select security settings for a PDF document, such as limiting access by assigning passwords and restricting printing and editing. (For more on using security options with PDF files, see Chapter 11.) Use these settings if you don't plan to distribute your eBook commercially through an online retailer or distributor. Note that if you do plan to market your eBook, you must leave these settings blank because security for commercial eBooks is determined as part of the distribution process. For more information, see the "Distributing Your eBooks" section, later in this chapter.

When the export job is finished, your new, tagged PDF opens automatically in Acrobat 6 for viewing, as shown in Figure 15-7. The first page of the document is displayed (in this case, the inside cover page of my Excel SkillBuilder eBook), and the Bookmarks palette shows the table of contents headings that were converted to PDF bookmarks. You can now test your links and use Acrobat's PDF editing features to make final adjustments to your eBook.

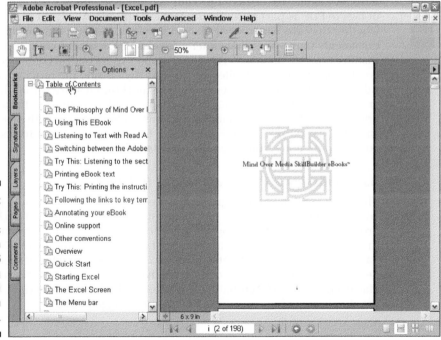

Figure 15-7: Your tagged PDF is opened in Acrobat 6 after being exported from PageMaker.

As of this writing, PageMaker 7.0 for Macintosh only runs in Classic mode on OS X. You can create an eBook as described in the previous sections, but when it comes time to exporting it to Acrobat, you'll run into problems because Acrobat 6 only runs under OS X version 10.2.2 or greater. If you have Acrobat 5, start up in OS 9 and create your eBook in PageMaker 7.0 from that environment. When it comes time to export your eBook to Acrobat, do so using Distiller 5.0, save the eBook, and then open it in Acrobat 6 from the OS X environment. If you have InDesign 2.0, which is OS X and OS 9 compatible, you could convert your PageMaker eBook document with that program (or better yet, build your eBook in that program to start with), and then export the InDesign eBook document directly into Acrobat 6 under OS X.

What about other layout programs?

As mentioned earlier, InDesign 2.0 is capable of converting its documents to tagged PDF, and the process is similar to the export function in PageMaker 7.0. It also has the added advantage of having Mac OS X and Windows XP versions, so there are no problems exporting documents directly to PDF in Acrobat 6. The following sections provide an overview of this program, as well as FrameMaker 7.0 and Quark 5, should you prefer using those authoring programs to create your eBook, rather than PageMaker.

Acrobat Distiller 6.0 does not provide the ability to specify the exporting of tags to PDF as part of configuring its job options. All layout programs, whether they are Windows or Mac OS versions, perform the conversion of documents to PDF by using either a Save as PDF, Export to PDF, or Print to Distiller type of command. The Save As and Export to PDF commands allow you to choose or edit Distiller job options right inside the program, and Adobe has only recently integrated the export tags feature within those programs listed at the beginning of this chapter. Older versions of these programs do not have this capability, and this is also the case with programs such as QuarkXPress 5 and FrameMaker 6.0 that use the Print to Distiller command for converting their documents to PDF.

Using InDesign 2.0 to create tagged PDF files

The latest version of InDesign is a feature-rich hybrid of layout and graphics editing programs. To date, it has the most advanced integration of Distiller properties of any Adobe program and allows complete configuration within the program. It also has the advantage of directly opening Quark 3.3–4.1 and PageMaker 6.5–7.0 documents. InDesign 2.0 is a great tool for designing and developing eBooks because of its extensive PDF conversion tools, and for Mac users, OS X and Acrobat 6 compatibility. But for this overview, here are the simple steps for exporting a document to tagged PDF:

1. **Open the document you want to export and choose File⇨Export.**

   The Export dialog box opens.

2. **In the Save as Type (Windows) or Formats (Mac OS) drop-down list, choose Adobe PDF.**

3. **Type a name for the converted PDF file, select a location on your hard drive, and click Save.**

   The Export PDF dialog box opens.

4. **In the Export PDF dialog box, shown in Figure 15-8, select an export style from the Style drop-down list.**

   To edit a selected style, choose the panel names on the left side of the dialog box and go to town.

5. **Click the Export button.**

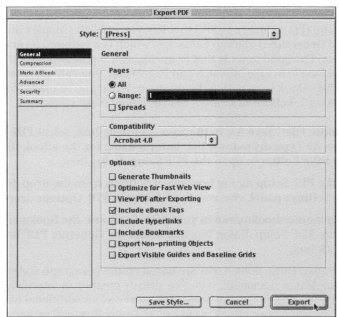

Figure 15-8:
The options-laden Export PDF dialog box in InDesign 2.0.

Converting QuarkXPress 5 documents to PDF

QuarkXPress 5 does not provide the export to tagged PDF feature for its documents that are converted to PDF. This may change with the release of Quark 6.0, which was in its pre-release stage at the time of this book's writing. To check out the program's new features, go online to:

```
www.quark.com/products/xpress
```

You can also get information about the PDF Filter XTension utility that integrates Distiller options into Quark. Otherwise, to convert a Quark 5 file to Adobe PDF, follow these steps:

1. **Open the document you want to export and choose File⇨Page Setup or File⇨Print.**

   The Print dialog box appears.

2. **Choose Acrobat Distiller (Windows) or Create Adobe PDF (Mac) on the Printer drop-down list.**

3. **Select the eBook job option on the PDF options drop-down list.**

4. **Click the Print button.**

Converting FrameMaker 7.0 documents to PDF

FrameMaker is much like PageMaker, in that you can create linked tables of content and indexes, as well as compile book publications from separate documents. It's designed to create long, content-rich documents and also comes in a version (FrameMaker SGML) that lets you publish complex documents in Standard Generalized Markup Language, which is a required format in some industries. The good news is that FrameMaker 7.0 now supports the export of tags to Adobe PDF. Like InDesign and PageMaker, you can now easily create a tagged PDF eBook from within the program. When you're ready to convert a FrameMaker 7.0 eBook document to PDF, follow these steps:

1. **Choose File⇨Save As; in the Save As dialog box, select PDF from the Save As Type drop-down list. Enter a name for the eBook file and click the Save button to open the PDF Setup dialog box.**

2. **In the PDF Setup dialog box, select Settings from the drop-down list; in the Settings panel, choose eBook from the PDF Options drop-down list.**

3. **To generate bookmarks in your eBook, choose the Bookmarks panel in the PDF Setup dialog box and select the Generate PDF Bookmarks check box.**

   Note that these bookmarks are based on the paragraph styles in your FrameMaker document. If you've already created an internally linked Table of Contents, these bookmarks serve as an additional navigation device when your eBook is viewed in Adobe Reader 6 or Acrobat 6.

4. **Click Tags on the Setup PDF drop-down list to display the Tags panel, and then select the Generate Tagged PDF Bookmarks check box.**

   This option ensures that your PDF eBook text can be reflowed when viewed on smaller devices, such as handhelds or cell phones.

5. **Click OK to close the PDF Setup dialog box and generate your Adobe PDF eBook.**

It's not the end of the world if your program doesn't export its documents to tagged PDF files. You can still add internal and external interactive links to your document in Acrobat 6, as you find out later in this chapter, and Windows users have the added ability to use Acrobat's Make Accessible plug-in to scan their PDF files and create tags that allow the document text to reflow. The plug-in is designed to create tagged files out of older PDF files so that they can be used in screen-reading programs for the visually challenged. Users of Acrobat 6 for Windows can download the plug-in at:

```
www.adobe.com/support/downloads/detail.jsp?ftpID=1161
```

There is not, as yet, a Make Accessible plug-in for Acrobat 6 for Macintosh (somebody write Adobe a letter!). After you've downloaded and installed the plug-in, open your PDF file in Acrobat and choose Document⇔Make Accessible. The utility scans your document's formatting structure, and if enough structure is available, it converts that information to reflowable tags.

Designing Library and Cover Graphics

You can definitely integrate graphics and digital photos into the design of your Adobe eBooks, especially those you create solely for viewing in Acrobat eBook Reader, Adobe Reader, or Acrobat 6. Because there is no added expense for color use in an eBook (as there is with printed books), you can feel free to embellish your eBook with colored text, borders, and fills. In addition to the graphics you might use to illustrate your eBook, you also need to consider the use of library and cover graphics. There are three different kinds of library and cover graphics: your actual eBook cover and two thumbnail versions of the eBook cover. Although none of these graphics are required to create a function-ing eBook, they add to the overall look and feel of your eBook and are required if you plan to market your eBook commercially.

When specifying color conversion settings in either the Distiller or the export settings of your eBook authoring program, always choose the sRGB model. Because computer screens use the RGB model, this device-independent color setting ensures that the graphics and colors in your eBook appear accurately in a wide variety of displays.

The Cover thumbnail is used for marketing purposes when you distribute your eBook online. (See the "Distributing Your eBooks" section, later in this chapter.) eBook sellers use the Cover thumbnail on their Web sites to identify and advertise your eBook. The Library thumbnail is displayed in the Acrobat eBook Reader Library, as well as the My Bookshelf feature in Adobe Reader 6 and Acrobat 6, and is used as a navigation button for selecting and opening an eBook. (See Chapter 2 for details about the Acrobat eBook Reader

Library.) The actual eBook cover graphic is set as the first page in your eBook in Acrobat 6 and appears full screen (momentarily) in Acrobat eBook Reader when a user double-clicks the library thumbnail graphic to open the eBook. You can create these graphics in any editing program, though recent versions of Photoshop (5.0 and up) have the advantage of using the sRGB color model as a default.

Here are the basic specifications for these three graphics:

- ✔ **Cover thumbnail:** Create a thumbnail of your cover graphic in GIF format. The image should be 100 pixels wide. A 3:2 aspect ratio works well, so at that width, your image would be 150 pixels tall by 100 pixels wide. Make sure to adjust the image resolution to 96 dpi, so that the thumbnail display is sharper with fewer artifacts or pixel distortions when viewed online in a Web browser.

- ✔ **Library thumbnail:** The image that appears in the Acrobat eBook Reader Library is slightly different than the Cover thumbnail. For this graphic, create a thumbnail of your cover graphic in JPEG format. The image should be 100 pixels wide with the same 3:2 aspect ratio as the Cover thumbnail. Make sure to use the sRGB color model if possible (RGB otherwise) and adjust the image resolution to 96 dpi.

- ✔ **eBook cover:** You should also create your eBook cover in JPEG format. To fill the Acrobat eBook Reader window, it should be 600 pixels tall and 400 pixels wide, using sRGB color and 96 dpi image resolution.

The graphics and illustrations you create for the body of your eBook can be developed in any graphic or photo editing program, such as Illustrator or Photoshop. When you export your eBook to PDF, these graphics are optimized for viewing via the Distiller job option you choose during the export process. (To find out how Distiller optimizes graphics to reduce file size for Web distribution, see Chapter 4.) Because the Library and cover graphics are added to your eBook in Acrobat 6 after it has been exported or converted to PDF, make sure to create GIF and JPEG format graphics and use the sRGB color model so that they are fully optimized for the Web when you upload the cover thumbnail to a bookseller's server or insert the cover and Library thumbnail in your eBook.

Adding a cover graphic to your PDF eBook

Because an eBook cover graphic is designed to fill the Acrobat eBook Reader window, it's nearly impossible to add this graphic to your eBook in a layout program, let alone a word processor, and achieve satisfactory results. Imagine placing a 300 dpi graphic that covers the entire page (beyond the margins) into a document created in your favorite layout program and then hoping that Distiller will compress it nicely for full-screen display in the eBook Reader. It's best to create the graphic separately and use Acrobat 6 to insert it into your eBook after it has been exported PDF. Here's how:

1. **Open the tagged PDF eBook file you exported from your layout program.**

2. **Choose Document⇨Pages⇨Insert.**

3. **Locate and select your JPEG cover image in the Select File to Insert dialog box and click the Select button.**

   (Note that you may have to choose JPEG in the Files of Type drop-down list to see your graphic in the dialog box window.) The Insert Pages dialog box appears. This dialog box lets you choose where in the eBook file you want the eBook cover graphic to appear. Luckily in this case, the default is before the first page in the document, which is where you want your eBook cover graphic to appear.

4. **Click Before in the Location drop-down list, and then click OK.**

   The cover image is imported into the PDF file as the first page in the document.

5. **Click the Pages palette tab to verify the location of the cover graphic at the beginning of the eBook document.**

6. **Note that because the cover graphic was appended to the beginning of the document, it was automatically given the first page number in the PDF. You can resolve this issue by choosing Number Pages on the Options pop-up menu at the top of the Pages palette.**

   Acrobat lets you renumber pages, as well as change numbering formats one section at a time, so that you can make sure the numbers you created for your eBook pages correspond to page numbers that appear in the page navigator bar in Acrobat eBook Reader. See Chapter 10 for details on using this feature.

Whenever you convert a document to PDF that is either a multisection book with different numbering schemes or a single document that starts with a page number other than the number one, you must use the Number Pages command in Acrobat 6 to renumber the PDF so that its page numbers mirror your original document's numbering scheme.

When you add a front cover graphic to your Adobe eBook, it's important to insert an inside front cover page, such as the page shown in Figure 15-7, though this page could be blank as well. Also, make sure that you end up with an even number of front-matter pages, using a blank page at the end of the front matter if needed. This ensures that your Adobe PDF eBook displays properly in Adobe Reader 6 and Acrobat 6, when viewing two pages at a time (by using the Facing Pages view), with odd-numbered pages on the right. It's best to create these pages in your eBook authoring program rather than inserting them into the eBook in Acrobat 6.

Adding a library thumbnail graphic to your PDF eBook

After you've created your Library cover thumbnail, you need to attach it to your eBook in order for it to appear in My Bookshelf in either Adobe Reader or Acrobat 6. Here's how:

1. **Open the eBook file and select the cover page graphic in the Pages palette (it should be the first page in the document) and then reduce the magnification so that the work area surrounding the page is visible.**

   A magnification of 75% usually works well for this with a screen resolution of 800 x 600.

2. **Select the Attach File tool located on the Advanced Commenting toolbar.**

   You can also hold down the Shift key while pressing the S key to cycle through the tools found on this menu. The cursor changes to a paperclip icon.

3. **Click in the workspace surrounding your cover page (not on the cover page itself), and in the Select File to Attach dialog box (Windows) or the Open dialog box (Mac) that appears, locate and select your Library thumbnail graphic, and then click the Select button.**

   The File Attachment Properties dialog box appears.

4. **Accept the default settings for your attachment and click OK.**

   A paperclip icon appears in the workspace next to the cover page, as shown in Figure 15-9. Make sure that the paperclip is in the workspace and not on the cover graphic page.

After you've attached your Library thumbnail graphic, you can open My Bookshelf in Adobe Reader or Acrobat 6 by choosing File⇨My Bookshelf to view the thumbnail, as shown in Figure 15-10.

Paperclip icon

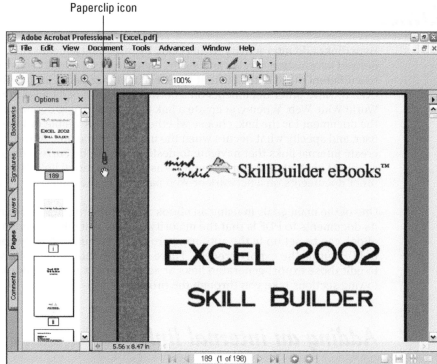

Figure 15-9:
The paperclip icon in the Acrobat workspace indicates an attached Library thumbnail graphic.

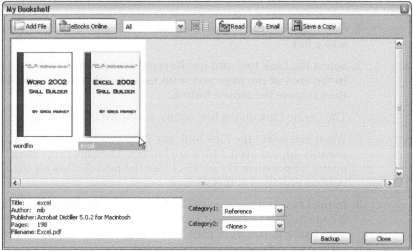

Figure 15-10:
The attached Library thumbnail appears in My Bookshelf in either Adobe Reader or Acrobat 6.

Links

Hyperlinks add interactivity to an eBook by providing a means of navigating to desired information quickly and easily. Using links, an eBook reader can jump to a different place in the current page, call up other pages in the eBook, and even retrieve other documents on a network or download pages from the World Wide Web. When you create a link in Acrobat 6, you define an area in the document for the link, choose whether it appears visible or invisible to the user, and specify what occurs when the user clicks the link. Acrobat 6 lets you create internal links that navigate to destinations in the current document — a table of contents link, for example — as well as external links that retrieve other documents on a network or Web pages from the Internet.

One of the main goals in using an eBook authoring program that can export its documents to PDF is that the majority of links you might need in your eBook can be set up in the authoring program and automatically converted to PDF during the export process. There are times, however, when you'll want to edit those export-generated links or add new links to your eBook. The following sections take you through the process.

Adding an internal link

You create all links with the Link tool, which is found on the Advanced Editing toolbar. To select the tool, click its button on the toolbar or press L. To add an internal link to your eBook, follow these steps:

1. **Open the eBook file and navigate to the page in which you want to add a link.**

2. **Select the Link tool and use its cross-hair pointer to draw a rectangle in the area of the page you want users to click to activate the link, and then release the mouse button.**

   The Create Link dialog box opens, as shown in Figure 15-11.

   When you select the Link tool, any links currently in the document temporarily appear even if they are hidden. The Link Properties toolbar also opens, as shown in Figure 15-11. See the next section for details on the options provided in this toolbar.

3. **In the Link Actions area of the Create Link dialog box, select the Open a Page in This Document radio button, enter the page number for your link's destination page in the Page text box, and select a Zoom setting from the Zoom drop-down list.**

   The zoom settings determine how the destination page is displayed in the PDF reader after clicking a link and are the same as those provided in Acrobat 6 — Fit Page, Actual Size, Fit Width, Fit Visible, and Inherit

Zoom, which uses the same view setting for the destination page as the page containing the link.

4. **Select the Open a File radio button to have the link open an external file.**

   Click the Browse button to locate and select the file. If the file is not a PDF document, those who click this link must have the associated program installed on their computers to view the file.

5. **Select the Open a Web Page radio button and type a URL address in the Address text box.**

   See the "Adding an external link" section, later in this chapter, for more on this option.

6. **Select the Custom link radio button to create a link with JavaScript actions attached to it, such as playing a sound file or movie clip.**

   These actions are specified in the Link Properties dialog box. See the next section for more about the Link Properties dialog box; for more on adding JavaScript action links to a PDF document, see Chapters 14 and 16.

7. **Click OK to close the Create Link dialog box and test your new link.**

   You can also use the Hand tool to test the link. Note that when you hover the Hand tool pointer over a link, it changes to a pointing finger.

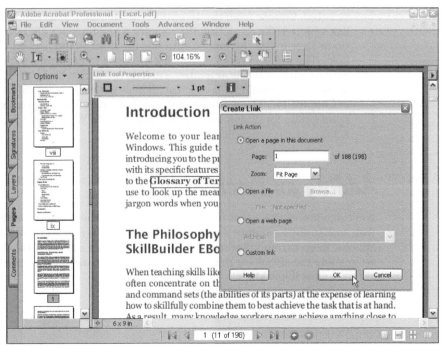

Figure 15-11:
The options provided in the Create Link dialog box and the Link Tool Properties toolbar that automatically displays when you select the Link tool.

Using Link Properties options

The Link Properties toolbar, like all Properties toolbars in Acrobat 6, pops up when you select an editing tool. This toolbar lets you specify the appearance of a link and what action occurs when you click the link. As you can see in Figure 15-11, each button on the Link Properties toolbar has a pop-up menu button (black triangle) attached for selecting the following options:

- ✔ **Color:** Click the Color button to choose a color for the link border on the palette that appears.

- ✔ **Line Style:** Click the Line Style pop-up menu to select No Line, Solid, Dashed, or Underline border style.

- ✔ **Line Thickness:** Click the Line Thickness pop-up menu (marked by either 1pt, 2pt, or 3pt line sizes in the Link Properties toolbar) and choose a Thin, Medium, or Thick outline border for the link.

- ✔ **Highlight Style:** The Highlight Style pop-up menu lets you specify a momentary change in appearance for a link when the user clicks it. The effect is displayed until the user releases the mouse button. These options are available for both visible and invisible links. Choose None to have no change in appearance, Invert to invert the colors of the link, Outline to highlight the border on a visible link or to display a thin line around an invisible link, or Inset to create a 3-D button effect.

- ✔ **More:** Opens the Link Properties dialog box with the Actions tab selected. Choose from the 16 options in the Add an Action drop-down list, which define an action that occurs when the user clicks a link. The Go to Page in the Document option is the default and is used for internal links. The other choices on this list are used to perform a variety of actions when a link is activated, such as opening a file, playing a sound or movie, or running a JavaScript. (These actions are explained in detail in Chapter 14.) The majority of the actions are either impractical or not appropriate for eBook use. An exception is the World Wide Web Link action, which is detailed in the next section.

Adding an external link

You can allow eBook users to jump back and forth between the World Wide Web and Adobe Reader or Acrobat 6, by adding external Web links in your eBooks. Keep in mind that users must have Internet access at the time they are reading the eBook for this to be possible. To create an external link in an eBook, follow these steps:

1. **Open the eBook file and navigate to the page in which you want to add a link.**

2. **Select the Link tool and use its cross-hair pointer to draw a rectangle in the area of the page you want users to click to activate the link.**

   The Create Link dialog box opens (refer to Figure 15-11).

3. **Select the Open a Web Page radio button.**

4. **Type the URL in the Address text box and click OK.**

   Note that URLs entered in the text box are stored for future use and can be selected by clicking the drop-down arrow. You can also copy a URL from your browser's address bar and paste it in this text box.

5. **To test your new link, select the Hand tool on the Basic toolbar and click the link in your document. To return to the original link, choose View⟲Go To⟲Previous View or press Alt+Left Arrow (⌘+Left Arrow on Mac).**

To delete, edit, or test (follow) a link you've created in Acrobat 6, right-click (Control+click on the Mac) the link with the Link tool, choose Edit on the context menu that appears, and then choose the appropriate command on the submenu. You can also open the Link Properties dialog box to edit a link by double-clicking it with the Link tool.

Controlling the Way Text Flows

After you've converted your eBook to tagged PDF, you may discover that the page elements don't flow properly, especially when the page is viewed on a smaller screen. For example, a text caption for a graphic might appear above the image rather than below it. In other cases, you might have an image that has a text wrap around it, but you want to have the image appear after the text when it is reflowed. In such cases, you can use the TouchUp Order tool in Acrobat 6 to edit the reflow order of tagged items in the document. The TouchUp Order tool is located on the TouchUp Text Tool pop-up menu. You can select the tool by either choosing it from this pop-up menu or by holding down the Shift key and tapping the T key to cycle through the TouchUp tools until the TouchUp Order tool appears.

To change the reflow order of elements on a tagged PDF page, follow these steps:

1. **Open the eBook file and navigate to the page containing the elements for which you want to change the reflow order.**

2. **Choose View⇨Navigation Tabs⇨Content to open the Content Navigation pane.**

The Content Navigation pane displays the content structure tree of your eBook document. When you click the Expand button (+) attached to your eBook icon, the pages of your eBook appear on the next level with Expand buttons of their own. Clicking these buttons displays containers that hold the separate elements on the page in the order that they appear in your eBook document, as shown in Figure 15-12. You can then drag the page elements either individually or their whole container to new positions in the structure tree to reorder the page elements.

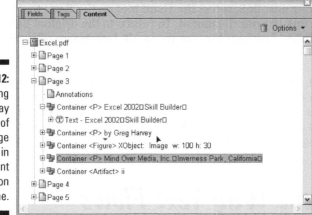

Figure 15-12:
Changing the display order of page elements in the Content Navigation pane.

3. **Drag the desired page element or container to a new position in the page structure tree.**

As you drag a page element or container, the mouse pointer changes between an International No symbol and a red downward arrow, indicating the positions you can or cannot drop the desired page element when you release the mouse button. A red underscore mouse pointer is displayed to indicate you are moving an element to an upper-level position.

4. **Repeat Step 3 until you're satisfied with the reordering of the eBook page elements, and then click the Close button to close the Content Navigation pane.**

5. **To view your reflow order changes first, choose View⇨Reflow or press Ctrl+4 (⌘+4 on Mac).**

Use the Zoom In and Zoom Out buttons to observe how the elements reflow under different page magnifications. (See Figure 15-13.)

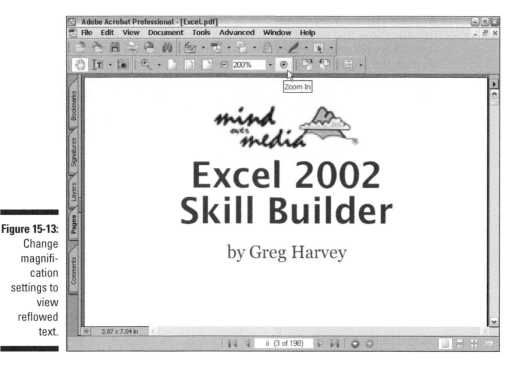

Distributing Your eBooks

When you're satisfied with the look and feel of your eBook, including the way its text reflows, and you have checked that all links are working properly, your next step is to decide how you want to distribute your eBook. Adobe sells a server software package called Adobe Content Server that online eBook distributors use to encrypt, store, and distribute eBooks for sale. The latest version is 3.0, and at $5,000.00 for the Standard Edition (which allows you to store 250 titles on a single Web site), it's definitely only for serious eBook publishers. To find out more about Adobe Content Server software, go to:

```
www.adobe.com/products/contentserver/main.html
```

If you're not quite ready to make the plunge into the world of eBook self-distributorship, a number of companies online have made the plunge and don't mind helping you distribute your Adobe eBooks for a percentage of your gross sales. Adobe provides a list of links to these digital fulfillment company Web sites for your convenience. Go to Adobe's eBooks Central page here:

```
www.adobe.com/epaper/ebooks/main.html
```

Whether you use your own server or sign an agreement with an online distributor, the actual process of uploading an eBook is fairly simple. The Content Server software provides an interface that takes you step by step through the process of filling out the necessary information about your book (including ISBN numbers, which you'll have to procure from the Library of Congress), specifying the level of encryption and printing privileges you'll allow for your eBook and, finally, uploading your Library and Cover thumbnails along with your PDF eBook to the server. After your eBook is uploaded to the Content Server, the distributor then makes it available to various online retailers, and you're in business!

Chapter 16

Making PDFs into Multimedia Presentations

*M*ore and more, paper easels and overhead transparencies are giving way to electronic presentations as a means of imparting information to groups of people. Whether in business or education, slide show-type presentations and their ability to incorporate multimedia components make everything from sales meetings and seminars to student academic reports more interesting and exciting.

In this chapter, you discover how Acrobat 6 lets you create interactive PDF presentations in graphics editing programs or from Web content. Plus, you find out how easy it is to convert existing slide shows created in Microsoft PowerPoint, as well as how to view eCards and slide shows created in Adobe Photoshop Album. On the way, you gain knowledge of how to add interactive elements, such as navigation buttons, and add multimedia objects, such as movies and sounds, to your PDF document. And, as if all this weren't enough, you find out how to design and display a project in Full Screen mode to give your Acrobat PDF presentation a more cinematic look and feel. Finally, you get a first-hand look at the new Pictures Tasks button that lets you export, edit, or print graphic images, as well as order photo prints online.

Converting a Presentation to PDF

Probably the easiest way to create a presentation in Acrobat 6 is simply to convert an already made Microsoft PowerPoint presentation to PDF. Users of Microsoft Office 2000 or XP and Office X for Macintosh are provided with the PDFMaker 6.0 macro utility when they install Acrobat 6. After the installation, when you open PowerPoint, Acrobat buttons appear on the PDFMaker 6.0 toolbar, and Acrobat commands appear on the menu bar that let you convert your PowerPoint presentations to a tagged PDF. Just click the Convert to Adobe PDF button on the PDFMaker 6.0 toolbar, or in the Windows version of PowerPoint, choose Adobe PDF⇨Convert to Adobe PDF, as shown in Figure 16-1. By default, your PDF presentation opens in Acrobat 6, as shown in Figure 16-2. (See Chapter 5 for more on converting Microsoft Office documents to Adobe PDF.)

PDFMaker 6.0 converts any hyperlinks you added in your PowerPoint presentation so that you don't have to re-create those interactive elements in your new PDF presentation. In addition, PDF portability makes it possible for you to easily distribute your PDF presentation over a company intranet or the World Wide Web and be assured that the greatest numbers of people are able to view it.

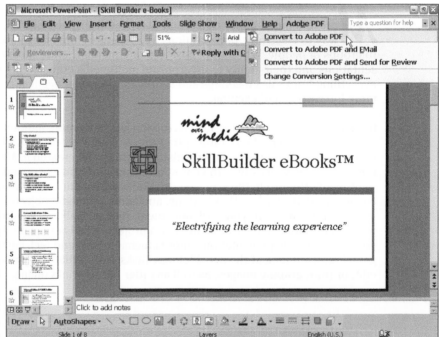

Figure 16-1:
Using the
Convert to
Adobe PDF
command in
Microsoft
PowerPoint.

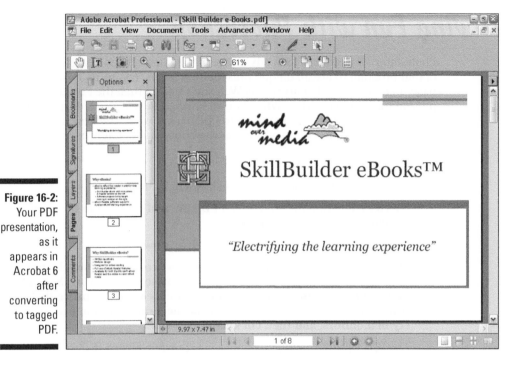

Figure 16-2:
Your PDF
presentation,
as it
appears in
Acrobat 6
after
converting
to tagged
PDF.

Building Your Own PDF Presentation

You might find that PowerPoint's design-template approach to developing a slide show presentation has limitations. For example, the simple slide show I created for my eBook publishing company, shown in Figures 16-1 and 16-2, doesn't match the design of my Web site. And, although I love PowerPoint's ability to create an appealing slide show in a hurry, it would take far longer to re-create the look and feel of my Web site in that program.

Acrobat 6, on the other hand, lets you use graphics editing or page layout programs to design a presentation to your exact specifications and then convert it to a PDF presentation. You probably already have a great deal of your own "branded" content developed in such programs, which makes the job of incorporating your designs in a PDF presentation all the easier. Check out Chapter 15 for details on page layout programs that convert their documents to Adobe PDF. On the graphics editing side, Illustrator or Photoshop are likely choices to use because of their close integration of Acrobat 6 features.

Having Fun with Photoshop

Photoshop 7.0 users can take advantage of the unparalleled design features of that program to create unique presentation pages. Figure 16-3 shows a page that more closely mirrors my Web site's design than the PowerPoint presentation shown earlier. When you've finished developing a design, you can convert a Photoshop document to PDF in two ways. The first is to use the Save As command in Photoshop 7.0, as described in the following steps:

1. **Choose File⇨Save As.**

   The Save As dialog box opens, as shown in Figure 16-4.

2. **Specify a location for your saved PDF file and type a title for your document in the Name text box.**

3. **Select Photoshop PDF in the Format drop-down list.**

4. **The Color area of the dialog box provides two options for selecting a color gamut conducive to either print or on-screen viewing. Select the Embed Color Profile: sRGB IEC61966-2.1 check box to ensure that the colors in your presentation will display accurately on the widest variety of monitors, and then click Save.**

   The PDF Options dialog box opens, as shown in Figure 16-5.

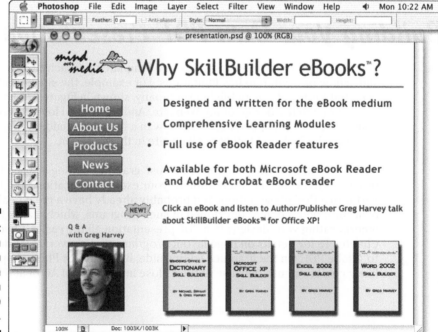

Figure 16-3: Creating a custom design for a presentation in Photoshop 7.0.

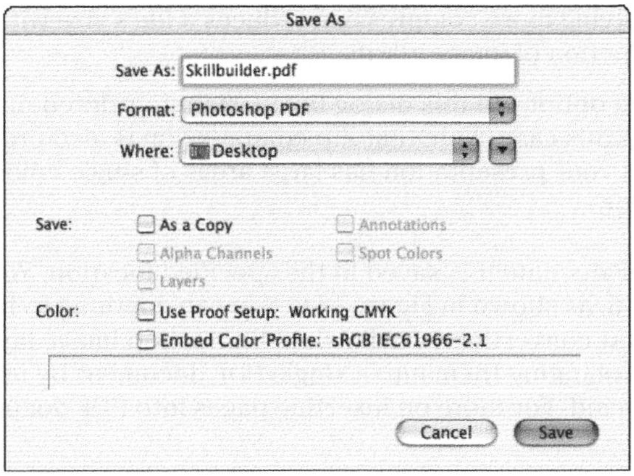

Figure 16-4:
Selecting
Save As
options
when
converting a
Photoshop
document to
PDF.

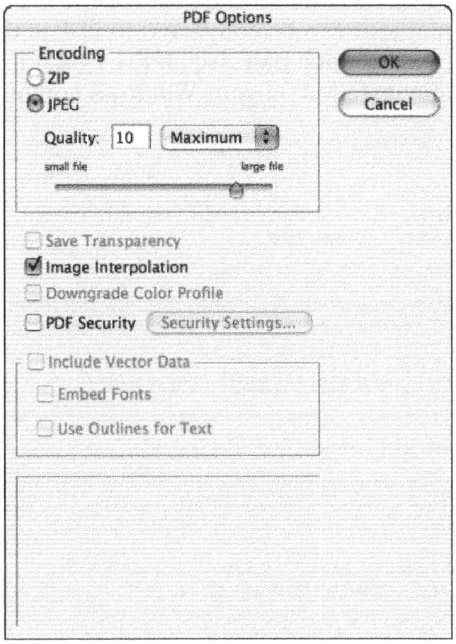

Figure 16-5:
Selecting
JPEG
encoding
options prior
to saving
your file.

5. **Select the JPEG radio button in the Encoding area.**

6. **You have three ways in which to select the amount of compression when using JPEG encoding: Type a number between 0 and 12 in the Quality text box, choose a fixed setting in the drop-down list, or use the slider. Then click OK to convert the document to PDF.**

Note that applying more compression reduces a file's size with a corresponding reduction of image clarity.

The remaining options in this dialog box pertain to printed output and don't apply in this case. Note that Zip compression is also provided and can be used if your presentation has large areas of single colors using 4- or 8-bit color.

The converted PDF document is saved in the specified location. You can then open it in Acrobat 6, as shown in Figure 16-6. You can continue to build a PDF presentation by first converting your finished Photoshop image layouts to PDF and then consolidating them into a single PDF document by using the Insert Pages command. For more on inserting pages into PDF documents, see Chapter 10.

You can also convert your Photoshop documents from inside Acrobat 6 by using the Create PDF command. Keep in mind that you have to first save your Photoshop document in a format that can be converted to PDF in this manner. Acrobat 6 supports these graphic formats: BMP, GIF, JPEG, PCX, PICT (Mac OS only, unless you have QuickTime installed on your Windows computer), PNG, and TIFF.

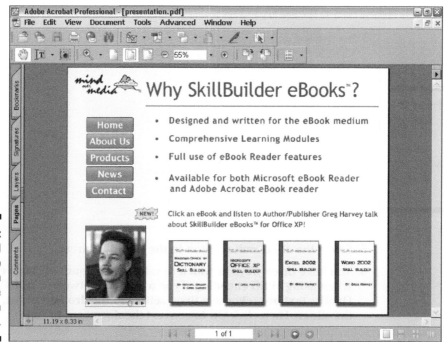

Figure 16-6:
A converted
Photoshop
presentation
page
viewed in
Acrobat 6.

To convert your Photoshop presentation page to PDF in Acrobat 6, follow these steps:

1. **Choose File➪Create PDF➪From File or choose From File on the Create PDF Tasks button menu.**

    The Open dialog box appears.

2. **On the Files of Type drop-down list, choose the file format in which you saved your Photoshop document, and then locate and select the file you want to convert to PDF.**

3. **Click the Settings button to choose a color, monochrome, or grayscale compression setting (JPEG, Zip, JBIG2, or CCITT G4) that Acrobat will use during the conversion process, and then click OK.**

    Note that if you left the default option, All Files, selected in the Files of Type drop-down list, this button will be grayed out.

4. **Click the Open button to convert the Photoshop document to PDF.**

5. **If you already have a document opened in Acrobat 6 when you open a Photoshop document as PDF, you get an alert dialog box that asks you what to do with your new PDF page. Select one of the following radio buttons and then click OK:**

    • **Create a New Document:** Select this radio button if you want to make a separate PDF file out of your Photoshop document.

    • **Append to Current Document:** Select this radio button if you want to add the Photoshop document as a new page in the currently opened PDF document.

You can invoke the Create PDF from File command by dragging an image file onto the Acrobat application icon located on your desktop (Windows) or Dock in OS X. Windows and Mac users can also drag an image to the open Acrobat 6 window to convert an image to Adobe PDF. In this case, if you already have a document opened in the Acrobat window when you drag a new image into it, Acrobat automatically creates a new PDF document with the same name as the image file. Your previous document remains opened and can be displayed by selecting its name at the bottom of the Window menu.

Using Multimedia Objects in a Presentation

Acrobat 6 lets you enhance a PDF presentation with the addition of movies and sounds. Before you add these objects to your PDF page, consider the following points about using these objects in your presentation:

✔ **Acrobat 5-Compatibility:** Acrobat lets you specify whether an inserted movie clip is Acrobat 5 or Acrobat 6 compatible. Acrobat 5-Compatibility does not allow you to take advantage of a number of new features found in Acrobat 6-Compatibility, but inserted movie and sound files are backwards compatible with earlier versions of Acrobat, which is not the case with Acrobat 6-Compatibility.

✔ **Acrobat 6-Compatibility:** This movie clip option provides new features, such as the ability to embed a movie in a PDF document, create a *poster* (an image displayed in the movie viewer or sound player prior to playing) from a separate file, specify content type, and use of alternate renditions, which allows a high-resolution movie to be played at a lower resolution if the user does not have a high-resolution player installed. When you choose Acrobat 6-Compatibility for movie clips, the PDF document must be opened in Acrobat 6 or Adobe Reader 6 to take advantage of these new features. When using Acrobat 6-Compatibility with sound files, you have the same embedding and poster features available with movies.

✔ **Formats:** Acrobat PDF documents play all video and sound files that are compatible with Apple QuickTime software. The most common (therefore, best to use) of these include MOV and MPG formats for movies and AIF, WAV, and MP3 for sounds. The user must have a minimum of QuickTime 2.5 for Windows or Mac (though versions 4.0–6.0 are recommended) or Windows Media Player to play these objects in your presentation. In addition, Acrobat supports the Macromedia Flash Player and RealOne Player, though viewers must have the proper hardware and software to play these media file formats.

✔ **Embedding:** If you choose Acrobat 6-Compatibility, sound clips are embedded in the PDF document, meaning that the actual sound file is attached to the PDF. (The same is true for movie clips added to a PDF document.) Because sound and movie files can be quite large, you should take care when using them, because they can increase the size of PDF files significantly. Movies and sounds using Acrobat 5-Compatibility are not embedded. They are linked to the PDF via a placeholder that points to the movie clip's location. For this reason, all linked movies and sounds must accompany a PDF document, so it's important to use the correct filenames and relative path locations for the actual movie clips when you distribute them to others. If your presentation is bound for network or World Wide Web distribution, playback quality will also depend on the user's network access speed. Movies and sounds using Acrobat 6-Compatibility must be viewed in either Acrobat 6 or Adobe Reader 6.

Inserting a movie in a presentation

Follow these steps to insert a movie in a presentation:

1. **Open the PDF presentation to which you want to add a movie clip.**

2. **Select the Movie tool on the Advanced Editing toolbar or press M.**

3. **Double-click a spot on your presentation page where you want the movie to play.**

   This spot represents the center of the movie frame, and the movie playback area will be the same size as the actual movie frame. Double-clicking with the Movie tool also opens the Add Movie dialog box, shown in Figure 16-7.

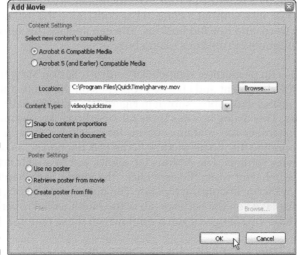

Figure 16-7:
Options provided in the Add Movie dialog box.

4. **In the Content Settings area, select either the Acrobat 6 Compatible Media or the Acrobat 5 (and Earlier) Compatible Media radio button.**

5. **Click the Browse button to locate the movie clip on your hard drive and click the Select button.**

6. **Select the Snap to Content Proportions check box to specify that the playback area snaps to the size of the movie clip frame. Select the Embed Content in Document check box to embed the movie clip in the PDF document.**

   Note that if you select the Acrobat 5 (and Earlier) Compatible Media radio button, the Embed Content in Document check box does not appear in the Add Movie dialog box.

7. **In the Poster Settings area of the Add Movie dialog box, select the Use No Poster, Retrieve Poster from Movie, or Create a Poster from File radio button.**

   Movie posters are image placeholders for the playback area in a PDF. They are usually the first frame of the linked or embedded movie clip.

Note that if you select the Acrobat 5 (and Earlier) Compatible Media radio button, the Create Poster from File radio button does not appear in the Add Movie dialog box. If you select this option, click the Browse button to locate and select a poster graphic in the Select a Poster File dialog box.

8. **When you're through selecting movie options, click OK.**

A border highlighting the play area appears in the PDF document. This border is displayed only when you're using the Movie tool for editing purposes. To play the inserted movie clip, select the Hand tool on the Basic toolbar and click the movie window in your PDF document. By default, Acrobat adds movies to PDF files without a control bar containing the usual Play, Pause, Stop, Forward, and Rewind buttons. You can specify this option and others in the Multimedia Properties dialog box.

To edit the movie clip properties, right-click (Control+click on Mac) the movie window in the PDF document and choose Properties on the context menu. The Multimedia Properties dialog box, shown in Figure 16-8 with the Settings tab selected, appears. This dialog box has three tabs: Settings, Appearance, and Actions. The Appearance tab contains options for specifying the appearance of the border surrounding the movie window in the PDF document, as well as changing the poster settings. The Actions tab allows you to attach JavaScript actions to mouse behavior when the user clicks the movie. See Chapter 14 for more on using JavaScript actions on this tab. The main movie editing options in Acrobat are displayed on the Settings tab of the Multimedia Properties dialog box. The following list gives you a rundown on these options:

- ✔ **Annotation Title:** Enter a title for the movie clip. This title is for annotation purposes only and does not determine which movie file is played.

- ✔ **Alternate Text:** Use this accessibility feature to enter descriptive text that can be read aloud using the Acrobat Read Aloud feature.

- ✔ **Renditions:** Acrobat creates *renditions* of a movie clip based on settings inherent in the selected movie clip and settings you select when you add a movie clip to a PDF document. The current rendition is displayed in the Renditions list box. You can create new renditions that allow the movie clip to be played under different hardware/software configurations, thus enabling playback on a greater number of user systems. Click the Add Rendition button to choose a movie file, URL address for a movie clip, or to copy a rendition in the list box to edit. Click the Remove Rendition button to delete a rendition from the list box. Use the Up and Down arrows to the right of the list box to set the order of rendition playback starting from top to bottom. When a movie clip is played, Acrobat tries to play the movie with the first rendition listed. If the user's hardware/software configuration does not allow playback, the next rendition is used until a suitable playback rendition is found. Click the Edit Rendition button to open the Rendition Settings dialog box. The Rendition Settings dialog box contains a whole slew of movie options on its five tabs: Media Settings, Playback Settings, Playback Location, System Requirements, and Playback Requirements.

To set the volume level of a movie clip, display movie player controls during playback, and specify repeat time, right-click (Control+click on Mac) the movie window and choose Properties on the context menu. Click the Setting tab in the Multimedia Properties dialog box and then click the Edit Rendition button. Click the Playback Setting tab in the Rendition Settings dialog box that appears and select your options. Click OK to close the Rendition Settings dialog box and then click Close to close the Multimedia Properties box and view your movie clip in the current PDF document.

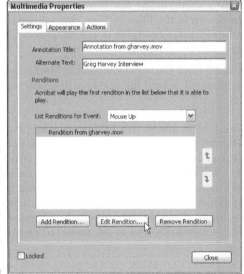

Figure 16-8:
Options provided in the Multimedia Properties dialog box.

When choosing a playback area with the Movie tool, you can not only double-click the area as described in the steps above, but you can also use the Movie tool cross-hair pointer to draw a marquee for a movie playback area. Regardless of which technique you use to add a movie to a PDF file, make sure that the Snap to Content Proportions check box is selected in the Add Movie dialog box (it is by default). This ensures that the playback area will be the exact size of the selected movie frame. If this feature is not activated, and you try and draw this area or resize it after the movie link has been created, it's very likely your playback area won't match the movie clip's aspect ratio, causing distorted playback. You should also set the magnification view of pages that have movies in them to 100% to avoid this type of scaling so that the user sees the best quality playback when viewing your presentation. If you find that a movie clip you want to use isn't the right size for your presentation, plan on using your movie editing software to make adjustments rather than Acrobat 6.

Inserting a sound in a presentation

The process of adding a sound clip to a presentation is nearly identical to that of adding a movie clip with the following exceptions:

- ✔ You drag the Sound tool (located on the Movie tool pop-up menu on the Advanced Editing toolbar) to define a rectangular playing area for sounds or double-click with the Sound tool (as you do for movies using the Movie tool).

- ✔ If you navigate to locate a sound in the Add Sound dialog box, the Most Common Formats are shown in the Files of Type drop-down list; you may have to select other formats available in the drop-down list in order for sound clips to appear in the navigation window.

- ✔ If you select the Acrobat 5 (and Earlier) Compatible Media radio button, the options for embedding the sound file and creating posters are not displayed.

You can test movie and sound clips added to a PDF presentation in this manner by selecting the Hand tool and then moving the mouse pointer over the playback area until it turns into the pointing finger cursor you see when hovering over a hyperlink. Click the playback area to play the movie or sound clip. To stop playback, click again or press the Esc key. Note that you can also attach movie and sound playback to buttons, as described in the next section. To get details on attaching actions to these and other Acrobat interactive elements, such as links, bookmarks, and so on, head to Chapter 14.

Making Your Presentation Interactive

You can add interactivity to a PDF presentation by adding links that navigate the user through the presentation and/or buttons that have actions assigned to them, such as playing movies or sound. (For details on inserting links into a PDF document, see Chapter 15. To find out about adding buttons created in Acrobat 6 to a PDF document, see Chapter 14.) If you decide to develop a custom-designed presentation in an editing program, such as Photoshop, it's better to create the graphics for your button in that program and add interactivity to it using Acrobat's Form tool. Here's how:

1. **Navigate to the presentation page in which you want to add an interactive button and select the Link Tool button on the Advanced Editing toolbar or press L.**

2. **Drag the Link tool pointer to draw a box in the desired field area of your PDF form, and then release the mouse button.**

   The Create Link dialog box opens. In Figure 16-9, I've created a button out of the Dictionary book cover that, when clicked, will play an interview movie in the area to the left.

3. **Click the Custom Link radio button and click OK to close the Create Link dialog box and open the Link Properties dialog box.**

4. **On the Appearance tab, choose Invisible Rectangle on the Link Type drop-down list and select None in the Highlight Style drop-down list.**

   Because the button graphic is already created in the document, you have no need for Acrobat's appearance embellishments.

5. **From the Select Action drop-down list, choose Play Media (Acrobat 6 Compatible), and then click the Add button.**

   The Play Media (Acrobat 6 Compatible) dialog box appears with any movies added the current PDF document listed by the annotation title in the Associated Annotations list box.

6. **Select Play on the Operation to Perform drop-down list.**

7. **Select the movie in the Associated Annotations list box.**

8. **Click the OK button, and then click Close to close the Link Properties dialog box.**

The button field appears in the PDF outlined in red to indicate that it is selected for editing. To test your button, select the Hand tool and click the button, as shown in Figure 16-9.

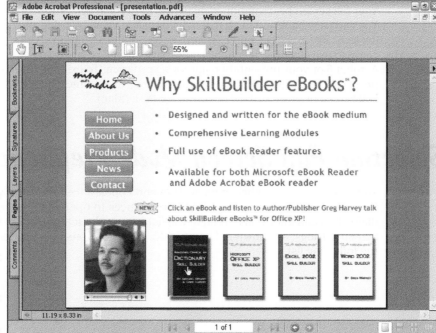

Figure 16-9: Testing an interactive button that plays a movie in a PDF presentation.

Viewing a Presentation Full Screen

Acrobat's Full Screen mode allows users to view your presentation without the distraction of the menu bar, toolbars, or window controls. Document pages fill the entire screen, allowing viewers to focus completely on your presentation. Acrobat lets you set full-screen presentations to run automatically by using timed page advancement and transition effects, and you can use the mouse pointer to activate on-screen controls, such as buttons or links, in your presentation. In addition, users can navigate and change views of a presentation by using standard keyboard shortcuts associated with Acrobat menu commands. To set up a PDF presentation so that it opens automatically in Full Screen mode, follow these steps:

1. **Open the PDF presentation you want to display in Full Screen mode.**

2. **Choose File⇨Document Properties to open the Document Properties dialog box. Click Initial View in the list box to display the Initial View settings.**

3. **In the Window Options area, select the Open in Full Screen Mode check box, as shown in Figure 16-10, and then click OK.**

4. **Save the presentation and then close and reopen it to view it in Full Screen mode.**

Your full-screen presentation is displayed in Acrobat 6, as shown in Figure 16-11. You can page back and forth through your slide show by using any of the following keys: Pg Up, Pg Dn, Enter, Return, or any of the arrow keys. Of course, you can also use any on-screen interactive navigational controls you've set up using Acrobat 6 or your presentation authoring program. To exit Full Screen mode, press Esc. To toggle Full Screen mode off or on at anytime, choose Window⇨ Full Screen or press Crtl+L (Windows) or ⌘+L (Mac).

Selecting Full Screen Mode Preferences

You can specify a number of navigation and appearance options that apply to PDF Full Screen mode. Choose Edit⇨Preferences to open the Preferences dialog box and click Full Screen in the list box on the left to display the Full Screen settings, as shown in Figure 16-12. Select options in areas described in the following list:

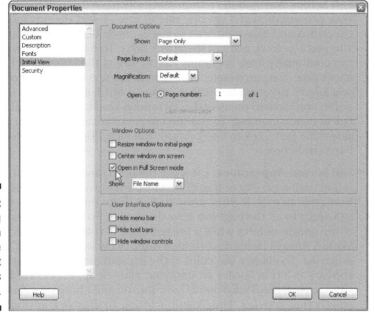

Figure 16-10:
Specifying
Full Screen
mode in the
Document
Properties
dialog box.

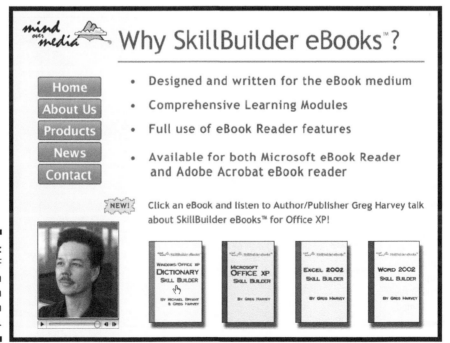

Figure 16-11:
A PDF
presentation
displayed in
Full Screen
mode.

✔ **Full Screen Navigation:** To automatically page through the slides in your presentation at a specific rate of time, select the Advance Every check box and type a number in the Seconds text box (activated when you place a check mark in the check box). To have your presentation run continually from beginning to end, select the Loop After Last Page check box. You can deselect the default Escape Key Exits check box, but you'll have to remember that in order to exit Full Screen mode at that point, you have to press Ctrl+L (Windows) or ⌘+L (Mac) to toggle the Full Screen command. To use the mouse to advance slides or go back, select the Left Click to Go Forward One Page; Right Click to Go Back One Page check box.

✔ **Full Screen Appearance:** Click the Default Transition drop-down list to select from a variety of transition effects that will display when moving from page to page in your presentation. Note that the selected transition will apply to all the pages in your document. To specify the appearance of the mouse pointer while a presentation is running, choose Always Visible, Always Hidden, or Hidden After Delay in the Mouse Cursor drop-down list. To change the color of the presentation background that appears as a thin border around your slide or appears during slide transitions, click the Background Color button and choose a color on the palette that appears. The default is black. To disable transitions in the presentation, select the Ignore All Transitions check box.

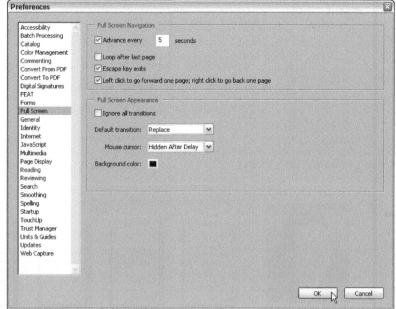

Figure 16-12:
Selecting
navigation
and
appearance
options for
Full Screen
mode.

Using the Image Viewer and Picture Tasks Plug-ins

Acrobat 6 comes with two new built-in plug-ins — the Image Viewer plug-in that allows you to view PDF slideshows and eCards created in Adobe Photoshop Album, and the Picture Tasks plug-in that lets you extract JPEG images sent in a PDF document created in Adobe Photoshop Album, Photoshop Elements 2.0, or Acrobat 6 using JPEG source files. You can export JPEG images and save them on your hard drive for editing in a graphics editing program like Photoshop, print them using standard photo print sizes and layouts, or send them over the Internet to an online service bureau that makes professional prints out of your digital images and mails them to you.

Viewing slideshows with the Image Viewer plug-in

Adobe Photoshop Album is a new program that lets you organize and share digital photos. When you get a whole bunch of photos organized in the program, you can then share the bounty with others by creating high-quality slideshows with music and transitions, as well as eCards (personal greetings sent via e-mail), calendars, books, and much more. Presentations you create in Adobe Photoshop Album can be converted to PDF and viewed using Acrobat 6 or Adobe Reader 6. When you perform a complete install of Acrobat 6, the Image Viewer plug-in is automatically installed. Note that the Image Viewer plug-in is only available in the Full rather than Standard version of Adobe Reader 6.0.

The first time you open a PDF slideshow, eCard, and so on, it is likely to start playing automatically in Full Screen mode because that is the default option when creating these presentations in Photoshop Album. After the slide show has run its course, an Adobe Picture Tasks message box appears, letting you know how special this particular PDF file is and how you can do so much more using the Picture Tasks features (described in the next section). Select the Don't Show Again check box in the bottom left corner of the message box (unless you like this type of reading every time you open a PDF graphic document), and then click OK to close the message box and view the presentation in Acrobat 6.

Figure 16-13 shows a typical Adobe Photoshop Album PDF slideshow displayed in Acrobat 6 after it has initially played. You can use the text and image selection tools on the Basic toolbar to select, copy, edit, or delete elements in the presentation. See Chapter 10 for more on editing PDF documents. You can also save it and even send it off to somebody else by choosing File⇨E-mail. Of course if you read the big, fat, Adobe Picture Tasks message box mentioned in the preceding paragraph, you'd know that you can also use commands on the Picture Tasks menu to further your fun with Photoshop Album presentations.

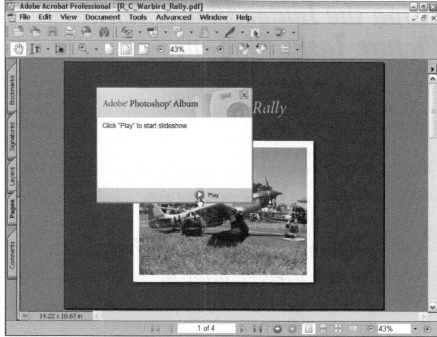

Figure 16-13:
Viewing
and edit-
ing a PDF
slideshow in
Acrobat 6.

Exporting images with the Picture Tasks plug-in

The Picture Tasks plug-in is automatically installed when you perform a complete install of Acrobat 6. You'll know it's available because it creates a button on the Tasks toolbar, appropriately titled Picture Tasks. The Tasks toolbar is displayed by default in Acrobat 6, but if you ever lose it, choose View➪Task Buttons➪Picture Tasks to bring it back up.

The plug-in is used to export images from presentations created in Adobe Photoshop Album, Photoshop Elements, or an Acrobat 6 document with JPEG source files. When you click the Picture Tasks button on the Tasks toolbar, as shown in Figure 16-14, a menu appears with commands that let you process images in a PDF document in some really useful ways. The following list describes these commands:

✔ **Export Pictures:** Export pictures from the current file and save them in a folder on your hard drive or a shared folder on a network. Choosing this command opens the Export Pictures dialog box, where you select individual or all pictures in Pictures area, specify whether to use Original or a Common Base Name in the File Names area, and choose a folder in which to save your photos in the Save In text box.

✔ **Export and Edit Pictures:** Export and edit pictures from the current file in your default graphics editing program. Choosing this command opens the Export and Edit Pictures dialog box, shown in Figure 16-15, where you select individual or all pictures in Pictures area, specify whether to use Original or a Common Base Name in the File Names area, choose a folder in which to save your photos in the Save In text box, and change your default graphics editing program in the Editing Application area.

✔ **Print Pictures:** Select images to print on photo paper using your own printer. Choosing this command opens the Select Pictures dialog box, where you make your photo selections in the Pictures area and then click the Next button to open the Print Pictures dialog box, as shown in Figure 16-16. Here you choose the paper size in the Layout Sizes area, select a print size, number of prints and how many per page, and automatic cropping in the Individual Print Format area. Options you selected are previewed in the Preview area. After selecting the options you want, click the Next button to display the standard Acrobat Print dialog box.

Figure 16-14:
Choosing commands on the Picture Tasks button menu.

Figure 16-15:
Choosing options in the Export and Edit Pictures dialog box.

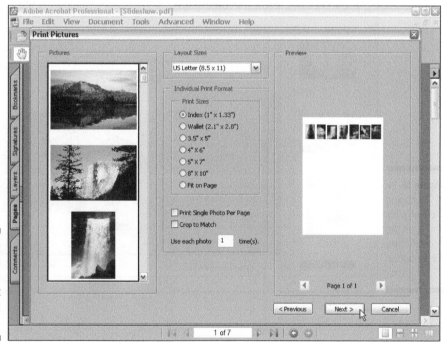

Figure 16-16:
Choosing options in the Print Pictures dialog box.

✔ **Order Prints Online:** Select photos to upload to the Shutterfly online photo printing service. Choosing this command opens the Select Pictures dialog box, where you choose the photos you want to upload and click the Next button to open the Online Services Wizard, as shown in Figure 16-17. Here you follow the instructions in the dialog boxes that let you sign up for an account or login and prepare your photo print order. Photos are then processed to your specification and delivered by mail to you.

✔ **Order Project Online:** PDF project files are those created exclusively in Photoshop Album or Photoshop Elements using one of their design templates, for example, a calendar or photo album. Choosing this command opens the Online Service Wizard that takes you step by step through the process of creating photo merchandise from a PDF project that is delivered to you by mail.

✔ **How To . . . Picture Tasks:** Choosing this command opens the How To window with links to all the help you need to use the Picture Tasks features.

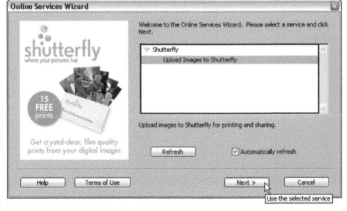

Figure 16-17:
The first
window of
the Online
Services
Wizard.

Part V
The Part of Tens

In this part . . .

Possibly the most fun and certainly the most dynamic
section of the entire book, the Part of Tens brings
you a cursory view of top ten things that make PDF and
Acrobat so special. Chapter 17 shows you how to extend
the functionality of Acrobat 6 through the use of what I
consider currently to be the top ten third-party plug-ins
for this already most versatile program. Finally, Chapter 18
rounds out the Part of Tens by giving you the top ten online
resources for extending your knowledge of Acrobat and
PDF files way beyond the basic introduction I've offered
you here in this book.

Chapter 17

Top Ten Third-Party Acrobat Plug-Ins

. . . .

As versatile as Acrobat 6 is right out of the box, you can make the program even more multitalented and yourself more productive by investing in third-party plug-ins for Acrobat. This chapter presents you with a smorgasbord of plug-ins that enhance various aspects of Acrobat. For more information on these plug-ins, including information on pricing and how to order them, as well as a listing of other third-party plug-ins currently available, visit

```
www.adobe.com/products/acrobatpro/main.html
```

and click the Third Party plug-ins link.

Quite a Box of Tricks 1.5

This plug-in from Quite Software enables you to recompress the graphic images in a PDF document without having to re-distill the file. In addition, it can convert any RGB (Red, Green, Blue) PDF document to CMYK (Cyan, Magenta, Yellow, Black), and get detailed information about any of the text and graphics in the file (including font and image dimensions).

Quite Imposing 1.5

The Quite Imposing plug-in from Quite Software enables you to compose PDF document pages on larger pages for printing and binding as books and booklets. This plug-in also enables you to reorder document pages and split or merge the even- or odd-numbered pages. It also enables you to compose foldable booklets from the pages of your PDF document.

Gemini 4.1 (Windows only)

The Gemini 4.1 plug-in from Iceni Technology enables you to quickly convert any PDF document into multiple text and image formats, allowing you to repurpose PDF content in numerous ways. Features include batch conversion; multiple format conversion for text, tables, and images; and an HTML customization of headers, footers, frames, background colors, and navigation links.

Jade 5.0 (Windows only)

This plug-in by BCL Software enables you to accurately extract normal text, tables, and graphics for editing in Windows applications, such as Microsoft Word and Excel, simply by selecting the text, table, or image and then copying it (using copy-and-paste or drag-and-drop methods).

Stamp PDF 2.7

This plug-in from Appligent enables you to add permanent text to a PDF document using watermarks, page numbers, colored text, and more. Stamps can be placed as headers or footer and at any angle in the PDF document.

ARTS PDF Tools

The ARTS PDF Tools by A Round Table Solution are a suite of 70 plug-ins that enable you to save time performing dozens of PDF editing tasks. The programs also allow you to create your own custom tools that give you quick access to predefined tasks and also allow you to copy and share custom tools with other users.

Magellan 5.0 (Windows only)

This plug-in from BCL Software enables you to accurately convert PDF files into Web pages. It converts the text, graphics, and structure of your PDF file to the appropriate HTML tags to ensure that all the elements on the PDF page are correctly positioned in the resulting Web page.

Portfolio

This plug-in by Extensis Software enables you to organize digital photos, illustrations, and scans and provides visual access to creative content workgroups. The program supports Adobe Photoshop, Adobe InDesign, and Acrobat 6, allowing those users to quickly share, organize, retrieve, and distribute digital files.

PageRecall (formerly Page Vault)

The PageRecall plug-in from Authentica enables you to control the distribution, printing, and use of information in a PDF document after it is downloaded by a recipient. The program lets you easily add protection to all types of confidential documents delivered over the Internet.

Crackerjack 4

This plug-in from Lantana enables you to perform a wide array of PDF-based color production tasks. The program allows you to preview color separations prior to printing, map spot colors, use ICC profiles to control conversion of RGB images to CMYK, and fix font embedding problems.

Chapter 18

Top Ten Online Resources

*L*ast, but never least, I present you with a list of ten of the top online resources for extending your knowledge of Acrobat and for getting service for PDF conversion jobs you're just not prepared to handle in-house. As you would expect, many of these top online resources are Web sites that are run and maintained by Adobe Systems.

Adobe Web Site

`www.adobe.com`

Check out the Adobe Web site for online support and to download all the free Adobe plug-ins for Acrobat 6, including the Make Accessible and Paper Capture plug-ins for Windows and the Save as XML plug-in for both Windows and Macintosh.

Acrobat Expert Center

`studio.adobe.com/expertcenter/acrobat`

This site offers white papers full of tips and tutorials on using Acrobat and integrating PDF into your workflow, access to the user forums and certified trainers, and the latest information on program updates and third-party plug-ins.

Adobe Access

`access.adobe.com`

Check out this site for general information on the accessibility features in Adobe Acrobat 6 and Adobe GoLive 6.

Adobe eBooks Central

www.adobe.com/epaper/ebooks

This site provides detailed information on creating, managing, and delivering PDF documents as Acrobat eBooks.

Create PDF Online

www.createpdf.com

Head for this site to have Adobe convert your documents into PDF files for you. You can test out this online conversion service by signing up for a free trial when you visit this Web page.

PDF Zone.com

www.pdfzone.com

This site provides all kinds of articles and tidbits on the Acrobat and PDF industry and professionals who inhabit it.

Planet PDF

www.planetpdf.com

Planet PDF offers all kinds of news and information on using PDF, including tips on how to get the most out of the file format, along with plenty of listings of PDF tools, consultants, and trainers that can help you get the job done.

Extensis Preflight Online

www.extensis.com/printready

This site provides a complete online preflight service for checking prepress PDF files against the parameters that you specify.

Texterity

www.texterity.com

Texterity is a complete online service for converting documents saved in a wide variety of file formats (including Word, WordPerfect, QuarkXPress, PageMaker, and InDesign) into ready-to-publish Adobe eBook PDF files.

Adobe eBook Site

ebookstore.adobe.com/store

At the Adobe eBook site, you can download some free Acrobat eBooks for your reading pleasure with Adobe Reader or Acrobat 6.

Index

Printed and bound by CPI Group (UK) Ltd, Croydon, CR0 4YY

27/10/2024

14580182-0003